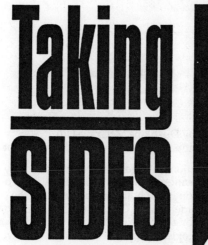

Taking SIDES

Clashing Views on Controversial Issues in World Politics

Eighth Edition

Edited, Selected, and with Introductions by

John T. Rourke
University of Connecticut

Dushkin/McGraw-Hill
A Division of The McGraw-Hill Companies

For my son and friend—John Michael

Cover Art Acknowledgment

Charles Vitelli

Library of Congress Cataloging-in-Publication Data

Main entry under title:
   Taking sides: clashing views on controversial issues in world politics/edited, selected, and with introductions by John T. Rourke.—8th ed.
   Includes bibliographical references and index.
   1. World Politics—1989–. I. Rourke, John T., *comp.*

909.82

0-697-39107-8   ISSN 1094-754X

 Printed on Recycled Paper

PREFACE

In the first edition of *Taking Sides*, I wrote of my belief in informed argument:

> [A] book that debates vital issues is valuable and necessary.... [It is important] to recognize that world politics is usually not a subject of absolute rights and absolute wrongs and of easy policy choices. We all have a responsibility to study the issues thoughtfully, and we should be careful to understand all sides of the debates.

It is gratifying to discover, as indicated by the success of *Taking Sides* over seven editions, that so many of my colleagues share this belief in the value of a debate-format text.

The format of this edition follows a formula that has proved successful in acquainting students with the global issues that we face and generating discussion of those issues and the policy choices that address them. This book addresses 18 issues on a wide range of topics in international relations. Each issue has two readings: one pro and one con. Each is accompanied by an issue *introduction*, which sets the stage for the debate, provides some background information on each author, and generally puts the issue into its political context. Each issue concludes with a *postscript* that summarizes the debate, gives the reader paths for further investigation, and suggests additional readings that might be helpful. I have also provided relevant Internet site addresses (URLs) on the *On the Internet* page that accompanies each part opener.

I have continued to emphasize issues that are currently being debated in the policy sphere. The authors of the selections are a mix of practitioners, scholars, and noted political commentators.

Changes to this edition   The dynamic, constantly changing nature of the world political system and the many helpful comments from reviewers have brought about significant changes to this edition. There are 10 completely new issues: *Is It Wise to Expand NATO Membership?* (Issue 2); *Is Geopolitics Still Relevant in the Era of Cyberspace?* (Issue 5); *Should China Be Admitted to the World Trade Organization?* (Issue 6); *Should Sanctions Against Cuba Under the Helms-Burton Act Be Abandoned?* (Issue 7); *Is the Current Trend Toward Global Economic Integration Desirable?* (Issue 8); *Does the Spread of Democracy Promote World Peace?* (Issue 13); *Should China Be Condemned as a Violator of Human Rights?* (Issue 14); *Are UN-Sponsored World Conferences Beneficial?* (Issue 15); *Is Nationalism Destructive?* (Issue 16); and *Is There a Global Population Crisis?* (Issue 18). Even where issues have remained controversial and have been carried over to this edition, new events and more current views have often led to the use of new readings: *Is Islamic Fundamentalism a Threat to Political*

Stability? (Issue 4); *Does the World Need to Have Nuclear Weapons At All?* (Issue 10); *Should a Permanent UN Military Force Be Established?* (Issue 11); and *Should Immigration Be Restricted?* (Issue 17). Of the 36 readings, 25 are new. My practice of searching a wide range of journals for more recent expositions on one side or the other of the various issues ensures that the readings are as fresh as the issues are current.

A word to the instructor   An *Instructor's Manual With Test Questions* (both multiple-choice and essay) is available through the publisher for instructors using *Taking Sides* in the classroom. A general guidebook, *Using Taking Sides in the Classroom,* which discusses methods and techniques for integrating the pro-con approach into any classroom setting, is also available. An online version of *Using Taking Sides in the Classroom* and a correspondence service for *Taking Sides* adopters can be found at www.cybsol.com/usingtaking-sides/. For students, we offer a field guide to analyzing argumentative essays, *Analyzing Controversy: An Introductory Guide,* with exercises and techniques to help them to decipher genuine controversies.

Taking Sides: Clashing Views on Controversial Issues in World Politics is only one title in the Taking Sides series. If you are interested in seeing the table of contents for any of the other titles, please visit the Taking Sides Web site at http://www.dushkin.com/takingsides/.

A note especially for the student reader   You will find that the debates in this book are not one-sided. Each author strongly believes in his or her position. And if you read the debates without prejudging them, you will see that each author makes cogent points. An author may not be "right," but the arguments made in an essay should not be dismissed out of hand, and you should work at remaining tolerant of those who hold beliefs that are different from your own.

There is an additional consideration to keep in mind as you pursue this debate approach to world politics. To consider objectively divergent views does not mean that you have to remain forever neutral. In fact, once you are informed, you ought to form convictions. More important, you should try to influence international policy to conform better with your beliefs. Write letters to policymakers; donate to causes you support; work for candidates who agree with your views; join an activist organization. *Do* something, whichever side of an issue you are on!

Acknowledgments   I received many helpful comments and suggestions from colleagues and readers across the United States and Canada. Their suggestions have markedly enhanced the quality of this edition of *Taking Sides.* If as you read this book you are reminded of a selection or an issue that could be included in a future edition, please write to me in care of Dushkin/McGraw-Hill with your recommendations.

My thanks go to those who responded with suggestions for the eighth edition:

Craig T. Cohane
University of Cincinnati

Willie Curtis
U.S. Naval Academy

Gary Donato
Three Rivers Community
   Technical College

June Teufel Dreyer
University of Miami

Marc Genest
University of Rhode Island

Mark F. Griffith
University of West Alabama

Ken Hall
Ball State University

Rosemary Hartten
Centenary College

Timothy Jeske
Yakima Valley College

Steven A. Leibo
Russell Sage College

Russell Leng
Middlebury College

Kathleen A. Mahoney-Norris
University of Colorado

Richard W. Mansbach
Iowa State University

J. Patrice McSherry
SUNY College at New Paltz

Kenneth E. Peters
University of South Carolina

David Purdy
Unity College

George Reed
New Mexico State University

John P. Stewart
Pennsylvania State
   University–Mont Alto

Jutta Weldes
Kent State University

I would also like to thank David Dean, list manager for the Taking Sides series, and David Brackley, developmental editor, for their help in refining this edition.

John T. Rourke
University of Connecticut

CONTENTS IN BRIEF

CONTENTS

Patrick Glynn, a former official in the U.S. Arms Control and Disarmament Agency, contends that the post–cold war world is a more dangerous place. Francis Fukuyama, a consultant at the RAND Corporation, argues that the current period of political instability will not necessarily lead to a more dangerous future.

Madeleine K. Albright, the U.S. secretary of state, argues that U.S. support of an expanded NATO will allow it to help shape a peaceful Europe in the future. Professor of political science Walter C. Clemens, Jr., contends that the risks and costs associated with expanding NATO outweigh any possible advantages that could be gained.

Doug Bandow, a senior fellow at the Cato Institute, argues that the United States should bring its military forces home and curtail expensive foreign aid programs. Anthony Lake, special assistant for national security affairs for the Clinton administration, maintains that U.S. national interests make full international engagement imperative.

Daniel Pipes, editor of *Middle East Quarterly*, argues that just as those who considered the Soviet threat a myth were naive, so are those who dismiss the threat from Islamic fundamentalists naive. Zachary Karabell, a researcher in the Kennedy School of Government at Harvard University, holds that it is wrong to view Islam as a monolith whose adherents pose a threat to the stability of the international system.

Colin S. Gray, a professor of international politics, asserts that geographical factors, such as size and location, are still dominant. Martin Libicki, a senior fellow at the Center for Advanced Concepts and Technology, National Defense University, contends that global communication links and computer capabilities have significantly lessened the importance of geography.

Professor of political science Robert S. Ross contends that the World Trade Organization (WTO) should admit China in order to incorporate that country into the global economy. Greg Mastel, vice president for policy planning and administration at the Economic Strategy Institute in Washington, D.C., argues that the integrity of the WTO would be damaged if China were admitted without significant legal and economic reform.

Stephen A. Lisio, an independent analyst with a particular focus on Western Hemisphere affairs, maintains that tightening economic sanctions against Cuba is likely to be counterproductive. Alberto J. Mora, an attorney with a specialty in international law, contends that abandoning sanctions against Cuba would be tantamount to endorsing despotism.

Business professor Murray Weidenbaum argues that the integration of the American economy with the world is both inevitable and desirable. Professor of political science Gregory Albo maintains that globalization is neither irreversible nor, in its present form, desirable.

United Nations executive James P. Grant contends that one way to jump-start solutions to many of the world's problems is to extend more assistance to impoverished countries. The editors of the *Economist*, a well-known British publication, suggest that the usual ways in which international aid is distributed and spent make it a waste of resources.

Tom Bethell, Washington correspondent for the *American Spectator*, contends that the drive toward denuclearization is likely to leave the United States exposed to its enemies. George Lee Butler, a retired U.S. Air Force general and former commander of the Strategic Air Command, advocates the elimination of all nuclear weapons.

Joseph E. Schwartzberg, a professor of geography, proposes a standing UN Peace Corps military force of international volunteers to better enable the UN to meet its peacekeeping mission. John F. Hillen III, a lieutenant in the U.S. Army and a doctoral student in international relations, criticizes the ideal of a permanent UN army on several grounds and concludes that such a force is unworkable.

Alan Tonelson, a fellow of the Economic Strategy Institute in Washington, D.C., contends that the United States' human rights policy ought to be jettisoned. Michael Posner, executive director of the Lawyers Committee for Human Rights, maintains that the United States should continue to incorporate human rights concerns into its foreign policy decisions.

James Lee Ray, a professor of political science at Vanderbilt University, contends that the evidence shows that the democratization of all the world's
countries would promote peace. Mary Caprioli, a doctoral candidate at the
University of Connecticut, argues that there is no conclusive evidence that
global democratization will result in world peace.

A report by the U.S. Department of State's Bureau of Democracy, Human
Rights, and Labor contends that China violates the human rights of its people
in a variety of ways. The State Council of the People's Republic of China
maintains that the report condemning China is culturally biased, inaccurate,
and violates China's sovereignty.

Timothy Wirth, a U.S. assistant secretary of state, contends that UN-sponsored
world conferences have helped shape a world that is more hospitable to
American interests and values. Christine Vollmer, president of the Latin
American Alliance for the Family, rejects what she sees as unwelcome policies
being promoted by UN-sponsored conferences.

John Keane, director of the Centre for the Study of Democracy, condemns nationalism as a destructive force that makes people self-absorbed, gives them a false sense of being invincible, and too often leads them to attack others. Professors of sociology Salvador Cardús and Joan Estruch contend that those who condemn nationalism either do not understand it or approach the subject with an antinationalist bias.

Yeh Ling-Ling, founder of the Diversity Coalition for an Immigration Moratorium in San Francisco, California, argues that immigration should be curbed because it detracts from the economic opportunities available to Americans. Stephen Moore, an economist with the Cato Institute in Washington, D.C., maintains that the net gains that the United States reaps from the contributions of immigrants far outweigh any social costs.

Al Gore, vice president of the United States, contends that rapid world population growth is outstripping the globe's ability to sustain it. Dennis T. Avery, director of global food issues at the Hudson Institute, argues that increased agriculture yields and other technology-based advances mean that the globe can sustain a much larger population.

INTRODUCTION

World Politics and the Voice of Justice

John T. Rourke

Some years ago, the Rolling Stones recorded "Sympathy With the Devil." If you have never heard it, go find a copy. It is worth listening to. The theme of the song is echoed in a wonderful essay by Marshall Berman, "Have Sympathy for the Devil" (*New American Review*, 1973). The common theme of the Stones' and Berman's works is based on Johann Goethe's *Faust*. In that classic drama, the protagonist, Dr. Faust, trades his soul to gain great power. He attempts to do good, but in the end he commits evil by, in contemporary paraphrase, "doing the wrong things for the right reasons." Does that make Faust evil, the personification of the devil Mephistopheles among us? Or is the good doctor merely misguided in his effort to make the world better as he saw it and imagined it might be? The point that the Stones and Berman make is that it is important to avoid falling prey to the trap of many zealots who are so convinced of the truth of their own views that they feel righteously at liberty to condemn those who disagree with them as stupid or even diabolical.

It is to the principle of rational discourse, of tolerant debate, that this reader is dedicated. There are many issues in this volume that appropriately excite passion—for example, Issue 4 on whether or not Islamic fundamentalism represents a threat to political stability or Issue 10 on whether or not the world needs to have nuclear weapons at all. Few would find fault with the goal of avoiding nuclear destruction—indeed, of achieving a peaceful world. How to reach that goal is another matter, however, and we should take care not to confuse disagreement on means with disagreement on ends. In other cases, the debates you will read do diverge on goals. John Keane, for example, argues in Issue 16 that nationalism is destructive and that we would be better off seeking new forms of political loyalty and organization. Salvador Cardús and Joan Estruch disagree, stressing the positive contributions of nationalism now and, they hope, in the future. Issue 15 also debates how we will organize ourselves politically and relate to one another in the future. The key issue is whether world conferences that meet to address global issues are making a contribution, as Timothy Wirth maintains, or imposing the will of a few on the countries and individuals of the world in violation of democratic principles and national sovereignty, as Christine Vollmer contends.

As you will see, each of the authors in all the debates strongly believes in his or her position. If you read these debates objectively, you will find that each side makes cogent points. They may or may not be right, but they should not be dismissed out of hand. It is also important to repeat that the debate format does not imply that you should remain forever neutral. In fact, once you are informed, you *ought* to form convictions, and you should try to act on those convictions and try to influence international policy to conform better with your beliefs. Ponder the similarities in the views of two very different leaders, a very young president in a relatively young democracy and a very old emperor in a very old country: In 1963 President John F. Kennedy, in recalling the words of the author of the epoch poem *The Divine Comedy* (1321), told a West German audience, "Dante once said that the hottest places in hell are reserved for those who in a period of moral crisis maintain their neutrality." That very same year, while speaking to the United Nations, Ethiopia's emperor Haile Selassie (1892–1975) said, "Throughout history it has been the inaction of those who could have acted, the indifference of those who should have known better, the silence of the voice of justice when it mattered most that made it possible for evil to triumph."

The point is: Become Informed. Then *do* something! Write letters to policymakers, donate money to causes you support, work for candidates with whom you agree, join an activist organization, or any of the many other things that you can do to make a difference. What you do is less important than that you do it.

APPROACHES TO STUDYING INTERNATIONAL POLITICS

As will become evident as you read this volume, there are many approaches to the study of international politics. Some political scientists and most practitioners specialize in *substantive topics*, and this reader is organized along topical lines. Part 1 (Issues 1 through 5) begins with a question about the present condition of the international system, currently an emphasis of many scholars. Patrick Glynn and Francis Fukuyama debate whether or not the world has become a more dangerous place since the end of the cold war. Beginning with Issue 2, the focus of Part 1 shifts to regional issues and actors. Debates here deal with the expansion of the North Atlantic Treaty Organization (NATO) to include Eastern European countries, the superpower role of the United States, and the role of Islam in the Middle East and elsewhere. Issue 5 then takes up the matter of whether or not regions and other geopolitical structures matter as much as they did in the past. Colin S. Gray argues that they do; Martin Libicki contends that information is supplanting geopolitics as a primary factor. Part 2 (Issues 6 through 9) focuses on international economic issues, including whether or not China should be admitted to the World Trade Organization (WTO); the wisdom of unilateral economic sanctions, especially the Helms-Burton Act; the desirability of the ever-increasing degree of economic interdependence; and whether foreign aid should be substantially increased or drastically reduced. Part 3 (Issues 10 and 11) deals with military security. The world has been threatened by atomic destruction for more than a half century. But some say that nuclear weapons have kept the peace. In Issue 10 Tom Bethell maintains that it would be a mistake for the United States to get rid of its nuclear weapons. George Lee Butler, a former commander of U.S. nuclear forces, takes the opposite point of view and says that it is time to create a world that is free of nuclear weapons. In Issue 11 the call to create a permanent UN peacekeeping force is debated. Part 4 (Issues 12 through 14) examines controversies surrounding the application of values in world politics. Debates here concern whether decision makers should apply moral standards when making policy, whether democracy should be promoted as a path to world peace, and whether China, possibly an emerging superpower, should be condemned for its human rights record. Part 5 (issues 15 through 18) addresses issues about global trends in international relations. Some analysts claim that the world is moving slowly but perceptibly toward international governance. The role of world conferences in that trend is discussed in Issue 15. By the same token, nationalism may be declining, as debated in Issue 16. Regardless of people's loyalties to their countries of birth, it is a fact that the movement of individuals across national borders is currently of epic proportions. This is the backdrop for Issue 17, which debates whether the United States should encourage or discourage immigration. The final debate addresses the future of the biosphere, in particular whether or not the world is reaching a point where it can no longer support its population.

Political scientists also approach their subject from differing *methodological perspectives*. We will see, for example, that world politics can be studied from different *levels of analysis*. The question is: What is the basic source of the forces that shape the conduct of politics? Possible answers are world forces, the individual political processes of the specific countries, or the personal attributes of a country's leaders and decision makers. Various readings will illustrate all three levels.

Another way for students and practitioners of world politics to approach their subject is to focus on what is called the realist versus the idealist debate. Realists tend to assume that the world is permanently flawed and therefore advocate following policies in their country's narrow self-interests. Idealists take the approach that the world condition can be improved substantially by following policies that, at least in the short term, call for some risk or self-sacrifice. This divergence is an element of many of the debates in this book.

DYNAMICS OF WORLD POLITICS

The action on the global stage today is vastly different from what it was a few decades ago, or even a few years ago. *Technology* is one of the causes of this change. Technology has changed communications, manufacturing, health care, and many other aspects of the human condition. Technology has also led to the creation of nuclear weapons and other highly sophisticated and expensive conventional weapons. Issue 10 frames a debate over whether or not, having created and armed ourselves with nuclear weapons, we can and should reverse the process and eliminate them. Technology has also vastly increased our ability to gather, analyze, and eliminate information. Issue 5 debates the degree to which information has displaced geopolitics as a primary determinant of power. Another dynamic aspect of world politics involves the *changing axes* of the world system. For about 40 years after World War II ended in 1945, a bipolar system existed, the primary axis of which was the *East-West* conflict, which pitted the United States and its allies against the Soviet Union and its allies. Now that the Warsaw Pact has collapsed as an axis of world politics, many new questions have surfaced relating to how security should be provided for Europe and the future of NATO. Some analysts advocate expanding NATO to include some or all of the countries of Eastern Europe and, perhaps, even Russia and some of the other former Soviet republics. This plan is the topic of Issue 2. Insofar as containing communism and the Soviet Union was the mainstay of U.S. post–World War II policy, the end of the Soviet threat also brings the United States to a pivotal choice about future foreign involvement. As Issue 3 explains, there is a growing tide of American sentiment that favors limiting the role of the United States abroad, but there are also those who argue that the United States should not abandon its activist, international superpower role.

Technological changes and the shifting axes of international politics also highlight the *increased role of economics* in world politics. Economics have always played a role, but traditionally the main focus has been on strategic-political questions—especially military power. This concern still strongly exists, but it now shares the international spotlight with economic issues. One important change in recent decades has been the rapid growth of regional and global markets and the promotion of free trade and other forms of international economic interchange. As Issue 8 on economic interdependence indicates, many people support these efforts and see them as the wave of the future. But there are others who believe that free trade undermines sovereignty and the ability of governments to regulate multinational corporations.

Another change in the world system has to do with the main *international* actors. At one time states (countries) were practically the only international actors on the world stage. Now, and increasingly so, there are other actors. Some actors are regional. Others, such as the United Nations, are global actors. Issue 15 explores the contribution of UN-sponsored world conferences to advancing the human condition. On the international military security dimension of the UN's role, Issue 11 examines the call for strengthening the peacekeeping and peacemaking capability of the United Nations by establishing a permanent UN military force.

PERCEPTIONS VERSUS REALITY

In addition to addressing the general changes in the world system outlined above, the debates in this reader explore the controversies that exist over many of the fundamental issues that face the world.

One key to these debates is the differing *perceptions* that protagonists bring to them. There may be a reality in world politics, but very often that reality is obscured. Many observers, for example, are alarmed by the seeming rise in radical actions by Islamic fundamentalists. As Issue 4 illustrates, the image of Islamic radicalism is not a fact but a perception; perhaps correct, perhaps not. In cases such as this, though, it is often the perception, not the reality, that is more important because policy is formulated on what decision makers *think*, not necessarily on what *is*. Thus, perception becomes the operating guide, or *operational reality*, whether it is true or not.

Perceptions result from many factors. One factor is the information that decision makers receive. For a variety of reasons, the facts and analyses that are given to leaders are often inaccurate or at least represent only part of the picture. Perceptions are also formed by the value system of a decision maker, which is based on his or her experiences and ideology. The way in which such an individual thinks and speaks about another leader, country, or the world in general is called his or her *operational code.* Issue 3, for example, explores the role of the United States in the world. How U.S. presidents and other Americans define their country's role creates an operational code governing relations. President Bill Clinton has shown himself to have more of an internationalist operational code than the public. Clinton, for example, launched military interventions into both Haiti and Bosnia and Herzegovina. The American public was opposed to both actions, demonstrating much less willingness than the president to cast their country in the role of defender of democracy, of human rights, or of what President George Bush called the "new world order." *ho did say it.*

Another aspect of perception is the tendency to see oneself differently than some others do. Partly at issue in the debate over China's desire to join the World Trade Organization, as discussed in Issue 6, is whether the country should be able to join as a less developed country (as China sees itself) and take advantage of fewer restrictions, or whether China should be admitted as a major economic power (as the United States sees it) and have to abide by all the WTO's rules requiring lowering barriers to trade and investment.

Perceptions, then, are crucial to understanding international politics. It is important to understand objective reality, but it is also necessary to comprehend subjective reality in order to be able to predict and analyze another country's actions.

LEVELS OF ANALYSIS

Political scientists approach the study of international politics from different levels of analysis. The most macroscopic view is *system-level analysis.* This is a top-down approach that maintains that world factors virtually compel countries to follow certain foreign policies. Governing factors include the number of powerful actors, geographic relationships, economic needs, and technology. System analysts hold that a country's internal political system and its leaders do not have a major impact on policy. As such, political scientists who work from this perspective are interested in exploring the governing factors, how they cause policy, and how and why systems change.

After the end of World War II, the world was structured as a *bipolar* system, dominated by the United States and the Soviet Union. Furthermore, each superpower was supported by a tightly organized and dependent group of allies. For a variety of reasons, including changing economics and the nuclear standoff, the bipolar system has faded. Some political scientists argue that the bipolar system is being replaced by a *multipolar* system. In such a configuration, those who favor *balance-of-power* politics maintain that it is unwise to ignore power considerations. The debate in Issue 3 about the future of U.S. international activity reflects the changes that have occurred in the system and the efforts of Americans to decide what role they should play in the new multipolar structure. That is also a part of the debate in Issue 2 on NATO expansion, both because of the willingness of Americans to take on new alliance responsibilities and because of the view of the Russians that the expansion of NATO is a U.S.-led move to threaten Russia by bringing the powerful alliance to her very borders.

State-level analysis is the middle, and the most common, level of analysis. Social scientists who study world politics from this perspective focus on how countries, singly or comparatively, make foreign policy. In other words, this perspective is concerned with internal political dynamics such as the roles of and interactions between the executive and legislative branches of government, the impact of bureaucracy, the role of interest groups, and the effect of public opinion. The Helms-Burton Act, which is debated in Issue 7, represents a case where the U.S. Congress passed strong sanctions against Cuba, and the president, even though he had serious reservations about the act, signed it into law because of the pressure of an upcoming presidential election.

A third level of analysis, which is the most microscopic, is *human-level analysis*. This approach focuses, in part, on the role of individual decision makers. This technique is applied under the assumption that individuals make decisions and that the nature of those decisions is determined by the decision makers' perceptions, predilections, and strengths and weaknesses. Human-level analysis also focuses on the nature of humans. Issue 12 explores the degree to which decision makers should apply their own or their society's moral standards to foreign policy decisions.

REALISM VERSUS IDEALISM

Realism and idealism represent another division among political scientists and practitioners in their approaches to the study and conduct of international relations. *Realists* are usually skeptical about the nature of politics and, perhaps, the nature of humankind. They tend to believe that countries have opposing interests and that these differences can lead to conflict. They further contend that states (countries) are by definition obligated to do what is beneficial for their own citizens (national interest). The amount of power that a state has will determine how successful it is in attaining these goals. Therefore, politics is, and ought to be, a process of gaining, maintaining, and using power. Realists are apt to believe that the best way to avoid conflict is to remain powerful and to avoid pursuing goals that are beyond one's power to achieve. "Peace through strength" is a phrase that most realists would agree with.

Idealists disagree with realists about both the nature and conduct of international relations. They tend to be more optimistic that the global community is capable of finding ways to live in harmony and that it has a sense of collective, rather than national, interest. Idealists also claim that the pursuit of a narrow national interest is shortsighted. They argue that, in the long run, countries must learn to cooperate or face the prospect of a variety of evils, including possible nuclear warfare, environmental disaster, or continuing economic hardship. Idealists argue, for example, that armaments cause world tensions, whereas realists maintain that conflict requires states to have weapons. Idealists are especially concerned with conducting current world politics on a more moral or ethical plane and with searching for alternatives to the present pursuit of nationalist interests through power politics.

Many of the issues in this volume address the realist-idealist split. Realists and idealists differ over whether or not states can and should surrender enough of their freedom of action and pursuit of self-interest to cooperate through and, to a degree, subordinate themselves to international organizations. This is one basis of disagreement in Issue 11, which contemplates a permanent UN military force. Realists and idealists also disagree on whether or not moral considerations should play a strong role in determining foreign policy. The proper role of morality is the focus of debate between realist Alan Tonelson and idealist Michael Posner in Issue 12. In a more applied sense, the U.S. Department of State takes the idealist position in condemning China for human rights violations in Issue 14, while the State Council of China argues that the condemnation is unfair. In Issue 13 James Lee Ray supports promoting democracy around the world in the interests of peace, while Mary Caprioli doubts that there is enough evidence to be sure that democracy promotes peace. Just as in *Faust*, as mentioned at the beginning of this introduction, the urge to do good is fraught with peril.

THE POLITICAL AND ECOLOGICAL FUTURE

Future *world alternatives* are discussed in many of the issues in this volume. Issue 1, for example, debates whether or not the current world situation portends anarchy. The debate in Issue 9 on the North providing aid to the South is not just about humanitarian impulses; it is about whether or not the world can survive and be stable economically and politically if it is divided into a minority of wealthy nations and a majority of poor countries. Abraham Lincoln once said, "A house divided against itself cannot stand." One suspects that the 16th president might say something similar about the world today if he were with us. Another, more far-reaching, alternative is an international organization taking over some (or all) of the sovereign responsibilities of national governments. Issues 11 and 15, for example, focus on the authority of the United Nations to assume even limited supranational (above countries) power. And Issues 6 and 8 touch on another supranational organization: the World Trade Organization under the new General Agreement on Tariffs and Trade (GATT) revision.

The global future also involves the ability of the world to prosper economically while, at the same time, not denuding itself of its natural resources or destroying the environment. This is the focus of Issue 18 on population growth.

THE AXES OF WORLD DIVISION

It is a truism that the world is politically dynamic and that the nature of the political system is undergoing profound change. As noted, the once-primary axis of world politics, the East-West confrontation, has broken down. Yet a few vestiges of the conflict on that axis remain. Issue 7 reviews the arguments for and against the United States lifting its economic sanctions against communist Cuba.

In contrast to the moribund East-West axis, the *North-South axis* has increased in importance and tension. The wealthy, industrialized countries (North) are on one end, and the poor, less developed countries (LDCs, South) are at the other extreme. Economic differences and disputes are the primary dimension of this axis, in contrast to the military nature of the East-West axis. Issue 9 explores these differences and debates whether or not the North should significantly increase economic aid to the South.

The maldistribution of wealth in the world leads many people in the impoverished South to try to emigrate, legally or illegally, to wealthier countries in an effort to find a better life for themselves and their families. The extent of this migration has caused the economically developed nations to increasingly resist the movement of people across international borders. The wisdom of severely constraining immigration is the subject of Issue 17.

Then there is the question of what, if anything, will develop to divide the countries of the North and replace the East-West axis. The possibility for tension is represented in several issues. Some believe that the remnants of the USSR, especially Russia, will one day again pose a threat to the rest of Europe. At least some of the East European countries that want to join NATO (Issue 2) are worried about that possibility. A provocative idea of political scientist Samuel Huntington is that cultures will be the basis of a new, multiaxial dimension of global antagonism. If that comes to pass, then it might be that an expanded NATO, including most of what Huntington calls the Western countries, will be one step in the formation of one part of the axis. A rising China, dominating parts of Southeast Asia (contemplated in

Issue 6), might form what Huntington calls the Confucian civilization, and politically resurgent Muslims (as discussed in Issue 4) might cohere as the Islamic civilization.

INCREASED ROLE OF ECONOMICS

As the growing importance of the North-South axis indicates, economics are playing an increased role in world politics. The economic reasons behind the decline of the East-West axis is further evidence. Economics have always played a part in international relations, but the traditional focus has been on strategic-political affairs, especially questions of military power.

Political scientists, however, are now increasingly focusing on the international political economy, or the economic dimensions of world politics. International trade, for instance, has increased dramatically, expanding from an annual world total of $20 billion in 1933 to $5.2 trillion in 1995. The impact has been profound. The domestic economic health of most countries is heavily affected by trade and other aspects of international economics. Since World War II, there has been an emphasis on expanding free trade by decreasing tariffs and other barriers to international commerce. In recent years, however, a downturn in the economies of many of the industrialized countries has increased calls for more protectionism. This is related to the debate in Issue 6 on China's application to join the WTO. Yet restrictions on trade and other economic activity can also be used as a diplomatic weapons. The intertwining of economies and the creation of organizations to regulate them, such as the WTO, is raising issues of sovereignty and other concerns. This is a central matter in the debate in Issue 8 between Murray Weidenbaum and Gregory Albo over whether or not the trend toward global economic integration is desirable. A further aspect of that issue has to do with the legitimacy and effectiveness of economic sanctions, such as the Helms-Burton Act, which is the focus of Issue 7.

The level and impact of international aid is another economic issue of considerable dispute. Issue 9 examines the question of whether massive foreign aid would help the less developed countries (and the developed countries as well) or actually hinder economic progress in the less developed countries.

CONCLUSION

Having discussed many of the various dimensions and approaches to the study of world politics, it is incumbent on this editor to advise against your becoming too structured by them. Issues of focus and methodology are important both to studying international relations and to understanding how others are analyzing global conduct. However, they are also partially pedagogical. In the final analysis, world politics is a highly interrelated, perhaps seamless, subject. No one level of analysis, for instance, can fully explain the events on the world stage. Instead, using each of the levels to analyze events and trends will bring the greatest understanding.

Similarly, the realist-idealist division is less precise in practice than it may appear. As some of the debates indicate, each side often stresses its own standards of morality. Which is more moral: defeating dictatorship or sparing the sword and saving lives that will almost inevitably be lost in the dictator's overthrow? Furthermore, realists usually do not reject moral considerations. Rather, they contend that morality is but one of the factors that a country's decision makers must consider. Realists are also apt to argue that standards of morality differ when dealing with a country as opposed to an individual. By the same token, most idealists do not completely ignore the often dangerous nature of the world. Nor do they argue that a country must totally sacrifice its short-term interests to promote the betterment of the current and future world. Thus, realism and idealism can be seen most accurately as the ends of a continuum—with most political scientists and practitioners falling somewhere between, rather than at, the extremes. The best advice, then, is this: think broadly about international politics. The subject is very complex, and the more creative and expansive you are in selecting your foci and methodologies, the more insight you will gain. To end where we began, with Dr. Faust, I offer his last words in Goethe's drama, *"Mehr licht,"* . . . More light! That is the goal of this book.

On the Internet . . .

http://www.dushkin.com

Welcome to Al-Islam.org
This site is an introduction to Islam (if you are a beginner) and a repository for advancing your knowledge about Islam further (if you are a Muslim).
http://www.al-islam.org

Jane's Electronic Information System
This is an online demonstration of the Jane Information Group's electronic information system. For nearly 100 years, Jane's has published accurate and impartial books on the subjects of defense, weaponry, civil aviation, and transportation. *http://www.btg.com/janes/welcome.html*

North Atlantic Treaty Organization
This site, distributed by the Canadian Forces College Information Resource Centre, links to the official servers of NATO and to information and archive sites.
http://www.cfcsc.dnd.ca/links/milorg/nato.html

U.S. Department of State Web Site Index
The information in this index of the U.S. Department of State is organized into categories, from foreign policy and the Middle East to regions and the United Nations.
http://www.state.gov/www/ind.html

PART 1

Regional Issues and Actors

The issues in this section deal with countries that are major regional powers. In this era of interdependence among nations, it is important to understand the concerns that these issues address and the actors involved because they will shape the world and will affect the lives of all people.

■ Has the World Become a More Dangerous Place Since the End of the Cold War?

■ Is It Wise to Expand NATO Membership?

■ Should the United States Abandon Its Superpower Role?

■ Is Islamic Fundamentalism a Threat to Political Stability?

■ Is Geopolitics Still Relevant in the Era of Cyberspace?

ISSUE 1

Has the World Become a More Dangerous Place Since the End of the Cold War?

YES: Patrick Glynn, from "The Age of Balkanization," *Commentary* (July 1993)

NO: Francis Fukuyama, from "Against the New Pessimism," *Commentary* (February 1994)

ISSUE SUMMARY

YES: Patrick Glynn, a resident scholar at the American Enterprise Institute and a former official in the U.S. Arms Control and Disarmament Agency, contends that post–cold war political and social fragmentation is destabilizing countries and making the world a more dangerous place.

NO: Francis Fukuyama, a resident consultant at the RAND Corporation and a former State Department official, argues that the current period of post–cold war instability does not necessarily mean that we face a more dangerous future.

The first half of the 1990s was truly remarkable. The world watched in amazement as the Soviet Union's empire in Eastern Europe disintegrated, and then as the communist and authoritarian political system of the USSR itself collapsed into 15 different countries and disappeared. For nearly three-quarters of a century, the communist Soviet Union had seemed to most in the West to loom threateningly. For 45 years an East-West rivalry had locked the Soviet Union and the United States, both militarily mighty and ideologically hostile toward each other, and their respective allies in a seeming death struggle The two alliances never engaged one another directly in combat, or a hot war. Still, the struggle was so intense and so potentially apocalyptic, given the two superpowers' nuclear arsenals, that *cold war* became the accepted term to describe the tensions that gripped international relations.

And then the foreboding was gone! The Soviet flag was lowered from atop the Kremlin in Moscow, and the Russian flag was raised in its stead. Russian president Boris Yeltsin pledged democracy and peace with the United States. The cold war is over, U.S. president George Bush told a national audience, and the Americans have won. The world seemed so much safer. There were pledges of friendship from the capitals of most of the former enemies as well as several new arms control initiatives and treaties. There were moves in the United States and elsewhere to slash defense spending. And people debated how to spend the surplus funds, the so-called peace dividend.

There was also great optimism about changing the world system for the better. As President Bush put it at the time, "A new world order [is] struggling to be born ... where the rule of law supplants the rule of the jungle. A world in which nations recognize the shared responsibility for freedom and justice. A world where the strong respect the rights of the weak."

Not everyone was so hopeful. Scholar John Mearsheimer, for one, in "Why We Will Soon Miss the Cold War," *The Atlantic Monthly* (August 1990), warned that we would one day look back nostalgically at the stability of the cold war. His view was determined in part by the view of many political scientists who theorize that when there are changes in the number of major powers (called poles) in the international system, or a significant shift in the strength of one or more of the poles, then several destabilizing trends may occur. One is that rising powers and declining powers may clash over territory, control of resources, or other matters. Second, areas once dominated by a fading power may fall into uncontrolled rivalries once the declining power's influence dissipates.

Soon after the cold war ended, the more dire image of the future projected by Mearsheimer and others seemed to come to pass. Nationalism was the most common cause of conflict around the world. Several of the 15 republics that established their independence by seceding from the Soviet Union now face their own secessionist movements. Elsewhere, the efforts of Kurds to break away from Iraq (and other surrounding countries), fighting between Muslims in the north of the Sudan and non-Muslims in the south, clashes among Bosnians, Croats, and Serbs in the former Yugoslavia, clan warfare in Somalia, tribal violence between Hutus and Tutsis in Rwanda, and other bloodletting have shocked the world. Such national and ethnic-based rivalries are, in the view of some analysts, part of a greater pattern of fragmentation that threatens to destroy the domestic social fabric of many countries. Whether the differences are based on race, gender, religion, language, or some other characteristic, numerous commentators argue that the national political systems that have so long been at the center of domestic order and a primary aspect of the international system are in danger of disintegrating.

There can be little doubt that there is instability in the international system as it seeks a new equilibrium. What is not certain, and what is the subject of this debate, is whether or not the current state of affairs is long-term and should make us relatively pessimistic about future global stability. Patrick Glynn and Francis Fukuyama take up this debate. Glynn argues that the world is becoming politically and socially fragmented and therefore unstable. Fukuyama contends that if we look beyond immediate distressing events, we need not be pessimistic about the future.

3

YES   Patrick Glynn

THE AGE OF BALKANIZATION

Today a fundamental change is under way in the character of global political life. A new era is in the making. Gone or fading are the great bipolar conflicts —between democracy and fascism, between democracy and Communism, and even perhaps between Left and Right—that shaped war and peace in the 20th century. In their place a new political struggle is emerging—more complex, more diffuse, but nonetheless global in character.

On every continent, in almost every major nation, and in almost every walk of life the overriding political reality today is that of increasing social separatism and fragmentation—a sometimes violent splintering of humanity by ethnic group, race, religion, and even (to a less dramatic extent) such characteristics as gender or sexual orientation. While the causes of this phenomenon are as yet imperfectly understood, its implications could hardly be more far-reaching.

The most dramatic manifestation of the change is found, of course, in the countries that used to be known as Yugoslavia and Czechoslovakia, and it is also showing itself in other parts of the defunct Soviet empire, not to mention the old Soviet Union itself. But the phenomenon is not merely one of Communism giving way to nationalism, nor is it confined to the old Communist world.

Indeed, everywhere one sees well-established nation-states threatened with disunion, and even in countries without explicit separatist movements, the unifying themes of political life are increasingly under attack. Canada copes with Quebec's secessionism, the United Kingdom with Scottish separatists, Italy with increasing tensions between its north and its south. In Germany, as well as in France and Britain, ethnically motivated violence has become a major factor in politics, and rebellious youths are inflamed by a puzzling new ideology of ethnic hatred.

Even in America—the proverbial melting pot—racial, ethnic, and other varieties of separatism are distinctly on the rise. Blacks assert their identity as "African-Americans"; homosexuals discover in their sexual orientation a basis for political action; Christian fundamentalists exert more and more influence as an organized political force.

Nor is this phenomenon merely political. It also finds its reflection in the highest reaches of contemporary culture and intellectual life. The controversial doctrine of "multiculturalist education" and the "postmodernist" philosophy now so current in American universities are both essentially codifications of the new experience of fragmentation.

Side by side with this splintering, paradoxically, has gone a fresh drive for unity. As the cold war was ending, George Bush, then still in the White House, hailed the advent of a Europe "whole and free," and in the lead-up to the Gulf war he spoke hopefully of a "new world order." Since then, European Community leaders have worked to forge a unitary Europe, while Germany's leadership has sought to make one nation out of two. In Russia, Boris Yeltsin fights a parallel battle, desperately trying to hold Russia together while moving toward democracy in the face of radical nationalism and mounting pressures for regional secession.

But these efforts at unification—including the effort to posit a new world order based on common democratic values—have thus far proved unable to stem the powerful counter-currents rooted in separatist identities. For this new cultural struggle is taking place not only within nations, but among them. Attempts to expand the postwar liberal trading order have been frustrated by intensified cultural conflict between America and Japan and, to a lesser extent, between America and Western Europe. Islamic fundamentalism poses a threat to moderate Arab regimes and increases the likelihood of eventual armed conflict between the West and radical Arab states.

Slowly this clash between, on the one hand, ethnic (and other types of) particularism and, on the other hand, what might be called democratic universalism seems to be replacing the old Left-Right and class polarities that have governed political life for nearly a century. It has every appearance of becoming the new bipolarity of global politics, the new dialectic of a new age.

* * *

What are the reasons for this great shift? The most obvious cause would seem to lie in the collapse of Soviet Communism. Communism repressed national differences; indeed, Marxist-Leninist ideology, rooted as it was in Enlightenment economic thinking, defined national and ethnic differences as epiphenomenal, stressing instead the primacy of class. Under Communism, nationalism was either disguised or stifled.

What we have seen since the breakdown of Communism—whether in the former Soviet Union, the former Yugoslavia, or the rest of Eastern Europe—is, to borrow a phrase from Sigmund Freud, a "return of the repressed," a resurgence of powerful national and ethnic feelings which had been simmering angrily beneath the surface.

But if Communist regimes ruthlessly imposed unity on their own peoples, they also evoked a more or less united response from the outside world they threatened. The unitary nature of the Communist threat inspired an unprecedented degree of cooperation—under American leadership—among heretofore uncooperative states. European adversaries laid aside age-old grudges to join NATO. New security relationships were forged among the United States and major Asian nations, including Japan.

To be sure, Woodrow Wilson and Franklin Roosevelt had earlier sought on their own initiative to structure a more or less unified world order, to export America's stated principles of ethnic tolerance, and to bring the many nations of the world together on the basis of common interests and goals. But it is far from clear that, absent the Soviet threat, so many disparate nations would have been so successful in achieving collaboration, not just on trade but on a host of diplomatic and security matters, as they were during the cold war. Long ago the sociologist Georg Simmel posited that human societies were cemented together by the need to cope with outside threats. This was clearly true of what we used to call the "free world."

Even within American politics, the anti-Communist imperative had a powerful unifying effect. It produced, albeit intermittently, bipartisanship in foreign policy. It also, at various times, unified each of the two major parties. In the early years of the cold war, the Democrats, and in the later years, the Republicans, found a basis for party solidarity in the anti-Communist cause. So much was this the case that when the Democrats and then the Republicans experienced ruinous internal division, it was owing in part to a perceived or real diminution of the Soviet threat—for the Democrats during the late 1960's and early 1970's, when many believed the cold war to have become obsolete, and for the Republicans in recent years, when it became plain that the cold war was in fact over.

The Republican case is especially interesting, for what else but fear of the Soviet threat could finally have held together the diverse elements of Ronald Reagan's winning electoral coalition: Christian fundamentalists, Jewish neoconservative intellectuals, free-market libertarians, blue-collar Democrats, and traditional Republican voters? Should it surprise us that with the subsidence of the Soviet threat, old party alignments would weaken? Is it illogical that with external dangers reduced we would turn inward as a society and discover social and political differences among one another that we had previously been willing to overlook?

Yet while the collapse of Soviet Communism remains the signal event of our age, many of the trends we are discussing were apparent before the Berlin Wall came down. Ethnic, national, and racial awareness was already growing, on both sides of the iron curtain. Here in America, for example, the multiculturalist movement—now so famous and controversial for its advocacy of heightened ethnic and racial consciousness in schools —was already making inroads into secondary and higher education. On both sides of the iron curtain, faith in central authority was declining and had been declining for some time. Even before the advent of Mikhail Gorbachev, Western Sovietologists debated whether Communist leaders still actually believed their ideology. Ironically, a weakening in the influence of received values—society's traditional unifying ideas—was apparent in our own culture as well, observed by intellectuals and documented by opinion polls.

* * *

In other words, it is hard to say whether the demise of Soviet Communism is the ultimate cause of the change we are witnessing, or whether Soviet Communism itself fell victim to some vaster trend, some grand Hegelian shift in human consciousness.

Certainly the contemporary experience of social and political fragmentation was foreshadowed by new directions in intellectual life, long before the social consequences were apparent. One of the major proponents of "postmodernist" thinking, Fredric Jameson of Duke University, has written of the postmodern idiom in contemporary literature:

> Perhaps the immense fragmentation and privatization of modern literature —its explosion into a host of distinct private styles and mannerisms— foreshadow deeper and more general trends in social life as a whole. Supposing that modern art and modernism—far from being a kind of specialized aesthetic curiosity—actually anticipated social developments along these lines; supposing that in the decades since the emergence of the great modern styles of society has itself begun to fragment in this way, each group coming to speak a curious private language of its own, each profession developing its own private code or idiolect, and finally each individual coming to be a kind of linguistic island, separated from everyone else?

Behind this new experience of cultural and intellectual fragmentation lies a loss of faith in general truths, and even, at its most radical, a loss of faith in the very possibility of general truths. Notably, the most sophisticated humanities instructors in our major universities today will no longer venture to assert that a proposition is "true," merely that it is "productive" or "intriguing," i.e., a basis for reflection or intellectual play. This premise lends a notable arbitrariness to "postmodern" modes of expression, robbing contemporary literature, criticism, and even philosophy of a certain weight, authority, or seriousness.

The same mixture of posturing and pastiche has become evident in our political discourse (think back to Bush's Gulf war speeches). However glorious the phrases—"freedom," "tyranny," "new world order"—they are uttered today with a certain self-conscious nostalgia.

We have lived through an era when people attached themselves to grand ideas—whether for good or for evil—and fought and sometimes died for them. But for some reason these ideas collectively seem to be losing their force. Such is the defining tendency of our age.

The resulting fragmentation is far from being a propitious development. At stake, one could argue, is the future of civilization itself. The struggle for civilization has always been a struggle for unity, universality, ecumenism. The great ages of civilization have been periods of concord and commonality, when large tracts of the globe were more or less united by common values, and sometimes even by a common language and common laws—the Roman empire, the era of Charlemagne, the Renaissance, the 19th-century Concert of Europe. These periods have been succeeded in turn by periods of fragmentation, factional strife, and relative barbarism: the Dark Ages, the feudal era, the Reformation with its religious wars, and of course the long "civil war" that wrenched Europe between 1914 and 1945. Looking back, one can see that Western history has been marked by a cyclical pattern in which unifying ideas triumph, only gradually to lose their hold on the imagination and to be replaced by factional struggle and particularism.

It is possible that we are on the threshold of a new such cyclical turn.

* * *

At the root of the problem lies the very large and very deep question of human identity. In a sense, the master-idea of Western civilization is the view that the identifying feature of the human being qua [as] human being is the faculty of reason. When the Greek philosophers hit upon this notion of man as the rational animal, they made possible the creation of large political orders on a basis other than that of pure despotism.

Furthermore, as Socrates and his students saw, this conception transcended differences of nationality and race: rational man could not be defined as Athenian or Spartan or even Greek or barbarian. And with this insight, the philosophers ceased to be good citizens of their cities, their *poleis,* at least in the terms of those cities: they became citizens of the rational universe—to use a somewhat later term, cosmopolitans—and they challenged the laws and gods of their fellow citizens....

Periods when [the classical idea of rational man] is in the ascendancy have been the great periods of civilization as we in the West know it. It is during such periods that peace reigns, learning spreads and advances, and the arts flourish. Yet experience shows that this idea does not hold indefinitely.

Perhaps the reason simply has to do with the inherent restlessness of human beings. When it first appears on the scene, the idea of rational man has a demythologizing force; it is an exploder of myth. Socrates' notion of rational man was subversive of the laws, customs, and gods of Athens—which is why he was condemned to death by his fellow citizens. Roman law, too, was subversive of local traditions and local religions; it was the "modern" idea of its era. The Renaissance was anti-traditional in the same sense—introducing ideas from the classics that raised questions about Christian beliefs.

Perhaps human beings have an over-riding need for myth, or perhaps the act of demythologization always contains within it the seeds of its own destruction. At any rate, periods of demythologization tend to be followed by periods of remythologization....

Remythologization and reversion to ethnic particularism have tended to go hand in hand. People cease to find satisfactory selfhood in large unities, become alienated from the larger whole, and begin to seek identity in smaller units. Such periods are characterized by diminished will on the part of those who stand for reason to defend reason, by a diminished appeal of reason to the human imagination. Civilization is destroyed by those whose attachment to religious or ethnic identity gives them the zeal which the defenders of reason come to lack. Civilization falls victim to barbarians from without and zealots from within. In such periods, as Yeats famously wrote, "The best lack all conviction, while the worst/ Are full of passionate intensity."

* * *

There are hints of all this in the emerging mood of our own time. The ferocious war in the Balkans is but one manifestation of a reemergent barbarism apparent in many corners of the earth. In the Balkans, the voices of the rational and the tolerant—for example, officials of the secular-minded Bosnian government—have been drowned out by the guns of ethnic fanatics. Efforts to secure democracy on the basis of rational Western principles have been crushed by the bloodthirsty exponents of "ethnic cleansing."

The new barbarians differ fundamentally from the old enemies of liberal democracy in feeling no need to justify themselves before the court of reason. The Communists, too, practiced barbarism, but they harbored a powerful imperative to vindicate themselves on the basis of some general truth: hence their elaborate ideology. Paradoxically, it was to prove they had the truth that they fashioned huge tissues of lies. Much the same was true of the Nazis, who invented the technique of the Big Lie.

The new tyrants—such characters as Slobodan Milosevic, Radovan Karadzic [both are Serbs], or for that matter Saddam Hussein—feel no such pressures. They offer as justification for their actions the thinnest pretexts. Their explanations are less an appeal to reason than a pure gesture of defiance.

Precisely because these tyrants lack intellectual seriousness, we are likely to discount them. But we forget that the great ideological struggle that characterized most of our century was the exception rather than the rule in history. Usually the enemies of civilization have not been so intellectually well-armed as the Communists (and even, in their way, the Nazis) were; but despite this they have often succeeded in prevailing. The once-mighty Romans, after all, were finally defeated by forces culturally, intellectually, and technologically inferior to them....

Nor is this problem merely one of foreign policy or regional conflict. The very idea of rational man—the cardinal concept of our civilization—is, as we have already seen, under explicit attack in our own universities. Our students are today being taught that such categories as "African-American," "female," or "person of color" are in effect more fundamental than the category of American, let alone of rational man, the human being qua [as] human being.

While the motives and consequences may be vastly different in the two cases, the multiculturalist doctrine that is fragmenting our universities as well as our intellectual life, and the "ethnic cleansing" of the Serbs, belong to the same troubling cultural and historical moment.

It is especially disturbing that this should be happening here, for America has always been the most rationally constituted of nations. It is the heir and perfecter of the great Roman idea of the *civis*, a country where nationality has nothing to do with ethnicity, a nation which has fought, through civil war and great domestic turmoil, to realize, however imperfectly, the principle of universality and tolerance.

We are now in an age that will move either toward ever greater fragmentation and violence or toward the ever wider spread of the tolerance and rationality by which we in the West have learned to live and prosper. As was true for most of this century, it is American leadership that will determine the path that history finally takes.

NO

Francis Fukuyama

AGAINST THE NEW PESSIMISM

The end of the cold war has brought about a remarkable consensus between former hawks and doves—at least those professionally involved in some fashion with international affairs, whether they be journalists, academics, or politicians—to the effect that the world has become a much worse place since the demise of the Soviet Union. The pessimistic analysis runs roughly as follows:

In 1989, with the fall of the Berlin Wall, everyone was filled with euphoria over the collapse of Communism and believed that the entire world was turning to democracy. But this expectation proved extraordinarily naive: the collapse of Communism led not to democracy but to the unleashing of virulent nationalism and/or religious passion. Now, about four years later, we see that the world is not progressing toward the "global village" but retreating into atavistic tribalism, whose ugliest expression is the "ethnic cleansing" witnessed in Bosnia.

Nor, according to the pessimistic account, is the former Yugoslavia an isolated case. Rather, Yugoslavia demonstrates that modernity is a very thin veneer indeed; what has happened there portends the resurgence of ethnic passions throughout Eastern Europe and the former USSR. And not just in that region. Even among the apparently stable democracies of Western Europe, attacks on foreign residents and immigrants are just the tip of a larger racist iceberg.

Our international institutions, by this same account, are woefully inadequate to the job of maintaining global order. The United Nations, which many people hoped would become far more effective after the cold war than it was in the days of the Soviet veto, has gotten overextended and is now presiding over policy failures in Bosnia, Somalia, and Haiti. The fecklessness of the European Community (EC) and NATO in failing to stop the slaughter in Bosnia shows how laughable was George Bush's concept of a "new world order." Instead of order we have a world far more dangerous and insecure than that of the cold war. Just as in 1914—so the pessimists conclude—the Balkans in our own day may serve as the tinderbox for a larger European conflict.

This litany, promoted by media and academic pundits around the world, makes the present situation sound very, very bad indeed. But I would argue that it misses the deeper reality of the contemporary situation, and vastly exaggerates the problems we face.

One reason it does so is that the pessimistic outlook is held primarily by Europeans or by Americans focused on European affairs, and represents a highly Eurocentric view. For a "return to tribalism" is not a helpful formula for understanding much of the rest of the world.

* * *

Let us begin at home. After having come through a bruising recession, the United States now leads the industrialized world in economic growth, hitting a rate of close to 4 percent in the fourth quarter of 1993. This latest recession performed the positive function of all recessions: it forced corporations to trim fat and focus on productivity, leaving American companies leaner and more competitive than they have ever been (albeit at a cost in certain jobs). Many of the productivity-enhancing innovations introduced in the 1980's, mostly related to information and communications technology, are now finally showing up on corporate bottom lines, particularly in the service sector. Who today would trade the American semiconductor, computer, aerospace, banking, or biotech industries for their Japanese counterparts? Or, for that matter, the American automobile industry for the German one?

As Henry S. Rowen of Stanford has pointed out, the new reality of the 21st century is that many poor people around the world are going to get rich. This is nowhere more true than in Asia, a region

that is hardly descending into tribal violence. Its problems are, rather, ones of adjustment to newfound prosperity. China, the world's largest country, grew an astonishing 13 percent in 1993, and every other country in the region (with the exception of Japan) forged ahead at comparable rates despite the recessions in other parts of the world.

Just as the proponents of modernization theory predicted in the 1950's, democracy has been following in the wake of economic development: the election of Kim Young Sam in South Korea last year represents a final break with that country's authoritarian past, while Taiwan will hold its first completely free elections in the near future. The most remarkable development is occurring in Japan. Despite Karel Van Wolferen's protestations that nothing ever changes in Japan, the Japanese political system is slowly moving away from the corrupt machine politics of the past couple of generations toward a more genuinely pluralistic democracy.

There are, it is true, serious security problems in Asia, the most important being North Korea's nuclear program. Further, the whole region will have to adjust to a very large and dynamic China, which in a decade may have an impact on regional politics comparable to the emergence of a unified Germany after 1871. But the likelihood seems low that in ten years China will still be a unitary, purposeful, authoritarian superpower with external ambitions, given the massive and rapid socioeconomic transformation it is now undergoing. A fragmenting or unstable China would also cause serious problems for the region, but not a balance-of-power threat.

In general, the character of internal relations in East Asia is remarkably different from that of Europe: security concerns have for some time now taken a back seat to economic issues as the chief preoccupation of the region's best minds. This perhaps explains why the countries most directly threatened by North Korean nuclear weapons—South Korea and Japan, as well as China—are decidedly more relaxed about the problem than is the distant United States. They believe that North Korea is one of the world's weakest states, economically and politically, and they maintain that its erratic behavior is the product of weakness rather than strength. Since time is working against the Kim Il Sung regime, it is in their view better dealt with through patience.

Finally, Latin America's prospects look brighter than at any time since the first decades of the century. Despite recent setbacks in Haiti and Venezuela, three of the region's large economies—those of Chile, Mexico, and Argentina—have liberalized substantially over the past decade, and have experienced low inflation and high growth. The code to economic development—a liberal one—has been cracked (or, more properly, relearned after decades of Marxist and Keynesian confusion), and those countries that have mustered the political will to follow its dictates are being rewarded.

Indeed, one of the great slanders of last fall's debate on the North American Free Trade Agreement (NAFTA) was Ross Perot's assertion that Mexicans were desperately poor people who could not afford to buy anything. In the next generation, Americans will have to get used to thinking about Mexico not as a political and economic basket case, but as an avid consumer and increasingly aggressive competitor. Even Peru, by most measures one of the world's most troubled countries, has seen a flood of new investment and positive economic growth since the Fujimori government's arrest of Abimael Guzman, the leader of the Shining Path guerrilla movement. With the passage of NAFTA and the successful conclusion of the Uruguay round of the General Agreement on Tariffs and Trade (GATT), the foundations have been laid for another generation of economic growth in Latin America.

*   *   *

Now let us turn to Europe. There, it is clear, nationalism and ethnic violence *have* been worse than anyone expected four years ago. Civil or interstate wars have been raging in Georgia, Azerbaijan, and Tajikistan, with many other potential conflicts just beneath the surface. But the chief indictment of the new world order centers, of course, on Bosnia, a horror the like of which has not been seen in Europe since the Holocaust.

The Bosnian conflict has four possible implications for the broader security of Europe. The first is that the war there could spread and involve other Balkan countries, and then the great powers of Europe. The second is that Yugoslavia will set an encouraging precedent for new conflicts among other intertwined ethnic groups in the former Communist world —Hungarians and Romanians, Poles and Lithuanians, Russians and Ukrainians. The third is that ethnic cleansing will legitimate racial and ethnic intolerance even in the apparently stable democracies of Western Europe, undermining their political fabric at a particularly delicate moment. And lastly, the ineffectiveness of international organizations like the EC, NATO, and the UN in dealing with the Yugoslav crisis will damage their credibility and encourage further aggression.

These fears are real, and should not be dismissed lightly. On the other hand, each one can and has been greatly overstated.

Take the question of escalation. The scenarios by which the Yugoslav civil war could lead to a larger conflagration tend to be rather nebulous. Other Balkan countries could indeed get involved if conflict spreads to the Serbian province of Kosovo, or to Macedonia. But of the interested outside powers, Albania—Europe's poorest and most backward country—wields virtually no power, while Greece would likely side with Serbia in crushing Macedonian independence.

Far more important than local Balkan considerations, however, is the absence of a larger great-power rivalry in Europe. In 1914, Europe was divided between two hostile alliances, and if war had not broken out over the Balkans, it could just as well have been sparked by Tangier or the Baghdad Railway. Today, the great powers of Europe are, if anything, struggling to avoid messy foreign entanglements as they try to deal with pressing domestic economic problems. Regional conflicts were of concern during the cold war because the superpower competition left open the constant possibility of superpower intervention and ultimately escalation. But the absence today of larger great-power rivalries means that sectional strife will remain regionalized in its impact, however horrendous the consequences may be for local populations. The ironic result is that even as the world is being united through communications technology, it is being regionalized and *dis*connected politically by the absence of a global great-power rivalry.

The second fear, that the Yugoslav example will be replicated among other ethnic groups, has already been realized in many places. But most of these conflicts, such as those in Transcaucasia and Central Asia, can and have been safely ignored by the outside world. (The only one that will pose direct security concerns for Europe is between Russia and Ukraine, an issue that will be dealt with below.)

The truth is that the mutual hatred of Yugoslavia's constituent groups is in many respects an extreme and atypical situation, and other parts of Eastern Europe look much less bleak. Economically, recent news is encouraging. Virtually all East European countries that have engaged in shock therapy or some variant of radical market reform have seen their inflation rates come down and their production bottom out and then rebound. Poland's GNP stopped falling in the second half of 1992 and is now rapidly on the way up. While recent elections in Poland brought back to power a left-wing coalition including the former Communists, this does not represent a rejection of reform so much as a desire to modulate its pace. Hungary, the Czech Republic, Slovakia, Slovenia, Lithuania, and Latvia are similarly poised for economic turnarounds, much like Western Europe in the early 1950's.

* * *

The third fear—that Bosnia will undermine tolerance and democracy in Western Europe—is supported by the wave of anti-immigrant violence in Germany, Italy, France, and most recently Austria. Nevertheless, the embourgeoisement of West Europeans has gone very far, and their situation is quite different from that of the rural Serbs and Croats driving the current struggle in Yugoslavia. If one scratches the typical Italian, German, or Frenchman of today, one is unlikely to find a vicious nationalist itching to come out. Such individuals certainly exist in Western Europe, but they have thus far been segregated at the margins of their societies. With any degree of sensible leadership, and in the absence of new discontinuities like war or depression, there is no reason to think they will not remain there.

The fourth and final fear concerns the weakness of international institutions in dealing with the war in Yugoslavia. The international community's single most important failure was actually an error of commission rather than omission—that is, the placing of a UN arms embargo on all the combatants in the civil war, and the subsequent failure to lift it so as to give the Bosnian Muslims a chance to defend themselves. An early ending of the embargo was the only policy option that had a chance of stopping Serb aggression at a reasonable cost to the outside world, and the fact that it was so bitterly opposed by the Europeans and so weakly advocated by the United States is both a moral failure and a political mystery.

On the other hand, the failure of various international organizations to intervene actively to promote order in the ways suggested by some does not reflect impotence so much as prudence. It is not self-evident that multinational, or even single-country organizations can intervene effectively and at reasonable cost in many conflicts that are primarily ethnic and/or civil in nature. Those, like Anthony Lewis of the *New York Times*, who argue that appeasement of Serbia encouraged the nationalists in Russia to vote for Vladimir Zhirinovsky in last December's parliamentary election should consider what lessons would have been drawn from a *failed* Western intervention.

The UN cannot function as a serious security organization except when it acts as a cover for unilateral American intervention, as in Korea or the Gulf. It has gotten into trouble in Somalia and Haiti because it did indeed outrun its mandate. As for NATO, it is an effective security organization, but primarily in those canonical big-war scenarios for which it was originally designed. Those who want to extend NATO's functions to include ethnic peacekeeping and the like seriously risk involving it in contingencies for which it is not particularly well suited, thereby unintentionally subverting its ability to execute tasks it is better able to perform. It is true that the world community does not have an effective instrument to promote order and security in regions like Eastern Europe today; but if the chance of escalation is low, this lack will not be critical.

* * *

The gloomy Europeanist assessment of the implications of ethnic conflict would be more cogent if there were an ongoing great-power rivalry. And in fact, many do postulate that one exists, latently if not overtly. Thus, a view is currently coalescing that Russia is well under way toward restoring the old union, using the cause of ethnic Russians stranded in the "near abroad" by the breakup of the Soviet Union to bully and threaten the other Soviet successor states. Some, like Zbigniew Brzezinski, believe it is almost inevitable that President Boris Yeltsin will fall and that Moscow will go back to its authoritarian, expansionist ways. Others, like Henry Kissinger, believe that Yeltsin himself harbors great-power yearnings, while analysts like William Odom argue that Yeltsin has already sold his soul to the Russian military in return for its support in his showdown with parliament....

Ultimately, those who take a jaundiced view of Russian intentions have already written off Yeltsin's democratic experiment. They argue—with much plausibility—that the political situation in Russia is unlikely to stabilize, or the economy to turn around, or democratic institutions to start putting down roots any time soon. Yet the policy question the United States faces is whether *we* want to be the ones to turn out the lights, especially when the new constitution adopted last December at least clears the way for a hyper-presidential regime that has some chance of promoting economic reform and a moderate foreign policy.

* * *

At any given historical moment there are always ominous clouds on the horizon. The current nightmares of specialists in international relations—nationalism or fundamentalism run amok; immigration; a growing gap between rich and poor countries; uncontrolled nuclear proliferation; and the like—many not be as dangerous as they are portrayed. Others less discussed may be more urgent....

* * *

It would be very surprising if the collapse of the largest empire in the world had not caused enormous instability and confusion. We are obviously in the midst of a prolonged transition period as political,

economic, and interstate systems transform themselves into something else. But it is vital not to take transitional turbulence for a permanent state of affairs, or to ignore the elements of order that exist while focusing on extreme cases of disorder in relatively unimportant parts of the world.

To be sure, it is primarily specialists in international affairs who are pessimistic; others, like investment bankers, who have to put money on the line behind their views of world order, tend to be much more sanguine. But among people professionally involved with international affairs, the liberals tend to be unhappy with the idea that the West won the ideological struggle of the cold war outright, and are eager to assert that the vindication of capitalism and liberal democracy is only apparent. Many conservatives, for their part, remain wedded to a dour view both of human nature and human institutions.

And then there is a simple matter of prudence: who, liberal or conservative, would not find it safer to be remembered as a Cassandra than as a Pollyanna? A Cassandra proved wrong (and there are many of them populating our TV talk shows and newspaper columns) is never held accountable; indeed, such people retain an aura of moral seriousness for their tragic sense of human history. Naive Pollyannas, by contrast, are routinely held up to ridicule. In the stock market, those who are unduly bearish are punished over the long run. The "market" for views on international affairs is, unfortunately, not quite so self-correcting.

POSTSCRIPT

Has the World Become a More Dangerous Place Since the End of the Cold War?

The international system is undergoing a significant shift. The debate among political scientists of the impact of such shifts on stability is extensive and can be reviewed, in part, by consulting Thomas J. Volgy and Lawrence E. Imwalle, "Hegemonic Perspectives on the New World Order," American Journal of Political Science (November 1995). (ind)

Is the world more dangerous in the post–cold war era? That depends on your assessment of various threats. Surely, there is more local instability in many regions, as the events in Bosnia, Rwanda, and elsewhere attest. Even the peaceful dismemberment of countries is unsettling to some. For an overview of how the system operates in a "lawless" environment, read Hedley Bull, The Anarchical Society (Columbia University Press, 1995) and James N. Rosenau, Turbulence in World Politics: A Theory of Change and Continuity (Princeton University Press, 1992). Turning to the future, analysts disagree about the level of conflict. The view that a new, more orderly world order is not in the offing is the theme of Hans-Henrik Hold and Gerog Sorenson, eds., Whose World Order: Uneven Globalization and the End of the Cold War (Westview Press, 1995). Benjamin Barber, in Jihad vs. McWorld (Times Books, 1995), takes the opposing view that growing global economic and other forms of interdependence will eventually lead to a homogenous, largely peaceful world.

What is certain, at least for now, is that the threat of a potentially civilization-ending nuclear exchange between the United States and its allies and the former Soviet Union and its allies has declined considerably. It is possible to argue that democracy and other positive approaches to governance are spreading, albeit slowly and unevenly, around the world. For this view, see Tony Smith, America's Mission: The United States and the World Wide Struggle for Democracy in the Twentieth Century (Princeton University Press, 1995).

At the pessimistic extreme is Robert Kaplan, who, in "The Coming Anarchy," The Atlantic Monthly (February 1994), predicts that the current system "is going to be replaced by a jagged-glass pattern of city-states, [poor] shanty-states, [and] nebulous and anarchic regionalisms," a virtual nonsystem in which "war and crime become indistinguishable" as "armed bands of stateless marauders clash with the private forces of the elites." Yet another pessimistic view is that of Samuel Huntington in The Clash of Civilizations and the Remaking of World Order (Simon & Schuster, 1996). He envisions a future fragmented by rivalries among religious, ethnic, and other cultures.

A related and important question is whether the future will be dark or bright. That depends. It depends in part on individuals and in part on whole populations of people. Many of the issues that need to be addressed to promote a hopeful future involve two main questions: How active internationally should each country be, and what role should each country take (unilaterally or collectively in association with the United Nations) to maintain or restore stability? Related issues involve how much monetary aid to give to help promote stability, the future desirability of nuclear weapons, and others. There is a great deal of uncertainty in the world; whether it will be more or less dangerous than what we experienced during the cold war depends in significant part on what we do to promote or allow instability, on the one hand, or to secure the peace, on the other.

ISSUE 2

Is It Wise to Expand NATO Membership?

YES: Madeleine K. Albright, from "The North Atlantic Treaty Organization: Partnership for Peace," *Vital Speeches of the Day* (March 15, 1997)

NO: Walter C. Clemens, Jr., from "An Alternative to NATO Expansion," *International Journal* (Spring 1997)

ISSUE SUMMARY

YES: Madeleine K. Albright, the U.S. secretary of state, argues that U.S. support of an expanded NATO will allow it to help shape a peaceful Europe in the future.

NO: Professor of political science Walter C. Clemens, Jr., contends that the risks and costs associated with expanding NATO outweigh any possible advantages that could be gained.

The North Atlantic Treaty Organization (NATO) is a military alliance that was established in 1949. It consists of the United States, Canada, 13 Western European countries, and Turkey. The initial purpose of NATO was to counter the threat that many in the West thought the Soviet Union posed.

When President Harry S. Truman was attempting to persuade the U.S. Senate to ratify the NATO treaty, the administration told Congress that U.S. troops would not be stationed in Europe. Truman agreed to language in the treaty that even if a NATO member were attacked, the other countries would decide what to do in accordance with their respective "constitutional provisions." This, Congress was assured, meant that the White House would have to get legislative approval before committing Americans to war in Europe. These assurances soon went by the board. The alarm about possible communist aggression set off by North Korea's invasion of South Korea in 1950 soon led to the dispatch of over 100,000 U.S. troops to Europe. With Americans stationed on the front line, any attack by the Soviet Union and its Warsaw Pact allies on NATO would have brought the United States into the war.

The threat posed by the Soviet Union is no more. Indeed, the Soviet Union, the Warsaw Pact, and the cold war are no more. One indication of the reduced sense of danger held by President Bill Clinton is his call during the 1992 presidential campaign to reduce U.S. forces assigned to NATO by about two-thirds. Clearly, the significant changes in the international climate have raised the question of NATO's future.

Many people who support a strong and even an expanded NATO see its purpose as evolving to become part of the growing emphasis on collective security that is evident in the expansion of UN peacekeeping missions and other collective international efforts to keep or restore the peace. This evolution has taken two paths.

The first path is the expansion of NATO's mission to include peacekeeping, perhaps even peacemaking. NATO never fired a shot in anger during the cold war. Indeed, NATO's first foray into combat was not against Soviet-led communist forces but against the Bosnian Serbs. In support of UN operations in the former Yugoslavia, NATO forces played an increasingly assertive role in the Balkan conflict. Warplanes attached to NATO sometimes bombed Serb positions, and after UN peacekeepers were taken hostage by the Serbs, NATO dispatched units from some of its European members to serve as a more potent force to protect the UN and, by extension, the Bosnian Muslims. The peace accord signed in November 1995 by the Bosnian Muslims, the Serbs, and the Croats rested in part on the dispatch of 40,000 to 50,000 NATO troops to Bosnia to supervise the peace. Advocates of this role for NATO insist that it is not one of altruism. Instead, they point out that World War I was ignited in 1914 by events that began in Sarajevo, Bosnia, when Serb assassins killed Archduke Franz Ferdinand of Austria-Hungary. It may be, NATO proponents contend, that preventing or limiting conflict in Bosnia and in other parts of Europe in the 1990s and beyond will prevent the kind of conflagrations that consumed Europe in 1914 and that dragged much of the rest of the world, including the United States, into the fighting.

The second path in the proposed future of NATO is the expansion of the alliance's membership to include countries to the east, including many former enemies. When Madeleine K. Albright made her speech and when Walter C. Clemens, Jr., wrote his article, which are excerpted in the following selections, they did so amid a debate on both sides of the Atlantic over whether or not Eastern European countries should be admitted to NATO and, if so, how many and which ones. That phase of the debate concluded in July 1997 when NATO extended membership invitations to the Czech Republic, Hungary, and Poland.

The invitations were hardly the end of the debate. First, adding new members changes the NATO treaty; thus, in the United States the membership change must be ratified by two-thirds of the U.S. Senate. Second, some NATO countries want to soon add even more countries. Third, expanding NATO will bring the alliance to the border of Russia. Under heavy pressure from Washington, an economically, militarily, and politically weakened Moscow suppressed its objections to the three-country expansion in mid-1997, but what Russia's attitude will be in the future remains to be seen.

There the matter rests for the moment. In the following selections, Albright argues for the expansion of NATO, while Clemens suggests that there is a better way to secure peace in Eastern Europe.

YES

Madeleine K. Albright

THE NORTH ATLANTIC TREATY ORGANIZATION: PARTNERSHIP FOR PEACE

Delivered before the North Atlantic Council, NATO Headquarters, Brussels, Belgium, February 18, 1997

[I]t was in 1947, a half century ago, that America made its fateful decision, in the aftermath of war, to remain a European power. Instead of settling for the illusion of security as it had, following World War I, America joined its European partners and built real security.

In March of that year, President Truman asked the American people, despite their weariness with sacrifice, and their wariness of new commitments, to re-join the battle for the future of this continent. He said that "the free people of the world look to us for support in maintaining their freedoms. If we falter in our leadership, we may endanger the peace of our world—and we shall surely endanger the welfare of our own nation." Out of that insight and the resolve of a Europe determined to remain free, there evolved first the Truman Doctrine, then the Marshall Plan and soon this great Alliance. I am pleased, at the very outset of my service in this new position, to re-affirm America's steadfast commitment to the sentiments expressed by President Truman fifty years ago.

America stands with Europe because Americans understand, without regard to political party, that it is in our national interests as well as our collective interest that we do so. Atlantic unity and European unity remain our common vision. And, as we look ahead to the next fifty years, we are determined that NATO will endure, and adapt, and become the essential foundation for an ever-widening Atlantic community.

To judge NATO's future potential, we must understand fully its past accomplishments. For NATO has always been more than a defensive shield. It was the roof over our heads when we rebuilt post-war Europe. It was the floor upon which the first structures of European unity were laid. It was the door through which one time adversaries were welcomed into our family of democracies. And because of its strength, and the courage of its members, it has been a mighty deterrent to aggression.

Today, we are privileged to live at a time of relative stability and peace. But we know from history that we cannot take the extension of these blessings for granted. Peace is not a gift. It must be earned and re-earned. And if it is to last, it must be constantly reinforced.

That is why, through our joint efforts, NATO—a great instrument of peace —has been transformed to meet the demands of a new era. Our military forces and strategy have changed. No longer is NATO arrayed in opposition to any one enemy. Its mission is peace and cooperation with all who wish to walk with it.

To this end, the Alliance has sparked unprecedented collaboration on European security through the Partnership for Peace. It has adapted to new roles, including the historic mission in Bosnia, which has halted the terrible carnage there and mobilized a remarkable coalition to help implement the Dayton Accords. It has undertaken a program of internal adaptation which offers greater visibility and responsibility to European members. And the prospect of its enlargement has contributed to the resolution of historic differences involving borders and minority rights in central and eastern Europe. In so doing, NATO has helped bring within our grasp the most elusive dream of this century: an undivided Europe, at peace, in which every nation is free and every free nation is a partner.

This vision of Europe is not the property of any one nation or group. It is an aspiration shared across the continent and on both sides of the Atlantic. And it is being realized through the efforts not only of NATO, but of the European Union, the OSCE [Organization for Security and Co-operation in Europe], the Western European Union, the Council of Europe and democratic reformers in every affected nation.

This is critical, for increasingly in this new era, security will not rest on a single pillar. It must be supported by democratic institutions and values; bolstered by the wealth of free peoples freely engaged in production, agriculture and commerce; and glued together by habits of cooperation and consultation on matters of mutual interest.

So, as we contemplate the next phase in the evolution of NATO, we understand that its development is part of, and complementary to, a larger process. But we also understand that if we are to achieve for Europe the kind of future we all want, we have to manage the evolution of this alliance correctly—we have to get it right.

That is why we have charted our course carefully, moved ahead deliberately, and acted together.

It is why we have chosen as our common purpose to do for Europe's east what NATO did fifty years ago for Europe's west: to integrate new democracies, eliminate old hatreds, provide confidence in economic recovery, and deter conflict.

And it is why the road ahead is clear.

Let there be no doubt.

NATO will complete its internal adaptation.

It will begin accession talks.

It will accept new members.

It will create an Atlantic Partnership Council and keep the door to membership open.

It will have an enhanced relationship with Ukraine and it will do all it can to force a long-term strategic partnership with Russia.

Our adherence to this course will keep NATO evolving and modernizing through the remaining years of this century and into the next. We must stay that course. We must stand by our commitments. And I am confident we will do so....

NATO's internal adaptation is already well advanced. The coalition assembled in Bosnia is evidence that a new NATO has already come into being; a NATO capable of undertaking new missions; a NATO capable of mobilizing members and non-members alike in support of European security; a NATO capable of performing tasks that must be done in a manner only NATO could achieve.

But the adaptation of NATO is also evident in other ways. We have agreed to the Combined Joint Task Force concept. We are building the Europeans Security and Defense Identity within the alliance. We have agreed to share NATO assets with the WEU [Western European Union] for European-led operations. We are streamlining our command structures and we are providing more senior positions for European commanders.

Our goal, in all these efforts, goes right to the bottom line. We want an Alliance that is stronger, broader, more cohesive and more effective.

That is also our goal in expanding the alliance.

The start of accession negotiations with a number of our central European partners will be a milestone in the history of the alliance. But it is no sudden event.

The process of enlargement began three years ago at the NATO summit here in Brussels. It will not end in Madrid. Nor will it end with a division between winners and losers, for ultimately all who are interested in a peaceful and democratic Europe—whether they are in NATO or partners of it—will win....

At its December [1996] meeting, this Council agreed on the goal that the first new members should join the alliance by 1999. At the Madrid summit, we should make that a firm commitment.

Those we invite should be confident that for them, this process is entering its final stage. And they should prepare to fulfill as many obligations of membership as possible on the day they join.

For those not invited to join this year [1997], but who wish to join, NATO's door must remain open. NATO has always been a dynamic alliance and has always been willing to take in qualified new members. Today, that open door has become a force for stability and an incentive for continued democratic reform throughout the region. This promise of enlargement is helping to bring Europe together. And it is a promise that must be kept.

The intensified dialogues we have conducted previously with potential NATO members have been vital. We need to conduct another round ... this spring to give every ally a chance for direct discussion with potential members, and to give every aspirant a fair hearing.

These dialogues must continue on some form beyond Madrid. We cannot make specific commitments, but we can and should offer a program to bring our partners up to NATO standards.

We should inform aspirants clearly what they must do to meet the political and military conditions for membership and we should be candid about shortcomings. In this way, NATO can continue to encourage the broadening of democratic institutions and values across the continent.

[A]t the Ministerial [Conference] here [in December 1996], this Council also agreed to strengthen the Partnership for Peace. We must go forward to implement the elements we have approved, and look to other possibilities for deepening our ties to Partner countries, especially those in the New Independent States.

We should also launch the Atlantic Partnership Council. . . . The Council will be the collective voice of the Partnership for Peace. It will deepen consultation and practical cooperation between the alliance and partner states and further strengthen their links to NATO.

Moreover, all of our partners should be invited to the summit in Madrid. Because the summit will help shape the future of Europe, all of Europe should be represented.

Our goal is an undivided Europe. We must ensure that every European democracy, whether it joins NATO sooner, later or not at all, has a role.

This includes Russia.

A critical task in the weeks ahead will be to build the partnership with Russia from which both Moscow and Europe will clearly benefit.

This is not a zero-sum game. On the contrary, NATO has recognized that we cannot build a Europe that is whole and free until a democratic Russia is wholly part of Europe. And I believe that most Russians understand, or will come to understand, that their great nation can best build a secure future for itself in a Europe without walls, with a transformed NATO as a partner.

The process of defining this new partnership is well underway.

We envision a NATO-Russia Joint Council that would promote a regular dialogue on major security issues, reach concerted decisions wherever possible, and seize opportunities for joint action.

Russian and NATO planners would work together at our major military commands. And we could begin immediately to develop a joint NATO-Russia brigade.

We have made progress on these issues and we have every chance through the efforts of Secretary General Solana, NATO's negotiator, to make more progress prior to Madrid.

We recognize that Russian leaders oppose the enlargement of our alliance and that this is not likely to change. But neither will we change. Russia has legitimate concerns that are being met: We have no plan, no need, and no intention to station nuclear weapons on the territory of new members. NATO's conventional and nuclear forces have been dramatically reduced.

In any event, our alliance is a positive alliance; it is not directed against any nation; and it need not be feared by any nation that does not seek first to instill fear in others.

To underline this point, last December, we agreed that the alliance should put forward a comprehensive proposal to adapt the CFE [Conventional Forces Europe] Treaty. I am pleased to learn that we are near agreement on the details of that proposal. Early tabling of Alliance ideas in Vienna will make an important contribution to our preparations for Madrid.

The alliance must be united, and I believe we are united in our policy towards Russia. We cannot realize our shared vision of a united, secure and democratic Europe without Russia. We will not delay or abandon our own plans. But we will be steadfast in offering to Russia our respect, our friendship and an appropriate partnership in providing for the future security of Europe.

Our relationship with Ukraine is also critical. Ukraine has made great strides against tremendous odds toward freedom and stability. It is clearly ready to play its part in building a secure and undivided transatlantic community....

Before I conclude, I also want to say a few words about Bosnia. Bosnia is a daily, practical challenge for NATO —perhaps the most complex we have ever undertaken. But it is also deeply connected to our larger challenge of building a New Atlantic Community. For four murderous years in Bosnia, we came face to face with the future we wish to avoid for Europe. For the last year, we have seen a glimpse of the future we are trying to build.

NATO-led troops have been on the ground in Bosnia for fourteen months. All 16 allies have been deeply involved, standing shoulder to shoulder with 14 Partnership countries and nations from around the world. They have not achieved perfection, but compared to what they found when they arrived, they have achieved a miracle.

Our troops no longer face the task of patrolling fixed fronts and former battlefields, but rather local threats to peace, such as the recent violence in Mostar, and the larger challenges of reconstruction, democracy and justice.

Working with the local parties and others in the international community, we must continue to diminish the need for an external military presence. We must establish a stable military situation, improve judicial and legal institutions, help more people return safely to their homes, and see that those indicted as war criminals are arrested and prosecuted....

I have said that the vision of a united and democratic Europe has been elusive, and that it extends back decades in history.

That reality could not better be illustrated than in a speech delivered fifty years ago by Mr. Winston Churchill. The aims he spoke of then, bear a striking resemblance to the aims we speak of now:

"It is not our task or wish to draw frontier lines," he said, "but rather to smooth them away. Our aim is to bring about the unity of all the nations of all Europe. We seek to exclude no state whose territory lies in Europe and which assures to its people those fundamental... liberties on which our democratic civilization has been created."

He went on to say that:

"Some countries will feel able to come into our circle sooner, and others later, according to the circumstances in which they are placed. They can all be sure that, whenever they are to join, a place and a welcome will be waiting for them at the European council table."

Twice before in this century, we have faced the challenge, in the aftermath of war, of building together a free, secure and united Europe.

We had the opportunity after World War I, but too many, in the United States and elsewhere, lacked the vision.

After World War II, as Churchill's remarks illustrate, and the memory of Marshall, Monnet, Bevin, Adenauer and their counterparts bears witness there was no shortage of vision. But across half of Europe, the opportunity was denied.

Today, we have both the vision and the opportunity, and together we are building that Europe.

It will be my great privilege to work with [NATO], on behalf of President Clinton and the American people, as we continue with this historic task. And by our success, we will ensure that the next century begins with a solid foundation for lasting liberty and enduring peace.

NO — Walter C. Clemens, Jr.

AN ALTERNATIVE TO NATO EXPANSION

Reluctant to let well enough alone, the administration of President Bill Clinton in the United States has persuaded its partners in the North Atlantic Treaty Organization (NATO) to push eastward. Who will be included and when they may join is still up for grabs. But expanding the Western alliance into the former Soviet empire will probably make Europe and the world less secure. For NATO to set up camp closer to Russia's borders is a recipe for strengthening Russian nationalism, militarism, and imperialism.

To be sure, NATO does not plan a new *Drang nach Osten* to bully or invade Russia. But any government would worry if its historic foe were to multiply its allies and edge closer. Russian leaders threaten a variety of counter-measures if NATO expands eastward. They are unlikely to be placated with saccharine words ('it is no longer you versus us') or by trivial concessions. Fortunately, weighty precedents suggest an alternative future for east central Europe— neutralization. This alternative would lower the chances that hardline expansionists would gain the upper hand in Moscow.

NOT THE ANSWER TO THE PROBLEM

Why enlarge NATO? Advocates say that NATO's 'opening' (an Orwellian euphemism) to the east is not directed against Russia. It aims rather to manage conflict, democratize and integrate all Europeans, and fill a power vacuum in east central Europe.[1] Despite sweet talk, however, NATO is still a military alliance against Russian attack. NATO's basic aim in the 1990s, as it was in the Cold War, is to prevent the world's largest country—now occupying one-seventh of the world's land—from expanding westward.

But NATO enlargement is the wrong answer to the problems it purports to solve. Taking new members into NATO is not necessary for managing ethnic conflicts, democratizing east central Europe, or uniting all Europeans. Under United States leadership, NATO as it now stands is quite capable of such operations as enforcing the Dayton accords in the Balkans. Without adding to NATO's ranks, the existing Partnership for Peace (PFP) facilitates closer co-operation among Russia, NATO members, and the non-aligned countries

From Walter C. Clemens, Jr., "An Alternative to NATO Expansion," *International Journal*, vol. 52, no. 2 (Spring 1997). Copyright © 1997 by *International Journal*. Reprinted by permission of The Canadian Institute of International Affairs. Some notes omitted.

of Europe. Countries such as Lithuania need not join NATO in order to send troops to serve with NATO peacekeepers. Even Russian troops are serving under tactical NATO command in Bosnia—with a Russian officer stationed in the Pentagon as part of the bargain.

Nor is NATO enlargement necessary for democracy in the former Soviet empire. Democratization depends in the first place upon internal conditions—development of the political and economic prerequisites for a civil society. Development of these conditions could suffer if NATO enlargement were to stimulate an anti-Western response in Russia. Moscow might choose to destabilize neighbours such as Ukraine and Latvia by mobilizing fifth columns of those who still identify themselves as Russians. To be sure, power vacuums can elicit dangerous interventions. For the foreseeable future, however, Russia has only limited means to reconquer its western neighbours. Its conventional forces are depleted both in quantity and quality from those that sustained the Soviet empire just a decade ago. Still, Russia's potential for military action remains vast; its existing forces are far larger than many observers acknowledge.

Piecemeal expansion of the Western alliance would accentuate the frailties of those countries in east central Europe omitted from the first wave of NATO expansion. Russia might well try to regain such non-aligned spaces before they, too, are occupied by the Western alliance. In 1992–3 some Kremlin leaders dreamed of NATO membership for Russia. When they were told that this was a dream, many Russian authorities warned that Moscow would treat NATO expansion as a threat to Russia's vital interests. From 1994 to 1997 most Russian officials averred that the Kremlin would interpret any NATO enlargement as a hostile act—little altered by offers of a NATO–Russia 'charter'..., by assurances that NATO has no desire or plans to station nuclear weapons closer to Russian soil, or by higher limits for Russia in permitted conventional forces. Even if Moscow settles for such sweeteners, the pill would still be bitter and could provoke a violent reaction.

Even if an enlarged NATO helped Europe to manage its conflicts, to become more democratic and better integrated, these gains would be nullified if—in consequence—Russians felt more isolated and became more bellicose. Surveys indicate that most Russian voters care little about NATO, whether or not it expands, but no aspirant for power in Moscow dares appear indifferent to this issue. Each must play the patriot card. According to Sergei Rogov, the moderate director of Russia's Institute of USA and Canada Studies, admitting former Soviet allies into NATO is likely to divide Europe once more—militarily and politically. 'Alienating Russia from the West again... will gravely affect economic and democratic reform' within Russia and bring on a 'besieged camp' mentality and 'harsh methods to mobilize the resources of society.'

One of the most alarmist scenarios was sketched by Russia's minister of nuclear energy, Viktor Mikhailov, and two colleagues writing in Vek on 20 September 1996: NATO enlargement could mean that 'Russia might be ousted from Europe completely, and that its influence on Ukraine and Belarus might wane as well. Failing to find new allies in Asia, Russia will be isolated on a scale unknown before. With former Soviet republics joining NATO, disintegration and separatism inside the Russian Federation might escalate, threatening its territorial integrity and national security.' Their conclusion: 'Russia cannot afford to give up nuclear weapons any time soon,' for 'there are no military means other than the nuclear deterrent to ensure Russian security.'

The prospect of NATO enlargement, combined with relentless upgrading of United States missile defences, leads many in Russia's Duma to argue against ratification of the second round of the Strategic Arms Reduction Talks (START II) and to reject the limits on conventional forces agreed to in 1990–2....

The Russian defence minister, Igor Rodionov, wrote in *Maskovskie Novosti* on 2 October 1996: 'Nobody will make us change our minds about NATO as a Cold War rudiment and a product of a bloc-type mentality.... Its ever growing military potential makes it hard for us to believe the much-publicized peaceful slogans of its leadership.' He went on to warn in *Nezavisimaia gazeta* on 28 November 1996 that Russia would consider counter-measures if NATO were to expand. These would include: intensified efforts to form a military alliance with members of the Commonwealth of Independent States and with other states; a massive military build-up in defiance of existing force limitations; a build-up of theatre nuclear weapons on Russia's western borders; retargetting missiles against new NATO members; and withdrawal from the START treaties.

Many Russians and some Westerners view NATO expansion as a violation of the understandings by which Moscow acquiesced in German unification. The man who approved these understandings, former Soviet President Mikhail Gorbachev, made this point in the *New York Times* on 10 February 1996....

The main alternative to NATO suggested by Russian leaders is an all-European security system, based perhaps on the Organization for Security and Co-operation in Europe. But this option gets little support in the West, if only because the OSCE can be hamstrung by any member's veto and has no forces at its command. Another option is for Moscow to close ranks with China. It is 'not by accident' that Chinese officials have been more critical of NATO enlargement since 1995, the same time that Moscow reaffirmed a 'one-China' policy and stepped up arms sales to the People's Republic....

WHY EAST CENTRAL EUROPEANS WORRY

While the prospect of NATO expansion disturbs many Russians, many—probably most—east central Europeans worry that Russia will again become menacing. Bitter experience has taught Russia's neighbours to fear expansion. Estonians and Finns are remnants of Finno-Ugric peoples once settled across much of present-day Russia but pushed to the Baltic Sea by Slavs. Estonians, Latvians, Lithuanians, Poles, Belarusians, and Ukrainians were dominated by Tsarist Russia for centuries before 1917. Communist Russia quickly regained Belarus and Ukraine after World War I and retook the Baltic and other borderlands during World War II.

All peoples of east central Europe remember the Soviet empire that neutered their sovereignty after 1945. Even Czechs and Bulgarians, well disposed to Russia, were treated by Stalin as subject peoples. Estonia and Latvia suffered greatly not only from Soviet killings and deportations but from an influx of Russian-speaking settlers whose magnitude still threatens the local culture and language. In the 1990s more than a third of the residents of Estonia and Latvia use Russian as their primary language. Those who are middle-aged or older have shown little interest in the local culture or language. Many are retired Soviet officers; some are members of the former KGB still actively involved in smuggling, money laundering, and political intrigue; some are ex-convicts not allowed to live in St Petersburg or Moscow.

The upshot is that most east central European governments want to join NATO to fend off Russian imperialism redux. They worry because even 'moderates' such as President Boris Yeltsin... invented a new version of the Brezhnev Doctrine—Russia's right to intervene in its 'near abroad.' Not surprisingly, the Baltic governments strongly criticized Yeltsin's war against Chechnya and complained of Western passivity toward Russian brutality there.

Imagine the effect on Estonians of two interviews published in the Tallinn daily, *Postimees*, on 26 and 27 April 1996. Talking with reporter Marko Mihkelson, Vladimir Zhirinovskii, a Liberal Democratic party presidential candidate, warned: 'I am doing everything to liquidate the Baltic states.' He predicted that... Estonia, Latvia, and Lithuania would disappear completely and finally from the world political map when the inevitable war broke out between Russia and the West between 2001 and 2011. He forecast that the Soviet-era Estonian president, Arnold Rüütel, or an Estonian communist sent from Moscow, would then rule Estonia. 'You small nations,' he concluded, 'are like small change' in the struggle for power by big nations....

A Latvian diplomat says that Balts feel they are living next to a very disorderly family. Some members lean out the window and shout: 'We'll burn your house down!' Others are less shrill. They say: 'Don't worry.' But then they go down the street and burn down another house—as in Chechnya. These Balts are like high-risk applicants for insurance—suspected of having a pre-existing condition or being in remission. Those who most need insurance are often denied coverage.

East central Europeans worry that 'moderates' in Moscow may bow to or be replaced by hard-line nationalists and militarists. They believe that Yeltsin's re-election in 1996 did not remove the strong forces and personalities in Moscow pressing for a more xenophobic, chauvinistic, or imperialist orientation.

WHO'S IN, WHO'S OUT?

Most governments of east central Europe would welcome NATO expansion—so long as they were included. The main exceptions are Ukraine, which has proclaimed its neutrality, and Belarus, which moves toward a military alliance and broad integration with Russia.

If NATO expands, it will probably do so in stages. The top candidates for inclusion in the first round are the Czech Republic, Poland, and Hungary. All have fairly strong armies, democratic institutions, and rapidly growing free market economies. Slovakia, Slovenia, and Romania are also possible first-stage candidates, but Slovakia is far from being a democratic state while Slovenia is too close to the Balkan powder keg. The complications are many. Without Slovakia, NATO has no land bridge to Hungary. To bypass Slovakia, Washington suggests admitting Slovenia, which would link Hungary and Italy.

This tack would increase pressures on Austria to renounce its neutrality. There are also strategic grounds to admit Romania—a useful staging ground in case of a Middle East crisis. Romania finally ousted its communist leaders in late 1996, but its economy is still in tatters. A common desire for NATO membership has pushed Hungary and Romania to mend fences, but what would the effect be on Romania's Hungarian-speaking minority if Hungary were included but Romania was not?

Since any expansion requires unanimity, any state admitted to NATO in the first [batch] could veto subsequent admission of its neighbours. For example, if the Czech Republic were admitted to NATO, it could keep out Slovakia; if Hungary were admitted, it could veto Romania. If three or four east central European states were to join NATO, the others would be left in an uncomfortable limbo. All those left out of the first stage—Balts, Bulgarians, Romanians, Moldovans, and Ukrainians—might feel more vulnerable than they do now.

The Baltic republics—Estonia, Latvia, and Lithuania—are especially nervous that they will be excluded until a second or third round of expansion. Each borders on Russia . . . ; Estonia and Latvia include large Russian-speaking populations; their armed forces are minuscule, poorly trained, and ill-equipped; and each doubts its ability even to slow a Russian advance without Western support. Here we meet a paradox: an expanded NATO might help shield the Balts from a resurgent Russian imperialism, but NATO enlargement up to Russia's border could trigger the very dangers that Balts and NATO governments fear. On the other hand, if NATO's defence perimeter excludes the Baltic states,

Moscow might infer that it enjoyed a free hand in that area.

. . . The three Baltic presidents—Brasauskas, Estonia's Lennart Meri, and Latvia's Guntis Ulmanis—issued a joint communiqué on 28 May 1996, asking for joint entry into NATO. To embrace Lithuania, NATO must leapfrog Russian Kaliningrad. If NATO takes in Estonia and Latvia, it will include many Russian-speaking non-citizens with dubious loyalties.

If NATO includes Poland but not the Baltics, Denmark and Norway, members of NATO, as well as neutral Sweden and Finland, could also be worse off than they are now. In time, each could come under greater Russian influence. Strategists in Stockholm and Helsinki have, therefore, spoken against NATO expansion into the Baltic.

Some countries of east central Europe —Bulgaria, Romania, Moldova, and Belarus—are not ripe politically or economically for membership in NATO. But if they were omitted, threats to their stability might increase from within and without. The Romanian president and chamber of deputies in May 1996 approved participation of NATO troops in six joint military exercises to be held on Romanian territory, but Socialist Labor party leaders objected, provoking much name-calling and a near fist fight in the chamber.

Ukraine has pursued a difficult balancing act. One of the largest and potentially richest countries in Europe, Ukraine proclaimed its neutrality on 16 July 1990; it has nicely accommodated its diverse language groups and avoided an open clash with Russia on Sevastopol and other issues. But if Poland joins NATO, Russian pressures on Kyiv [Kiev, Ukraine's capital] to align with Moscow will mount. Should Ukraine join NATO, however, it could be the last straw for Russians who see Kyiv as their original capital. Still, in 1995–6 some Ukrainian leaders welcomed the prospect that Poland might join NATO and began to call for a special partnership between Ukraine and NATO.

If NATO admits some but excludes others, Europe will be divided among NATO members, a Russian sphere of influence, and a group of anxious states in between. There are many suggestions for an Atlantic partnership council and other formats to blur divisions between 'ins' and 'outs'. In December 1996 NATO offered Moscow some kind of 'charter' requiring both sides to consult and, on some issues, to reach unanimity before acting. But all such half-way measures are as likely to fan as to diminish anxieties.

WESTERN INTERESTS AND RESPONSIBILITIES: CHICAGO FOR WARSAW OR NARVA?

All NATO members have a deep interest in the peace and prosperity of east central Europe. Their foremost concern is to avoid conditions that elicit Russian efforts to retake all or parts of the region. A second priority is to dampen regional disputes, as between Romania and Hungary. A third goal is to improve economic conditions there and multiply opportunities for comparative advantage in a world of free trade. Fourth, West Europeans hope to reduce emigration flows from east central Europe.

Kinship and shared cultural ties also matter. Many West Europeans and North Americans are kin to peoples in east central Europe. They want their relatives, no matter how distant, to be free and prosperous. The West's debts to the scientists, writers, and musicians of east central Europe are manifold. Westerners

who know the cultural achievements of, say, Bohemia, and all those who have struggled with east central Europeans to throw off the Soviet yoke may feel a strong rapport with what were once 'captive nations.' Anyone who knows their aspirations will want them to be free and, if they wish, to join or rejoin the West.

Still, it is not clear that most NATO countries—indeed, *any* NATO members —are willing to risk the lives of their own citizens to defend the countries of the former Soviet empire from external threat. It was never certain that an American president would wager Chicago for West Berlin or for Hamburg. It is even less clear that a future United States president would stake Chicago for Warsaw. Most of east central Europe is moving toward democracy, even though ex-communists have been elected in many capitals. But some governments resemble dictatorships more than democracies. Should citizens of Western democracies move into harm's way to protect a racist dictatorship in Slovakia or to assure Estonia's hold on Narva—a town dominated by Russian speakers?...

Unless NATO members are willing to pay the costs of deploying eastward and helping the countries of east central Europe to upgrade their forces, NATO should not be expanded. Poland and some other countries of the region have sizeable armies; others, as in the Baltic, have very small forces. None is close to meeting NATO standards. Most depend heavily upon the equipment and training methods of the former Soviet coalition. Morale is low in many armies, partly because pay, living conditions, and equipment are poor. Corruption and alcohol abuse are rife.

No less important than hardware and dependable communications are intangibles—mastery of a common language (English), military organization, and style of command. Many east central European officers have already studied in Western military schools and have imbibed something of NATO's leadership culture. But the differences between the top-down hierarchical discipline inherited from their Soviet masters and the more democratic ethos in Western forces will take years to overcome.

To bring the Czech Republic, Poland, and Hungary up to NATO standards of communication and equipment could cost at least US$20 billion over ten years; to station Western forces in east central Europe could push the bill to well over $100 billion.…

Are citizens of the existing NATO countries willing to subsidize modernization of the armed forces of east central Europe? If not, should the citizens of Poland and Estonia direct funds from programmes designed to promote domestic well-being into defence at this juncture? To both questions the answer is probably 'no.'…

NATO enlargement could become a self-fulfilling prophesy if it pushed Russia to become more aggressive. Here is the security dilemma writ large: the steps that one side takes for its 'defence' may goad the other into countermeasures that multiply tensions and dangers. If NATO does not expand, Russia may remain quiet. If NATO expands and funds are found to pay for modernizing the armed forces of east central Europe, Russia may be aroused. Expansion is a gamble.

But in no case should politicians in North America, where there are large numbers of citizens of central and East European background, gamble with security just to win votes in the ethnic wards of Pittsburgh, Cleveland, Chicago, Toronto, or Winnipeg. In the United States in particular, the baleful effects of electoral politics have long been evident in foreign policy toward many countries, from Israel to Cuba. If United States senators agree that NATO expansion is a risky and unnecessary proposition, they can and should block it. They could hand Clinton the same kind of defeat senators delivered to Woodrow Wilson in 1920 when they voted to keep the United States out of the League of Nations. Thus, in his attempts to enlarge NATO, Clinton might instead end up gutting American security ties with Europe altogether.

MODELS OF NEUTRALITY

Is there any way to improve the security of east central Europe without antagonizing Russia? One option would be to adopt the principle of neutrality that has helped Austria, Switzerland, Sweden, Finland, and Ireland to become havens of peace and prosperity. Neutrality means that a state may not join an alliance or permit foreign bases on its soil. Switzerland's neutrality has been recognized since 1815; Austria's, since 1955—by an Austrian constitutional law and in formal notes by each of the Big Four states —Britain, France, the Soviet Union, and the United States—that occupied Austria in 1945.

It is not only Europe's neutral countries that benefit from neutrality. The great powers, by denying one another the right to take a pawn or a rook, simplified their chess game. To be sure, the Kremlin had special reasons to withdraw from Austria and to agree to Austrian neutralization, namely preventing Austria from following West Germany into NATO. The West allowed Austria to become neutral, but felt it could not do the same for Germany. 'The result was that part of Germany was destined for decades of life under communism, whereas the Austrians, although militarily neutral, were part of the West.' A divided Germany, moreover, became a line of confrontation between East and West while 'Austria was a peaceful backwater.' Had the West agreed to German unification premised on the country's neutrality, a ripple effect might have radiated into Eastern Europe. Instead, Moscow herded its satellites into the Warsaw Treaty Organization in reaction to West Germany's admission to NATO.

Neutrality need not mean demilitarization or non-alignment. The Austrian State Treaty signed with London, Moscow, Paris, and Washington in May 1995 set no limits on the number of troops Vienna might train to deploy. But it stipulated that Austria could possess no weapons of mass destruction, no guided missiles, no guns with a range of more than 30 kilometres. The Big Four reserved for themselves the right to prohibit Austria from acquiring other weapons that might be spawned by scientific development. Less than two generations after Austria regained its independence, its soldiers, military observers, and civilians have served in United Nations peacekeeping missions from Cyprus to Syria and from Tajikistan to Bosnia.

Another model is heavily armed neutrality.... Switzerland and Sweden have maintained strong, well-equipped armed forces. Universal military training for males has permitted Switzerland to field a large, well-equipped army with modern tanks and aircraft intended to stop invaders at the frontiers without retreating to the Alps. Despite Switzerland's refusal to join the United Nations, Swiss

observers have joined United Nations peacekeepers in Bosnia, Georgia, Korea, the Middle East, Macedonia, and Tajikistan.

Switzerland and Sweden invested a great deal in defence during the East-West Cold War while Austria, Finland, and Ireland spent less. In any case, Europe's neutrals avoided international war and became prosperous.

No former satellite or border republic of the USSR approaches the defence spending of neutral Austria, not to speak of Sweden or Switzerland. Even Ukraine (population 51,334,000) spends only $1 billion on defence on its active forces of 400,800 and reserves of 1,000,000. Russia, with three times the population of Ukraine, probably spends closer to $50 billion....

Neutrality need be no more costly for states such as Poland and Hungary than membership in NATO would be. Warsaw and Budapest might decide that they must invest in forces like those of Switzerland or Sweden to discourage any invader. But they would also be compelled to spend heavily if they joined NATO. The biggest variable would be that their major potential foe would probably be less menacing if they remain outside NATO.

Informal co-operation on security affairs helped tie Europe's neutrals to NATO and raised the risks for Moscow if it assayed an advance anywhere on the periphery of the alliance. Still, Austria, Switzerland, Sweden, Finland, and Ireland have had no formal security commitment from other powers. Each of the Big Four recognized Austria's neutrality but did not guarantee it. Soviet as well as Western interests were well served by Austria's neutrality.

Unless NATO governments are willing to station troops in east central Europe and to fight there, they should not lightly extend NATO guarantees eastward. Trying to square the circle, the German defence minister, Volker Rühe, in late 1996 suggested that the alliance should unilaterally declare that it would not place any foreign troops on a permanent basis east of NATO's current borders. Other Western leaders have also offered not to deploy nuclear weapons in the territory of new NATO states....

Security guarantees mean little if the will and means to uphold them are lacking. Belgium's neutrality was formally recognized and guaranteed by its neighbours, but Germany invaded Belgium in 1914. This action triggered Britain's entry into World War I but did not spare Belgium. France allied with Czechoslovakia but betrayed Prague in 1938–9. Britain and France then warned Hitler they would fight if he attacked Poland. But neither the promises nor subsequent actions of London and Paris protected Poland.

Austria has gained more from a four-power recognition of its neutrality than did Belgium, Czechoslovakia, and Poland from an irresolute guarantee system that did not deter German aggression. The countries of east central Europe might be worse off if they obtain a NATO 'guarantee' but have no NATO troops on their soil.... In a crunch some Western powers might prove reluctant to defend 'a distant land of which we know nothing.' A NATO guarantee for Poland or Lithuania today would mean little unless other NATO forces, including American, were stationed there prior to any conflict—the 'trip-wire' meant to deter an attack on West Berlin in the Cold War.

Much can and already has been done to buttress the security of east central Europe without enlarging NATO. Forswearing membership in NATO need not stop the countries of east central Europe from continuing their broad integration with Western Europe through the European Union, the PFP, and the OSCE. Ties with these organizations assure that the countries of east central Europe will not be forgotten or neglected even if they do not join NATO....

The security of all east central Europe has improved thanks to the withdrawal of Russian troops from their soil and the weakening of Russia's military power. But it also gains from Russia's economic dependence upon the West and its preference for looking like a civilized country.... For its part, the West could accentuate the positive with Russia. 'Forget expansion. Broaden... the Partnership for Peace... Support Russia's admission to the World Trade Organization and eventually, to the European Union. Foster trade. Encourage commerce. Invest in prosperity. Ultimately, trust and confidence will bring security to Europe.'

HOW WOULD RUSSIA RESPOND?

Moscow would probably welcome neutralization of east central Europe. Russia could not place its troops on the soil of its western neighbours, but Moscow would be assured that no Western armies or nuclear weapons would be deployed closer to Russia. Probably all PFP members (including Russia) could continue to train and serve together for peacekeeping, but such exercises would not endanger Russia. Lacking Western allies, no country of east central Europe could threaten Russia militarily....

Neutralization of east central Europe would help Russian liberals oppose chauvinists and keep Russia in the PFP and the OSCE. It would probably reduce militarist pressures in Moscow and help Russia to integrate with the First World. Neutralization would exploit Russia's interest in being treated as a partner rather than a foe.

Russian peacekeepers [have served] in Bosnia under the tactical command of a NATO officer—an American. Russian and United States defence secretaries watched the destruction of each others' missiles and bombers under START I. They also observe joint exercises of their troops in each other's heartlands. But Moscow might halt such co-operative security efforts if NATO were to appear more foe than partner.

WHY STICK TO A COLLISION COURSE?

Officials in many NATO countries admit in private that expansion is unwise. One Pentagon planner sums up the choice: 'Would you rather have a NATO like today that is strong or one that is larger but weaker?' The choice seems obvious, but he and many other Western officials devote themselves to limiting the damage caused by what they see as a misguided but inexorable policy. Having decided to expand NATO, Western governments are seeking to square the circle: to convince Russians that their security is not threatened even though their recent Cold War rivals ally with ancient foes such as Poland close to Russia's doorstep....

Why should the West continue on a collision course not required by any present danger? Why pursue a larger but weaker NATO likely to multiply insecurity and fear? Why opt for a course that will cost billions to make the Soviet-equipped armies of east central Europe more compatible with NATO standards? Instead of isolating and antagonizing Russia, why not invite Moscow to respect the territorial integrity and independence of all countries between NATO and the Russian Federation? Instead of fuelling Russian paranoia, why not calm Russian fears and grant Russia some of the great-power status it craves? Instead of treating Russia as a potential outlaw, why not make it a partner in a system that threatens no one?

Absolute security is impossible in or outside alliances. To be sure, neutrality can be violated. But the dangers for east central Europeans will be less if they accept neutrality than if their quest for allies abets Russian militarism. A contented Russia, at ease with the West, will be a safer neighbour. No Russian government is likely to jettison positive ties with the West to reconquer a captive-nation empire that cost Moscow more than it gained. Mutual advantage through trade and co-operation can profit peace and prosperity far more than zero-sum confrontation.

NOTES

1. East central Europe here refers to Austria, Slovakia, the Czech Republic, Hungary, Poland, Bulgaria, Romania, Estonia, Latvia, Lithuania, Ukraine, Moldova, and Belarus. If the Balkans stabilize, the neutralized zone could include Albania and the republics of the former Yugoslavia.

POSTSCRIPT

Is It Wise to Expand NATO Membership?

The issue of NATO and its membership is part of a larger series of questions that are related to current changes in the world system. With the cold war over and with much of Europe becoming increasingly integrated within the structure of the European Union, the future security arrangements for the continent are subject to a great deal of debate. There are a number of articles that address this issue in Alexander Moens and Christopher Anstis, eds., *Disconcerted Europe: The Search for New Security Architecture* (Westview Press, 1994).

There are numerous questions for Americans and others to think about when considering the wisdom of expanding NATO. One is whether or not the United States and other NATO countries should be committed to defending not only the three countries that have been invited to join but also other countries that wish to join. A 1994 poll found that only 42 percent of the American public supported the idea of extending NATO membership to Poland, Hungary, and the Czech Republic. And only 32 percent of Americans were willing to support sending U.S. troops to defend Poland if it were invaded by Russia. Indeed, only a narrow majority (54 percent) of Americans were willing to respond "yes" to the statement, "I favor the use of U.S. troops if Russia invaded Western Europe." In addition to East European countries that wish to join, there are former Soviet republics, including the three Baltic states (Estonia, Latvia, and Lithuania) and Ukraine, that have expressed interest in membership in or association with NATO.

Another matter is the addition of peacekeeping to the traditional mission of NATO to deter external invasion. Writing in the *Harvard International Review* (Spring 1995), NATO deputy secretary general Sergio Silvio Balanzino envisioned "trying to move beyond [NATO's] core principle of collective defense to make [it]... available for collective security tasks such as crisis management and peacekeeping." Bosnia has provided the first test of the alliance's new mission. The reviews have been mixed. After several years of internal disagreement and ineffective action, NATO finally moved more resolutely in 1995. Military action via NATO air power against the Bosnian Serbs helped to bring them to the peace table. The multinational Implementation Force (IFOR) that moved into Bosnia in accordance with the November 1995 Dayton Peace Accord was essentially a NATO operation. Whether that has brought peace, or whether Bosnia will explode again once IFOR is withdrawn, remains uncertain.

Then there is the issue of the cost of bringing new NATO members into the alliance. The modernization of just Czech, Hungarian, and Polish forces to NATO level will cost, according to one NATO estimate, $1.3 billion dollars a year over a 13-year period.

Another concern is the Russian question. A severely weakened Moscow had little choice but to give way to pressure from the United States in 1997 and accede to the expansion of NATO. There are, however, voices in Russia and elsewhere that strongly object to the expansion and warn that it will cause a nationalist backlash in Russia in the future. For one such view by a Russian scholar and diplomat, read Yuri Rahkmaninov, "The Reasons for and Possible Consequences of NATO Expansion," *International Affairs* (Moscow) (Fall 1996).

Yet for all the uncertainties of expanding NATO (and, therefore, U.S.) defensive commitment eastward to the borders of Russia, it may be that the move is wiser than leaving the relatively small and weak states of Eastern Europe undefended and a source of possible confrontation between their larger, more powerful neighbors to the east and west. That, to a degree, is what led to World War I and to World War II. Perhaps, then, the old advice that "an ounce of prevention is worth a pound of cure" is worth remembering, even heeding.

ISSUE 3

Should the United States Abandon Its Superpower Role?

YES: Doug Bandow, from "Keeping the Troops and the Money at Home," *Current History* (January 1994)

NO: Anthony Lake, from "The Price of Leadership: The New Isolationists," *Vital Speeches of the Day* (June 1, 1995)

ISSUE SUMMARY

YES: Doug Bandow, a senior fellow at the Cato Institute and a former special assistant to President Ronald Reagan, argues that while the United States should remain engaged globally in many ways, it should bring its military home and curtail expensive foreign aid programs.

NO: Anthony Lake, special assistant for national security affairs for the Clinton administration, maintains that calls from the ideological left and right to stay at home rather than being engaged abroad are ill-considered and that U.S. national interests make full international engagement imperative.

Isolationism was one of the earliest and most persistent characteristics of U.S. foreign policy. In his 1796 Farewell Address, President George Washington counseled, "Our detached and distant situation invites and enables us... to steer clear of permanent alliance with any portion of the world,... taking care always to keep ourselves... in a respectable defensive posture."

Washington's view played a strong role in U.S. foreign policy making until World War II. It is not true that the country was isolationist until that point and then became internationalist. It is more accurate to say that there has always been among Americans a tension or an ambiguity about isolationism and internationalism. Even during the 1700s and 1800s the world could not be ignored, as U.S. foreign trade, sporadic clashes with other countries, and other factors occasioned U.S. international involvement. In the late 1800s and increasingly in this century, U.S. global interaction intensified as trade grew in volume and importance; as U.S. military and economic power gave the country world-class strength; and as the speed of communications, transportation, and military movement shrank the world operationally.

Still, isolationism remained both a strong and respectable policy through the 1930s. World War II brought an end to that. The emergence of the United States from that conflict as the world's richest and most militarily powerful country combined with the perceived global threat from communism—

backed by Soviet military strength—combined to thrust the United States into virtually unchallenged internationalism. The very term *isolationism* became discredited.

Isolationism did not altogether disappear, however. Although distinctly a minority view, surveys throughout the cold war period showed that public support for isolationism existed among Americans. Gallup polls from 1945 through 1986 indicate that the percentage of Americans surveyed who said the United States should "stay out" of world affairs averaged 27 percent. There was a slight uptrend over the years, rising from an average of 23 percent during the first 10 years of the survey to 32 percent during the last decade of the period covered to 1986. Over the years, an average of 7 percent had no opinion; 66 percent favored the United States playing an "active part" in world affairs.

Now the isolationist–internationalist debate has resurfaced. Three factors have been the main causes for this renewed debate. First, the cold war and the perceived threat from the Soviet Union have ended. Therefore, one of the main thrusts behind U.S. internationalism, the containment doctrine that countered the communist and Soviet military threat, has become irrelevant. Second, U.S. economic power has declined, at least relative to the rest of the world, and the country is experiencing troubling economic conditions. Americans now want to concentrate on the home front. A poll taken in 1995 found that 73 percent of all Americans thought that their country should reduce further its involvement in world affairs in order to concentrate on domestic problems. Another recent survey indicated that 83 percent of Americans believe that protecting the jobs of American workers from foreign competition should be an important U.S. foreign policy goal. Third, the upsurge in global instability in Bosnia and elsewhere seems to many Americans to threaten to draw their country's human and financial resources into a never-ending series of expensive, frustrating engagements that seem unrelated to the safety and prosperity of the United States. Because of these and other factors, many Americans are convinced that huge defense budgets, gaping trade imbalances, increasing foreign ownership of U.S. economic assets, and other symptoms demonstrate that internationalism has become too expensive a policy to pursue. In particular, they are unwilling for the United States to continue to bear the cost of being a hegemon, a dominant superpower.

Doug Bandow is among those who would have the United States step back from superpower status. He argues that the United States should calculate military interventions and foreign aid on a strict cost/benefit basis and that if Americans do so, they will see that it is wiser most often to keep their troops and money at home. Anthony Lake, in contrast, contends that the prosperity and safety of Americans are inextricably bound up with the economic health and stability of the world and that the United States must maintain its leadership of the world.

YES
Doug Bandow

KEEPING THE TROOPS
AND THE MONEY AT HOME

We are living in exciting times. Who would have believed when George Bush was elected president that a year later the Berlin Wall would fall? That non-Communist governments would take power throughout Eastern Europe, Germany would reunite, and the Soviet Union would disintegrate? That the menace of aggressive Soviet communism would disappear? That the chairman of the Joint Chiefs of Staff Colin Powell would admit, "I'm running out of villains. I'm down to Castro and Kim Il Sung."?

In this dramatically changed world the interventionist stance that has dominated United States foreign policy for nearly five decades must be reexamined. The United States will be a global power, but what kind of power? Should it continue to seek global hegemony, or should it go back to being, in former ambassador to the UN Jeane Kirkpatrick's words, a "normal country"?

THE INTERVENTIONIST'S OUTLOOK

Today the American military is spread around the globe. President Bill Clinton says that 100,000 United States troops in Europe is the minimum required, despite the disappearance of any credible threat to the West and the ability of the prosperous European Community—which includes two nuclear powers, Britain and France—to deter a resurgent Russia in the future. Indeed, George Bush went so far as to state that he did not foresee that "utopian day" when all America's soldiers might come home arriving for perhaps another hundred years.

The Clinton administration, following the lead of its predecessor, also seems committed to retaining at least 100,000 troops in East Asia. Japan is the world's second-ranking economic power and faces no serious military threats; nevertheless, Tokyo apparently is slated to continue as an American defense dependent indefinitely. South Korea has 12 times the GNP [gross national product] and twice the population of Communist North Korea, yet Clinton suggests that United States forces will remain so long as Seoul wants them, which could be forever.

From Doug Bandow, "Keeping the Troops and the Money at Home," *Current History* (January 1994). First appeared in *Orbis: A Journal of World Affairs* (Fall 1992). Copyright © 1992 by The Foreign Policy Research Institute. Reprinted by permission of JAI Press.

And many would like to further expand America's role as global policeman. Three years after the mercifully short war against Iraq in the Persian Gulf, the United States remains entangled in Kuwait, Saudi Arabia, and the affairs of Iraq's Kurdish minority, risking a long-term presence in one of the world's most volatile regions. Bulgaria, the Czech Republic, Hungary, and Poland all want United States defense guarantees, preferably through formal membership in NATO [North Atlantic Treaty Organization]. America is enmeshed in Somalia and has threatened to intervene in the Balkans. Some press for involvement in Liberia's three-sided civil war, to bring peace, or against Haiti's military regime, to bring back democracy. Others write of America's obligation to guarantee Taiwan's security, prevent North Korea, Iran, and others from building weapons of mass destruction, and wage low-intensity conflicts around the world —in Latin America, Asia, the Middle East, and Africa. And columnist Ben Wattenberg wants the United States to go on making weapons simply to stay "Number One."

Given the expansiveness of the United States role abroad, it is time to ask: Is there anything the American people are not forced to pay for? Is there anything young Americans are not expected to die for?

THE IMPORTANCE OF JUSTIFYING POLICY

To answer these questions, one must first decide on the purpose of the national government. But rarely, alas, is this issue even addressed. The current administration speaks of a foreign policy of "enlargement"; hyper-internationalists cite the alleged need to spread democracy and enforce peace; and unreformed cold warriors warn of new enemies and threats requiring a military as large as that which successfully contained the Soviet Union. None consider whether their grand designs are consistent with America's organization of government, however.

Among the primary duties of the United States government, the first is to safeguard the country's security in order to protect citizens' lives and property. (The federal government also has some obligation to attempt to protect American citizens traveling abroad, but ultimately those who do business outside the United States must voluntarily incur the risks of doing so. Thus the formal justification for the entry of the United States into World War I—to uphold the right of Americans to travel on armed belligerent merchantmen carrying munitions through declared submarine zones—was patently absurd.) The government's second primary duty is to preserve the constitutional system and liberties that make America unique and worth living in. Every foreign policy action should be consistent with these two functions, and the president, legislators, and other officials can have no higher goals.

This is not, of course, to say that there are no other important ideals in life. For instance, the apostle John wrote in his first epistle, "This is how we know what love is: Jesus Christ laid down his life for us. And we ought to lay down our lives for our brothers." But the moral duties that individuals acknowledge are very different from duties established by the civil institutions that govern all. John did not suggest that we should force our neighbors—indeed, everyone in our entire country—to lay down their lives for others.

Yet many people no longer perceive any moral dimension to taxing and drafting citizens to implement government policies. Joshua Muravchik of the American Enterprise Institute, for example, sees no problem in promoting "common purposes" so long as such actions "don't involve curtailing the rights of our own citizens, but involve only taxing them." Yet taxation, and conscription, the policy used for years to obtain the needed personnel for Washington's extensive overseas commitments, certainly "involve curtailing the rights of our own citizens." An activist foreign and military policy should, therefore, require a justification that warrants circumscribing—often severely—people's freedom.

A FOREIGN POLICY OF HIGHER PRINCIPLES?

Advocates of an interventionist foreign policy have, of course, advanced many lofty justifications: To promote democracy. To ensure stability. To protect human rights. To stop aggression. To enforce international law and order. To create a new world order. And on and on. Such appeals to higher principles and values are very seductive; suggesting that foreign policy should be based on the promotion of the national interest sounds decidedly cold and selfish in comparison.

The moral goals articulated by many interventionists are important, but citizens should have no illusions about the ability of the United States government to promote, let alone impose, them. Furthermore, recourse to such principles is often simply a rationalization for pursuing strategic or political ends. A cursory survey of activist foreign policy decisions ostensibly taken in the name of higher moral principles reveals ample evidence of both naïveté and sophistry.

For instance, in 1990 policymakers in Washington proclaimed their love of democracy and the free market, but years later there is still little sign of reform in Kuwait City, which was "liberated" during the Gulf War; American troops fought to make the Middle East safe for a monarchy that has largely evaded fulfilling its promises of greater domestic freedom. Despite its professed ideals, the United States used its armed forces to prop up authoritarian regimes in Korea and Vietnam. In two world wars it cultivated grand alliances with, respectively, an authoritarian Russia (although by the time the United States officially declared war, the czar had been overthrown) and a totalitarian Soviet Union. It viewed its bases in and defense treaty with the Philippines as equally important during the presidencies of autocrat Ferdinand Marcos and democrat Corazon Aquino.

Not only has American intervention often been motivated by factors other than disinterested selflessness, but Washington has equally often bungled the job. Financial assistance to a host of third world autocracies has strengthened the enemies of freedom and democracy. Aid and support tied the United States to failing dictatorships in Iran and Nicaragua; the two regimes' collapses resulted in neither democracy nor allies. America's entry into World War I to promote a utopian world order had perhaps the most disastrous consequences of any international meddling by any state ever; by allowing the allies to dictate an unequal and unstable peace, it sowed the seeds of the planet's worst conflagration, which bloomed just two decades later.

Even more important than the question of Washington's sincerity and realism in promoting higher principles in its foreign policy is the question of cost. How much money—and how many lives—should be sacrificed to bring American principles to other countries? Restoring Kuwait's sovereignty proved surprisingly cheap, but there were no guarantees United States and coalition casualties would be so light. How many American lives did policymakers think Kuwait's liberation would be worth? Five thousand? Fifty thousand? And even if Iraq was the aggressor, the deaths of estimated tens and possibly even hundreds of thousands of Iraqis, many of them either civilians or military conscripts, must also be recognized as a very real cost of United States intervention.

How many body bags per foreign life saved would make intervention elsewhere worthwhile? Why did Iraq's earlier brutal assaults on its Kurdish minority not warrant war? What about Syria's depredations in Lebanon? China's swallowing of Tibet? The war between India and Pakistan? Or Pol Pot's mass murder in Cambodia?

If young American males—and now females—are born to give their lives overseas to forestall aggression, protect human rights, and uphold a new world order, should not the United States have gone to war to unseat the two dictators who (unlike, say, Ho Chi Minh, Iraq's Saddam Hussein, or Serbia's Slobodan Milosevic) truly *were* the moral equivalent of Hitler—Stalin and Mao? Why was protecting human rights in these instances not worth war? If the answer is that the cost would have been too great, then those who attempt a moral explanation for sacrificing 58,000 Americans for Vietnam but refusing to

offer up some unspecified larger number to free more than 1 billion Chinese need to elucidate their methodology—unless, of course, they believe the United States should have ignited World War III in the name of some more just world order.

In fact, the United States did not intervene to liberate the two largest Communist states because doing so was not perceived to be in America's interest, owing to the catastrophic costs that such actions surely would have entailed. For all the idealism embodied in the moral explanations for United States behavior, American intervention is generally animated by a spirit of realpolitik [politics based on practical factors]....

As unsatisfactory as an emphasis on the national interest may be to some, it is the only proper basis for American policy. Such an approach reflects the purpose of the United States government —to protect the security, liberty, and property of the American people— in a way the international pursuit of utopian ideals does not. Reasons of national interest and security are the only legitimate justification for United States intervention abroad.

WEIGHING COSTS

It is not enough, however, to decide that the United States has one or more interests at stake in some foreign matter, because interests are not of unlimited value. The benefits of gaining desired objectives have to be balanced against the cost of intervention.

Perhaps the most obvious expense is financial. NATO accounts for roughly half the entire United States military budget; the defense of the Pacific runs to about $40 billion. Operation Desert Shield cost

$60 billion or more (though that bill was largely covered by coalition states). Foreign aid adds another $12 billion annually to the deficit. All told, roughly 70 percent of America's military outlays goes to prepare for conventional wars abroad. As General Wallace Nutting, former commander in chief of the United States Readiness Command, has observed, "We today do not have a single soldier, airman, or sailor solely dedicated to the security mission within the United States."

American domestic freedoms also suffer as a result. World Wars I and II resulted in massive assaults on civil liberties, including the suppression of dissent and free speech, and culminated in the incarceration of more than 100,000 Japanese Americans. Much more modest, but still unsettling, was the anti-Arab Sentiment unleashed during the short war against Iraq. Moreover, a panoply of security restrictions that grew out of the cold war continues to limit Americans' freedom.

Both wars also vastly expanded the government's economic powers. Federal spending in 1916 was just $713 million; it shot up to $18.5 billion in 1919, eventually settling back to the $3-billion level throughout the 1920s, more than quadruple its prewar level. Similarly, federal outlays in 1940 were $9.5 billion. Spending increase nearly tenfold, to $92.7 billion, fell to $29.8 billion in 1948—triple prewar figures—and then began its inexorable climb. Burton Yale Pines of the National Center for Public Policy Research argues that "today's mammoth federal government is the product not so much of the New Deal but of the massive power assembled in Washington to wage Wold War II and the Cold War." Some of the government's regulations have never been reversed: New York City, for instance, still suffers from the destructive effects of rent control, a supposedly temporary wartime measure.

Similarly, America's interventionist foreign policy has malformed the domestic constitutional system. We have seen both a centralization of power in the federal government and the aggrandizement of the presidency. How far we have come is reflected by the fact that serious thinkers who purport to believe in jurisprudential interpretation based on the original intent of the framers argue that the president can launch a war against another sovereign state without congressional approval. And although United States participation in formal UN forces is rather limited, it represents an even greater abrogation of congressional authority, since the act allowing participation dispenses with the need for a declaration of war when such troops are involved.

Further, intervention has a great human cost. Woodrow Wilson's fantasies of a new world order drove him to take the country into the mindless European slugfest of World War I, which left 116,000 Americans dead and led to the outbreak within one generation of an even worse war, which killed another 407,000 (mostly young) Americans. Since the end of the second world war, more than 112,000 American citizens have died in undeclared conflicts. It is one thing to ask Americans to die for the United States Republic. It is quite another to expect them to sacrifice their lives in the interest of power-projection politics more characteristic of an empire.

Finally, intervention could one day threaten the very national survival of the United States. Biological, chemical, and nuclear weapons are spreading and ballistic missiles [are] increasingly available. Terrorism has become a fixture of international life. With the growing ability of even small political movements and countries to kill United States citizens and to threaten mass destruction, the risks of foreign entanglements increase. No longer are the high costs limited to soldiers in the field. In coming years the United States could conceivably lose one or more large cities to demented or irrational retaliation for American intervention. A modest Strategic Defense Initiative program would reduce these risks, but it would never be able to provide full protection.

DIFFERENT WAYS AND MEANS

How, then, should the United States formulate a foreign policy? Every action taken abroad should reflect the purpose behind the creation of the government: namely, to serve the interests of American society and the people who live in it. Washington's role is not to conduct glorious utopian crusades around the globe. It is not to provide a pot of cash for the secretary of state to pass out to friendly regimes to increase United States influence abroad. It is not to sacrifice the lives of Americans to minimize other peoples' sufferings. In short, the money and lives of the American people are not there for policymakers, or even the president, to expend for purposes other than defending the American community.

Of course, some analysts argue that promoting moral values, particularly democracy and human rights, advances American national interests by making conflict—or at least war—less likely. The link is tenuous, however. Indeed, in the Middle East, North Africa, and some other states, true democracy is as likely to unleash destabilizing as stabilizing forces, particularly Islamic fundamental-

ism. The end of the totalitarian rule that kept simmering ethnic tensions in eastern Europe under control has already resulted in violent conflict in the Balkans: it was "democratic" decisions to secede from Yugoslavia after free elections in Slovenia and Croatia that sparked war. The best we can say is that democracies generally do not attack their neighbors.

Further, America's ability to advance democratic values is inconsistent at best. There is little the United States can do to make Haiti a free country, for example; sustaining in power a demagogue like Jean-Bertrand Aristide, even an elected one, certainly will not. And Washington's policies often throw United States commitment to democracy into question. Foreign aid, in particular, has assisted authoritarian rulers more often than liberal forces all over the third world. In the absence of any direct link between important United States objectives and the imperative to advance democracy in a particular country, American resources should not be used in this way.

Furthermore, to decide that a specific intervention is consistent with the purpose of the United States government is not enough to justify it. Decisionmakers also need to assess whether there are alternative means of achieving the goal. A free Europe is certainly important to the United States, but keeping 100,000 troops there is not necessary. The Soviet threat has disappeared, while Europe's ability to defend itself has expanded. A sharply reduced potential Russian threat may remain in coming years as Moscow struggles with daunting economic, ethnic, and political problems, but civil war is far more likely than aggression against the West. Indeed, according to the International Institute for Strategic Studies, Russia now spends less than Germany alone on the military. Thus there is no reason the Europeans, with three times the economic strength of a decaying Russia (and a larger gross national product than America) and a new buffer in the former Warsaw Pact states, cannot create their own security system to deter any potential threat.

Indeed, those who should be most concerned about a Russian revival—the Germans—aren't. Last year Chancellor Helmut Kohl announced his nation was going to cut troop levels 40 percent through 1995. If Bonn sees no need to maintain a large military for its protection, there is certainly no cause for America to maintain troops in Germany. Washington is increasingly begging the Europeans for the right to defend them.

Similarly, South Korea is vastly stronger than North Korea by every measure except current military strength. Seoul's growing edge has become increasingly obvious as South Korea has stripped away all of the north's allies, particularly Russia and China. The south is fully capable of eliminating the military imbalance on the peninsula. South Korean officials do not deny their country's ability to sharply increase its defense efforts; instead, they tend to complain about having to bear the added expense. This is hardly a justification for an American presence. Seoul could gradually increase its military spending—which would be unnecessary if the north enters into meaningful arms control negotiations— as United States forces were phased out. The potential North Korean acquisition of a nuclear weapon is serious, but the continued presence of American ground forces will do nothing to stop nuclear proliferation; rather, the troops would simply serve as nuclear hostages....

It might be difficult to fashion alternative solutions that do not involve direct United States intervention, and Washington might not always be fully satisfied with the outcome. But it is unrealistic to expect the United States to assume the responsibility for maintaining global order. Instead, Washington should seek to promote cost-effective policies that yield results most consistent with the government's duty to protect Americans' security and constitutional freedoms.

Even if there appear to be no alternatives to a United States commitment, the United States must weigh benefits against costs before it intervenes, and avoid or extricate itself from tragic but ultimately irrelevant conflicts. For example, more people died in 1993 in Angola than in Bosnia. Starvation stalks Liberia and Sudan, both victims of vicious civil wars. Yet there has been no groundswell for intervention in Angola, and no UN relief mission for the latter two. The Trans-Caucasus is suffering from seven separate conflicts. All are human catastrophes, but none affects a single vital American interest or warrants the death of even one United States soldier. The point is not that American lives are worth more than others', but that the primary duty of the United States government is to safeguard the lives of its own citizens—servicemen included—not sacrifice them for even seemingly worthy causes.

What if United States policymakers concluded that South Korea would not defend itself if Washington pulled out its troops? In fact, Seoul would probably be the last American ally to give up, but what if it decided to do so? A northern takeover of the south would be a tragedy for the latter, but it would have little impact on the United States, whose security would remain largely unchanged and whose economy would suffer only marginally from the loss of a midsize trading partner. The threat to go to war should be reserved for cases involving vital American interests. Korea is a peripheral, rather than a substantial, interest of the United States, and does not justify spending billions of dollars and risking tens of thousands of lives every year, especially if the peninsula goes nuclear.

A similar analysis could have been conducted for the Gulf. Even if the other regional powers had not taken steps to contain Iraq, the likelihood of Saddam Hussein striking Saudi Arabia was overplayed, since this would have left him dangerously overextended. (In fact, United States intelligence knew at the time he was withdrawing his best units to Iraq after seizing Kuwait.)

The consequences even of a highly unlikely conquest of the entire Gulf were overstated. In this fantastic worst-case scenario, Saddam would have controlled about one-fifth of international petroleum production; enough to nudge prices up, to be sure, but not enough to control them or wreck the international economy. Nor did Saddam's invasion of Kuwait threaten America's ally Israel. On the contrary, Iraq only attacked Israel in a desperate attempt to split the coalition; absent the United States presence, Baghdad would surely not have attacked Israel since it was fully capable and willing to retaliate.

THE LUXURY OF UNINVOLVEMENT

The United States enjoys many advantages that provide it with the luxury of remaining aloof from geopolitical conflicts that engulf other countries. American benefits from relative geographic isolation, for example. (This does not insulate it from nuclear attack, of course, which is why it should try to develop some form of missile defense.) The United States is also the world's largest single economic market, which reduces the impact of the loss of one or more trading partners. (Germany and Japan, for example, would suffer far more if the American market was denied them.) Moreover, the United States has a constitutional system and political philosophy that have endured for more than 200 years and have proved to be popular around the world.

This unique status allows America to balance the costs and benefits of intervention differently from most other states. Alliances make a lot more sense among European states threatened by a Soviet Union, for instance, or between Saudi Arabia and its neighbors when they are threatened by Iraq. Observes political commentator and former presidential candidate Patrick Buchanan, "Blessed by Providence with pacific neighbors, north and south, and vast oceans, east and west, to protect us, why seek permanent entanglements in other people's quarrels?"

For this reason, the United States is rarely open to charges of appeasement, such as are sometimes rightly leveled at other countries, for intervention is seldom required to protect its vital interests. For example, had France and Britain accurately perceived the potential threat posed by Nazi Germany, they should have blocked the remilitarization of the Rhineland and they certainly should not have helped dismember Czechoslovakia (through active intervention, it should be noted). Washington's failure to leave its expeditionary force in Europe in 1919 or to raise a new one in 1933, however, did not constitute appeasement. Similarly, it would not be appeasement for the United States to decline to defend a populous and prosperous South Korea; for Seoul to choose not to augment its forces once United States troops were gone, however, would be.

In fact, there is nothing wrong in principle with appeasement, if this means only diplomatic accommodation and avoidance of war. In the late nineteenth and early twentieth centuries, Austria-Hungary, Britain, France, Germany, and Russia all resolved potentially violent disagreements without conflict by making concessions to one another that could be termed "appeasement." The case of Nazi Germany was different, because Hitler wanted far more than could be given to him, and because the allies materially weakened themselves—for example, by eviscerating Czechoslovakia—in attempting to satisfy him.

The end of the cold war has resulted in a new world order, whether or not the United States defines or polices it. The Russian military remains a potent force, of course, but it is far less capable than that possessed by the Soviet Union, and Moscow's will to use it in an aggressive fashion appears to have dissipated. Moreover, the ability of American allies —a Japan that is the second-ranking economic power in the world, a reunited Germany that dominates Europe, and so on—to contain Russia has grown. These two changes alone give the United States an opportunity to refashion its foreign policy.

A new, noninterventionist policy should rest on the following bedrock principles:

- The security of the United States and its constitutional system should remain the United States government's highest goal. Individuals may decide to selflessly risk their lives to help others abroad; policymakers, however, have no authority to risk their citizens' lives, freedom, and wealth in similar pursuits.

- Foreign intervention is usually expensive and risky, and often counterproductive. Many smaller nations may still need to forge preemptive alliances to respond to potentially aggressive regional powers. Because of America's relative geographic isolation and other advantages, however, intervention is rarely necessary to protect our security and free institutions. This is especially true today, with the disappearance of a threatening hegemonic power.

- America's most powerful assets for influencing the rest of the world are its philosophy and free institutions, the ideas of limited government and free enterprise that are now sweeping the globe, and its economic prowess as the world's most productive nation. These factors ensure the nation's influence irrespective of the size of its military and where its soldiers are stationed. The United States can best affect others through private means—commerce, culture, literature, travel, and the like.

- The world will continue to suffer from injustice, terror, murder, and aggression. But it is simply not Washington's role to try to right every wrong —a hopeless task in any event. The American people are entitled to enjoy their freedom and prosperity rather than having their future held hostage to unpredictable events abroad. Their lives and treasure should not be sacrificed in quixotic crusades unrelated to their basic interests.

The world is changing faster today than it has at any time since the end of World War II. As a result, the United States has no choice but to refashion its foreign policy. While Washington should remain engaged throughout the world culturally, economically, and politically, it should bring its military home and curtail expensive foreign aid programs. After bearing the primary burden of fighting the cold war, Americans deserve to enjoy the benefits of peace through a policy of benign detachment. War may still be forced upon them, of course. But as John Quincy Adams observed shortly after the nation's founding, America should not go abroad "in search of monsters to destroy."

NO

Anthony Lake

THE PRICE OF LEADERSHIP: THE NEW ISOLATIONISTS

Delivered at The National Press Club, Washington, D.C., April 27, 1995

Let me begin with a simple but alarming fact: The United States could be on the brink of unilateral disarmament. Did that get your attention? I hope so, because it is true. No, we are not about to junk our jets or scuttle our ships. Our military is strong and ready—and there is a strong bipartisan consensus to keep it so. But we are on the verge of throwing away—or at least damaging—many of the other tools America has used for 50 years to maintain our leadership in the world. Aid to emerging markets, economic support for peace, international peacekeeping, programs to fight terrorism and drug trafficking, foreign assistance: Together with a strong military, these have been key instruments of our foreign policy.

Presidents since Harry Truman have used these tools to promote American interests—to preserve our security, to expand our prosperity and to advance democracy. Their efforts were supported by Democrats and Republicans—and the broad majority of the American people. Congress consistently provided the needed resources for these tasks. Because of this resolve, coupled with our military might, we prevailed over the long haul in the Cold War, strengthened our security and won unparalleled prosperity for our people.

Now, I deeply believe our success is in danger. It is under attack by new isolationists from both left and right who would deny our nation those resources. Our policy of engagement in world affairs is under siege—and American leadership is in peril.

A few of the new isolationists act out of conviction. They argue that the end of the Soviet menace means the serious threats are gone—that we should withdraw behind our borders and stick to concerns at home. Fortress America, they say, can shut out new dangers even though some of the new threats facing us—like nuclear proliferation, terrorism, rapid population growth and environmental degradation—know no boundaries.

But most of the new isolationists do not argue such a position or even answer to the name isolationist. They say they are part of the postwar bipartisan consensus… that their goals are its goals—democracy, security, peace and prosperity. But they won't back up their words with deeds.

These self-proclaimed devotees of democracy would deny aid to struggling democracies. They laud American leadership, but oppose American leadership of coalitions, advocating only unilateral action instead.

Yes they praise peace. But then they cut our help to those who take risks for peace. They demand greater prosperity. But they shy away from the hard work of opening markets for American workers and businesses. Under the cover of budget-cutting, they threaten to cut the legs out from under America's leadership.

These are the back-door isolationists—and they are much more numerous and influential than those who argue openly for American retreat. They can read the polls, and they know that the American people want the U.S. to be engaged in the world. Support for American leadership in the world is about as strong as ever—a Chicago Council on Foreign Relations survey [published in *Foreign Policy* (1995)] shows two-thirds or more want us to remain deeply engaged. So these back-door isolationists and unilateralists cast themselves as the true guardians of American power. But through their actions, they could become the agents of an America's retreat. They champion American leadership, but they want it the one way you can't have it: and that is on the cheap.

They want America to turn its back on 50 years of success. They are working—whether they know it or not—to destroy part of the foundation for our peace and prosperity, the great legacy of our postwar leaders: Vandenberg, Truman, Marshall, Acheson. These men faced their own challenge from isolationists. But they saw the cost of our earlier withdrawal after Versailles was terribly, terribly damaged—saw it in the wreckage of Europe and Asia after World War II and the casualties America suffered liberating those continents. And they understood that investing in a vigorous foreign policy was the only way to prevent another catastrophe.

They knew the price of leadership. They spent what was necessary to maintain America's security. And they went further, creating the United Nations and the Bretton Woods institutions [such as the International Monetary Fund] and covering those bills, pouring Marshall aid into Western Europe to save it from despair and communism, and they and their successors in later Administrations developed the new tool of technical assistance—so that democracy and prosperity got a better chance around the world.

Look at the results: the map is almost covered with democracies, many of them strong allies. Markets that fulfill needs and dreams are expanding. A global economy supports American jobs and prosperity. These are the returns on 50 years of American political and economic investment abroad—the benefits of 50 years of bipartisan engagement.

But these achievements are not cut in stone. We will not go on reaping these benefits automatically. Back-door isolationism threatens to propel us in the wrong direction at a real moment of hope —when our engagement can still make a dramatic difference, by securing rather than frittering away our victory in the Cold War.

We could forfeit that victory because in many places, democracy still needs nurturing. Some market economies have not sunk deep roots. And the post-Cold War world has brought into new focus real and powerful dangers that threaten what we have worked for: aggression by rogue states, international terrorism, economic dislocation. These are new forms of an old conflict—the conflict between freedom and oppression, the conflict between the defenders of the open society and its enemies.

There is no expiration date on these lessons from five decades: Defeating these threats requires persistent engagement and hands-on policies. Defeating them demands resources. Throwing money at problems won't make them go away—but we also cannot solve problems without money. The measure of American leadership is not only the strength and attraction of our values, but what we bring to the table to solve the hard issues before us. That is why President Clinton has said that he will not let the new isolationism prevail.

Make no mistake. The American people want their nation to lead. Americans know the world is growing closer; they know our security and prosperity depend on our involvement abroad. And they agree with President [Clinton], who has said before and since he took office: "For America to be strong at home, it must be strong abroad."

Plenty of Americans also say they want us to spend less abroad—until they know the real numbers. Most think that we spend 15 percent or more of the federal budget on foreign aid. They think 5 percent would be about right.

They would be shocked to know that little more than 1 percent—$21 billion out of a $1.6 trillion dollar budget—goes for foreign policy spending, and less than $16 billion to foreign assistance. That's a lot of money, but not the budget-buster that neo-isolationists pretend. And that is 21 percent less in real terms than spent in FY 1986. They would also be surprised to learn that others recognize the reality of necessary resources far better than we. The richest, most powerful nation on Earth—the United States—ranks dead last among 25 industrialized nations in the percentage of GNP devoted to aid.

These are facts that should be better known. And more of our citizens should know that our foreign policy resources are devoted towards goals that the American people support.

- $6.6 billion a year promotes peace—including our efforts in the Middle East, the help we give U.S. allies to defend themselves, and our contribution to UN peacekeeping missions around the world, such as those on the Golan Heights, the Iraq-Kuwait border and in Cambodia.
- $2.4 billion builds democracy and promotes prosperity—helping South Africa, for example, hold free elections and transform itself peacefully.
- $5 billion promotes development—that includes jobs programs in Haiti to increase employment, improve infrastructure and help that nation get back on its feet.
- $1.7 billion provides humanitarian assistance—like caring for refugee children in the former Yugoslavia—because Americans have always wanted their country to alleviate suffering in areas of the most compelling need.
- And the remainder is for the State Department and other agencies that work every day to advance America's interests abroad.

This is the price of American leadership—and the backdoor isolationists don't want us to pay it. But imagine how the world would look if we did not. Take what I call the George Bailey Test. You remember George—he is the character played by Jimmy Stewart in the Christmas classic "It's a Wonderful Life." In that film, the angel Clarence shows George how Bedford Falls would have fallen apart without him.

Allow me to play Clarence briefly and take you through a world without American leadership. Imagine:

- If Ukraine, Belarus and Kazakhstan joined the club of declared nuclear weapons states because we couldn't do the deals to denuclearize them.
- If Russian missiles were still pointed at our cities, because we couldn't push to de-target them.
- If thousands of migrants were still trying to sail to our borders, because we had not helped restore democracy in Haiti.
- If nearly 1 million American jobs had not been created over the last three years alone—because we had not promoted U.S. exports.
- If we had to fight a war on the Korean peninsula—the implication of what some critics urged—because we did not confront the threat of a North Korea with nuclear weapons.
- If another quarter of a million people had died in Rwanda because we had not deployed our military and they had not done such a fine job in the refugee camps.
- Or, if we had paid tens of billions of dollars more and suffered more casualties because we insisted on fighting Operation Desert Storm against Iraq by ourselves.

Imagine that. Each of these efforts cost money and the hard work of building international coalitions. But you and I are safer, better off and enjoy more freedom because America made these investments. If the backdoor isolationists have their way, much of what we have worked for over two generations could be undone.

Speaker [Newt] Gingrich recently described what the world might look like if America retreats. He described "a dark and bloody planet... in our absence you end up in Bosnia and Rwanda and Chechnya." He added, "They are the harbingers of a much worse 21st century than anything we've seen in the half century of American leadership."

It does not have to be that way. If we continue to invest in democracy, in arms control, in stability in the developing world, in the new markets that bring prosperity, we can assure another half century of American leadership.

But already, because of decisions in the last few years, we sometimes cannot make even modest contributions to efforts that deserve our support. America is a great nation—but we cannot now find the small sum needed to help support peacekeepers in Liberia, where a million people are at risk of renewed civil war. Or the money to fund adequately UN human rights monitors in Rwanda. We can barely meet our obligations in maintaining sanctions on Serbia. This is no way to follow the heroic achievements of the Cold War. And I can't imagine that this fits any American's vision of world leadership. It doesn't fit mine.

Nickel and dime policies cost more in the end. Prevention is cheap—and doesn't attract cameras. When the all-seeing eye of television finds real suffering abroad, Americans will want their government to act—and rightly so. Funding a large humanitarian effort after a tragedy or sending in our forces abroad to assist will cost many times the investment in prevention.

Some costs of shortsighted policies must be paid in our neighborhoods: In 1993, Congress cut by almost one-third our very lean request for funding to combat the flow of narcotics into our country—and that funding has been declining in real terms ever since. As a result, we are scaling back programs to wipe out production of drugs and block their importation, as well as training programs for police, prosecutors and judges in foreign countries. America pays a far higher cost in crime and ruined lives.

These are some of the constraints we have lived with in the past few years. And now, however, American leadership faces a still more clear and present danger. Budget legislation being prepared in Congress could reduce foreign affairs spending by nearly a quarter—or $4.6 billion. That would mean drastic cuts or the elimination of aid to some states of the former Soviet Union, and into the security assistance programs that help U.S. allies and friends provide for their own defense. It would sharply reduce or eliminate our contributions to international peace operations. It would lame the agencies—like... the [Export-Import] Bank—that have played a key role in expanding U.S. exports. It would threaten our non-proliferation efforts and the Arms Control and Disarmament Agency. It could eliminate assistance for some programs that save children's lives.

These cuts would cripple our legacy of leadership. The strength to lead does not fall from heaven. It demands effort. It demands resources.

A neo-isolationist budget could undercut our strategic interest in democracy in Russia and the former Warsaw Pact. And it would directly affect America's security: We must continue to fund the farsighted programs begun by Senator [Sam] Nunn and [Richard] Lugar to reduce nuclear arsenals in the former Soviet Union. The $350 million in Nunn-Lugar funds made it possible for Ukraine to dismantle its arsenal and accede to the Non-Proliferation Treaty. That made it easier for us to pull back from the Cold War nuclear precipice—and save some $20 billion a year on strategic nuclear forces. That is just one of the more dramatic examples of how our foreign spending literally pays off.

A neo-isolationist budget could harm our efforts to prevent rogue states and terrorists from building nuclear weapons. We are spending $35 million over three years to employ thousands of weapons scientists in the former Soviet Union on civilian research projects. That helps keep them off the nuclear labor market—and from selling their skills to an Iraq or Iran.

A neo-isolationist budget could nearly end our involvement in UN peace operations around the world—operations that serve our interests. Presidents since Harry Truman have supported them as a matter of common sense. President [George] Bush in particular saw their value: last year nearly 60 percent of our UN peacekeeping bill went to operations begun with his Administration's support. His Secretary of State, James Baker, made a strong defense for these operations when he remarked that "We spent trillions to win the Cold War and we should be willing to spend millions of dollars to secure the peace."

This is burdensharing at its best. UN peace operations:

- Save us from deploying U.S. troops in areas of great importance—for example, Cyprus or the Indian subcontinent.
- They help pick up where our troops left off—for example, along the border of Iraq and Kuwait. In Haiti, UN troops are saving us resources by replacing most of our own withdrawing troops.
- They are building democracy in Namibia, Mozambique and Cambodia —all missions we helped design. In Cambodia, the UN negotiated the withdrawal of Vietnamese forces and then held the country's first democratic election. After the years of the Killing Fields, 90 percent of the electorate turned out to vote—while UN peacekeepers protected them from the Khmer Rouge.

We would pay much more if we performed even a small number of these missions unilaterally. Instead, the price we pay now in manpower and money is reasonable: Of the 61,000 UN peacekeepers deployed around the world, only some 3,300 are American. We pay the equivalent of half of one percent of our total defense spending for UN peace operations —less than a third of the total UN cost and less than the Europeans pay in proportion to their defense spending. We participate in these operations only after careful consideration of the command arrangements and costs—but we gain immense influence through our ability to lead multinational efforts.

And a neo-isolationist budget would severely undercut our work for peace. The President has said that "America stands by those who take risks for peace." This is true in Northern Ireland, in South Africa, the Middle East and around the world.

For the Middle East peace process to continue—and for negotiations in other regions to succeed—we must have the resources to support the risk-takers. We cannot convince the holdouts from the peace process that we will stand behind a just and lasting settlement if we back away from our current commitments. That means maintaining aid to Israel, Egypt and the Palestinians and fulfilling our pledge of debt relief to Jordan. In the Middle East, our vital security and economic interests are on the line. We must not fold our hands—and leave the game to the opponents of peace—just when we are so close to the verge of winning.

A neo-isolationist budget could throw away decades of investment in democracy. In the last 15 years, the number of democracies in the world has almost doubled—and USAID provided assistance to most of the newcomers. For example, in Mozambique, a nation emerging from years of strife, AID assistance helped register 6 million out of a possible 8 million voters and turn the polling there into a success. Now, when these societies are most fragile, is not the time to cut this lifeline for democracy.

And a neo-isolationist budget would directly damage our own livelihoods. Our economy depends on new markets for U.S. goods and high-paying jobs for American workers. That is why President Clinton led efforts to expand free trade with the landmark GATT agreement, NAFTA, and the free trade agreements in the Asia-Pacific region and in the Americas. And this Administration has worked harder, I believe, than any other to promote American exports. Imagine, for example, where we would be without the Commerce Department's efforts on this score. Secretary [Ron] Brown's staff worked with other agencies last year on export deals that support 300,000 U.S. jobs.

In many cases, we were in a position to close deals because America had been engaged in those countries for years. Consider two statistics: AID programs in some countries have helped increase life expectancy by a decade. And every year, AID's immunization program saves 3 million lives. These are statistics not only of humanitarian hope. They are part of efforts to help create stable societies of consumers who want to buy our goods—not masses of victims in need of relief.

In addition, our support of the multilateral development banks also helps nations grow and their economies prosper. We contribute $1.8 billion while other nations contribute $7 billion—and that capital leverages more than $40 billion in lending. If we stopped our contributions, we would lose our influence. And others might also follow our lead, and that would cripple these important institutions.

The backdoor isolationists who claim they are saving America's money cannot see beyond the green of their own eyeshades: Our assistance has repaid itself hundreds and hundreds of times over. That was true when Marshall aid resuscitated European markets after the war. And in South Korea, which now imports annually U.S. goods worth three time as much as the assistance we provided in nearly 30 years.

And while we preserve our tradition of assistance, we are reforming its practice. AID has become a laboratory for Vice President [Al] Gore's efforts to reinvent government—it is eliminating 27 overseas missions and cut its workforce by 1200.

Now, with the "New Partnership Initiative," we will improve our assistance programs even more—by focusing on the local level. This will enhance the efforts of non-governmental organizations and raise the percentage of our aid that is channeled to them to 40 percent—because these organizations are on the ground and more responsive than distant national governments. This puts our resources to better use, helping nations so they can become self-sufficient.

Every one of us in this room knows that winning support for an activist foreign policy has never been easy in America.

Throughout the history of our Republic, we have never lived in literal isolation. In a world of instant communication and capital flows, we cannot do so now. That is not the issue. Literal isolationism is not an option.

What is at issue is whether we will have the policies and resources that can shape and support our involvement in ways that benefit our people in their daily lives—whether by opening markets or by preventing conflicts that could embroil us. It is at those times that our government failed to engage in such efforts that our people have paid the greatest price—as in World War II, following a period of irresponsible American retreat.

The genius of our postwar leaders was to see that technology and American power had changed the world and that we must never again remain aloof. But they had a hard time winning support even with the memories of war still fresh.

As he put his case forward, President Truman had an uphill struggle. But a foreigner saw that it was America's moment to lead—and told us so. [British Prime

Minister] Winston Churchill stirred the nation with his appeal for an engaged foreign policy. Today, we remember his address as the Iron Curtain speech, but Churchill called it "The Sinews of Peace." The phrase plays on a saying of the Romans: "Money is the sinews of war." Churchill's message was that preserving peace—like waging war—demands resources.

Today, that message rings as true as ever. This is a moment of extraordinary hope for democracy and free markets. But nothing is inevitable. We must remain engaged. We must reach out, not retreat. American leadership in the world is not a luxury: it is a necessity. The price is worth paying. It is the price of keeping the tide of history running our way.

POSTSCRIPT

Should the United States Abandon Its Superpower Role?

The 1990s have radically altered the previous four decades of world politics and the accompanying assumptions about U.S. foreign policy. Not only did the bipolar era and the cold war end, so did the Soviet Union. These changes obviated a significant part of the popular rationale for the extended U.S. presence in the world. The anticommunist foreign policy consensus has been replaced with discord. What role should the United States play in the world? What are the country's vital interests, and how much internationalism can Americans afford?

It would be incorrect to assume that most Americans are isolationists. In 1994, 65 percent of the public thought that it would be best for the United States to take an "active part" in world affairs. Americans also support the United Nations, with 65 percent of the respondents to a 1995 survey saying they agreed that "the United States should cooperate fully with the United Nations." A good, recent survey of American attitudes can be found in John E. Rielly, "The Public Mood at Mid-Decade," *Foreign Policy* (Spring 1995).

Yet, as pointed out in the introduction to this debate, the public also wants first to safeguard American wealth and energy at home, and it is wary about overseas, especially military, involvement.

The term *globocop* has been commonly used to disparage the idea that the United States should try to act like the world's police officer. Instead, as one quip goes, many Americans now lean toward the role of "globoGarbo," a reference to actress Greta Garbo's famous phrase, "I want to be alone." Those who favor the internationalist position are apt to characterize this viewpoint as isolationist. President Bill Clinton, for one, warns that "domestic renewal is an overdue tonic . . . [but that] isolationism and protectionism are still poison." Others disagree. Robert Zoellick, undersecretary of state for the Bush administration, says that Americans now practice "show-me internationalism" and "want each case demonstrated on its own terms why the U.S. should engage." As far as American emphasis on domestic-oriented foreign policy goals, such as protecting jobs and stopping the inflow of drugs, Zoellick maintains, "That's a pretty good common-sense position."

It is important to understand that *isolationism* is often used in a perjorative way to label those who would restrict to a greater or lesser degree U.S. involvement, particularly military intervention, abroad. First, it should be noted that the American elite (those who hold positions of influence in government, business, the media, and other American societal institutions) are considerably more internationalist than is the American public. This is readily obvious in the Rielly article, which, for example, found that 82 percent of the elite, but only 39 percent of the mass, would use American troops to counter a North Korean invasion of South Korea. Second, the sometimes touted image of the public as ignorant, apathetic, and therefore wrong, is not necessarily accurate. There are numerous studies that conclude that wisdom resides in the mass, not in the elite. One good example is Bruce Jentleson, "The Pretty Prudent Public: Post-Vietnam American Opinion on the Use of Military Force," *International Studies Quarterly* (1992).

Labels such as "internationalist" and "isolationist" are helpful in classifying foreign policy views. But they go only so far. To determine your position and to evaluate the positions of others, the next step is to identify specifically what U.S. interests are and what Americans are or should be willing to do to maintain them.

ISSUE 4

Is Islamic Fundamentalism a Threat to Political Stability?

YES: Daniel Pipes, from "Same Difference," *National Review* (November 7, 1994)

NO: Zachary Karabell, from "Fundamental Misconceptions: Islamic Foreign Policy," *Foreign Policy* (Winter 1996–1997)

ISSUE SUMMARY

YES: Daniel Pipes, editor of *Middle East Quarterly*, argues that just as those who considered the Soviet threat a myth were naive, so are those who dismiss the threat from Islamic fundamentalists naive.

NO: Zachary Karabell, a researcher in the Kennedy School of Government at Harvard University, holds that it is wrong to view Islam as a monolith whose adherents pose a threat to the stability of the international system.

Several Islamic political concepts are important to this issue. Some tend to bring Muslims together; others work to divide Muslims.

One of the forces that serve to promote Muslim unity is the idea of the *ummah,* the spiritual, cultural, and political community of Muslims. In part, this means that Muslims are less likely than people from the Western cultural tradition to draw distinct lines between the state, religion, and the individual. Belief in the *ummah* also implies that the adherents to Islam should join spiritually and politically in one great Muslim community.

A sense of common history is another factor that works to bring Muslims together. After a triumphant and powerful beginning, including the spread of Islam and its culture into Europe and elsewhere from its Middle Eastern origins, the political fortunes of the Muslims declined slowly after about the year 1500. Part of this decline was due to losses to predominately Christian European powers. By the 1920s almost all Muslim lands were under the control of colonial powers, which were mostly European and Christian.

There are also strong forces that tend to divide Muslims. One of these is the frequent rivalry between the majority Sunni sect and the minority Shi'ite sect. A second factor that divides Muslims is the degree to which they believe in the strict adherence to the *shari'ah*—the law of the Koran, which is composed of God's (Allah's) teachings—to govern both religious and civil conduct. Muslim traditionalists (fundamentalists, according to common usage) want to frame legal systems based on the *shari'ah* and to establish theocratic rule.

As one Muslim theologian argues, "The notion that a majority should rule and the notion of the political party are all Western notions. Islam calls for obedience to the rule, the unification of the nation and advice by religious scholars to the rules." Other Muslims, who are often called secularists, believe that religious and civil law should be kept relatively separate and that Koranic law is flexible enough to allow changes in tradition, such as permitting greater entry of women into business, politics, and other aspects of civil society. There is considerable strife occurring in Algeria, Egypt, and several other Muslim countries based on the traditionalist-secularist struggle.

Nationalism (primary political loyalty to a national state) is a third factor that divides Muslims. Individual Muslim countries are fiercely nationalistic. Achieving full Muslim political unity would necessarily entail giving up patriotism and other manifestations of nationalism. A fourth factor, and one that further solidifies nationalism, is the major ethnic and sectarian differences within Islam. Iranians, Kazakhs, Pakistanis, and many other Muslim peoples are not ethnic Arabs and do not speak Arabic.

These forces of unity and division among Muslims started to be a matter of global concern with the Muslim world's change of fortune since its nadir after World War I. There are now many more independent Muslim countries. Moreover, Muslim countries are becoming increasingly dependent on, among other things, the wealth that petroleum has brought them. By extension, Muslims everywhere have begun to reclaim their heritage in what might be called a "Muslim pride" movement.

The Muslim revival has many interrelated parts. One involves rejecting direct interference by outside powers. Rejection of outside domination entails reaction against the European–North American West, which Muslims closely identify with the Christians and imperial powers that long beset the house of Islam. There is also an intensifying of the efforts of many Muslims to "get back to their roots." That has strengthened the appeal of traditionalism, and there is a struggle in many Islamic countries between the secularists (usually in power) and the traditionalists for control of the government.

The resurgence of Islam as a political force has ramifications for world politics. First, the secularist-traditionalist struggle within countries will, depending on the outcome, influence their foreign policies. Second, intra-Islamic strife has in part already led to international conflict, such as the Iran-Iraq war. Muslims have also tended to unite, be that in support of Afghans, Palestinians, or others who in the Muslims' view are being oppressed. Some Muslims have also reverted to terrorism.

The issue is whether or not resurgent Islam, especially its traditionalist/fundamentalist aspects, represents a threat to political stability. In the following selections, Daniel Pipes argues that the traditionalists are indeed fundamentally antithetical to stability. Zachary Karabell disagrees, arguing that Islamic fundamentalism in the worst-case scenario is confined to one region and that it poses no threat to other regions or to the global system.

YES

Daniel Pipes

SAME DIFFERENCE

The Western confrontation with fundamentalist Islam has in some ways come to resemble the great ideological battle of the twentieth century, that between Marxism–Leninism and liberal democracy. Not only do Americans frame the discussion about Iran and Algeria much as they did the earlier one about the Soviet Union and China, but they also differ among themselves on the question of fundamentalist Islam roughly along the same lines as they did on the Cold War. Liberals say: Co-opt the radicals. Conservatives say: Confront them. As usual, the conservatives are right.

At first glance, how to deal with fundamentalist Islam appears to be a discussion unrelated to anything that has come before. Islam is a religion, not an ideology, so how can the U.S. Government formulate a policy toward it? A closer look reveals that while Islam is indeed a faith, its fundamentalist variant is a form of political ideology. Fundamentalists may be defined, most simply, as those Muslims who agree with the slogan: "Islam is the solution." When it comes to politics, they say that Islam has all the answers. The Malaysian leader Anwar Ibrahim spoke for fundamentalist Muslims everywhere when he asserted some years ago that "we are not socialist, we are not capitalist, we are Islamic." For the fundamentalists, Islam is primarily an "ism," a belief system about ordering power and wealth.

Much distinguishes fundamentalism from Islam as it was traditionally practiced, including its emphasis on public life (rather than faith and personal piety); its leadership by schoolteachers and engineers (rather than religious scholars); and its Westernized quality (e.g., whereas Muslims traditionally did not consider Friday a Sabbath, fundamentalists have turned it into precisely that, imitating the Jewish Saturday and Christian Sunday). In brief, fundamentalism represents a thoroughly modern effort to come to terms with the challenges of modernization.

The great majority of Muslims disagree with the premises of fundamentalist Islam, and a small number do so vocally. A few... have acquired global reputations, but most toil more obscurely. When a newly elected deputy to the Jordanian parliament last fall called fundamentalist Islam "one of the greatest dangers facing our society" and compared it to "a cancer" that "has to be surgically removed," she spoke for many Muslims.

Americans can in good conscience join them in criticizing fundamentalism. As an ideology, fundamentalist Islam can claim none of the sanctity that Islam the religion enjoys.

BATTLE LINES

In responding to fundamentalist Islam, Americans tend, as I have suggested, to divide along familiar liberal and conservative lines. More striking yet, the same people hold roughly the same positions they held vis-à-vis that other quasi-religious ideology, Marxism–Leninism. A left-wing Democrat like George McGovern advocates a soft line, now as then. A right-wing Republican like Jesse Helms argues for a tough line, now as then. Consider the following parallels:

Causes. The Left, in keeping with its materialist outlook, sees Communist or fundamentalist Islamic ideology as a cover for some other motivation, probably an economic one. The Russian Revolution expressed deep-seated class grievances; fundamentalist violence in Algeria, the State Department tells us, expresses "frustration arising from political exclusion and economic misery." In contrast, the Right sees radical utopian ideology as a powerful force in itself, not just as an expression of socio-economic woes. Ideas and ambitions count at least as much as the price of wheat; visions of a new order go far toward accounting for the revolutions of 1917 and 1979.

Solutions. If misery causes radicalism, as the Left argues, then the antidote lies in economic growth and social equity. The West can help in these areas through aid, trade, and open lines of communication. But if, as the Right believes, ambitious intellectuals are the problem, then they must be battled and defeated. In both cases, liberals look to cooperation, conservatives to confrontation.

The West's responsibility. The Left sees Western hostility as a leading reason why things have gone wrong. According to one journalist, the West "made its own sizable contribution" to the current crisis in Algeria. It's the old "blame America first" attitude: just as Americans were responsible for every Soviet trespass from the Gulag to the arms race, so they are now answerable for the appearance [in Iran] of the Ayatollah Khomeini (due to U.S. support for the Shah) and for the many Arab fundamentalist movements (due to U.S. support for Israel). The Right adamantly denies Western culpability in both cases, for that would absolve tyrants of their crimes. We made mistakes, to be sure, but that's because we find it hard to contend with racial utopian movements. Along these lines, [one analyst] argues that "we are at the beginning of what promises to be a long war in which new moral complexities... will present themselves as once they did in the days of Soviet Communism."

A single source. When the State Department disclaims "monolithic international control being exercised over the various Islamic movements," it uses almost the same words it once used to speak of Marxism–Leninism. For decades, American "progressives" insisted that Communist organizations around the world had indigenous sources and did not owe anything to Moscow (a claim easier to make so long as Moscow's archives remained closed). To which conservatives typically replied: Of course there's no "monolithic international control," but there is an awful lot of funding and influence. Teheran administers a network akin to an Islamic Comintern, making its role today not that different from Moscow's then.

The antis. For many decades, the Left saw those Russians, Chinese, and Cubans whose firsthand experience turned them into anti-Communists as marginal elements. In similar fashion, the Left today looks at anti-fundamentalist Muslims as inauthentic. Churches are among the worst offenders here. For example, in one recent analysis, a German priest presented the extremist element as the Muslim community per se. The Right wholeheartedly celebrates the new antis, like the old, as brave individuals bringing advance word of the terrors that result from efforts radically to remake society.

Do moderates exist? The Left distinguishes between those ideologues willing to work within the system (deemed acceptable) and those who rely on violence and sabotage (deemed unacceptable). The Right acknowledges differences in tactics but perceives no major difference in goals. Accordingly, it tends to lump most Communists or fundamentalists together.

Motives. When the other side strikes out aggressively, the Left often excuses its acts by explaining how they are defensive. Invasions by Napoleon and Hitler explain the Soviet presence in Angola; a legacy of colonial oppression accounts for the depths of fundamentalist rage. The Right concludes from events like the downing of a Korean Airlines flight or the World Trade Center bombing that the other side has offensive intentions, and it listens to no excuses.

Fighting words. The two sides draw contrary conclusions from aggressive speech. Liberals dismiss the barrage of threats against the West (Muslim prisoner in a French court: "We Muslims should kill every last one of you [Westerners]") as mere rhetoric. Conservatives listen carefully and conclude that the West needs to protect itself (French Interior Minister Charles Pasqua: fundamentalist groups "represent a threat to us").

Threat to the West. If they are approached with respect, says the Left, Marxist–Leninists and fundamentalist Muslims will leave us alone. Don't treat them as enemies and they won't hurt us. The Right disagrees, holding that all revolutionaries, no matter what their particular outlook (Communist, Fascist, fundamentalist), are deeply anti-Western and invariably target the West. Their weaponry ranges from ICBMs to truck bombs, but their purpose is the same: to challenge the predominance of modern, Western civilization.

And if truck bombs are less threatening than missiles, it should be noted that fundamentalists challenge the West more profoundly than Communists did and do. The latter disagree with our politics but not with our whole view of the world (how could they, as they pay homage to Dead White Males like Marx and Engels?). In contrast, fundamentalist Muslims despise our whole way of life, including the way we dress, mate, and pray. They admire little more than our military and medical technologies. To appease Communists means changing the political and economic spheres; to appease fundamentalists would mean forcing women to wear the veil, scuttling nearly every form of diversion, and overhauling the judicial system.

Future prospects.   In the 1950s, the Left portrayed Marxism–Leninism as the wave of the future; today, it ascribes the same brilliant prospect to fundamentalist Islam. In other words, these radical ideologies are an unstoppable force; stand in their way, and you'll not only get run over, you might even spur them on. But conservatives see utopianism enjoying only a temporary surge. The effort to remake mankind, they say, cannot work; like Communism, fundamentalism has to end up in the dustbin of history.

CONCILIATION OR CONTAINMENT?

Summing up, the Left is more sanguine than the Right about both Communism and fundamentalist Islam. It's hard to imagine a conservative calling the Ayatollah Khomeini "some kind of saint," as did Jimmy Carter's ambassador to the United Nations, Andrew Young. It's about as uncommon to hear a liberal warning, along with France's Defense Minister François Léotard, that "Islamic nationalism in its terrorist version is as dangerous today as National Socialism was in the past." On the scholarly level, a liberal Democrat like John Esposito publishes a book titled *The Islamic Threat: Myth or Reality?*, in which he concludes that the threat is but a myth. In sharp contrast, Walter McDougall, the Pulitzer Prize–winning historian and sometime assistant to Richard Nixon, sees Russia helping the West in "holding the frontier

of Christendom against its common enemy," the Muslim world.

These contrary analyses lead, naturally, to very different prescriptions for U.S. policy. The Left believes that dialogue with the other side, whether Communists or fundamentalist Muslims, has several advantages: it helps us understand their legitimate concerns, signals that we mean them no harm, and reduces mutual hostility. Beyond dialogue, the West can show good will by reducing or even eliminating our military capabilities. Roughly speaking, this is the Clinton Administration's position. In Algeria, for instance, the Administration hopes to defuse a potential explosion by urging the regime to bring in fundamentalist leaders who reject terrorism, thereby isolating the violent extremists.

The Right has little use for dialogue and unilateral disarmament. Communists and fundamentalists being invariably hostile to us, we should show not empathy but resolve, not good will but will power. And what better way to display these intentions than with armed strength? Now as then, conservatives think in terms of containment and rollback. For conservatives, Algeria's regime fits into the tradition of friendly tyrants —states where the rulers treat their own population badly but help the United States fend off a radical ideology. It makes sense to stand by Algiers (or Cairo), just as it earlier made sense to stick by Ky in Saigon or Pinochet in Chile.

Of course, the schemas presented here do not align perfectly. The Reagan Administration searched for "moderates" in Iran (an effort led by none other than Oliver North), and the Bush Administration enunciated a soft policy toward fundamentalism. The Clinton Administration, in contrast, has pursued a quite resolute policy toward Iran.

Interests sometimes count for more than ideology. Circumstance on occasion compels the U.S. Government to aid one enemy against another; thus, we have recently helped fundamentalist Afghans against Communist ones, and Communist Palestinians against fundamentalist ones. The liberal Clinton Administration speaks out against a crackdown on fundamentalists in Algeria, where the stakes are low for Americans, but accepts tough measures in Egypt, where the United States has substantial interests. The conservative French government bemoans the crackdown in Egypt (not so important for it) but encourages tough measures in Algeria (very important).

Still, the basic pattern is clear. And as the lines of debate sort themselves out, the two sides are likely to stick more consistently to their characteristic positions. This suggests that while Marxism–Leninism and fundamentalist Islam are very different phenomena, Westerners respond in similar ways to ideological challenges.

They do so because of a profound divide in outlook. American liberals believe that mankind is by nature peaceful and cooperative; when confronted with aggression and violence, they tend to assume it is motivated by a just cause, such as socio-economic deprivation or exploitation by foreigners. Anger cannot be false, especially if accompanied by high-minded goals. Less naïvely, conservatives know the evil that lurks in men's hearts. They understand the important roles of fanaticism and hatred. Just because an ideology has utopian aims does not mean that its adherents have lofty motives or generous ambitions.

The Left's soft approach to fundamentalist Islam predominates in Washington, and in the universities, the churches, and the media. Indeed, to recall one of the Left's favorite phrases, it has become the hegemonic discourse in the United States. On the other side stand nothing but a handful of scholars, some commentators and politicians, and the great common sense of the American people. Americans know an opponent when they see him, and they are not fooled by the Left's fancy arguments. That common sense prevailed in the Cold War and no doubt will suffice yet again to overcome the follies of the New Class.

NO

Zachary Karabell

FUNDAMENTAL MISCONCEPTIONS: ISLAMIC FOREIGN POLICY

For all the furor surrounding Islamic fundamentalism, there has been surprisingly little attention given to fundamentalist foreign policy. True, Iranian foreign policy has been analyzed and excoriated, and generalizations have been made on the basis of this one case. It is often assumed that fundamentalists approach foreign affairs with the same set of goals as those that drive domestic policy: namely, rejection of the secular state and the establishment of religious law as the foundation of society. It is further thought that lurking behind Islamic fundamentalist foreign policy is a commitment to holy war (jihad) with the non-Muslim world. And there seems to be a consensus among Western powers that fundamentalism poses a threat to the international system.

The Clinton administration has consistently stated that it opposes violence and extremism, but not Islam. The State Department has spoken out against the repressive measures taken by the Algerian government in its ongoing civil war with fundamentalist insurgents. At the same time, the administration has supported with economic and military aid the pro-Western regimes in Egypt, Saudi Arabia, and Turkey. While the U.S. government has taken great pains to differentiate between its opposition to violence and its respect for Islam, it has nonetheless supported governments like Egypt and Algeria that at times use extreme violence to suppress even nonviolent Muslims who oppose those regimes on religious grounds.

The recently passed Iran-Libya Sanctions Act penalizes foreign companies that do business with those two "rogue" states. Administration officials were careful to say that the target of the legislation is terrorism sponsored by these governments and not Islamic fundamentalism. Yet evidence does exist that associates the Saudi government with fundamentalist insurgents, the Pakistani government with the fundamentalist Taliban guerrillas who seized Kabul [Afghanistan], and the Turkish military with violent, extraterritorial reprisals against the Kurds. No action is taken against these regimes; indeed, these countries are courted by the U.S. government as valuable allies. The discrepancy leads to the speculation that policy toward Algeria, Iran, and the

From Zachary Karabell, "Fundamental Misconceptions: Islamic Foreign Policy," *Foreign Policy*, no. 105 (Winter 1996–1997). Copyright © 1996 by The Carnegie Endowment for International Peace. Reprinted by permission.

Muslim world in general is colored by an antipathy toward Islamic fundamentalism and a strong, if unstated, presumption that fundamentalism is a volatile and dangerous force in international affairs. These assumptions are predicated on a misunderstanding of Islamic fundamentalist foreign policy.

We cannot understand fundamentalist foreign policy simply by inferring from the domestic ideology. Fundamentalist foreign policy is different from the realpolitik or the liberal internationalism of U.S. policymakers. It is different from the raison d'état of France and the communism of the People's Republic of China. Islamic civilization is not destined to clash with the rest of the world, and Islamic fundamentalists in power do not necessarily represent a threat to international security. Instead, outside of the Islamic world, most Islamic fundamentalists have no ambition other than the most anodyne desire for security. While fundamentalism is an expansive force within the Islamic world, it neither seeks jihad with nor domination of the non-Muslim world. In this respect, Islamic fundamentalism ought to matter no more to the non-Muslim world than Québécois nationalism matters to Thailand.

There is considerable disagreement about what precisely constitutes "Islamic fundamentalism." At one time or another the label "fundamentalist" has been attached to groups as diverse as Hamas in Israel/Palestine; Hizbollah in Lebanon; the Refah (Welfare) Party in Turkey; the al-Nahda Party in Tunisia; the Muslim Brotherhood in Egypt, Jordan, and Syria; the Armed Islamic Group (GIA) in Algeria; and the Jamaat-i-Islami in Pakistan. Yet there is no unitary Islamic fundamentalism any more than there is a unitary Christian fundamentalism. In the Middle East, fundamentalism ranges from pietist organizations to revolutionary groups committed to the violent overthrow of what they perceive to be un-Islamic regimes.

While there is no monolithic Islam—and no monolithic fundamentalist movement—there is an ongoing struggle in the Islamic world. On one side are largely secular governments; on the other, there are individuals and groups who believe that politics and religion are one and who reject the secular Western division between the state and religion. As the scholar Nazih Ayubi has observed, for fundamentalists, Islam is understood as *din* (a religion), *dunya* (a way of life), and *dawla* (a state). Fundamentalists call for a return to an earlier, supposedly more pure Islam. They want to replace secular, civil law with the *sharia* (Islamic law), and they view the modern state system in the Islamic world as an illegitimate and immoral division of the *umma* (the community of believers). Fundamentalists share this basic ideology, but different groups adopt varying strategies to realize their vision.

FOREIGN POLICY AND IDEOLOGY

What exactly is an Islamic foreign policy? Many of the ruling Iranian elite say that Iran's foreign policy is Islamic, but what does that mean? Does the foreign policy of the state of Iran depart in significant ways from the foreign policies of states in general? The governments of Saudi Arabia and (non-Arab) Pakistan are avowedly Islamic (as opposed to secular), yet they are rarely considered fundamentalist. Though each of these countries attempts to fashion its laws in accordance with the *sharia,* and though the Saudi monarchy is deeply influenced by a group of Islamic puritans (the Wahhabis), they act in foreign policy matters in a more realist fashion than do leaders in Iran and Sudan, who pursue a distinctly fundamentalist foreign policy.

These questions lead to the further conundrum of whether there is anything that can be characterized as an Islamic foreign policy or as a fundamentalist foreign policy. For example, do the policies that fundamentalist Iran pursues as a self-declared Islamic state differ from the policies of the other, more secular Muslim governments in the Middle East, such as Syria or Jordan? In addition, do the policies of Iran, whose citizens follow Shiite Islam, depart in noticeable ways from the policies of another self-declared Islamic state, Sudan, whose Muslims are Sunni?...

The default setting for foreign policy is realism. Most policymakers, whether American, European, Asian, or Middle Eastern, perceive international politics to be a competition between states for power, influence, and profit. Over time, diplomats and world leaders have developed what amount to rules of engagement.

One of the strongest of these dictates is that the state is inviolable. Even in war, modern states do not usually attempt to obliterate one another. When they do—as Iraq tried with Kuwait in 1990—they are deemed to have broken the cardinal law of international politics and are punished accordingly.

Some states, however, champion an ideology that challenges the legitimacy of states. Cold War Soviet communist rhetoric, for instance, labeled Western states as bourgeois, capitalist tools of oppression. In due time, workers would recognize their common interests, unite, and liberate themselves from the capitalist state. That ideology, as well as the policies pursued by the Soviet Union that were designed to carry it out, profoundly disturbed the governments of the West.

Like communism, Islamic fundamentalism is an ideology. Where communism rejected capitalist rules of engagement in international affairs, Islamic fundamentalism rejects the notion that the state is an inviolable unit. But unlike communism, Islamic fundamentalism confines its aspirations to one portion of the world—the Muslim world. Thus, when fundamentalists challenge the state, it is the state within the Muslim world that is the target of their animus. Communism sought, and free market capitalism still seeks, world domination. Islamic fundamentalism does not and never will.

Any successful ideology is malleable, and Islamic fundamentalism is no exception. It does not dictate specific action and can—in the hands of adept leaders or intellectuals—justify almost any behavior. Furthermore, the relationship between ideology and actual policy is notoriously opaque. State leaders are perfectly capable of articulating a governing ideology and then acting in ways that contravene that ideology. Any regime often needs an ideology to legitimize its use of force, both internally and externally. This ideology may mask realist motives, but ideology and realism can also coexist. In the particular case of Islamic fundamentalism, ideology matters a great deal. Fundamentalists conceive of the world as two broad but distinct realms: the community of believers and the non-Islamic world. While there are great variations and divisions within each of those worlds, policy toward one is radically different from policy toward the other.

THE UMMA AND
THE MODERN STATE

In a realist world of states, or in an international system in which the United Nations recognizes and sanctifies the state as the primary and morally approved actor in international relations, foreign policy is anything beyond the borders of the state. Yet, for an Islamic regime, state borders within the Islamic world are artificial constructs, created largely by the former colonial or imperialist powers of Europe. Hence they lack true legitimacy.

The lack of respect that political Islam extends to the state as understood by the West characterizes not just fundamentalists in power (Iran and Sudan) but fundamentalists in opposition (Algeria, Lebanon, and Tunisia). As Hassan al-Turabi, the spiritual leader of Sudan's military regime, has said, "The international dimension of the Islamic movement is conditioned by the universality of the *umma* ... and the artificial irrelevancy of Sudan's borders." In the tradition of one of the foremost spokesmen of modern fundamentalism, Egypt's Sayyid Qutb, many of today's fundamentalist groups attempt to realign the traditional relationship between Islam and the state from one in which Islam serves to legitimize state authority into one in which Islam delegitimizes the state by branding it un-Islamic. The Ayatollah Ruhollah Khomeini did this frequently in his years of opposition to the shah, and even more moderate opposition leaders like Tunisia's al-Ghannouchi label the attempts of the Tunisian and Algerian governments to suppress fundamentalism as "anti-Islamic."

Not all fundamentalist movements seek to undermine the state. Some movements (such as the Muslim Brotherhood in Jordan) seek accommodation with the state, while others (such as Algeria's GIA) are insurgent. Almost all fundamentalist movements nonetheless seek to infuse Islamic principles into the governments of states within the Muslim world. The attempt to invalidate the state is, on the whole, more pronounced in Middle Eastern and African Islamic fundamentalist movements than in those of Southeast Asia. Indonesian and Malaysian movements call for Islamic law and an Islamic state but they do not as frequently assail the concept of the state itself.

Most fundamentalist movements in the Middle East, however, view states as artificial colonial-era dividers of the *umma*. Western powers drew the state lines of the Gulf emirates, Iraq, Israel, Jordan, Saudi Arabia, and Syria. At the same time, the boundaries of Algeria, Egypt, Iran, Morocco, and Turkey were not invented by the colonial powers. Fundamentalists in these countries cannot attack the state as a Western invention. Instead, they call the rulers of these countries "un-Islamic" and in so doing brand them as illegitimate.

In theory, the *umma* is one unit. All Muslims, regardless of sect, constitute the *umma*; hence, division among the believers is a degenerate state of affairs. In the view of many contemporary political fundamentalists, the entire community of believers makes up the universe of action. States are nothing more than lines on a map. Thus, the policies of the Iranian government toward Central Asia or the policies of Sudan toward North Africa are not really "foreign policy" at all. As al-Turabi remarked in 1995 when discussing his Popular Arab and Islamic Conference, "It represents all Muslim nations. First, because these nations cannot express their views in their countries, and, second, because the whole world is drawing closer together. It behooves the Muslims as a single nation to meet and express their views."

The same view is espoused by the Ayatollah Ali Khamenei, the spiritual leader of the Islamic Republic of Iran. As he stated in a March 1995 sermon,

The Islamic *ummah* should try to preserve unity, cohesion, and solidarity, as the term *ummah* suggests. Today, this great community has a duty to its esteemed prophet, savior, and teacher, to a person who as God's testimony among the *ummah* is the most popular personality. This duty is to preserve the honor and integrity of the Islamic *ummah* through unity and cohesion. This is the duty of the *ummah* today.

Today the enemies of Islam and the Islamic community are doing their best to pit the members of this community against each other. This is not peculiar to the present time, as the situation has been the same in the past. However, today, this dastardly mission of the enemies is being implemented through systematic thought and comprehensive planning. The reason is that they feel that the Islamic spirit is growing among Muslims, Islam has awakened hearts, and with our nation's great revolution, arrogance has received a blow from Islam. This is why they want to create enmity in the Islamic community.

All the Muslims who today in some way or another feel the bite of arrogance's lashes on their bodies and souls—such as the nations of Palestine, Bosnia, Chechnya, Kashmir, and Lebanon, and other Muslim nations in Africa and Asia —are subjected to pain and suffering because of the lack of unity and solidarity in the Islamic community. If the Islamic community had enjoyed solidarity, none of these would have happened.

Fundamentalism significantly expands the strategic universe for fundamentalist states and groups. Prior to the 1979 Iranian revolution and the accession of the government of Umar al-Bashir and al-Turabi in Sudan in 1989, neither Iran nor Sudan would have considered events in Bosnia, Chechnya, Kashmir, or Malaysia to be foreign policy concerns. Foreign policy in these countries now rests on the principle that the *umma* is a cohesive political unit. As a result, the universe has expanded. But at the same time, that universe has a finite scope: It stops where Islam stops and therefore is not expansionist toward the Western world or the East Asian world outside of Malaysia and Indonesia.

Ideologically, then, the policies that Iran or Sudan pursue toward the Muslim world are not foreign but rather are aimed at reconstituting the *umma*. No matter that this *umma* was never politically unified as a self-conscious nation stretching from Morocco to Indonesia, the ideal of fundamentalist policy is that the Muslim community is unitary. That position is shared by many of the more prominent opposition fundamentalist groups, such as the al-Nahda Party in Tunisia, the Jamaati-i-Islami in Pakistan, and the Muslim Brotherhood in Jordan, as well as by the Refah Party in Turkey, which is now in a coalition government. They therefore view the *umma* as a community of interests, and other Islamic countries as potential allies.

Within the Islamic world, the ideology of the *umma* is sometimes trumped by pure realpolitik. Iran might ideologically oppose Syria's Hafez al-Assad, but during the Iran-Iraq war Iran and Syria drew closer against the common enemy of Saddam Hussein's Iraq.

In dealing with the non-Islamic world, however, fundamentalist states and opposition groups adopt a more variegated and pragmatic foreign policy that closely approximates the realist paradigm. While Iran and Sudan support, either rhetorically or with arms and money, fundamentalist revolutionary groups that operate within the *umma*, their policies toward China, Europe, India, and the United States are less subversive. Iran might be antagonistic toward the United States and friendly with India, while Sudan might be friendly with China and less so with Japan. Certainly, there is profound antagonism toward the United States, overall, but it is an antagonism that more closely resembles state competition for power. Within the *umma*, fundamentalism rejects the state and thus sees no constraints on actions that might undermine the states in the region; outside of the *umma*, fundamentalists see an antagonistic world dominated by the United States in allegiance with other states and a system that rarely serves Muslim interests. The aim is not to undermine Western states, or to destroy them, but to try to compete internationally for influence, prestige, and power.

FUNDAMENTALIST GOALS

All fundamentalist movements, whether they accommodate the state or challenge it violently, whether they are pietistic or revolutionary, strive for the unification of the *umma*: Yet they differ greatly over how this goal is to be achieved. In part, the differences among the governments of Iran, Sudan, and the numerous opposition groups, such as Tunisia's al-Nahda Party, may have to do with the life-cycle of ideologies: Iran is entering a postrevolutionary

phase, Sudan's Islamic regime is newer to power, and the al-Nahda Party is still an outlaw movement subject to intense repression. The al-Nahda Party is so consumed with local problems that its leader, Rashid al-Ghannouchi, talks hardly at all of exporting ideology. In both word and deed, Iranian leaders were more eager to export fundamentalism a decade ago. With the passing of the early revolutionary fervor, Iran's foreign policy is decidedly less ambitious. Even in its relations with the new Muslim states of Central Asia, its policy is more realist and pragmatic, though it is not necessarily status-quo oriented.

The regime in Sudan emphasizes rhetorically an expansionist, revolutionary foreign policy within the *umma*, and at times al-Turabi even suggests that world Islam is the ultimate goal. Asked by a Spanish newspaper if Sudan is destined to save the world, al-Turabi responded, "We are the spearhead of a movement which must free the world from the moral turpitude and atheism in which it is living." The leaders of Sudan sound much like the leaders of Iran did in the first decade of the revolution. Sudan has been accused by the U.S. government and by Egypt and other Arab states of training guerrilla forces at several camps in its northern region. While Sudan denies the allegations, evidence overwhelmingly indicates that the camps do exist. The primary targets of these guerrilla groups are the secular regimes of Algeria and Egypt. However, these insurgent groups do not appear to be directly controlled by the Sudanese government.

Beyond seeking to unify the *umma*, two additional goals of fundamentalist foreign policies are an opposition to Israel and a rejection of U.S. hegemony in international politics. The two are linked, since the existence of the state of Israel is seen by many as the most naked example of Western imperialism and intrusion on the *umma*. The Iranian republic is especially vehement in its rejection of the U.S.-dominated international system. "The Islamic Republic," said Khamenei, "opposes the hegemony of the United States and its influence and interference in Islamic countries and in all oppressed countries." In this view, the international system is the creation of the West and its current standard-bearer, the United States. The rules of the international system—the rules of realism and state power—work to the disadvantage of Iran and, by extension, Islam. And the most visible local way of rejecting that influence is by negating or refusing to recognize the legitimacy of Israel. This attempt to reject "hegemony" is both a function of Islam and a natural reflection of state interests in acquiring a greater share of the international pie.

POLICY IMPLICATIONS

Fundamentalist foreign policy has several discernible characteristics: an embrace of the unity of the *umma*; a refusal to respect the sovereignty of secular states within the *umma*; a rejection of Western hegemony within the Muslim world; and an animus toward Zionism as the most glaring local manifestation of the Western state system that artificially divides the *umma*.

The intensity with which fundamentalist groups and governments seek to realize the goal of a unified *umma* and a destruction of the Western state system within the *umma* differs depending on a variety of factors. In Iran, an initial expansionist ideology has faded as that nation

enters a postrevolutionary phase, and its behavior may in part be explained by theories of revolution. Sudan's al-Turabi has donned the mantle of Islamic revolution, but Sudanese society is not undergoing revolutionary transformations, and the behavior of Sudanese elites can be explained by the demands of their fundamentalist ideology more than by the pressures of revolution. In Tunisia, where the al-Nahda Party represents a nonviolent variant of fundamentalism, local concerns are dominant.

The policy implications of fundamentalist foreign policies differ depending on the nation in question and its perceived relationship to the *umma*. The implications for Israel are not (or should not be) the same as the implications for the United States or France. For the French, the outcome of the civil war in Algeria has substantial economic and political consequences. The prospect of hundreds of thousands of Algerians fleeing to France, combined with French investments in North Africa and French support for the military government, makes the GIA's violent ideology an immediate security concern. Similarly, the rejection not just of Zionism but of Israel that characterizes Hamas and Hizbollah means that fundamentalism is a security concern for the Israeli state.

Yet the ideology of fundamentalism should not be threatening to France itself. The effects of that ideology on a region in which France has vested interests are problematic, but the fact that fundamentalist ideology so rigorously distinguishes between the *umma* and the non-Islamic world means that the boundaries of ambition of the GIA or of the al-Nahda Party do not cross the Mediterranean.

For the United States, then, Islamic fundamentalist foreign policy can be read in several ways. As an ideology that seeks to disrupt the state system of the Middle East, South Asia, Saharan Africa, and Central Asia, it could create severe chaos. Though there is little hard evidence implicating the Iranian or Sudanese governments in many of the plots they are alleged to have masterminded, it is certainly true that Iran financed the Hizbollah in Lebanon, which kidnapped American citizens in the 1980s and helped to perpetuate the Lebanese civil war. The Palestinian fundamentalist faction, Hamas, seems to have received some financial support from Iran, but it also seems to have received support from the Saudis and the Gulf emirates. Given that U.S. foreign policy is geared toward maintaining the status quo, chaos is threatening. As an ideology that more immediately jeopardizes the health and security of allies such as Israel, Hosni Mubarak's regime in Egypt, and, to a lesser extent, France, fundamentalism does pose a threat. And to the extent that the foreign policy of fundamentalism challenges U.S. "hegemony" in the Muslim world, it is antagonistic to the United States.

None of the above need be interpreted as threats to the United States, however, if the United States interprets its security more narrowly. Islamic fundamentalist ideology does not challenge either the United States or the West on its own turf. Fundamentalism is not a global ideology like communism or capitalism, and hence it should not trigger alarm bells in Western states to anywhere near the degree that it currently does. The more U.S. foreign policy seeks global power and the greater the demand for an international system of liberal democracies, the greater will be the threat posed by an Islamic fundamentalism that adamantly and violently rejects that hegemony and the norms of liberalism. If U.S. goals remain relatively limited and the United States attends to issues such as global prosperity and domestic security, then Islamic fundamentalism should not be considered a threat to the United States.

When asked about fundamentalism in the Middle East, most officials, whether at State, CIA, the White House, or the Pentagon, say that it is a pressing concern and that it has become an even more pressing concern in the past few years. Opinions over why it is a concern differ widely. The major U.S. interests in the region are oil, stability, American power, and the Arab-Israeli peace process. U.S. officials see fundamentalism as a potential threat to each of these.

It is difficult to see how political Islam jeopardizes access to oil. After all, even if every oil-producing country were governed by a radical Islamic regime, they would still wish to sell oil to the West, and there would be a rather low limit to how high they could price that oil. One of the lessons of the 1973 and 1979 oil crises was that once the price of oil exceeds a certain maximum, it becomes cheaper for industrial economies to switch to alternate sources of energy. In the interim, producers outside of the Middle East could increase production to compensate for the decline in supply. Therefore Islamic fundamentalism does not constitute a potential threat to oil.

The other issues are trickier. Regimes such as Iran and Sudan are indeed hostile to the Arab-Israeli peace process, and they wish to see the United States removed as a presence in the Middle East.

It is true, therefore, that a fundamentalist sweep of the Middle East could weaken U.S. influence in the region. It could also so radicalize Arab sentiments that it would prevent a comprehensive Middle East peace and undermine Israeli-Palestinian relations. But judging from the problematic Arab-Israeli peace process so far, the more Israel recognizes Palestinian autonomy, the less antagonistic its Muslim neighbors are.

In addition, the diffuse nature of Islamic fundamentalism and the disunity among such fundamentalists suggests that a Middle East dominated by fundamentalism would be less of a problem for the United States than a secular dictator with illusions of grandeur. As the Persian Gulf war ought to have demonstrated, there is a far greater likelihood that U.S. hegemony will be diminished by secular autocrats than by Islamist puritans. There is a long history of Saddam Husseins. Khomeinis, however, are far more unusual, and Khomeini's Iran never posed the kind of military challenge to the region that Hussein's Iraq has.

As for terrorism, fundamentalist ideology suggests that it is the exception rather than the rule. Indeed, outside of a number of highly publicized incidents in the 1980s, such as the highjacking of TWA flight 847 in 1985 and the World Trade Center bombing in 1993, fundamentalist violence outside of the *umma* has been rare. Where it does occur, the motivation is usually retaliation for perceived infringement of the territorial integrity of the *umma* by the United States or other Western nations. The Iranian government has violated the state sovereignty of several European governments by sending assassination teams to murder Iranian opponents of its regime, but as outrageous as that extraterritorial violence is,

it is not violence directed against the non-Islamic world. Nor is the assistance that Iran and Sudan give to fundamentalist insurgencies directed against the West as much as it is directed against governments that Islamic ideologues perceive to be un-Islamic. Indeed, the ideology of fundamentalism suggests that in foreign policy toward the non-Muslim world, there is no reason for antagonism unless the non-Muslim world cooperates in the continued division of the *umma*.

Furthermore, the policies taken by the United States in response to the perceived threat of fundamentalism may well exacerbate the situation. U.S. officials apparently view authoritarianism in the Middle East as an evil preferable to fundamentalism. The United States ends up supporting the very factor that gives the Islamic opposition its greatest strength: the sense that the secular regimes of the Middle East are illegitimate because they are creations of Western hegemony and not true products of Islam and the *umma*.

Because Islamic fundamentalism is expansive within the *umma* and limited without, U.S. policymakers can set aside notions that fundamentalists will not abide by international norms in foreign affairs. Within the *umma*, they may not, but outside of it, they will. Outside of the *umma*, they have no ideological reason not to abide by international norms, and the demands of the international system exercise the same constraints on them as on traditional nation-states.

Once again, the lack of a compelling ideological reason for violence against the United States has meant that fundamentalist governments do not tend to attack the United States with anything other than words. Attacks and plots against the United States and American citizens have been carried out by "freelance" fundamentalists such as Sheikh Omar Abdel Rahman and his followers. The recent bombing of an American military base in Saudi Arabia was probably carried out by an outlaw group opposed to the Saudi government. Despite efforts to link conclusively the policies of groups such as Hizbollah and Hamas to directives from Tehran, no such evidence appears to have been found. If monetary links make Tehran (or Riyadh) responsible for the actions of these groups, then the U.S. government bears responsibility for the victory of the fundamentalist Taliban in Afghanistan through its covert financing of *mujahedeen* rebels fighting Soviet forces in the 1980s.

The United States must avoid the temptation to treat all fundamentalist governments as rogues. Given the lack of action taken against the Saudis and Pakistanis for behavior that elicits condemnation and embargoes against the Iranians, it seems that at present the United States treats fundamentalist foreign policy as inherently lawless and hence threatening.

The United States should reconsider its stringent policy toward Iran, as well as its excessive support for the repressive regimes in Algeria and Saudi Arabia. Fundamentalist Iran has created far fewer difficulties for the United States than has either secular Iraq or divided Lebanon. While relations between Iran and the United States are not likely to be warm, little is gained by current policy toward Iran.

Finally, the United States can afford to pay less attention to Islamic fundamentalism. If fundamentalist foreign policy is understood to be inherently circumscribed, then fundamentalism in the worst-case scenario is confined to one region. Policymakers have been able to normalize relations with communist China because China is not expansionist. So too could policy be normalized with fundamentalist governments. The United States can afford to accommodate fundamentalism, and it should. The attempt to contain it will almost certainly fail, and there is no better way to guarantee continued tension between political Islam and the West.

POSTSCRIPT

Is Islamic Fundamentalism a Threat to Political Stability?

There are nearly 1 billion Muslims in the world, constituting a majority among the Arabs as well as in several non-Arab countries, including Algeria, Indonesia, Iran, Kazakhstan, Morocco, Pakistan, the Sudan, and Turkey. There are other countries, such as Nigeria and the Philippines, in which Muslims constitute an important political force. Indeed, only about one of every four Muslims lives in the Middle East. To learn more about Islamic history, read *The Middle East: A Brief History of the Last 2,000 Years* by Bernard Lewis (Scribner, 1996) and Graham E. Fuller and Ian O. Lesser, *A Sense of Siege: The Geopolitics of Islam and the West* (Westview Press, 1995).

There can be little doubt that the interplay between Islam and politics remains an important issue in world affairs. Fundamentalism remains strong. The civil wars continue in Afghanistan, Algeria, and elsewhere. A fundamentalist prime minister came to power democratically in Turkey in 1996, only to be forced to step down by the country's military in 1997. Hamas and other radical groups continue to wage terrorist attacks on Israel.

From a Western point of view, the images are mixed and the future ramifications are uncertain. Muslim countries, like most less developed countries, face many difficulties in preserving their traditional values while adopting so-called modern practices, which are mostly those promoted by the dominant European–North American powers. Indeed, the rush of technological advancement associated with modernity, the loss of cultural identity, and other aspects of a rate of change unparalleled in world history are troubling for many people in many countries around the world. It is important to note that the traditionalist movement in Muslim countries is part of a larger effort of people to find belonging and meaning in a rapidly changing world dominated by huge, impersonalized governments, businesses, and other organizations. It is possible to argue that some of the causes of Islamic fundamentalism are the same factors that have strengthened the so-called Christian right in the United States and Hindu fundamentalists in India.

Amid the turmoil, there are many signs that Muslim countries are adjusting to what is arguably a spreading homogenization of global culture. As elsewhere, democracy has taken hold in some Muslim countries and struggles to survive or begin in others. Two worthwhile readings on these matters are S. V. R. Nasr, "Democracy and Islamic Revivalism," *Political Science Quarterly* (Summer 1995) and Rex Brynen, Bahgat Korany, and Paul Noble, eds., *Political Liberalization and Democratization in the Arab World: Theoretical Perspectives* (Lynne Rienner Press, 1995).

ISSUE 5

Is Geopolitics Still Relevant in the Era of Cyberspace?

YES: Colin S. Gray, from "The Continued Primacy of Geography," *Orbis* (Spring 1996)

NO: Martin Libicki, from "The Emerging Primacy of Information," *Orbis* (Spring 1996)

ISSUE SUMMARY

YES: Colin S. Gray, a professor of international politics, asserts that geographical factors, such as size and location, are still dominant.

NO: Martin Libicki, a senior fellow at the Center for Advanced Concepts and Technology, National Defense University, contends that global communication links and computer capabilities have significantly lessened the importance of geography.

Linking the academic fields of geography and political science is political geography, which focuses on the interrelationship of geography, power, and international politics. First formulated in the late 1800s, geopolitical theory fell into considerable disrepute after the Nazis used it to justify German expansion in order to gain *lebensraum* (living space). They and many of the early advocates of geopolitics maintained that the state had an organic dimension and that it had to expand or die. This theory has been discredited.

Other geopolitical theories, however, have influenced history and continue to do so. Alfred Thayer Mahan, an American naval officer, in *The Influence of Seapower on History* (1890), argued that world power was determined by control of the seas and by the acquisition of colonies for that purpose. Mahan's theory supported and even encouraged imperial expansion. Kaiser Wilhelm II was influenced by Mahan, and his policies led to Germany's naval expansion and search for colonies in the years before World War I.

Taking the opposite view, British geographer Sir Halford Mackinder, in *Democratic Ideals and Reality* (1919), classified Europe, Asia, and Africa as the "world island, at the center of which was the East European heartland." From this perspective, Mackinder held,

> Who rules East Europe commands the Heartland;
> Who rules the Heartland commands the World Island;
> Who rules the World Island commands the world.

A third classic political geographer, American Nicholas J. Spykman, in *Geography and Peace* (1944), took a geopolitical position between those of Mahan and Mackinder. Spykman emphasized the "rimlands" of Europe—the Middle East, Africa, South America, and Asia—as the key to U.S. national security. These lands, Spykman theorized, constitute a barrier that, if controlled by friendly or neutral forces, serves to keep other powers out of the Western Hemisphere. Conversely, if the rimlands were controlled by a hostile power, then that antagonist could encircle the United States.

Even if one does not subscribe to geopolitical theories, the impact of specific geographic factors on history is axiomatic. Geography, for instance, is at the core of the way most people define themselves politically. Nationalism—the sense of being American, Russian, German, or Japanese—involves seeing one's political identity attached to a territorial state (a country). In another way, significant protection has been afforded Switzerland by the Alps, Great Britain by the English Channel, and the United States by its flanking oceans. Napoleon and, later, Hitler learned that Russia's huge size and frigid winters were formidable allies of the Russian army. Conversely, Poland's unfortunate location between Germany and Russia or the Korean people's equally vulnerable position between China and Japan have often brought destruction and outside domination.

Technology has certainly changed the importance of geography, perhaps even weakening the state. Some claim that the military relevance of geography has been eclipsed, that, for example, the safety provided to Americans by the Atlantic and Pacific oceans has diminished in an age of nuclear-tipped, continent-spanning missiles. The growth of multinational corporations, trade dependency, and other aspects of the global economy also mean that the territorial state is less important as an economic entity.

There are also analysts who argue that, in an age of easy long-distance travel and almost instantaneous global communication, the territorial loyalties that bound people together with national identities may be weakening as new, transnational ties are being strengthened. For example, women from around the world have found that they have common causes, and that sense of being a political woman supplements—perhaps competes with or even supplants—the sense of being a political American, Canadian, or Mexican.

Technology is changing at an ever-increasing rate. One list of the most important scientific/technological discoveries and innovations throughout human history indicated that 50 percent have occurred in this century alone and 90 percent have occurred over the last two centuries.

The authors of the following selections discuss the impact of rapidly changing technology on relatively stable geography. Colin S. Gray maintains that geopolitical factors continue to have primary importance. Martin Libicki contends that information is overtaking geography in importance. This debate focuses mainly on military relevance, but it is also part of a much wider speculation about the future of political identifications and relationships.

YES
Colin S. Gray

THE CONTINUED PRIMACY
OF GEOGRAPHY

Because "geopolitics" is a word—as well as a basket of associated ideas—
that all but begs to be abused by the unscrupulous, the following definition
may prove useful: geopolitics refers to "the relation of international political
power to the geographical setting."

But what, then, is "geography"? The concept of geography is perilously
all-embracing and, like other factors that purportedly explain everything,
has the potential to end up explaining nothing in particular. One can speak
of physical geography, human geography, economic geography, political ge-
ography, cultural geography, military geography, strategic geography, and
many more. Unfortunately for neatness of analysis, the geographical setting
for international political power must embrace all of these.

That is not to deny that "geography" and "geographical" are frequently
used as if they implied only the physical setting for human activity. After
all, geography in its narrowest sense is the descriptive science of the earth.
But the earth is the physical setting for human activity of, say, an economic,
political, or strategic kind. Thus, though geography is conceptually distinct
from economics, politics, and strategy, it influences each of these categories of
human behavior, and the relationships between geography and economics,
politics, and strategy can therefore be studied as geoeconomics, geopolitics,
and geostrategy.

In addition to these objective geographies, as one might call them, there is
also psychological geography, a concept closely associated with the notion
of culture. Physical conditions limit what a polity can achieve at any one
time by particular methods, but what that polity seeks to achieve, as well as
the methods it prefers, depends in part upon what it has taught itself about
itself and the world. Historically, such geographical backing for political and
strategic ideas has proved powerful, even seductive.

Today, notwithstanding the reality and exaggeration of transnational phenomena, world politics is still keyed to territorially based and defined states.
The challenge, therefore, is not to defend or assault the proposition that there
is geopolitical influence upon international security; so much is evident. The

challenge, rather, is to identify important truths about the forms, structure, and intensity of that influence.

GEOPOLITICS: SOME BASICS

Strictly speaking, geography does not require political behavior of any particular kind. Nonetheless, it: 　*lglited*

- defines the location of the national (or multinational) territory;
- describes the physical character of that territory in all respects;
- distinguishes the (national) territory of the state from the territories of other states (in one important sense geography selects neighbors and, more arguably, friends and foes);
- defines a polity's cultural zone or civilization (e.g., in the American case, was the region colonized by the Spanish and Portuguese, or by the French and British?); and
- conditions, shapes, and influences the course of a polity's historical choices.

Thus, though the geographical setting does not determine the course of history, it is fundamental to all that happens within its boundaries. Writing a history of modern Europe, one would not mention casually that the German Empire. was located in the continental heart of Europe or that Great Britain is an island. German and British statesmen can pursue a wide variety of policies and adopt a wide range of strategies from their respectively continental and maritime geographical settings. But those different settings impose distinctive constraints and provide distinctive opportunities that have profound implications for policy and strategy.

The argument, therefore, is neither that geographical setting determines policy and strategy in some all-but-mystical way, nor that the implications of that setting remain constant as technology evolves, but rather that geographical factors are pervasive in world politics. Geography defines the players (which are territorially organized states, or would like to be), frequently defines the stakes for which the players contend, and always defines the terms in which they measure their security relative to others.

Admittedly, it can be difficult to rein in the claim for geopolitical influences upon international security, and those who think geopolitically are often accused of determinism. But to discern geopolitical patterns in the course of strategic history is not deterministic. For example, it is simply accurate to note that in modern times maritime powers and coalitions have either won or drawn all the great wars they have waged with continental powers and coalitions. Thus, in what British geographer Sir Halford Mackinder called the Columbian Age of 1500–1900, maritime powers apparently enjoyed a strategic advantage in their struggles with continental powers. In ancient and medieval times, exactly the reverse was true: the conditions of, including the geographical setting for, continental polities' strategies appear to have been more tolerant of fault than was true for maritime polities.

Obviously, maritime states like Britain and maritime coalitions like NATO have not been fated to win in the modern era. Individuals and individual decisions matter. Poor statecraft, strategy, or tactics; a shortage of men and material; inferior technology; and the workings of what Carl von Clausewitz generically termed war's "friction" can negate the most systemic of advantages. Nonetheless, a prima facie case can be made that, over the past five hundred years, errors in policy and strategy were more likely to be fatal when committed by a continental power than when committed by a maritime power. Louis XIV, Napoleon, and Adolf Hitler might have won their wars, but there were strong geopolitical reasons why final victory was unlikely for any of those continental imperialists. The strategic histories of the Netherlands, France, Germany, and Russia/USSR all demonstrate why, for reasons of geography, a continental homeland means an inability to sustain prudently a bid for preeminent sea power.

It is useful to supplement these observations on the grand sweep of historical outcomes with a specific geopolitical argument. The American historian and strategic theorist Alfred Thayer Mahan argued that a state with a land as well as a maritime frontier was at an enduring and usually fatal geostrategic disadvantage when in naval competition with a wholly insular opponent. Mahan developed this argument in a 1902 essay focused upon the growing Anglo-German rivalry, though against the backdrop of the historical experiences of Britain in her past competitions with the Dutch and the French. Mahan, reasoning geopolitically but not determistically, wrote that

it is *clear* that an insular state, *if attentive to the conditions that should dictate its policy*, is inevitably led to possess a superiority in that particular kind of force [sea power], the mobility of which enables it most readily to project its power to the more distant quarters of the earth, and also to change its point of application at will with unequaled rapidity.

The relevant geostrategic question is not one of land power versus sea power; it is the translation of superiority in one geographical environment to superiority overall. In modern times, powers superior at sea have more easily generated complementary, superior land power than powers superior on land have developed a fighting advantage at sea. Whether or not the coming of air power, missile weapons, space power, nuclear weapons, and, for the latest wave, "information warfare" has wholly overtaken yesterday's continental-maritime geostrategic relationships is a topic to which this essay will return. But over the past five hundred years, despite all the changes in civil and military technology, and particularly in communications and transportation technologies, and notwithstanding all the "might-have-beens," an essential continuity has existed in geopolitical and geostrategic relationships between continental and maritime powers. English grand strategy against Habsburg Spain—later repeated against royal, republican, and imperial France, and then against imperial and Nazi Germany—was very similar to much of the struggle between NATO's essentially maritime coalition of Western powers and Moscow's "evil empire." By the 1980s, the leader of the NATO coalition was thinking more and more about protracted non-nuclear conflict on a global basis, via the U.S. maritime strategy.

A maritime alliance in conflict with a continental foe generally will need to succeed on land, for until recently that was the only geographical environment in which a continental power could be defeated. NATO was, indeed remains, a maritime alliance in the sense that its leading member has a maritime rather than a continental orientation and its "internal" lines of essential communication are maritime rather than continental. Land power typically is a vital complement to sea power, even in the era of air power, missiles, and nuclear weapons, as the United States and NATO demonstrated throughout the cold war. The Eurasian continental allies of the United States comprised important stakes in the conflict and served as a continental, or (in the case of Britain and Japan) barely off-continental, barrier to a Soviet maritime breakout from its continental imperium.

GEOPOLITICS TODAY?

Paradoxically, perhaps, a useful approach to the question of contemporary geopolitical influence on international security is via topics sometimes held to be unfriendly to it.

Technology and geography: Is the geographical setting still important, as exploitation of the electromagnetic spectrum and modern transportation technologies defy and conquer distance, terrain, and climate?

Communications and culture: If we increasingly live in "one world" because of the global communications revolution, how can geography much matter?

Geopolitics and geoeconomics: Are not the stakes, terms, and instruments of conflict becoming economic rather than political, let alone political-military? Whether or not geopolitical ideas had relevance yesterday, how can they say anything important about tomorrow's economic and financial struggles?

Joint warfare: With the pervasive interdependence of the armed forces today and their organization and preparation for joint (i.e. multi-service) operations, how can environmentally

specific ideas of military power retain relevance? *Do they mean Branches ochnes-unit?*

Technology and geography. That modern technology has conquered geography to the point where geographical factors can be regarded as mere details is a notion popular among three groups of people. First are those who are deeply ignorant of the management science of logistics. Secondly, there are those who believe that some newly omni-competent military technology has miraculously canceled the traditional limitations imposed by "brute geography." Lastly, there are people who believe that the possible military salience of the geographical setting has been trumped by the advance of a truly global community.

That technology has canceled geography contains just enough merit to be called a plausible fallacy. It is true that electronic advances now allow for genuinely global communication in real time (albeit not reliably in time of war against an equally competent foe). It is true that long-range air-breathing vehicles can transit oceans and continents in hours, that missiles can reach their targets in minutes, and that control of earth orbit permits a global presence (for some limited purposes, at least). New weapons technologies can offset distance, terrain, and even climate to an important degree, but their strategic value is limited by at least three major considerations.

First, technological progress cannot be owned or retained by one security community alone. Aircraft, radio, and nuclear weapons all have considerable utility. That utility, however, is more than a little reduced by the achievement or acquisition of militarily parallel instruments by potential foes. Secondly, it remains a fact of enduring significance that *"the ultimate determinant in war is the man on the scene with the gun."* Man is a territorial animal in many senses, and he must inhabit continental physical geography. Human beings can be intimidated by threats from afar, blown apart by bombardment from altitude and spoken to at the speed of light. But the exercise of continuous influence or control requires the physical presence of armed people in the area at issue. In some important ways, conflict cannot occur "beyond geography." (Makers of U.S. policy in the Balkans, please note.)

The third major consideration of relevance here pertains to the material needed by "the man on the scene with the gun." People can reach the scene of action at fairly high subsonic speeds, but coming by air they will arrive with little other than personal weapons, light artillery, and an embarrassingly small ammunition load. In other words, one can all but cancel geographical distance by the rapid air insertion of paratroops, or by the less rapid forward deployment of troops to air bases in the combat theater, but with what will they fight, and for how long? If anything, Mahan understated the matter when he wrote that "notwithstanding all the familiar and unfamiliar dangers of the sea, both travel and traffic by water have always been easier and cheaper than by land." For the movement of heavy and bulky goods, marine transportation continues to enjoy a decisive, nay an absolute, advantage over air transportation. If wars reliably could be concluded decisively and victoriously by means of "raids" of various kinds, then indeed modern technology might be said to have canceled out the influence of much of what we term geography.

Outside the abstract realm of some modern strategic theory, conflict occurs within particular geographical environments. For example, it mattered enormously that the Falklands War of 1982 was waged in a maritime theater and that the reconquest of Kuwait in 1991 was effected in a desert environment. The maritime character of the Falklands War dictated the notably slow pace of military events, while the desert environment of Kuwait and Iraq magnified the strategic effect of air power (as had been true in Palestine in 1917–18 and the Western Desert in 1941–42).

Communications and culture. What can geopolitical analysis have to say to a world where CNN can transmit to all societies, where facsimile transmission makes a mockery of attempts at state censorship, and where billions of dollars, yen, or deutschemarks can be traded electronically in near real time? Whatever the political and military institutions that still appear to stand guard for international order, is it not a fact that the "global village" has arrived at long last?

The geopolitical theorist properly attentive to "the relation of international political power to the geographical setting" would never assert some absolute position that disregards the trend towards global cultural homogeneity. But the relevance of geopolitical reasoning does not depend upon particular conditions of cultural assimilation. All that geopolitics asserts is that the geographical setting matters for the course of international security relations. And thus far, at least, the "spatial study of the relationships among states and the implications of these relationships for the morphology of the political map as a whole" —to quote a recent definition of geopolitics—has yet to assume the character of an antiquarian interest. If the nineteenth century was the century of nationalism, so too has been the twentieth. Even in the more globally interdependent 1990s, hearts do not beat faster at the sight of the U.N. or EU [European Union] flags. War may be all but unthinkable among the debellicized peoples of Western Europe, but even in that multidimensionally integrated region, true Europeans are thin on the ground.

Communications technologies undoubtedly have produced some features key to the growth of a global community. The O. J. Simpson trial could be followed live in Chinese villages and throughout Europe and the Americas. To date, though, the rich variation in geographical circumstances and relationships among societies has produced more or less distinctive world views—cultures, broadly conceived—and distinctive sets of national interests that are still territorially connected. Indeed, scholars of statecraft and strategy are only in the early stages of appreciating the identities, roots, characteristics, and consequences of national "thoughtways" in security attitudes and behavior. Far from discounting the significance of local conditions and traditions, geographical commentary, unlike the more austere versions of neorealism, allows full play to the influence of particular political and strategic cultures. In fact, the scholar of geopolitics considers strategic culture to be shaped importantly by the geographical setting.

Thus, even in the age of CNN there are —to simplify—Russian, German, British, American, and Polish preferred "ways" in international security behavior and relevant habits of mind. The British continue to be unsure just how "European" they are, or need to become, while Amer-

icans in large numbers fail to understand why they might have a vital interest in the course and outcome of the tragedy in the former Yugoslavia. Psychological world maps can encourage an insularity in judgment regardless of the immediacy of electronic images of distant conflict in places with unpronounceable names.

Geopolitics and geoeconomics.   Geopolitical theory is not at all hostile to the idea that conflict among security communities is increasingly taking on financial and economic forms, rather than overtly political and military ones. Bearing in mind the central role of economic dynamics in the Marxist world view, it is understandable that one commentator has said of communism that "its roots in Western geopolitical theory are obvious."

Nevertheless, it is probably naïve (and certainly optimistic) to believe that future prospects for international security will be shaped primarily, let alone exclusively, by economic rather than political-military struggles. That hopeful view has much to recommend it for the post-military societies of the European Union, but for the rest of the world, and particularly for those states in fracture zones between cultural areas or "civilizations," the idea appears absurd. Nonetheless, careful study of geographical settings can yield relevant economic analysis just as it can treat military matters. The geopolitician and national or international security analyst must study all of the instruments of grand strategy, not just the military one.

But there can be no economic escape from "the struggle for power." Every international economic and political order requires guardians, lest villains locate and exploit victims; economic success may be more attractive than is competitive military success, but the former can be canceled by military failure. This is not to deny security has an economic dimension and that military capability is necessarily an expression of economic achievement. But military capability is also an expression of political choice. Polities that elect to devote little of their wealth to military defense tend, ultimately, to lose the basis of that wealth. _/hcfs not true Sops_

Geopolitical analysis, therefore, sees international political meaning in economic competition. But it remains holistic. Just as it cannot be exclusively political-military, neither can it accede to a school of thought that believes the future of conflict to be wholly economic.

Joint warfare. One hundred years ago, the military world was relatively simple in its structure. States had armies and navies that operated on land and on the surface of the sea. Today, the structure of the military world is far more complex. Armed forces now function on land and sea, in the air and in space, across the electromagnetic spectrum, and with what amounts to an extra dimension in the nuclear realm. The world's leading navy, that of the United States, has integral sub-surface, surface, amphibious, and air forces, and in addition, it is the principal American military user of space systems.

By the middle years of World War II, naval and land forces had so fused with air forces that, except in particularly well-covered or rugged terrain, or in poor weather, the concepts of land power and sea power incorporated adjunct air power. By 1944, as Field Marshal Erwin Rommel appreciated fully from his experience in Africa, armies could not as a general rule succeed if the enemy ruled the skies. Similarly, in 1941–42, events in European waters and in the Pacific demonstrated the futility of maritime operations undertaken in the absence of effective air cover.

The air age had been heralded in 1914–18; it arrived between 1939 and 1945 and was in a sense completed by the advent of the atomic weapon in 1945. Unsurprisingly, the leading turn-of-the-century geopolitical theories were not eloquent on the subject of air power. Mahan's most influential book—extolling the strategic effect of sea power—was published in 1890, while Mackinder's great lecture, which expressed British anxiety over the growth of integrated continental empires, was delivered in January 1904. The first heavier-than-air flight was achieved by Orville and Wilbur Wright only in December 1903. As a historical sidelight, however, it may be noted that in the discussion period following Mackinder's lecture, R. S. Amery observed:

> Both the sea and the railway are going in the future—it may be near or it may be somewhat remote—to be supplemented by the air as a means of locomotion, and when we come to that... a great deal of this geography must lose its importance, and the successful powers will be those who have the greatest industrial base.

I could see that

But as for Mahan and Mackinder, they both wrote about a geopolitics that involved a persisting struggle between continental and maritime polities. Mahan (1840–1914) scarcely had time to revisit his theory of sea power in the light of the accelerating developments in aviation between 1903 and 1914, but Mackinder (1861–1947) and others certainly had ample time to recast geopolitical analysis thoroughly, so as to take full account of the maturing of air power. Suffice it to say that in neither the 1918–19 nor the

1943 revision to his theory did Mackinder systemically reorganize his thoughts to allow sufficient importance to air power. Furthermore, notwithstanding the appearance of a library of writings on air power, an air equivalent to the theories of Mahan and Mackinder has not appeared. That is not to demean or discount the theories of Giulio Douhet, Sir Hugh Trenchard, "Billy" Mitchell, Alexander P. de Seversky, and others. But it is to suggest that geopolitical analysis has not been persuaded that an independent air orientation has achieved a significance comparable to a continental or maritime perspective. Part of the reason, of course, is that armies and navies have co-opted, or even "owned," air forces.

The air instrument, or weapon, has contributed massively to transformations in military operational art and tactics in this century, but it has not transformed, let alone canceled, the relevance of geopolitical analysis. A brief nuclear World War III might do that, but mutual deterrence has helped keep geography in play.

Air power unquestionably is useful; indeed, in desert terrain or when other military elements are roughly in balance, it can be decisive. But with the possible exception of the United States, states are not yet air powers in the same way that they are land powers or sea powers. Aircraft can show resolve—or lack of resolve, as when the use of air power to the exclusion of a ground or local naval commitment signals lack of will. Aircraft can bombard, and they can execute missions rapidly. But aircraft cannot transport goods in bulk or goods of great weight, and they cannot exercise control of the ground continuously or reliably, for they are present only briefly.

In this information age, the armed forces of advanced nations will wage "third wave war"—information warfare —organized task for task more or less "jointly." This latest revolution in military affairs has the microchip as its generic tool and information as the key to performance. The armed forces will consist of "information warriors," rather than soldiers, sailors, airmen, or spacemen. The electronic engines of advanced military achievement will be fitted, and retrofitted, onto vehicles specialized for operation in each environment, but electronically managed information warfare will be characteristic of, and common to, combat in all geographical realms. In the words of one commentator:

> The information age has altered the whole nature of time and space and distance. Weapons can be launched from any place on the globe, in the air or the sea. The information will flow over electronic means. The commander can sense the battlefield regardless of where he's located. —maybe

Some recent commentary on information warfare is probably more fashionable than profound; in any case, the implications for the relevance of geopolitical analysis are less than startling. Defense planning and the conduct of war are approached more and more as joint, multi-service endeavors (at least in principle: note the less than fully joint character of Desert Storm). But such jointness does not cancel the importance of the geographical setting. The electromagnetic spectrum may be exploitable by all kinds of armed forces, but technological advance cannot cancel differences among the land, sea, air, and space environments. Information is vital, but alone it sinks no submarines, blows no bridges, and threatens no villains. The tip of the military spear continues to consist of men and women who operate on land, at sea, and in the air, and who must command spacecraft in compliance with the laws of orbital motion.

The tools of land, sea, air, and space warfare are improving dramatically (when considered absolutely; net consideration—against defense—may yield a different answer), but warfare remains environmentally specific to a significant degree. Jointness may be king, but for an air force to perform well jointly it must first perform well in the air. There may be a trend towards greater fungibility among armed forces, allowing for a healthy measure of improvised substitution, but that is a trend only. Warriors will cope ever more competently with a variable geographical setting, but realistically, they cannot aspire to operate beyond the scope of significant geographical constraint.

I do not agree w/ that at all sooner or later branded soldiers (?) or servicos(?)

CONCLUSION

So pervasive are geographical images and facts for statecraft and strategy—not to mention tactics, logistics, and intelligence—that it is hard to understand why geopolitical analysis is controversial. Is it plausible that there could be no significant geopolitical influence upon international security? The problem is more apparent than real. When a broad but commonsense definition of geopolitics is asserted—"the relation of international political power to the geographical setting"—the ubiquity of and necessity for, geopolitical analysis becomes apparent. How could one argue that the Atlantic Ocean does not much matter for the U.S. role in the security of Europe?

Likewise, how could one doubt that the particular territorial space a people occupies on the earth has a shaping influence upon that people's history and culture. Would Russians be Russians regardless of the political geography of Russia? The suggestion is absurd. Culture changes, but does so slowly. Russians (or Britons or whoever) have fairly distinctive attitudes, preferences, and habits that have been significantly shaped by their unique historical experiences in particular geographical settings.

Geopolitics is neither deterministic nor inexorably aggressive in its policy implications. "The geographical setting" is only a stage; it is not the script, though it does suggest the plot and influence the cast of characters. Geopolitics, in common with the broader discipline of international relations, cannot but have implications for public policy.

For the same reasons that the authors of *The Federalist Papers* were concerned to deny European polities the opportunities to play some American states off against others, their successors have been determined to keep what Mackinder called the World-Island of Europe and Asia (and Africa) politically divided. By far the most influential geopolitical concept for Anglo-American statecraft has been the idea of a Eurasian "heartland," and then the complementary idea-as-policy of containing the heartland power of the day within, not to, Eurasia. From Harry S. Truman to George Bush, the overarching vision of U.S. national security was explicitly geopolitical and directly traceable to the heartland theory of Mackinder.

Mackinder's relevance to the containment of a heartland-occupying Soviet Union in the cold war was so apparent as to approach the status of a cliché; much more challenging is the problem of geopolitical interpretation for this post–cold war world. There is urgent need for constructive geopolitical analysis for the twenty-first century.

The influence of the geographical setting upon international power relations is so pervasive that it can escape notice. But that influence can be seen by contrasting the sharply different geostrategic implications of hypothetical developments in two very different regions: South America and continental East Asia. With respect to the former, Henry Kissinger was almost brutally to the point when he observed dismissively that South America is a dagger pointed at the heart of Antarctica. In other words, adverse developments south of Panama would probably threaten nothing of great importance to the United States. Geopolitically and geostrategically, despite the long-standing U.S. rhetoric about hemispheric security (not to mention the Monroe Doctrine), what happens in South America does not matter very much to U.S. citizens.

The contrast with continental East Asia could hardly be more stark. The emerging Chinese superstate is located in Eurasia, as the Eastern "rimland" of the historical "heartland," while its long sea coast flanks the principal sea lines of communication of the great maritime, manufacturing, and trading empire of Japan. China has weight and position. Unlike the unlamented, erstwhile USSR, China is not a landlocked power, and she cannot be landlocked by a prudent U.S. containment policy.

That is not to say China matters to the United States whereas Brazil does not. It is to say that, for reasons of geography, China is vastly more important than Brazil. Indeed, because of size, character of territory, population, social habits, and location, it would be difficult to exaggerate the potential positive or negative contribution of China to international order.

To recognize the relevance and importance of geopolitical thinking is not unlike recognizing that we speak in prose and that most of us see in color. Some appreciation of the meaning of the geographical setting for international political power pervades thought and action, but that appreciation can be so habitual and uninspiring as to blind us to geopolitical insight and understanding.

NO

Martin Libicki

THE EMERGING PRIMACY
OF INFORMATION

Thanks to cyberspace—which may be understood as the sum of the globe's communications links and computational nodes—any piece of data can show up anywhere almost instantly.

Will cyberspace kill geography? Colin Gray's excellent article argues, and correctly so, that the answer is no, that we are not at liberty to disregard the geographical setting for international political power. But is this the right question? Could the geography of national security be so transformed as to be unrecognizable? If so, how?

As long as mankind uses instruments bound to its slow media—such as ground or sea transportation—much of what we know about geography and geopolitics will still apply. Yet with each new medium comes a new geographical logic; as the importance of new media grows, their logics will not only dominate those of old media but transform them as well. With the invention of aircraft, for instance, Great Britain could be attacked directly from Europe, regardless of the British fleet. The same instrument dominated the U.S. campaign against Japan: each island was sought for its successively closer air approach to Japan. When ballistic missiles made space a medium of conflict, that permitted the United States and the Soviet Union to hold each other directly at risk. And that factor, in turn, governed the superpower confrontation across central Europe.

Two of Colin Gray's four topics—the relevance of geography in the face of technology and its relevance in the face of jointness—are the subject of this essay. The essential considerations that argue for geography are the persistence of logistics (which in turn argue for naval forces) and the requirement for ground control (ditto for ground forces). The counterargument is that, with enough information, warfare becomes sufficiently precise to obviate much of logistics, and control need not be a local phenomenon (at least as far as the United States is concerned).

Cyberspace, to be sure, is a medium that lies largely in the future. As broadly defined, however, it already permits the near-real-time management of multinational enterprises, the extension of command and control across oceans, the creation of international markets, the creation of transnational media (e.g., CNN), and the global interchange of scientific and technical information via the Internet. Yet today's uses may pale before tomorrow's. The Third World's stock of telephones is slated for huge increases over the next twenty years. Fiber is being laid at rapid rates across land and under oceans. Computer applications that can be used across networks are only in their infancy. It is virtually certain that electronics will be ten times more cost effective in five years, and, probably, a hundred times more cost effective in ten years. It is this more pervasive cyberspace of tomorrow that is the proper realm of consideration.

Those who argue that cyberspace will erase geopolitics usually claim that cyberspace (like aerospace) creates institutions and interests that transcend national lines. Such institutions and interests both weaken a nation's ability to mobilize resources for nationalistic reasons and also create valuable ties that war would destroy, raising the cost of war and lowering its likelihood.

That argument, though valid to some extent, often descends to sterile debates. For instance, over the last fifty years, the world's rich countries did not threaten one another. Was it because they had moved beyond force, or because they had banded together in the face of a larger enemy (with inertia explaining the lack of rupture since the Berlin Wall fell)? A different argument is made here: cyberspace will tend to eliminate geopolitics through its influence on military security, rather than (or at least in addition to) its influence on international politics.

Such an argument may seem paradoxical, for it is a fundamental cliché of nation-state theory that trade promotes international cooperation while security promotes international competition. Thus, it is assumed, trading elites tend to be global while military elites tend to be local—and whatever reduces the cost of globalism favors the former. So, if cyberspace does not erase geopolitics through trade, why would it tend to do so through security?

The argument begins with what has been called the revolution in military affairs and extracts from it new instruments of national power that erase geography, culminating in new instruments for international security management that tend to erase classic geographical formulations. It is based on three fundamental observations:

1. Modern weaponry, notably precision-guided munitions (PGMs), has magnified the relative importance of tactical information in conflict. It required 2,500 bombs to hit a single target point during World War II. To hit a single target in Vietnam, using more accurate targeting systems, required roughly 50 bombs. To do so in the Gulf War required one laser-guided bomb. Devotees of information warfare speculate that twenty years hence we should know precisely which one of fifty potential targets must be bombed to achieve the desired effect.

2. By separating information from force, it is possible to influence distant conflicts without the usual logistical accoutrements, and hence geographical constraints, of war.

3. By combining bitstreams from global sources, both private and government, commonly accessible networks may help nations go a long way

toward securing themselves against their neighbors' intentions.

Given enough time, cyberspace may become the medium in which security information is generated and traded, mediating the production and consumption of such information just as electronic economic markets—the confluence of quite different bitstreams—mediate the production and consumption of goods and services.

AS INFORMATION SUBSTITUTES FOR FORCE

The military transformation of geography stems from the development of precision-guided munitions whose defining characteristic has been to mate precisely the coordinates of force and target. Today's modern arsenals generally contain three types of PGMs: those with active manned guidance (e.g., reflected laser signals and fly-by-wire anti-tank weapons); those that chase given signatures (e.g., infrared missiles and acoustic torpedoes); and, the most recent class, those that travel to specific coordinates (e.g., map-based cruise missiles, inertially navigated ballistic missiles, and tomorrow's coordinate-guided weaponry). PGMs are being developed that can hit moving targets by adjusting their own flight path to continually updated coordinates. As the transition from human-guided to signature-guided weapons obviated the need for on-the-spot guidance, the further transition from signature-guided to coordinate-guided weapons could transfer the smarts from the PGM itself to the system that builds its flight path.

Where PGMs are sufficiently abundant, to be seen and recognized on the battlefield means to be hit and hurt. Granted, targets can avoid destruction by spoofing (i.e., creating false and confusing signatures), armor, evasion, and shooting back. Although the contest between seeker and sought is hardly over, every passing year favors the seeker.

Such technology, in turn, alters the entire calculus of conventional conflict. Victory used to be determined largely by who brought the most force to bear first. Today, conventional conflict is akin to hide-and-seek.

The technology of search is advancing rapidly, principally because it uses the same electronics and other microdevices as those emerging from the global commercial electronics revolution. America's comparative advantage, so far, has been its ability, first to militarize the application of these devices, secondly to integrate them into a system whose whole exceeds its parts, and lastly to couple them with very long range attack systems (e.g., cruise and ballistic missiles, refuelable bombers, and blue-water ships with extended times on station).

Tomorrow's searches will be conducted by what Admiral William Owens (vice chairman of the [U.S.] Joint Chiefs of Staff) has called a "system of systems" that is complex and multilayered. The top layer of this system will orbit in space. Today's satellites, which collect detailed imagery every few days, will gradually be superseded by a system better equipped for real-time tasks. The next layer will be airborne. Today's expensive manned systems should give way to much denser clouds of unmanned aerial vehicles (UAVs—mostly flying, but perhaps some floating). The bottom layer will consist of sensors at sea (for traditional anti-submarine pursuits, but also for hunting mines and sensing littoral spaces) and above ground. The latter will include optical devices; devices that read radar reflections; improved sensors of thermal, pressure, magnetic, biochemical, and perhaps gravimetric phenomena; and devices for seismic and acoustic sensing from both close-in and stand-off range. Complementing them will be emitters to create echoes, data-fusion processors, and communications devices that permit the information to be shuttled where needed. Over time, the various sensors, emitters, and processors will be structured to work with one another: a space sensor detecting a questionable phenomenon may ask a UAV to collect further readings; those readings may cue various ground sensors to turn themselves on for longer periods, and then to obtain for themselves scarce spectrum space in order to report more detailed findings than the sensors usually collect.

Why dwell on all this detail? One reason is to sketch the new dimensions of jointness. Colin Gray argues that although "the tools of land, sea, air, and space warfare are improving dramatically ... warfare remains significantly environmentally specific." But consider this vast set of devices—sensing, emitting, communicating, redirecting, cuing, filtering, pinpointing, classifying, and creating target determinations—and then picture artificial lines among them segregating them into air force, navy, marine, and army assets, each reporting up their separate chains of command. Silly, no doubt—yet all that today's jointness aspires to is to be able to define, after years of wrangling, the various ways in which these devices may be allowed to talk to each other if given permission. The problem is not, as Colin Gray posits, that for a service to perform well in joint operations it must first perform well in its medium.

The problem is that, with the range and interconnectivity of today's weapons and sensors, a unique medium is almost undefinable.

The detail given above also helps illustrate some differences in each sensor's entrée into the battlespace. Sensors that sit in space, blue water, or across borders (e.g., over-the-horizon radar) can be used in peace and war. Sensors that must traverse another state's land, air space, or coastal waters may require permission from the state being watched. (The consequences of catching an unmanned sensor in one's space have yet to be determined.) Open-skies agreements recognize the international interests in air-breathing surveillance but are only an early manifestation of the new terms of trade in information on another's nation.

If the system of systems works, a traditional invasion across recognized borders would be suicidal against the United States or any other similarly equipped force. Moving targets generate copious signatures, and well-armed stand-off forces (or hard-to-see forces such as stealthy aircraft) can pick them off with relative ease. For many contingencies, the logistics load can be dramatically reduced. The United States took roughly 93 percent of its supplies to the Gulf by sea —a reflection of what Colin Gray calls the "embarrassingly small ammunition load" of an aircraft. Yet, in the end, most of what was shipped came back home. Advances in precision have already reduced the requirements for ordnance. If airlift capability does not fall dramatically, precision targeting—coupled with the use of cyberspace for remote control, and sensors rather than humans for local sensing—may permit a comparable war to be supplied mostly by air.

Although cross-border assaults constitute a minority of security threats, their potential demise as tools of power politics should be noted with at least some respect, for that is precisely the scenario against which most militaries are organized.

In more ambiguous situations and more difficult terrain (e.g., Bosnia prior to the Dayton accords), a system of systems has to do much more work. Assets may come and go with less signature, and observation has to be closely coupled with engagement. But the actual degree of engagement need not be that great. Suppose the location and identity of hostile assets, once detected, are broadcast—and only then attacked. After sufficient demonstration of the correlation between visibility and destruction, future broadcasts may call for the offending target to be visibly disabled. The savings in logistics (not to mention televised gore) would remove yet one more geographical barrier to U.S. intervention.

How might a potential adversary counter such a system of systems? Clearly, it needs to keep intervening forces as far from the battlefield as possible. Weapons of mass destruction may be one method, perhaps best used not by making threats against interveners but by threatening the nations that could host them. However, in an era of proliferating information technology and burgeoning arms markets, a competitor could keep the United States at bay without such weapons (and their risks). A relatively low cost system of systems can be cobbled together using third-party satellite imagery, UAVs, digital cameras, cellular communications, and detailed terrain imagery on CD-ROMs. With it, less-than-rich countries can make U.S. assets visible and hence put them at greater risk in, or even near, theaters of conflict.

Forcing the United States to work from farther away may not make enemy assets less visible, but it increases the required range, and hence cost, of striking those assets—which is the point. Against an enemy that has successfully distributed its military force amongst many units, a stand-off strike is expensive. Compelling the expenditure of million-dollar cruise missiles against a military composed of "technicals" (pick-up trucks with automatic weapons) may suffice to exhaust an intervention.

So is Colin Gray correct to say the "ultimate determinant in war is the man on the scene with the gun"? Yes and no. For the United States, it may suffice in future conventional scenarios to disarm the other side's heavy weapons. Thereafter, local allies, retaining their own heavy forces, can dominate on the battlefield, even if initially outmatched. Alternatively, if heavy forces are altogether absent, the same architecture that produced all those bitstreams to illuminate the battlefield for U.S. forces can also be used to help allies. By so doing, force and geography are even further displaced—for the United States.

ARMING ALLIES WITH INFORMATION

Five times this century, the United States fought major overseas wars to defend one or more allies: France and Britain in World War I, Britain in World War II, and then Korea, South Vietnam, and Saudi Arabia. If anything, with the absence of a hostile peer competitor, this arrangement is even more likely to characterize the next twenty years. That is, the primary purpose of U.S. military combat intervention will be to protect and defend other nations. The objectives at hand will be determined by the relative security of our allies when the fighting stops.

Information can make such intervention easier and reduce the still immense geographical impediments to conventional military assistance. If warfare evolves to hide-and-seek, and seeking systems can be unplugged from the forces they serve, the United States may be able to help almost as much as it now does with conventional arms and personnel, but more frequently and for far longer with indirect rather than direct assistance. By extending information dominance to allies, Washington can itself remain concealed while multiplying its allies' power—in some respects, by ten- or a hundred-fold. It would do so by sending bitstreams to its allies: primarily real-time information of the battlespace but also background archives (e.g., map data) and software for systems integration, simulation, and maintenance. Such help presumes an ally who can use it; one with precision weaponry that waits for target locations to be plugged into its computer program is best, but even less well equipped friends can profit immensely by knowing exactly where the other side's assets are in real time.

In some ways, extended information dominance is a version of traditional arms shipments. But supplying bitstreams has several advantages over supplying arms. First, bitstreams do not leave the kind of fingerprints that arms do. Secondly, bitstreams multiply forces while arms add to them. Thirdly, bitstreams are easier to deliver and easier to turn off. (How certain is anyone that Stinger

missiles supplied to Afghan rebels did not wind up in the hands of terrorists?) Fourthly, once a bitstream is generated, making a second copy is cheap, while a tank sent abroad is a tank one no longer has. Lastly, offering allies a specific illuminated vision of the battlespace does far more to lend them one's own perspective on conflict than the mere provision of material can. In practice, however, the United States is unlikely to help an ally with bitstreams alone—that is, without manpower and material. Even sophisticated allies may need smart PGM warheads and ground sensors. Military liaison and special operations officers would have to help allies with this integration.

(Another analogy with the arms bazaar should also be noted: Although the United States is likely to be the first country that can offer real help without actually showing up, much of what enables extended information dominance originates in the commercial marketplace. Very little requires tightly controlled technology. These capabilities thus lie within the reach of many other potential great powers as well.)

To illustrate the possible application of extended information dominance, consider Operation Vigilant Warrior. In October 1994, in response to what looked like an Iraqi move south, the United States conducted a very visible exercise with Kuwait to demonstrate its willingness and ability to stop a potential invasion. That little exercise cost upwards of a billion dollars (against a feint that probably cost Iraq far less). Now consider the same billion dollars spent a different way. Kuwait would purchase several thousand anti-armor missiles and bury them amid perhaps ten times as many holes. If armor were to cross the border, real-time updatable target designations, courtesy of the American system of systems, would replace the dummy target designations in these missiles so that a large share of the attacking force could be hit and disabled. Although armor is probably the most favorable example for this capability, the basic ideas can be used against an air threat or a stealthier subversion across rougher terrain by technicals. Rather than send forces into harm's way, the United States can achieve the same end, with far greater freedom, if it sends bitstreams to a well-prepared defender. In so doing, it widens the usable space between engagement and passive observation.

Arming allies with information has other applications. Suppose the United States wishes to support one side in a murky conflict—the Muslims in Bosnia, say—without risking U.S. troops or compelling other great powers to intervene. Surreptitiously provided bitstreams could multiply the effectiveness of the favored side's operations and weaponry. Major powers friendly to the other side of the conflict might suspect the United States is providing such assistance, but its covert nature would elicit less of a reaction than would overt assistance.

The United States could also fulfill alliance commitments by extending information dominance instead of deploying troops. In particular, such assistance could ease the integration of new countries into its alliances. Indeed, the United States is already emphasizing the provision of intelligence-based systems to Partnership for Peace countries as a step toward full integration. Unlike alliance membership, such information assistance can be doled out in degrees to specific countries depending on their readiness for closer ties (e.g., the Czech Republic might get better help than Tajikistan). Data collected remotely (which grows more cost effective every year) can substitute for costly and risky border patrols. So armed, allies can protect their borders against infiltration with less need for cross-border incursions (such as Turkey's 1995 pursuit of Kurdish PKK rebels into Iraq).

Similarly, extended information dominance could help bolster regional security. Nations distrustful of their neighbors often turn to stocking armaments; that, in turn, feeds arms races. If each nation could see what its neighbor was up to (thanks to U.S.-supplied bitstreams), and if each understood that access to U.S. information depended on abjuring offensive weapons and maintaining good behavior, the impetus to acquire arms would be blunted. For example, in Asia, where countries formally aligned with the United States (South Korea, Japan, and Australia) nonetheless eye each other with suspicion, such help might assuage old fears without generating new ones.

Peacekeeping can be another application. The Sinai agreement between Israel and Egypt is reinforced by U.S. sensor systems that permit each side to monitor movements by the other that might signal attack. Information systems that may be deployed in some future Golan Heights zone could generate not only indications of impending attack but targeting information as well—putting at risk those who would encroach into demilitarized zones. Both the regional security and peacekeeping examples illustrate how the United States could exercise considerable influence in distant lands in the interests of stability and peace without having to supply a "man on the ground with a gun."

Developing and maintaining such a capability will require some changes in how forces are equipped. The most capable sensor systems in U.S. inventories (i.e., the Aegis cruiser and the AWACS [airborne warning and control system] and JSTARS [joint surveillance and target attack radar system] aircraft) are themselves quite visible; such capability needs to be distributed among more numerous but less valuable targets. Also needed are technologies to integrate bitstreams with other countries' operations, munitions, and fire-control systems, and with their own sensor systems. Because tomorrow's allies may include countries initially diffident (e.g., Kuwait in 1990) or outside U.S. defense responsibilities (e.g., South Korea in 1950), integration may have to take place in near real time.

If extended information dominance becomes a useful way to assist others, its impact on the verities of geostrategy is relatively straightforward. For example, once a bitstream has to go through space, it is roughly the same cost to get it anywhere in the world. Physical access to the United States is not necessary for assistance.

Geographical considerations will nevertheless matter for the collection of information. The closer the battlespace lies to friendly soil, or at least international waters, the easier it is to use airborne and blue-water sensors. Simulation software is difficult to build and test without on-sight knowledge of the battlefield. And, as noted, a pure bitstream approach is often unrealistic; the delivery of items and liaison personnel means physical connectivity matters. Thus, the notion that assistance can be offered regardless of geography is exaggerated—but less so with every given year.

HOW CYBERSPACE PROMOTES STABILITY

Extending information dominance to allies may permit great powers to influence events with far less regard for geography. The fact remains, however, that the United States, since 1945, has shown itself capable of using armed forces in the most distant corners and commanding them in real time. To be able to guide other nations' forces in real time would be quite a feat but would not, by itself, alter the basic nation-state calculus of military security.

What might alter this calculus is the potential that cyberspace offers for adding more players to the security game, not only nation-states of a lesser affluence, but also non-governmental organizations, transnational organizations, and even concerned individuals.

The basic mechanism is simple: while only nation-states are granted the legitimacy of force, and only affluent ones can afford the complex systems that permit the application of force, the essential information on which tomorrow's military operations rest is becoming swiftly globalized. Transparency makes offense harder than defense; it makes challenging the security status quo harder than maintaining it. As such, globalized information can begin to dominate the raw use of military force.

To understand why, consider the World Wide Web, the Rodney King affair, Croatia's Krajina offensive and the Clementine spacecraft as harbingers of the factors affecting global security in the twenty-first century.

(a) The Web, already a familiar element in American popular culture, has become a vehicle by which anyone can post messages to the universe. Regardless of whether it becomes the world's greatest library or the billboard advertising of the information highway, the overall concept of easy-to-get global message posting, coupled with the emergence of software that can roam and gather enough cyber-lint to make a decent suit, is here to stay. If a fact can be made presentable, it can be put on the Web; once there, it can ultimately be found by the interested and assiduous.

(b) The Rodney King affair demonstrates how easily street life can become the province of ubiquitous private surveillance. How much more opportunity might exist for such ubiquity in one of tomorrow's Asian mega-cities? A combination of abundant street traffic and accelerating expenditures on consumer goods such as videocameras and digital telephone systems means that the leap from incident to imagery to bitstream to global posting may be a few short hops. Most postings will, of course, be junk. But enough of them, sampled widely, filtered finely, and fused intelligently can suffice to ensure that nothing of significance goes unwatched.

What amateurs miss, professional newsmen may capture. Technologies such as direct broadcast satellites (coupled with digital compression to squeeze four to ten times as much signal per channel) plus the global competition to get more and more international journalists into various theaters promise yet more information proliferation. At a summer 1995 conference sponsored by the National Strategy Council outside Chicago, it was clear that U.S. military leaders are conceding the ubiquity of the press in tomorrow's conflicts and the consequent impossibility of managing what can be hidden from them.

(c) Croatia's Krajina offensive—by an army that lost a third of its territory to Serbian rebels in 1992—is testimony to the value of private contractors in shaping a military. (Reputedly, the effectiveness of Croatia's army was significantly enhanced by the help of a U.S. consulting firm based in the Washington D.C. area.) Contractors did very little for U.S. warmaking in the Korean War; they played a small but vital role in the Vietnam conflict; they were critical in the Gulf War (in order to work, JSTARS required Grumman employees on board); and they proved essential to the Haiti operation. Information, a growing facet of war, can be privatized with far fewer legal restrictions than can force. So far, U.S. firms have acted consistently with U.S. interests (most customers are allied with the United States in one way or another). Even so, American aerospace companies are offering imagery services to various countries, and Raytheon has begun building an environmental surveillance network for Brazil with potential dual-use applications. (Indeed, Raytheon hopes to leverage its experience to garner similar wide-area surveillance work in places such as Bosnia and the Golan.) Ultimately, nothing prevents rootless multinationals from free-lancing their talents globally. They, too, will be drawing from the Web and posting to it as need arises.

(d) The Clementine I spacecraft was an experiment in the use of small, relatively cheap spacecraft to gather detailed imagery. Eighty million dollars purchased a half-dozen sensors plus a trip to the moon, whose surface was then mapped for less than a tenth of what NASA thought it would cost. Just one of these sensors was capable of resolving down to a few meters from the typical height of a surveillance satellite. Clementine was an experiment (and perhaps not every nation has the skills to put so much capability in so small a package), but several U.S. aerospace firms are lining up financing to offer near-real-time space-based imagery at a very militarily useful one-meter resolution to (almost) any and all customers. Even India is preparing to launch environmental satellites with ten-meter resolution soon. State-gathered bitstreams from UAVs, commercial space, and industrial-grade sensors may mean that more events are recorded than would otherwise get caught up in the accidental effects of mass ownership of consumer appliances.

What does such a future portend for security? Consider how information is used in defense: in collection, distribution, processing, and actuation. Collection may become the province of private and media surveillance, coupled with on-line information from global sources. Global distribution is a feature of cyberspace. Processing can be handled by contractors. This leaves just actuation— the conversion of information into physical violence. With every given year, the ratio of information to force declines. Force, of course, remains the sine qua non of security. But more of the security burden can be effectively globalized —particularly by security spiders sitting patiently on the Web looking for flies. Such a firm—around whose existence national security strategies can be spun— could be anywhere and nowhere at the same time.

It would seem that the security interests of the United States would be confounded by a world increasingly dominated by the information web. After all, if America's emerging core competence on the battlefield is dominant battlespace

knowledge (and the ability to pass it selectively to its friends), will its edge not be considerably dulled if such a capability to gather gobs of information is available to everyone? There is growing awareness within the U.S. military that its operations are becoming increasingly visible (stealth aside) as information technology spreads. And there is considerable debate on how to counter such visibility. But when third-party assets generate militarily significant imagery and encrypted bits sluice from satellite to satellite, generating a set of specific targets to destroy or neutralize without causing politically unacceptable harm to third parties may not be at all easy.

Yet, from a broader perspective, a global watch on the global village may actually be conducive to the kind of world the United States seeks. Why that may be true can be examined under two circumstances: first, if it comes about willy-nilly; secondly, if the architecture of this emerging system reflects deliberate U.S. policy.

The generic argument for transparency has new meaning against the background of the cold war's end. A certain amount of chaos aside, the unipolar moment is good for American security (and, by extension, its friends' security as well). The longer the emergence of a hostile peer competitor can be deferred or deterred, the better. With the United States's global military dominance essentially assumed, every other power operates at a disadvantage—it must challenge the status quo to achieve equality. The more visible societies are, the harder time they have building, mobilizing, or deploying forces, or, in general, creating mischief. Against random surveillance (and that is all such a system can aspire to), a sufficiently clever opponent may be able to get away with some things, but randomness itself makes it harder to know what other eyes are watching. At the very least, a country building its forces would be expected to give a reasonable explanation of why it was doing so (presumably, other than as an open challenge to the United States), which, if nothing else, limits the destabilizing element of surprise.

A nation could, in theory, cherry-pick the system, tuning into those bitstreams that allow it to watch others but denying its space to outside eyes and the video-cameras of internal lay reporters. Clearly, China and Singapore are trying to finesse their participation in cyberspace in this way, so that their businesses can prosper from global information but their citizenry cannot. Many believe that those states will ultimately fail in their attempts, that cyberspace does not permit such distortions. Yet there is no sentiment for denying nations connectivity because they want the modems without the mores. It is too soon to know whether such hands-off attitudes will prevail should cyberspace acquire a security as well as a business role.

If the emergence of cyberspace as a medium of security is inevitable, are there advantages for the United States (or the West in general) in accommodating and shaping this phenomenon? Yes, under the following strategy:

- The United States would take some of its existing bitstreams—many from satellites—and open them to subscribers (e.g., other nations) or to all (as precedence, the declassified pictures from its once top-secret Corona program are becoming available on-line). In time, more general data files, as well as bitstreams from ongoing monitoring

systems such as transportation control, and network regulation could also be added. (Needless to say, some things would not go on-line: classified systems, those that reveal what sensitive targets are under watch, those built to track assets in which the United States has an enduring superiority, and so forth.)

- Software tools could be put into circulation to extract various pieces of information, correlate them with other pieces, recognize patterns, generate conclusions, use such evidence to update logic systems, and prepare the evidence for display in alternative formats. With it would follow the standards, protocols, and architectures implied in these tools.

- Tacit or explicit agreements could be made with others that induce them to contribute their own tools and bitstreams (from both external surveillance and internal monitoring—e.g., for transportation and the environment) or at least open themselves to external and internal watching.

By accelerating the use of cyberspace for common security purposes, the United States could serve itself in both operational and strategic ways.

Most of the operational benefits stem from the subtle but pervasive advantages that accrue to whoever can set the standards, architectures, and terms of trade of any information realm (just ask Microsoft). For instance, familiarity with how the system works would help other nations, particularly those who request our assistance on short notice, take better and faster advantage of whatever extended information dominance (e.g., specifically deployed sensors) the United States might offer allies. When it comes time to form coalitions, other countries will find it easier to link up with the United States than with one another.

More important is how the standards of any security cyberspace reflect its architecture (i.e., who can say what to whom), which, in turn, reflects the interests (i.e., what the system ought to do well and what it does poorly) of its designer. Thus, the system would focus on what the United States fears most (e.g., armaments for a major regional war) and not focus on matters it cares less about (e.g., dissidents) or on things it alone owns in quantity (e.g., satellites, long-range mobility assets, or blue-water submarines). Buying into the system would mean buying into these choices; it would be easier for others to look for what we look for and harder for them to look for what we do not look for.

As for the strategic advantages, there is a case that such magnanimity from a nation in its unipolar moment would be disarming (in both senses of the word) —but the more compelling case comes from inducing friendly (or at least not actively hostile) countries to buy into a global system and thereby rely on it. Over time, if access to a system of bitstreams persisted across minor international differences, its reliability would come to be more widely assumed (a process that is slowly taking place with navigation information from the Global Positioning System satellites). Access per se would not induce nations to junk their own systems, but it could inhibit them from expanding (and ultimately upgrading and maintaining) what are expensive and troublesome capabilities. U.S. policymakers already understand tradeoffs between giving intelligence to our allies and watching them develop their own independent capability. A

security cyberspace extends this logic to potential great powers with which we are, for the nonce, on speaking terms. Over time, if the strategy worked (that is, if nations abjured independent capability), the barriers to the emergence of a hostile peer competitor would creep higher and higher. A determined nation could, of course, back out of dependence, but catching up would grow ever more difficult and visible. (Figure at least ten years to make new investments and re-learn the systems integration.) In the interim, such a nation must visibly stand on the outs with the United States and its allies. A period of extended vulnerability buys time for countermoves and creates opportunities for any fortuitous event that may set its competitor on a new course.

A full-fledged security cyberspace will not, in and of itself, protect nations; its coverage is necessarily spotty and specific, allies still matter, and, yes, the geography of threat is not totally irrelevant. Yet, by taking the most rapidly growing component of military security —information—and making it globally accessible, a security cyberspace may alter the waning influence of the other media of warfare—no small feat.

Some presumptions. The notion of cyberspace as the arena of international security rests on two presumptions. The first is that today's relatively peaceful world continues for a while. The unexpectedly sudden re-emergence of intense rivalry among major powers would subdivide the great atrium of cyberspace into jealous cubicles. Similarly, the world's descent into crime, chaos, corruption, and craziness would require that too much energy be spent to protect civilization and too little to expand cyberspace.

The second presumption is that cyberspace does not distinguish itself by becoming a medium through which one nation attacks another (e.g., by unleashing viruses, worms, Trojan horses, logic bombs, and so forth into its information infrastructure). Clearly, such a threat grows in importance as information systems wend their way into everyone's high-technology economic sectors. Yet, such a threat is easy to exaggerate in a culture grown dependent on machines that very few understand. With rare and uninteresting exceptions, there is no such thing as forced entry in cyberspace. Hackers do their damage because the systems they attack have forgone security that technology makes possible (whether such security is cost effective depends on the threat and the value of what is being protected). If the threat is grave enough, a system can adapt by making entry difficult or, in some cases, impossible. Such adaptations are not free but are nevertheless trivial compared with defending nations against conventional invasion or nuclear weapons.

Because the architecture of the security cyberspace cannot help but favor some interests more than others, those left out may want to corrupt or degrade the means by which the security cyberspace comes together. If a data-level attack is unproductive (e.g., viruses defeated because of computer security), perhaps an information-level attack (e.g., the insertion of ambiguously misleading bitstreams) may be more effective.

CONCLUSION

The application of information to military power has three fundamental elements: perceiving reality and representing it in bits (intelligence), processing and distributing bits, and using bits to act on reality (operations). In air-combat terms, this parses to observing, orienting/deciding, and acting. As cyberspace (broadly defined) expands, the impact of geography on each segment declines apace. Already, processing and distributing information is almost entirely liberated from spatial concerns. The remaining geographical distinction in surveillance is between the information that can be acquired from beyond borders (e.g., from space or blue waters) and that which cannot be (and in a pinch, cheap, untraceable sensors such as UAVs may be used to augment properly collected data). Lastly, although the application of information to force is still bound by geography, those who generate and deliver information (i.e., the United States) need not be the same as those who act on it (i.e., nations under threat).

Any speculation on cyberspace must include the caution that the inevitable often takes longer than first thought, and institutions differ in their appreciation of what is, in retrospect, obvious. Logistics (or at least tonnage) still matters, and so does being there. Colin Gray argues that media also matter, and hence geography does too. But the importance of both is rapidly fading. The race may not necessarily go to those who grasp the new pride of placelessness, but, in cyberspace, that is increasingly the way to bet.

POSTSCRIPT

Is Geopolitics Still Relevant in the Era of Cyberspace?

Geography still plays a distinct role in politics. The reality that most of the world's oil is produced in one geographic region of the world and consumed in other geographical regions goes far to explain why the Persian Gulf War occurred in 1991. If the United States was physically attached to the land mass of Europe, the viewpoint of many Americans about the future of NATO might be different than it is today. Two works on modern geopolitics are Saul B. Cohen, *Geography and Politics in a Divided World* (Oxford University Press, 1973) and Michael D. Ward, ed., *The New Geopolitics* (Gordon & Beech, 1992).

There can be little doubt that technology is having a major impact on international politics, as explained in Mark D. Alleyne, *International Power and International Communication* (Macmillan, 1995). The current cyberspace age, as Libicki refers to it, is affecting our political relationships in many ways. Croats, Muslims, and Serbs have periodically slaughtered one another in the Balkans without outside humanitarian intervention. Now the United States and other troops are in Bosnia partly due to the fact that for the first time, through television, the death and destruction in the region have invaded the outside world's consciousness and conscience.

On another dimension, the growth of the transnational feminist movement has been facilitated by technology. Almost instantaneous, relatively inexpensive means of international communication have allowed women to interact with one another, to discuss their common concerns, and to plan their common advance. High-speed transportation has also promoted face-to-face interactions, including the last UN-sponsored World Conference on Women that was held in China in 1996.

Technology is also revolutionizing security relationships among states (countries) and even impacting the viability of the state as a core political entity. There is a theory, for example, that the origins of the modern state can be traced to the fact that as warfare became more technologically sophisticated and required more soldiers and economic support, there was a need for stronger and more centralized government. This, in turn, gave rise to the state beginning some five centuries ago. Some analysts believe that this nexus of factors will lead to even more powerful, authoritarian states. Bruce D. Porter, in *War and the Rise of the State* (Free Press, 1994), reflects this view in expressing his concern that the cost and danger of high-technology weapons may well create the "Scientific Warfare State—a new kind of political system in which society would be intensely organized toward the aggressive exploitation of high technology for military purposes."

On the Internet ...

CNN World News
CNN World News is updated every few hours and includes full stories of events with pictures and film. This site includes a search mechanism and links. *http://www.cnn.com/WORLD/index.html*

International Development Exchange (IDEX)
This is the Web site of the International Development Exchange (IDEX), an organization that works to build partnerships to overcome economic and social injustice. IDEX helps people to gain greater control over their resources, political structures, and the economic processes that affect their lives. *http://www.idex.org/*

National Bureau of Economic Research's Online Data
The National Bureau of Economic Research (NBER) is a private, nonprofit, nonpartisan research organization dedicated to promoting a greater understanding of how the economy works. The NBER's Online Data site makes economic data available for downloading, including the NBER Macro History Database and Penn World Tables. *http://www.nber.com/data_index.html*

W.T.O. Pages
This site is intended to be a stimulus for research, reflection, and debate about the World Trade Organization (WTO). It contains links to articles, forums, and other resources. *http://www.eleves.ens.fr:8080/home/boyd/wto.html*

PART 2

International Economics

International economic and trade issues have an immediate and personal effect on individuals in ways that few other international issues do. They influence the jobs we hold and the prices of the products we buy—in short, our lifestyles. In the worldwide competition for resources and markets, tensions arise between allies and adversaries alike. This section examines some of the prevailing economic tensions.

■ Should China Be Admitted to the World Trade Organization?

■ Should Sanctions Against Cuba Under the Helms-Burton Act Be Abandoned?

■ Is the Current Trend Toward Global Economic Integration Desirable?

■ Should the Developed North Increase Aid to the Less Developed South?

ISSUE 6

Should China Be Admitted to the World Trade Organization?

YES: Robert S. Ross, from "Enter the Dragon," *Foreign Policy* (Fall 1996)

NO: Greg Mastel, from "Beijing at Bay," *Foreign Policy* (Fall 1996)

ISSUE SUMMARY

YES: Professor of political science Robert S. Ross contends that the World Trade Organization (WTO) should admit China in order to incorporate that country into the global economy.

NO: Greg Mastel, vice president for policy planning and administration at the Economic Strategy Institute in Washington, D.C., argues that the integrity of the WTO would be damaged if China were admitted without significant legal and economic reform.

China is a country in transition. It is attempting to move from a poor, largely agricultural economy to a wealthier, industrial economy. China retains its authoritarian, communist government, but it has adopted many of the trappings of a capitalist economy. Where once China rejected global trade and other international economic organizations, now it is trying to join them. Once called a "country without lawyers," China is now moving toward enacting commercial codes and other laws that regulate business and other activities. As with many transitions, the results are unevenly formulated, uncertainly applied, and unpredictable as to their future viability.

China's unfulfilled desire to become a member of the World Trade Organization (WTO) is caught up in the issues of transition. It is possible to argue that China should be regarded as a less developed country (LDC) and admitted to the WTO as such. From a micro, per capita perspective, China is one of the world's poorest countries. China's 1994 per capita gross national product (GNP) of $530 place it in the bottom 25 percent of all countries. Admission to the WTO as an LDC would give China a number of advantages not available to an industrialized, economically developed country (EDC). One of these advantages is a greater ability to use tariffs and other trade barriers to protect newly developing, "infant" industries.

But it is also the case that from a macro perspective, China has one of the largest economies in the world. China's 1994 gross domestic product (GDP) was $522 billion, the ninth largest economy in the world. Adding the GDP of Hong Kong, which is now part of China, would have moved China to seventh place. With $232 billion in goods exports in 1995, China was the world's sixth largest exporter in that category. Adding Hong Kong would have moved China to fourth place behind the United States, Germany, and Japan.

Whatever perspective one takes, there can be no disagreement that China is one of the world's fastest-growing economies. From 1990 through 1995, China's real GDP expanded an average of 10.5 percent annually. Moreover, China is rapidly industrializing. Its industrial sector has led the GDP growth, amassing an average 18.8 percent growth during the period. China is the world's twelfth largest producer of automobiles and commercial vehicles and is the third greatest steel manufacturer. The country's exports have also increased rapidly, climbing 14.8 percent annually during 1990–95. Again, manufactured goods led the way, jumping from 48 to 81 percent of all exports.

One result of China's rising economic importance is that the United States and other EDCs are devoting increased attention to their economic relations with China. One key issue is its burgeoning trade surplus with the United States. During 1995 China exported $48.8 billion in merchandise to the United States but took in only $11.8 billion in U.S. imports. The U.S. $37 billion trade gap trailed only the U.S. deficit with Japan and has evoked criticism from Washington that Beijing is practicing one-way free trade.

One response, along with some other EDCs, has been to deny China's application for membership in the WTO. The WTO is the organizational structure that administers the General Agreement on Tariffs and Trade (GATT). This treaty was concluded in 1947 to promote free trade. For most of its existence, the name GATT caused confusion because it was both the name of a treaty and the name of the organization, which is headquartered in Geneva, Switzerland. That confusion ended in 1995 when the GATT organization was renamed the WTO.

By whatever name, the organization is at the center of global trade policy. GATT's initial membership was 23 countries; there are now 117 members of the WTO. These members account for more than 85 percent of all world trade. Membership in the WTO is important to China for a number of reasons. Among these is the fact that under WTO rules, the United States could not impose unilateral sanctions on trade with China because of concerns over human rights violations or other practices internal to China.

China contends that it should be admitted to the WTO with the status of an LDC, which would give it greater ability to protect its economy than is given to EDCs. Washington wants Beijing to forgo many of the protections because of its large economy. Washington also opposes Chinese membership based on Beijing's alleged unwillingness to enforce other countries' patents and other intellectual property rights. In the following selections, Robert S. Ross and Greg Mastel take up the debate. Ross supports a WTO membership for China, while Mastel argues that China should be denied admittance until it institutes significant trade and market reforms.

YES

Robert S. Ross

ENTER THE DRAGON

The completion of the Uruguay Round of the General Agreement on Tariffs and Trade (GATT) and the establishment [in 1995] of the World Trade Organization (WTO) were truly major accomplishments. Together, they are helping to construct an international economic order characterized by liberal trade norms and dispute-settlement procedures that follow agreed-upon rules.

Challenges to the stability of this trade order could nonetheless arise from many sources. Economic factors such as unequal rates of growth and national recessions could elicit counterproductive foreign economic policies. Challenges could also come from powerful countries that refuse to play by the established rules of the WTO liberal trade regime and thus lead to destructive countervailing protectionist measures from their economic partners.

The post–World War II trade system faced such a challenge from Japan, whose effective export-promotion policies undermined the domestic industries of the advanced industrial economies, while its protectionist import restrictions prevented these industries from competing in the Japanese domestic market. Unfair Japanese trade practices brought about growing protectionism from Japan's major trading partners, including the United States and the European Union. Although Japan and its competitors have been able to contain the impact of their protectionist measures, Japanese protectionism has been a major factor contributing to the recent regionalization of the international economy and the emergence of trading zones characterized by special privileges for select WTO members.

THE CHALLENGE OF A RISING CHINA

Japan remains the country with the world's largest trade surplus, and its economic system remains mostly impenetrable. Nonetheless, the openness of the world economy may well be facing an even greater challenge from China's emergence as an economic power. If China's economy continues to grow at current annual rates of 8 to 10 per cent, and if it acquires advanced-technology capabilities, China's impact on the international economic system will dwarf that of Japan, even considering Japan's most influential period, during the

From Robert S. Ross, "Enter the Dragon," *Foreign Policy*, no. 104 (Fall 1996). Copyright © 1996 by The Carnegie Endowment for International Peace. Reprinted by permission.

1970s and 1980s. With favorable domestic economies of scale and a nearly unlimited supply of cheap labor, China could become a major export power capable of prevailing in the domestic markets of its economic competitors. If China simultaneously were to fail to offer opportunities for participation in its own domestic market, its policies could lead to destabilizing responses by all of the major economic powers.

Clearly, the challenge for the international community is to incorporate China into the global economy so that its behavior reinforces the contemporary trend toward trade liberalization. What is in dispute is the means by which this can be achieved. Chinese membership in the WTO is at the center of this debate. Correct management of China's application would have considerable implications for Chinese economic policy, for the role of the WTO in managing a liberal trade order, and for global economic stability. The dilemma is that there is no easy response to China's application.

Current Chinese trade practices are at wide variance with the WTO obligations assumed by the world's major trading powers. China's state-owned enterprises, which contributed approximately 31 per cent to China's total industrial output in 1995 and control strategic sectors of the economy, receive big subsidies and enjoy preferential access to government investment projects. Equally important, high tariffs and nontransparent government regulations protect China's private, collective, and state-owned manufacturers of consumer and industrial goods, further interfering with free trade. China's economic reforms and trade liberalization process have a long way to go before its economic policies meet WTO standards.

An equally important factor is the central government's failure to enforce a range of domestic policies meant to protect the rights of foreign businesses. China's ineffective protection of intellectual property rights is only the most obvious failure. Pervasive corruption throughout China and the absence of an effective central regulatory system weaken the government's ability to enforce international economic obligations on local governments and businesses. The absence of an effective legal system enforced by an independent judiciary compounds these problems, insofar as judicial recourse often is not an available remedy for injured parties. Corruption rather than law often determines the outcome of economic disputes in China.

China's growing economic power and its detrimental economic practices present the international community with a clear-cut policy objective: To persuade China to abandon its current practices for an economic system that complements the WTO's rule-based order. Moreover, if this process is delayed, China will develop sufficient economic power to resist pressures for reform. The United States faced this situation in its relations with Japan. By the time Washington actively sought change in Japan's trading system in the 1980s, Japan had developed the economic power to resist U.S. pressure. Washington failed to act when it had maximum leverage.

THE FAILURE OF CURRENT U.S. POLICY

The United States and its economic partners seek Chinese compliance with the WTO guidelines applicable to the major economic powers. Chinese membership in the WTO should be evaluated in terms of its contribution to this important agenda. Uncompromising adherence to rules and legal norms is a prerequisite to domestic order, but it is inappropriate for achieving interests in a world of states. Whether China today meets WTO standards is less important than adopting policies to promote the development of a Chinese economy compatible with the WTO. Practical pursuit of interest, rather than rigid adherence to principle, will best serve U.S. interests.

While it is in the interest of the United States and other industrial countries that China establish a liberal economic system as soon as possible, it is in China's interest to prolong its current policies. Although China has succeeded in expanding exports, the long-term expansion of its industrial base requires the use of the protectionist measures that Indonesia, Japan, South Korea, and Taiwan employed to assist their nascent industrial system prior to liberalization.

There is a conflict of interest between China and the global trading system that requires negotiation. Mere insistence that China abide by the rules before it is admitted to the WTO will not lead to a negotiated settlement. On the contrary, Chinese foreign trade officials argue that the U.S. price for Chinese admission into the WTO—rapid compliance with the trading rules applicable to the other major economic powers and a weakened industrial base—is too high. They have thus decided that China should remain outside of the WTO until the entry requirements are eased.

It is clear that WTO membership provides insufficient benefits to persuade China to liberalize its economy prematurely. Most-favored-nation (MFN) trade status assures China continued access to global markets. Although WTO textile regulations will eventually prove more advantageous than those of the Multi-Fibre Textile Agreement, the changing structure of Chinese trade is reducing the importance of textile exports to the Chinese economy. Equally important, improved access to international textile markets will not compensate China for a weakened industrial base. Given China's current ability to access markets, the benefit of WTO membership is primarily prestige. Beijing has determined that prestige is of little use in making China strong or in raising the standard of living of the Chinese people.

In this respect, contemporary China is different from the Japan of the 1960s. Whereas the United States had significant leverage over Japan in the early years of its post–World War II development, it lacks comparable leverage over China at a similar stage in China's development. The reason is that China has a far more open economy than Japan had at a similar stage of its development. Whereas Japan's trading partners could not sell to the Japanese market, China's trading partners have developed a significant interest in maintaining their access to the lucrative Chinese markets in consumer goods, aircraft, and infrastructure projects. This is not to say that the advanced industrial countries have no leverage over China, but that they have less leverage to compel China to open its markets fully. The result is a failed effort to use the prospect of Chinese membership in the WTO as an incentive for Beijing to liberalize its foreign economic policies.

The most profound implication of U.S. policy intransigence will be for China's future economic behavior. Not only has China *not* made the concessions demanded by Washington, but U.S. policy will merely encourage Beijing to persist in its current policies. Chinese isolation from the WTO and the resulting Chinese resentment of the major trading powers will likely enhance Beijing's proclivity to pursue mercantilist policies for national power rather than merely short-term protectionist policies for economic development.

Denial of Chinese membership in the WTO will not minimize the global impact of Chinese protectionism. China will affect the world trade system through its bilateral relationships: WTO member countries will seek bilateral accommodations with China in order to profit from its vast market, thus weakening the liberal trading order. This was the impact of U.S. and European bilateral arrangements with Japan. Denying China membership in the WTO may reflect principled adherence to the rules of trade and allow America to hold the moral high ground, but it will not realize American interests or the interests of America's major trading allies in maintaining a stable liberal economic order. Keeping China out of the WTO provides only the illusion of isolating the problem; it will not solve the problem.

A NEW DIRECTION

The United States has been negotiating Chinese admission into the GATT/WTO since 1988. The two sides remain far apart. It is time to reconsider the premises of U.S. policy.

Washington should support an accession agreement that acknowledges China's interest in protecting its industrial base. The agreement should also include a schedule for Chinese trade reform. The schedule might delay the reforms for longer than Washington would

like, but, once in the WTO, China will be required to follow through on the schedule. Indeed, one of the great missed opportunities of Washington's China policy was its failure to achieve Chinese membership in the GATT on terms negotiated by the Bush administration in 1989. If China had entered the GATT in 1989, it would be committed to a far more open trade system than is currently the case. Following the June 4, 1989, suppression of the Chinese democracy movement, Washington withdrew support for the agreement. Now China is under no obligation to conform to any GATT/WTO guidelines.

Moreover, the longer agreement is delayed, the longer the actual period of adjustment will be. The clock for Chinese adherence to WTO regulations does not start ticking until China joins the WTO. In addition, the longer China's entrance is postponed, the more powerful it will become, thus diminishing the organization's ultimate leverage. It is in the interest of the major economic powers to get the WTO clock ticking as soon as possible.

Chinese membership in the WTO will increase international leverage over China. Current efforts to coerce China to reform its economic system depend entirely on U.S. efforts. One of the reasons that U.S. negotiations with China for market access have failed is that the United States lacks support from its allies. By conducting negotiations within the multilateral setting of the WTO, the likelihood of maintaining a "united front" would be far greater, and the pressure on Beijing to compromise, more compelling. In addition, it would be politically easier for Chinese leaders to bow to WTO pressures than to unilateral U.S. insistence.

For any international regime to succeed, it must reflect the interests of its most important members. The United States acknowledged this fact throughout the Cold War when it allowed significant protectionism for its NATO allies and Japan in numerous economic sectors. It continued to do so during the Uruguay Round when it made concessions to Japan and France over agricultural products. While those compromises resulted in a less liberal trade agreement than the United States would have liked, they have enabled Europe and Japan to contribute to the integrity of the overall regime. As a result, the WTO may well be more stable and enduring. Accommodating Chinese interests may require concessions similar to those offered to Europe and Japan. But failure to include China in WTO negotiations will only ensure that the regime will develop in a direction inimical to Chinese interests. Asian countries understand this point. They have admitted China into the Association of Southeast Asian Nations Regional Forum and the Asia-Pacific Economic Cooperation forum because they understand that a Chinese commitment to these institutions requires a Chinese voice in their development. The same truth holds for the WTO. By incorporating China, the WTO will develop in a direction that reflects a consensus of all the major powers. This is the prerequisite to global economic stability. The alternative is a trade regime that encourages Chinese policies that are likely to destabilize a system that does not reflect its interests.

Chinese membership in the WTO will also strengthen the hand of Chinese policymakers who want to promote a more liberal Chinese trading system. Prior to Chinese membership in the World Bank and the International Monetary Fund,

many analysts argued that China would be a destructive force—that its communist bureaucrats would undermine these institutions' commitments to international norms. Just the opposite occurred. Not only did China become a constructive member of these institutions, but its membership has allowed implicit alliances to develop between the institutions and proreform policymakers, strengthening their hand within China. Chinese membership in the WTO could create similar partnerships.

Finally, Chinese membership in the WTO would serve American bilateral interests with China. The United States has assumed the burden of obtaining Chinese compliance with international economic norms. This is the case in intellectual property rights negotiations. The primary causes of Chinese intellectual property rights violations are the political and economic decentralization of post-Mao China, the lack of an effective legal system to enforce government regulations, and the corruption of those authorities who participate in the piracy of intellectual property. Copyright infringement is rampant in China, affecting domestic producers of cigarettes, drugs, and food products as well as the profits of China's own software and entertainment industries, and the regime's legitimacy has suffered. By all appearances, the Chinese government would like to end much of the piracy in the Chinese economy. It simply lacks the authority.

There seems to be little that U.S. policymakers can do to fundamentally improve Chinese enforcement of intellectual property rights violations—foreign economic sanctions will not enhance central Chinese government authority over local activities. The threat of sanctions has only encouraged Chinese leaders to commit to improved intellectual property protection by local officials who are not susceptible to government policy, creating periodic crises with Washington when agreements are not fulfilled. Moreover, when Beijing shuts down factories that pirate intellectual property, they often quickly reopen elsewhere in connivance with corrupt local officials. The economics of piracy almost guarantees it; the cost of new duplicating facilities is significantly less than the potential profit. Focusing on Chinese policy toward these high-profile factories merely creates the illusion that rapid progress is possible and heightens American acrimony when expectations are unmet.

As with Chinese protectionism, the issue is how to encourage constructive Chinese behavior. Current U.S. policy has failed. Multilateral WTO sanctions would impose costs on the central government for its failure to control localities, while removing the burden on Sino–U.S. relations for inevitable Chinese infractions. Moreover, the WTO could be an effective channel for technical assistance in developing a Chinese system for regulating intellectual property. Over the long run, a better Chinese regulatory and legal system will do the most to promote global interests.

Without doubt, Chinese foreign economic practices will remain troubling for many years to come. The evolution of the Chinese political and economic systems will primarily reflect long-term domestic trends—a growing respect for law and the institutionalizaton of political authority. International pressures will not fundamentally affect the pace of change. Whether or not China is admitted into the WTO, it will remain a problematic trading partner.

In these circumstances, foreign policies can only help to ameliorate a difficult situation; they cannot resolve it. Moreover, Chinese membership in the WTO entails some risk—allowing a blatant violator of international economic norms to join the WTO may well erode the organization's credibility. Nonetheless, Chinese membership in the WTO sooner rather than later remains the best option for improving a difficult situation.

China's admission to the WTO will subject it to multilateral pressures for adherence to a self-imposed agreement to adopt liberal trading practices within a specified time. Currently, China has not agreed to any multilateral commitments to reform its trading system. Isolating China will not compel China to change nor will it protect the international economic system from counterproductive Chinese trade practices. Rather, it will ensure that China's gap with WTO standards will grow, along with Chinese resentment and the incentive to adopt destabilizing trade policies.

Current American policy fails either to minimize the likelihood of international economic instability or to improve Chinese trading practices. There is no more opportune time than now to promote China's support for a liberal trade order that can endure into the twenty-first century.

NO

Greg Mastel

BEIJING AT BAY

With the Sino-American relationship under much stress, many "China hands" have viewed China's application to join the World Trade Organization (WTO) as an issue on which the United States could compromise in order to keep the peace. The United States, with the support of other major countries, has been delaying China's entry into the WTO until China commits to sufficient trade and market reforms. Arguing, however, that the Clinton administration is too legalistic in its approach to China's application, some China experts have urged that the administration put aside its concerns and support China's immediate entry into the WTO.

This view places political and security concerns above economic concerns. It has the ring of classic U.S. Cold War foreign policy decision making, a paradigm that has dominated U.S. policy toward China for decades. This viewpoint is dated and out of touch with current realities. China is an important player in the global economy. It is already one of the world's top 10 exporters and is expected to be the world's largest economy early in the next century. As a result, economic and trade issues with China are at least as important as security and political issues.

More importantly, the integrity of the WTO would be severely damaged if China were admitted without significant legal and economic reform. The WTO is more than a simple club of trading partners. The WTO—originally the General Agreement on Tariffs and Trade (GATT)—is a postwar institution founded to establish and promote the principles of free markets and free trade. Thus, simply being a big player in international commerce does not warrant WTO membership. The acceptance of key market principles—even if they are not always rigorously applied—should be the key test for WTO membership. Viewed in this light, China's compatibility with the WTO is open to question. In fact, there are three basic reasons to question China's current compatibility with the organization.

Chinese trade barriers. The most visible impediments to China's membership in the WTO are its formal trade barriers, including tariffs, import licenses, and subsidies. In recent years, these formal trade barriers have been

From Greg Mastel, "Beijing at Bay," *Foreign Policy,* no. 104 (Fall 1996). Copyright © 1996 by The Carnegie Endowment for International Peace. Reprinted by permission.

lowered; however, others have appeared, and China still has considerably more formal trade barriers that are inconsistent with WTO membership than any other major country. These barriers have been the focus of WTO accession negotiations so far.

The negotiations on formal trade barriers have already proven contentious. In theory, however, the issues under discussion—tariffs, investment policy, etc.—have been addressed in previous negotiations (NAFTA [North American Free Trade Agreement], Uruguay Round). Thus, if the political will exists to reach an agreement, traditional trade barriers do not pose a conceptual obstacle to China's accession.

Rule of law.   The formal trade barriers, however, are only the tip of the iceberg. It is very difficult to ensure that any trade agreement will translate into changes in Chinese policy. China simply does not yet have a reliable rule of law. The current generation of leaders frequently pronounces that establishing the clear and consistent rule of law is a primary goal. The... leader of the National People's Congress, Qiao Shi,... spoke of the importance of establishing the rule of law, as opposed to the rule of a strong leader, which has led to tragedies like the Cultural Revolution.

This issue may seem initially to have little to do with international trade negotiations, but China's lack of a rule of law presents almost insurmountable problems for WTO membership. In China, trade regulations and tariffs are set by national policy, but their implementation in different provinces and ports is inconsistent. Officials often are open to bribes, a practice that results in further inconsistency. Some laws are simply not enforced,

particularly if it is profitable not to enforce them.

The severity of this problem was brought into sharp focus in a recent dispute over the protection of intellectual property. The United States has criticized China for not enforcing the bilateral understanding, struck last year, on the protection of intellectual property rights. In defense, Chinese officials cite the lack of central government control over provincial governments—and even over some operations affiliated with the People's Liberation Army.

The lack of a reliable rule of law governing Chinese behavior in international commerce raises serious concerns about China's readiness for WTO membership. After all, it does little good to negotiate trade agreements with a government that, by its own admission, is unable or unwilling to live by the agreements it negotiates. Before China can be considered a serious applicant for WTO membership, it must establish a reliable rule of law, at least in relation to trade and investment.

The Communist system.   Another difficulty, closely related to the lack of a rule of law, is the presence of a still nearly totalitarian government. One of the issues that illustrates the problem, and is currently under discussion in the context of WTO membership for China, is the issue of "trading rights." Essentially, trading rights are granted to private enterprises to enable them to engage in foreign commerce without governmental approval. But Chinese citizens, or enterprises operating in China, do not automatically enjoy these rights. In WTO negotiations, China has proposed granting these rights, in a limited sense, to foreign entities operating in China but has been silent on extending similar rights to Chinese citizens. This issue highlights the expansive role of the Chinese government in commercial decision making. After all, if consumers do not have the right to purchase imports, what sense does it make to negotiate on tariffs and quotas?

The WTO, like the GATT before it, normally ignores the degree of political freedom a government permits: A number of WTO members have authoritarian governments. But now there is an increasing focus on the link between social freedom and the potential for conducting normal commerce. In the debate over congressional approval of the North American Free Trade Agreement, Senator Patrick Moynihan (D-New York) posed the question, "How can you have free trade with a country that is not free?" In his argument, Moynihan focused on the absence of both an independent judiciary and a corruption-free government to enforce trade and commercial regulations in Mexico, but an even more compelling argument can be made with regard to China.

There are several problems caused by the expansive powers and influence of the Chinese government. The first and most obvious is the continuing role of government planning in the Chinese economy. Since the late 1970s, China has undertaken considerable economic reforms and has moved toward creating a more market-oriented economy. Yet China is still—and intends to remain—largely a centrally planned economy. Although China is undertaking reforms, state-run industries are still responsible for a significant portion of China's gross domestic product, and they employ an enormous number of people and provide a major source of exports. China recently adopted another five-year economic plan and maintains extensive plans to support what it calls "pillar industries." Reaching beyond those industries directly owned by the state, new sectoral guidelines have been issued for the automotive and pharmaceutical industries, and there is reportedly a similar blueprint for the electronics industry.

CHINA SIMPLY DOES NOT HAVE A RELIABLE RULE OF LAW

These plans contain many policy elements inconsistent with the WTO, including import-substitution directives, local-content requirements, onerous investment requirements, and foreign-exchange balancing requirements. Even more troubling is the fact that the Chinese government clearly has no intention of ending the issuance of industrial guidelines. Despite assurances that future plans would be WTO-consistent, there is no evidence that recent industrial plans are moving in that direction.

Beyond the formal role of central planning, the pervasive presence of the government in Chinese society raises serious questions about the possibility of establishing a normal trading relationship with China. A large percentage of trading decisions, particularly with regard to infrastructure projects and agriculture, are made directly by government agencies, and the Chinese government has explicitly used foreign purchases and business deals as tools to promote foreign policy objectives.

Where the government's role in commercial decisions is direct, perhaps WTO provisions regulating government procurement and state trading could be of some help in regulating Chinese trading decisions. The Chinese government, however, has innumerable opportunities to tilt regulatory decisions in favor of, or against, any enterprise. The opportunities to harass foreign businesses are numerous, and the opportunities for WTO policing are limited, because there is rarely any formal paper trail, and there is often no formal decision.

More difficult still is moderating the informal role the government plays throughout society. The official Chinese press has been pounding away regularly at the United States on a variety of foreign policy issues, accusing the United States of seeking to "contain" China. In such a political environment, and given the need for government approval to thrive and even survive, can any Chinese citizen ignore government rhetoric when selecting business partners? With memories of the Cultural Revolution and Tiananmen Square very much in mind, the answer is almost certainly "no."

Historically, the GATT/WTO was conceived in part as an organization of market economies convened to assist the market world in its competition with the nonmarket world. Viewed in this context, the problem presented by the fact of the world's largest nonmarket economy seeking to join the WTO comes into focus. The Chinese government's influence over its economy may be so pervasive that the WTO trading rules will prove inadequate to create a "level playing field." Simply put, China retains too many features of the communist system to be easily married with the WTO.

The U.S. Interest

Ultimately, China's membership in the WTO seems clearly to be in the best interest of the United States, China, and the world. Assuming China is enticed to operate its economy within the terms of the WTO, membership would commit China to further economic reform. Such reform is likely to improve the life of the average Chinese citizen, make China a more reliable trading partner, increase trade opportunities, and stimulate economic growth worldwide.

China's membership is not, however, urgently required. Currently, the United States can regulate trade with China through bilateral negotiations and the application of domestic laws. Other countries can and have taken similar steps. For its part, China's trade with the world is already growing at an astounding rate. Over the last 15 years, Chinese exports have grown at three times the world average rate. In short, all parties have alternatives to China's immediate membership, and, even if China is not able to join the WTO for some time, no serious problems will result.

Unfortunately, if China were allowed to enter the WTO without undertaking substantial reforms, the fallout *would* be serious. Under the accession agreement, China has suggested it would make no additional, immediate reforms and would do the minimum required of the world's weakest trading countries in order to join the WTO—while immediately gaining all the benefits of membership.

From the American perspective, the immediate implication of China's entry into the WTO is that the United States would have dramatically less leverage with which to address trade concerns. Currently, the United States can negotiate with China to improve the protection of intellectual property, to enhance market access, or to address other trade problems under threat of imposing sanctions on Chinese exports if the negotiations do not succeed. If China were a WTO member, WTO rules would bar sanctions on Chinese exports unless the WTO ruled in favor of the United States in the matter being disputed. Since China presumably would be bound only to the WTO's minimum standards and would be entitled to special treatment as a developing country, it is unlikely that the WTO would rule in any major country's favor.

The difference between what can be achieved bilaterally and what would be possible under the WTO is dramatic. For example, the bilateral commitments for the protection of intellectual property are in many respects superior to those required by the WTO. Of course, there have been serious problems in convincing China to abide by these bilateral commitments, but it is unlikely that China would be any more enthusiastic about honoring WTO commitments. Bilaterally, the United States has negotiated strong trade reforms that have benefited U.S. trading interests and Chinese economic reforms.

The negative consequences of allowing China to enter the WTO without committing to substantial reform go beyond harming the economic interests of China's trading partners and slowing the pace of reform in China. Another negative consequence is the precedent China's application would establish for other countries seeking WTO membership, including Russia, Saudi Arabia, Taiwan, and Vietnam.

In practice, these applications are not likely to proceed until after disputes over China's application are resolved. As a result, the terms of China's accession are likely to set a powerful precedent for these negotiations. Given the success of Chinese industry in world markets and the strength of the Chinese economy, WTO rules bent or broken to allow China's entry would almost certainly be bent or broken for weaker economies. As

a result, the credibility of the WTO as the policeman of world trade would be severely damaged. The immediate effect would be that many countries would emulate China and refuse to dismantle their trade barriers. After all, if such a major trading country can successfully ignore WTO discipline, certainly smaller countries can keep their trade barriers in place. The longer-term result could be an increase in the already significant political dissatisfaction with the global trading system—in the United States and perhaps elsewhere—which threatens the system itself.

In the past, the trading community allowed a number of countries, notably Japan, to join the world trading system without demanding substantial adherence to its principles. The result was an erosion of the trading system's credibility, which the negotiations that created the WTO aimed to restore. Clearly, allowing countries to enter the world trading system without opening their markets has hurt the system in the past, and allowing China to follow suit risks placing the exception above the rule.

The global trading system is far from perfect. Despite flaws, however, the WTO provides discipline in international trade and has created some order where anarchy would otherwise prevail. Trade liberalization created under the GATT/WTO system has been one of the great engines of global growth in the postwar era, and there is the potential for further progress for decades to come. Weakening or destroying the system as a political favor to China would be an enormous economic and political mistake.

A Transitional Mechanism

The decision on China's accession need not come down to a black-or-white choice of either allowing China's immediate entry into the WTO or permanently blocking its membership. The challenges that must be confronted to integrate China into the WTO are larger than those faced in other accession agreements, such as those with Japan and Mexico. Nonetheless, in the 1960s there was an effort to integrate three non-market economies—Hungary, Poland, and Romania. This experience suggests some possible elements of a transitional arrangement to do the same for China.

A three-part transitional arrangement could be devised for China's WTO accession. First and foremost, China would agree to accept WTO discipline within a fixed period of time. Second, since during the phase-in China would continue to maintain WTO-inconsistent policies, other WTO members would retain the right to unilaterally limit China's exports to their markets, either to prevent a market disruption or to retaliate for China's failure to fulfill its commitments. Finally, to ensure that the Chinese market would continue opening to imports, China would be obligated to increase imports by a fixed percentage each year. A similar approach was used both with Poland and, more recently, as part of the effort to open agricultural markets worldwide. With vigorous oversight and a real effort by China, such an approach could integrate China into the WTO.

It is certainly possible that negotiation of such an arrangement would take years. However, the trade relationship between China and the world has advanced over the last two decades without China's admission to the GATT/WTO. China's exports have grown strongly, its imports have increased, and many trade issues have been dealt with bilaterally. It is also possible that China may decide that it is not prepared to undertake such a negotiation at this time. Far from being a disaster, either outcome is preferable to allowing China to enter the WTO without making meaningful reforms.

Most of the "China hands" who suggest that China be allowed immediate entry into the WTO unfortunately are not "WTO hands," or even "trade hands." The more one understands the cost of such a gesture, the clearer it becomes that it would amount to granting an enormous trade concession in order to achieve ill-defined political benefits. Both the United States and China have compelling interests in developing a stable and mutually beneficial economic, security, and political relationship, and both must work to establish that relationship. Sacrificing a sound economic and trade relationship in the hope of achieving some temporary gains in other areas would be unwise policy. China should become a full-fledged member of the world trading system, but it should do so in a way that strengthens the system instead of undermining it.

POSTSCRIPT

Should China Be Admitted to the World Trade Organization?

Relations between the United States and China have long been difficult, as discussed in Robert Garson, *The United States and China Since 1949: A Troubled Affair* (Farleigh Dickinson Press, 1994). China's membership in the WTO is just one in a complex skein of issues involving relations with China. Concerns about whether China should be condemned as a violator of human rights have regularly roiled China-U.S. relations since the massacre of protesters by People Liberation Army troops in Tiananmen Square in 1989. There have been periodic attempts in Congress to impose U.S. sanctions on China. As a candidate, Bill Clinton advocated such sanctions, but he changed his view once he became president. One reason for this is because trade relations with China do not exist in a vacuum. China is arguably an emerging superpower, and trade disputes spill over into many other areas. Clinton explained his change of heart; as president, he came to appreciate that "China has an atomic arsenal and a vote and a veto in the UN Security Council. It is a major factor in Asian and global security." On China's potential as at least a regional hegemon, see Denny Roy, "Hegemon on the Horizon? China's Threat to East Asian Security" and Michael G. Gallagher, "China's Illusory Threat to the South China Sea," *International Security* (Summer 1994).

China's strategic importance has caused Washington to avoid economic confrontations with China when possible. Normal trade relations have continued despite attempts in Congress to impose sanctions. American negotiators have accepted China's pledges to act against intellectual piracy and ignore charges by critics that Beijing has done little to end the practice.

Washington, however, has continued to block Chinese membership in the WTO. A significant part of that has to do with the huge and growing trade deficit with China and with the mounting pressure by adversely affected U.S. businesses and workers to end alleged Chinese trade abuses.

The Clinton administration has continued to block China's admission to the WTO. The Clinton Administration hopes this will force Beijing to agree to meet most of the rules that apply to industrialized countries for opening their economies to free trade and investment. "We would like to see [the Chinese] become a member of the WTO," said one U.S. diplomat, "but the other part of the equation, of course, is that they must make a much better offer, in terms of market access and adhering to WTO disciplines, than they have so far."

Given the complexity of relations with China, one consideration is whether to "link" issues such as human rights or strategic concerns with trade or to treat each matter separately. Another uncertainty is how to best encourage reform in China. Is that done by making demands on China or by interacting with China more fully so that reforms flow from friendship and mutual confidence? For an overall view of China's foreign relations, see John R. Faust and Judith F. Kornberg, *China in World Politics* (Lynne Rienner Press, 1995). Then there is the future. China is not considered a superpower today, but tomorrow it might be. How will current practices impact future Chinese attitudes toward the United States and other EDCs? President Clinton indicated how mindful of these he is when he observed, "I believe among the great security questions of the twenty-first century... one of them is how will China... define [its] greatness."

ISSUE 7

Should Sanctions Against Cuba Under the Helms-Burton Act Be Abandoned?

YES: Stephen A. Lisio, from "Helms–Burton and the Point of Diminishing Returns," *International Affairs* (vol. 72, no. 4, 1996)

NO: Alberto J. Mora, from Statement Before the Committee on Foreign Relations, U.S. Senate (July 30, 1996)

ISSUE SUMMARY

YES: Stephen A. Lisio, an independent analyst with a particular focus on Western Hemisphere affairs, maintains that tightening economic sanctions against Cuba is likely to be counterproductive.

NO: Alberto J. Mora, an attorney with a specialty in international law, contends that abandoning sanctions against Cuba would be tantamount to endorsing despotism.

The issue of Cuba and the Helms-Burton Act involves two different matters. One is U.S. relations with Cuba and the impact of sanctions on the communist government of President Fidel Castro. The other is the legality of the United States' unilaterally applying sanctions not only against Cuba but against other countries that do business with Cuba.

The intimate interaction between the politics of Cuba and those of the United States goes back to the origins of the Monroe Doctrine of 1823. President James Monroe declared that year that the Western Hemisphere was not subject to "further colonization" and that any attempt by an outside power aimed at "oppressing... or controlling by any other manner" part of the so-called New World would be viewed "as the manifestation of an unfriendly disposition toward the United States."

Although Monroe's dictum did not immediately affect Cuba, which remained a colony of Spain until the Spanish-American War of 1898, the Monroe Doctrine did create in American minds the notion that they exercised some special, legitimate authority over the hemisphere, especially Central America and the Caribbean. This sense was heightened when, as a result of the U.S. victory over Spain in 1898, Cuba and Puerto Rico in the Caribbean, as well as the Philippines and Guam in the Pacific, came under either direct or indirect U.S. control. The 1904 (Theodore) Roosevelt Corollary to the Monroe Doctrine asserted the U.S. right to intervene in the affairs of other Western Hemisphere nations to stop actions that are unacceptable to the United States. The corollary justified to Americans repeated interventions in the region, including occupying Cuba (1898–1922).

Like many other countries in the hemisphere, Cuba was frequently controlled by dictators, who were supported or tolerated by Washington. This situation changed in Cuba when rebels led by Fidel Castro toppled right-wing dictator Fulgencio Batista in 1959. Americans were alarmed by Castro's leftist sentiments, and escalating U.S.-Cuba tension saw Castro align his country with the Soviet Union.

After attempts to topple Castro by force or assassination failed, the United States settled down to a continuing series of economic sanctions against Cuba. These have continued even after the end of the Soviet Union, the cold war, and, therefore—some would argue—the reasons for isolating Cuba and trying to unseat Castro.

Instead of ending, however, the sanctions became even stricter in early 1996. As Stephen A. Lisio reports, Cuba shot down two unarmed light planes that had flown from Florida over Cuba to drop anti-Castro leaflets. The United States reacted by enacting the Liberty and Democratic Solidarity Act (popularly known as the Helms-Burton Act). In addition to its impact on Cuba, the Helms-Burton Act raises a second point, which rests on the fact that the legislation imposes penalties on foreign companies and individuals for doing business with or in Cuba. The issue is whether or not this is good or even legal policy.

Whatever Americans might have thought of the U.S. law, there was a strongly negative reaction overseas. Addressing Canada's Parliament with Prime Minister Jean Chrétien at his side in June 1996, President Ernesto Zedillo of Mexico declared, "Mexico and Canada consider inadmissible every measure that... erects [barriers] to the detriment of international investment and business." The European Union (EU) joined in condemning what it considered a U.S. intrusion into the sovereign authority of the EU member countries. "We remain strongly opposed to the legislation,... You don't export your laws and principles to other countries," protested an EU spokesperson. The Organization of American States, with only the United States voting no, also condemned the U.S. initiatives, calling them actions that "obstruct international trade and investment" and "the free movement of persons" in violation of international law.

In the following selections, Lisio, who provides details of the Helms-Burton Act, makes common cause with those who reject sanctions on Cuba in general and condemn the act in particular. Alberto J. Mora takes the opposite view, arguing that the Helms-Burton Act is both good policy and a good law.

YES

Stephen A. Lisio

HELMS–BURTON AND THE POINT OF DIMINISHING RETURNS

On 12 March 1996 US President Bill Clinton responded to the Cuban shooting down of two US-registered Cessna aircraft by signing into law the Cuban Liberty and Democratic Solidarity Act. This law, known as Helms–Burton after its congressional sponsors Senator Jesse Helms (Republican, North Carolina) and Representative Dan Burton (Republican, Indiana), tightens the US economic embargo on Cuba as an expression of outrage over that country's 'blatant violation of international law' on 24 February, when Cuban ground control authorized the destruction of the civilian aircraft over international airspace. Ironically, however, rather than simply punish the Cuban government for its actions, Helms–Burton instead punished nine Canadians and their families by barring them from entering the United States. By seeking to punish any foreign citizen, company, or government that does not adhere to the America embargo, the United States itself is testing the limits of international law. Although some believe that tightened economic sanctions provide the best opportunity to end Fidel Castro's regime, it remains to be seen how far the United States is willing to jeopardize its diplomatic relations by punishing its allies in the process. Also, in light of Cuba's continuing economic transition, the current path of US policy promises to be less than profitable.

With the end of the Cold War and the dissolution of the Soviet Union, Fidel Castro's Cuba suffered a major economic contraction which lasted nearly five years. Now 'independent' of Soviet subsidies, the island economy is struggling. Nevertheless, while six years have passed since the multibillion dollar subsidies stopped flowing from the Soviet Union, some 36 years have elapsed since the United States first tried to force Castro from power through the use of economic sanctions. Castro's tenacity, despite these pressures, inspired Senator Helms and Representative Burton to sponsor the Cuban Liberty and Democratic Solidarity Act.

Since its introduction in Congress in early 1995, Helms–Burton has been steeped in rhetoric reminiscent of the Cold War. Burton proclaimed the bill a 'tool of democracy', and 'an expression of faith and solidarity with the people of Cuba, who have suffered for far too long'. Meanwhile, Helms insisted that, 'as Chairman of the Senate Foreign Relations Committee, doing everything possible to bring freedom and democracy to Cuba and the Cuban people is at the top of my priority list.... Let me be clear: whether Castro leaves Cuba in a vertical or horizontal position is up to him and the Cuban people. But he must —and will—leave Cuba.' The sponsors' rhetoric illustrates an important flaw in the new policy. It maintains that no other country or issue in the world is more important to the foreign policy of the United States than Cuba. Both Helms and Burton agreed, in action if not in words, that US policy towards Cuba held precedence over relations with Canada, Mexico, the European nations or Russia. Moreover, the provisions of the new law require the United States to maintain such a tight embargo that US economic and political relations with its allies will surely suffer. Such an inflexible policy cannot hope to serve US interests.

The most critical shortcoming of Helms–Burton is that it does not constitute an effective tool with which to promote democracy. Indeed, a tightening of the embargo on Cuba may be more counterproductive to the cause of democracy than its sponsors admit. Although distressed, the Cuban economy is not about to collapse and is unlikely to do so under the pressure of the new sanctions. In fact, the embargo notwithstanding, the Cuban economy is already recovering from its major economic crisis, at its most acute between 1989 and 1993. The Cuban government has been implementing a host of piecemeal reforms, which have generated a market dynamic in the newly liberalized sectors of its economy. And, despite the regime's recent denunciations of capitalism, the reforms have established a momentum which will continue to encourage additional gradual changes as Cuba legalizes the activities necessary for sustainable growth. Such an economic transformation will ultimately render Cuba less vulnerable to US efforts to influence its internal political structure.

Helms–Burton became law at a critical juncture in Cuba's history. The Cuban economy, as well as its politico-legal regime, was already in a state of flux, independent of US influence. Thus, the 'one final push' championed by Helms and Burton is unlikely to yield more than slight political change and could ultimately weaken the US influence over a situation in which it has, for the past 36 years, exercised minimal control. Cuba's economic transition presented an opportunity for a different US policy, one which used the progress of economic liberalization to encourage political reform; instead, Helms–Burton by contrast, will probably strain US relations with its allies and yield diminishing returns in Cuba.

THE PROVISIONS OF HELMS–BURTON

Although it is prudent for the United States to consider modifying its policy in ways that might expedite Cuba's transition towards democracy, Helms–Burton is too inflexible to achieve that goal. Before the United States will recognize any Cuban government, much less begin negotiations with it, Helms–Burton requires the legalization of all political activity, the release of all political prisoners, the protection of human rights, the existence of an independent judiciary, the abolition of the Department of State Security, the organization of free elections under international supervision, and a new leadership exclusive of Fidel and Raúl Castro. Moreover, Helms–Burton places heavy emphasis on sanctions and compensation for US assets lost during the revolution. Such demands are more appropriately made upon the long-term goals of a permanent government, not the immediate goals of a transitional one. Also, the tighter sanctions may hinder a peaceful transition to democracy in Cuba, in which the United States has a strong interest. Generally, the Cuban Liberty and Democratic Solidarity Act purports to encourage a free and independent Cuba. However, measures concerning democracy are the subject of only one title, Title II, of a four-title bill. The other three titles are concerned with sanctions and US property rights.

Title I

The first title concerns the economic embargo against Cuba. This title involves a prohibition against providing loans, credits or other financing to any entity that uses, or conducts trade with, US assets confiscated by the Cuban government. It also opposes Cuba's membership in the international financial institutions, such as the World Bank and the International Monetary Fund (IMF), and requires a reduction of US payments to the said institutions equal to the amount of any loan or other assistance provided to Cuba by those institutions. Furthermore, Helms–Burton contains a provision to withhold assistance from any state of the former Soviet Union by an amount equal to the sum of assistance provided by that state in support of military and intelligence facilities in Cuba, such as the nuclear facility at Cienfuegos and the intelligence facility at Lourdes. Another provision prohibits trade in sugar or sugar products from any country that has traded in such goods with Cuba unless that country can prove that the sugar

products it exports to the United States are not of Cuban origin. Finally, Section 102 'codifies' the embargo, thus ensuring that the embargo cannot be lifted by presidential initiative until Cuba has established a transition government, as outlined in Title II.

Title II

The second title outlines the support to be accorded to a transition government in Cuba. Provisions include the end of all economic sanctions and the resumption of diplomatic relations with Cuba when the US President determines that the island has established a democratically elected government with an independent judiciary and free elections. Also, Helms–Burton allows for assistance to a transition government in the form of food, medical supplies and emergency humanitarian assistance. However, the definition of 'democracy', which specifies the exclusion of Raúl and Fidel Castro, coupled with the strict requirements which any transition government must meet to receive assistance, negate the policy's democratic intentions.

Title III

The third title of Helms–Burton centres on the punishment of those who have made use of American property seized during the Cuban revolution. It allows that any person or government that 'traffics' in—trades, invests in, or expands —confiscated US property is liable for monetary damages in US federal district courts. This provision establishes a private 'right of action' for US citizens to receive compensation for the current market value of such property, or its original value plus interest (whichever is greater), plus reimbursement from the trafficker for court costs and reasonable attorneys' fees. However, the President has the authority to delay the enforcement of Title III indefinitely, in successive six-month periods, if he determines that it 'is necessary to the national interests of the United States and will expedite a transition to democracy in Cuba'....

Title IV

Finally, Title IV establishes the mandatory denial of visas to individuals (like the Canadians mentioned above) who traffic in confiscated property. Thus, any aliens who traffic in confiscated property, or are corporate officers or shareholders of an entity involved in the confiscation, trafficking or unauthorized use or benefit from confiscated US property, are denied access to the United States for residence, business or travel. Exemptions to this provision will be made on a case-by-case basis only to allow entry for humanitarian medical reasons or to face litigation under Title III.

Together, these provisions purport to end the Cuban regime by ensuring that other countries respect the US embargo. However, Cuba's recovery from economic crisis, the progress of its transition, and the objection of several US trading partners to the extraterritorial nature of Helms–Burton may oblige the United States to invest a tremendous amount of its resources (including political capital) in order to attain its goal of removing Castro from power.

CUBA'S ECONOMIC SHOCK AND INSUFFICIENT ADJUSTMENT, 1989–1993

Cuba's loss of Soviet subsidies, and nearly all other sources of external financing from 1989, initiated a six-year production crisis which resulted in a major economic contraction. From 1989 to 1993 Cuban earnings from exports dropped from $5.4 billion to $1.7 billion. One prominent casualty of the decline was the Cuban sugar crop. After the termination of the annual Soviet subsidy of $2.1 million, sugar production fell by 50 per cent. As exports and foreign earnings decreased, imports also declined, from $8.1 billion in 1989 to $2.2 billion in 1993. The removal of Soviet economic assistance created a financial vacuum between 1989 and 1993: the lack of subsidies caused a reduction in export production, which resulted in lower foreign exchange earnings, which in turn resulted in the purchase of fewer foreign inputs of production, crucial to the production process. In the same period, gross domestic product decreased by more than 40 per cent....

In a market economy, such a drastic contraction would necessitate a massive currency devaluation that would eventually return the economy to equilibrium through a reduction in the demand for imports and an increase in the demand for domestic goods and exports. This phenomenon of returning to equilibrium is widely acknowledged to be the product of free market forces. However, currency devaluation is also tantamount to a reduction in wages. Rather than place such a strain on a people living at subsistence level, the leaders of the Cuban centrally planned economy forfeited the use of free market forces and instead allocated the country's meagre foreign exchange earnings to wherever they were most needed. This involved reducing the already low levels of financing in various sectors while maintaining prices at artificially low levels....

Cuba's economic shock, and its insufficient attempt at adjustment, generated an enormous fiscal deficit which by 1993 equalled 40 per cent of GDP.... The government simply could not reduce its expenditures quickly enough to offset the reductions in its exports and fiscal revenues. Given the absence of both external financing and internal capital markets, the government had almost no alternative but to print money to cover its deficit. Consequently, the economy was flooded with liquidity. The amount of pesos in circulation increased from 5 billion in 1990 to 11.4 billion in 1993. In a capitalist regime, such an increase in liquidity would have created inflation; however, in Cuba's centrally planned economy, the effects were different. Since official prices did not change, people suddenly had more money to spend than products to buy. Huge shortages spurred the proliferation of black markets, which paved the way for the development of a separate economy within Cuba.

DIFFICULT DECISIONS, 1993–1995

Confronting the reality of his country's economic situation, Fidel Castro announced to his people on 26 July 1993: 'Today life, reality ... forces us to do what we would have never done otherwise ... we must make concessions.' Among the concessions made to salvage the Cuban economy were agricultural reforms, provisions for self-employment, the legalization of foreign hard currency, the liberalization of foreign investment, exchange rate and monetary reform, and fiscal reforms.

Agricultural Reforms

The two main concessions that the Cuban government made in the agricultural sector were the dismantling of the state farm system and the creation of a capitalist-style farmers' market.

First, in July 1993, Fidel Castro announced the dismantling of the large state-run farms and the leasing of state land to private producers, such as families and village cooperatives. Under this reform, the Basic Cooperatives of Production, or UBPCs (Unidades Básicas de Producción Cooperativa), received the right to use the land they worked for an indefinite period of time, own their harvest, hold bank accounts, and freely elect their own management. Although the cooperative production system does not provide for private ownership of the land, it is designed to give farmers greater control over the factors of production....

Second, Castro's brother, Raúl, announced that beginning on 1 October 1994, a free market system in agricultural products would encompass the entire agricultural sector. After selling to the state an obligatory quota of 80 per cent of their crops, in accordance with the state procurement system, individual farmers and cooperatives could sell their products at farmers' markets, where goods are sold at prices determined by supply and demand. In the farmers' markets, located in each of Cuba's provinces, prices can be several times greater than the prices paid by the government for the same product. Despite higher prices, the farmers' market has helped to alleviate shortages in the food supply and to moderate the highly inflationary black market for food. It has also created a system of incentives to spur production in the once heavily regulated, and thus highly inefficient, crop harvests.

The agricultural sector has become one of the most liberalized sectors of the Cuban economy. A large amount of foreign investment has helped to ease shortages of inputs and has provided farmers with even higher incomes. In fact, farmers are becoming a somewhat affluent group in Cuban society. By the end of 1995, their savings represented nearly 75 per cent of all private savings in Cuba. As a result, farmers have begun to ask for more freedom and less government intervention in their industry.

Self-Employment

A second concession made by Castro occurred in mid-1993 when the Cuban National Assembly allowed self-employment in over 100 occupations. By late 1995 there were over 130 vocations which Cubans could practise privately. These included the 'profession' of bicycle repairman, hairdresser, plumber, electrician, taxi driver, cook, shoemaker, babysitter, and 'restorer of dolls and other toys'. Although private employment is subject to restrictions, such as licensing and an income tax, until recently it was permitted more by exceptions than by formal permision....

In order to be eligible for self-employment, applicants must be government employees, home-makers, handicapped or displaced state workers receiving unemployment compensation. By December 1994 over 110,000 Cubans had joined the ranks of the self-employed. Moreover, of the 2.2 million people currently employed by public enterprises in Cuba, some 500,000–800,000 are likely to be relieved of their jobs and encouraged to become self-employed.

While self-employment has curbed some black market activities, it is encouraging other illegalities. As in other sectors, self-employed production is limited by input shortages. Since inputs are provided by the state, and are often unavailable, entrepreneurs must acquire their inputs illegally in a growing black market for supplies that are usually stolen from state companies. Until the government can acquire the foreign exchange necessary to fulfil the demand for inputs, there will be continued illegal growth in the self-employed sector.

Legalization of Foreign Hard Currency

Commonly referred to as 'dollarization', this third concession was a direct response to black markets. Through remittances, tourism and foreign investment, the dollar economy began to expand in Cuba, and black market activities soared. Since illegal dollar transactions were already commonplace among Cubans, the government decided it must redirect dollar flows through regulated internal trade. [In 1993,] Cubans were allowed to hold foreign currency, have bank accounts in dollars, and to pay for services in dollars. Eventually, in December 1994, the government made its national currency convertible to the dollar. Finally, the government established several stores that sold goods to the Cubans in dollars.

By these measures Castro enabled his government to monitor and control the flow of dollars in Cuba, and provided his country with another channel of foreign exchange earnings. In fact, the Cuban 'dollarization' was intended to attract dollar remittances from Cuban families in the United States by providing a market in which the dollar could circulate legally. However, in August 1994 the US government prohibited these cash flows to Cuba in response to an increase in unauthorized immigration. Despite the restriction, dollar remittances from Cubans in exile still total approximately $500 million a year. Moreover, those Cubans who have access to dollars through remittances from relatives in exile, or from ties to the external sector via foreign investment, can do better financially than those who have access only to pesos. Given the emergence of this apparent stratification in Cuba, 'dollarization' will have important implications for Cuba's economic and political future.

Foreign Investment

Perhaps the most effective concession the Cuban government has made in addressing its economic crisis has been the opening of the economy to foreign investment. The National Assembly... established a legal framework within which state property could be transferred to joint ventures with foreign investors.... Cuba lured potential investors by offering them financial incentives such as tax holidays and debt-for-equity swaps. In November 1994 Cuban officials reported that they had established 165 joint ventures with partners from 35 different countries. Parallel to the joint-venture agreements, Cuba signed investment protection agreements with its partners, guaranteeing the right of the investor to repatriate profits as well as the abstention of the Cuban government from nationalizing physical capital. Finally, in September 1995 the Assembly passed a new foreign investment law, which allowed foreign investors 100 per cent ownership of their enterprises.

Cuba's joint-venture agreements in 1994 totalled more than $2 billion in promised investment... by the following year, nearly $5 billion in promised investment was reported.... Initially, the majority of investments were in the tourism industry, namely hotels and beach resorts. In fact, in 1994, tourism displaced sugar as the principal source of foreign exchange, earning $800 million, or 35 per cent of Cuba's total dollar revenue, against $700 million generated by the sugar industry that year. In 1995, tourism became a $1 billion industry. Meanwhile, the demand for inputs and financing in other sectors led to joint ventures in agriculture (mainly tobacco and citrus), mining (nickel, lead, gold and chrome), oil and coal, telecommunications, and textiles.

Through foreign investment provisions alone, Cuba has been able to acquire the foreign capital necessary to alleviate its chronic input shortages, which in turn has allowed resumption of production. Consequently, foreign investment has proven to be one of the most significant engines for growth in Cuba. Nevertheless, it has also created within Cuba a dual economy: a free-market, dollar economy, in which foreign investment occurs, and a centrally planned, peso economy. As Cuba's economic recovery proceeds, the free-market economy will continue to make inroads upon the centrally planned economy. The encroachment of capitalism poses a dilemma for a socialist country in desperate need of continued, sustainable economic growth.

Exchange Rate and Monetary Reform

The dollar has been circulating legally in Cuba since [1993,] and official 1995 estimates claimed that 21 per cent of the population had access to dollars. [In 1993] the peso, which had official parity against the dollar, was being traded in the free, 'unofficial' market at rates as low as 150 pesos per dollar. By 1994 the unofficial exchange rate of the peso had appreciated from 150 to 35 pesos per dollar, and it continued to appreciate slightly over the next year to between 20 and 30 pesos per dollar. This appreciation of the peso occurred in part because of a contraction in the money supply, which in turn made people more willing to exchange dollars for their improved domestic currency. However, despite the appreciation, the difference between the private and official exchange rates remained quite large and generated huge distortions in the economy. For example, in 1995 the price of rice and beans in an 'unofficial market', such as a farmers' market, where dollars can be used, equalled about 9 pesos per pound, while the government paid farmers approximately 0.27 pesos per pound in the official market.

The difference in prices between the official and the unofficial markets was a direct reflection of the difference in official and unofficial exchange rates. Such a difference was the result of what the Cuban minister for finance and prices, José Luis Rodriguez, called 'monetary overhang'. In essence, monetary overhang is the circulation of a currency, such as the US dollar, which exerts inflationary pressures on the domestic currency. Despite the fiscal discipline of 1994 and the contraction of the peso supply, the US dollar still distorted prices in trade that occurred beyond government regulation.

At the end of 1994 the National Assembly decided to create the convertible peso in an effort to unify exchange rates and reduce monetary overhang. Consequently, Cuba now has three currencies in circulation: US dollars, pesos and convertible pesos. Thus far, there is no indication that Cuba has made any progress towards unification of exchange rates....

Fiscal Reforms

Finally, the Cuban government was forced to balance its own fiscal account. To do this, the government had to increase its revenues, and its sources of revenue, while reducing expenditures, namely government subsidies and salaries. These reforms have enjoyed a significant degree of initial success: the fiscal deficit fell from 40 per cent of GDP in 1993 to 7.4 per cent of GDP in 1994, and then to 3.6 per cent in 1995.... But the continued successful management of Cuban fiscal policy underscores the inherent contradiction of Cuba's transition: that the command structure of the economy attempts to marginalize the market reforms upon which Cuba depends exclusively for its growth.

In pursuit of increased revenues, in August 1994 the National Assembly announced a tax on property and income that would take effect the following year. The income tax affected the newly self-employed as well as UBPC members and independent farmers. In all, taxes were increased by 24 per cent. Also, as part of an earlier initiative, the Assembly raised prices on a variety of state goods and services including postal services, transport, fuel and electricity.

Concurrently, in order to rein in government expenditures, the National Assembly made perhaps its most difficult decision: it eliminated 15 ministries from the central government and reduced subsidies for education, and health. In ideological terms, this decision was tantamount to a compromising of the revolution....

Of all these reforms, Cuba's fiscal restructuring will continue to have some of the most profound effects on the social, political and economic transition of the island. In streamlining state government and enterprises, the Cuban leadership acknowledged that it would have to expand the number of people who are self-employed in trades and crafts. But so far the expansion process has been hampered by internal debate among leaders over the degree to which they are willing to withdraw state control in order to reduce structural unemployment. Meanwhile, as the structure of the economy remains in flux, the Cuban leadership must decide whether it is willing to ignore, in the name of socialism, the consequences of its urgently needed fiscal reforms. . . .

It is upon this potentially fragile moment in Cuba's history, when Cuba is enduring the social, economic and political strains of transition, that Helms–Burton seeks to prey. However, it is difficult to imagine that a leader like Castro, whose keen sense of survival has enabled him to outlast eight American presidents and the end of Soviet subsidies, would ignore the need to make further concessions in the name of his regime's political and economic survival. Although Castro has admitted that he tried to avoid making the difficult decisions he has had to make, he nevertheless made them, and it is certain that he would allow his country's new market dynamic to progress far enough to evade the effects of Helms–Burton. Indeed, the political and economic developments on the island this year suggest that Castro may have reached a safe distance from the dangers of sanctions abroad and unrest at home.

PERSPECTIVES ON CUBA'S ECONOMIC REFORMS, 1996

The reforms enacted so far have halted Cuba's economic decline, but they do not represent a coherent plan for recovery. Cuba's piecemeal reforms do, however, bear some resemblance to a China-style growth strategy. By allowing foreign investment in certain sectors, the Cuban government hopes to generate growth in exports and employment sufficient to spur overall growth; meanwhile, it continues to avoid reform in other sectors. This strategy, which stands in contrast to the 'big-bang' approach followed in eastern Europe and the former Soviet Union, requires Cuba to manage a dual economy: the majority of the economy remains under central planning while a market sector, operating under free market forces, develops next to it. . . .

From 1993 to 1995, the Cuban government had to make difficult new reforms in order to counteract the consequences of its previous insufficient adjustment. . . . The Castro regime has grudgingly acceded to the use of isolated exposures to free market forces as safety valves for the wounded economy. However, the safety valves have proven themselves to be the only effective engine for growth in Cuba. In the resulting dilemma, the socialist regime has had to sacrifice its ideals in order to survive.

Cuba's economic shock has ended. In fact, the economy posted a slight increase in activity in 1994 and 1995. More important, several key sectors have reported tremendous growth in 1996 including tourism and agriculture (both over 30 per cent). These gains resulted in a 40 per cent growth in exports, a 5 per cent increase in GDP and a fiscal deficit of less than 3 per cent of GDP. . . . However, it is too soon to argue that the Cuban economy is well on its way to recovery. Cuba has endured an intense contraction in its economy over a short period of time. The high subsequent growth rates of some sectors must be measured in relation to the extremely low previous levels of income. Nevertheless, double-digit growth rates in such key sectors of the economy demonstrate the effectiveness of the free-market reforms, and reinforce the notion that the economic shock has ended. Cuba's greatest challenge may be to sustain its growth in the future and prevent the distortions between the two coexisting economic systems from producing dramatic social inequality and corruption, while maintaining an economic balance between the two systems such that the success of the capitalist reforms does not precipitate the dissolution of the socialist regime....

To be sure, Castro made his difficult policy decisions not because he had abandoned the ideals of socialism, but because he found himself with no other choice. He stated publicly that he hated doing what he felt he had to do for the good of his country. However, given his decision, it became possible to envision a US policy towards Cuba that might capitalize upon the fact that Castro must make concessions, thereby leading Cuba into a new economic and political era. Yet, at a crucial phase in Cuba's transition, the United States has frittered away the opportunity to craft such a productive policy through harsher economic sanctions and legal squabbles over property rights.

IMPLICATIONS OF HELMS–BURTON: US INTERESTS

Helms–Burton has negative implications for the new phase in US–Cuba relations now opening. In particular, Helms–Burton will erode the more cooperative tone of the relationship between the two countries which had emerged prior to the events of 1996. More widely, it threatens to undermine US influence in the world by straining America's relations with its allies and former enemies alike; and, ultimately, it compromises the US interest of fostering a peaceful transition in Cuba from dictatorship to democracy.

Specifically, tightening the economic embargo on Cuba strains the new US–Cuba immigration accord. The agreement of 2 May 1995, negotiated by Cuban National Assembly President Ricardo Alarcón and US Under-Secretary of State Peter Tarnoff, effectively ended a 30-year open-door immigration policy for refugees fleeing Cuba. For the American part, this agreement requires a more liberal screening process of Cuban emigrés who seek political asylum through the proper legal channels in Havana. On the Cuban side, it secures a promise not to harass those nationals seeking asylum, and simultaneously prohibits the regime from encouraging massive boatlifts of illegal immigrants to the United States, as it did from Mariel Harbor in 1980 and in August 1994. Now, any Cuban national attempting to enter the United States illegally will be intercepted by the US Coast Guard and repatriated.

Although the Tarnoff–Alarcón agreement appeared to be a stop-gap solution to the immigration crisis begun in August 1994, it is, more importantly, a crucial step towards fostering a negotiation process between two bitter enemies. Tarnoff–Alarcón has enjoyed almost complete success, but tighter sanctions could eventually force Castro to reopen the infamous economic safety valve of Mariel. Such a development would completely undermine the small, hard-won progress that the United States has made towards negotiations on immigration and civil rights issues. Moreover, by codifying the embargo, Helms–Burton limits the authority of the President to refine and conduct US Cuba policy in pursuit of the national interest.

Helms–Burton undermines US influence in the world community by testing the limits of international law. By allowing US citizens to sue traffickers of confiscated property in US federal courts, Title III threatens the principles of the international legal system. Such recourse, if [ever allowed,] would be contrary to the principle of international law which holds that the United States must accept as legal the expropriation of property by a sovereign country. Although Helms–Burton does not accept Cuba's sovereignty, it also rejects, in effect, the sovereignty of virtually every major US ally and trading partner.

Quite apart from international legal principle, Helms–Burton may violate the General Agreement on Tariffs and Trade (GATT), the North American Free Trade Agreement (NAFTA) and the procedures of the World Trade Organization (WTO). On 17 June 1996 Canada and Mexico announced efforts to convene an official dispute-resolution panel under NAFTA to contest the denial of visas under Title IV provisions, maintaining that by denying free entry into the United States to business executives and their families for doing business with Cuba, Helms–Burton violated provisions of the free trade agreement.

Furthermore, all of the most important US trading partners—Japan, Mexico, Canada and the 15-nation European Union (EU)—have raised a cacophony of protest against Helms–Burton and lodged complaints with the WTO. In particular, the EU began proceedings in May to challenge the 'extraterritorial implications' of the US 'secondary boycott'. The results of these complaints and actions could weaken future US complaints in the WTO against members such as Japan, where some markets remain relatively closed to US competitors. Thus the compensation acquired through Helms–Burton sanctions hardly seems worth the loss of political capital that the United States stands to suffer with its trading partners in the WTO and NAFTA.

The conflict inherent in Helms–Burton lies in the issue of the sovereignty of US allies in the conduct not simply of economic policy, but of foreign policy as well. Canada and the nations of western Europe have maintained normal economic relations with Cuba and simultaneously promoted a transition to democracy. Most notably, Spain has both advised Cuba on its fiscal reforms and also promoted a dialogue between the Cuban government and moderate opposition groups in an attempt to create greater political pluralism. Moreover, Spanish initiatives have led to the release of scores of political prisoners in Cuba each year. Although British ties with Cuba have been mainly commercial, its signals of support for reform have manifested themselves in high-level delegations and aid for development projects. Finally, Canada's improved relations with Cuba have been marked by development aid, support for the end of Cuba's exclusion from the Organization of American States, and the encouragement of regular visits by Cuban government ministers. Proponents of these policies of engagement argue that sustained contacts through commerce, aid and diplomacy are more effective in leading Cuba towards a peaceful transition to democracy than the punitive and confrontational measures of the United States.

Helms–Burton is inconsistent with post–Cold War US policy of reconciliation with its former communist adversaries. The 1995 agreement with North Korea on its nuclear policy and the 12 July 1995 decision to normalize relations with Vietnam stand in stark contrast to US policy towards Cuba. Furthermore, the United States already has substantial trade relations with another infamous violator of human rights: China. In addition to its most favoured nation trade status with the United States, China is a member of US-based international lending institutions. Furthermore, the most potentially dangerous external effect of Helms–Burton could be to strain relations between the United States and Russia. The provision for monetary reprisal against Russia for its support of the Lourdes intelligence facility threatens a crucial link in US–Russia relations, since the Russian government could choose not to ratify the START II Treaty without the ability, provided by Lourdes, to monitor US treaty compliance. Thus, not only is Helms–Burton inconsistent with overall US post–Cold War policy, it also contains the makings of a step backwards, towards a cooling of US–Russian relations. The cost of enforcing Helms–Burton in an era of improved international relations is incalculable. Ridding the world of Fidel Castro does not warrant the potential damage it does to the US national interest.

Finally, Helms–Burton goes beyond the point of diminishing returns by compromising the very US interest it purports to achieve: the peaceful transition in Cuba from dictatorship to democracy. Increased sanctions are not the most effective tool for hastening a peaceful transition. Moreover, according to the latest full-scale Pentagon-commissioned report on US–Cuba policy, 'Cuba is already a nation in historic transition', and will 'continue to change over the next two to four years'. The report notes that Cuban military leaders, who occupy an important niche in Cuba's political framework, support transition towards market reform. This means that Castro is likely to retain his leadership in the future, provided that he continues his economic re-

forms, and any discontent will probably dissipate with further economic progress. However, as the report also indicates, social and economic instability (a primary aim of Helms–Burton) would have 'profound' implications for the United States, such as unstoppable waves of refugees or 'large scale violence in Cuba (for example, mass resistance to the Castro Government or civil war between organized military units) [which] would generate intense pressure for US intervention.' Thus Helms–Burton needlessly propels US policy in a direction opposite its own interests.

CONCLUSION

In recent years, the Cuban government has had to carry out difficult new reforms in order to recover from the loss of Soviet subsidies. Cuba has enjoyed relative success in its piecemeal reforms, as it has demonstrated with at least two years of initial growth. Nevertheless, it has also created a dual economy in which the government must constantly confront the dilemma of a command structure that depends on free-market forces for its recovery. Desperate for sustained growth, the Cuban government is likely to continue to concede additional reforms, albeit at a decreasing pace. Thus the Cuban economy, as well as its politico-legal regime, is already in a state of flux independent of US influence. The economic progress achieved by Cuba in the absence of Soviet aid bodes ill for the notion that Castro can be toppled through increased economic sanctions.

For over 35 years, economic sanctions have not proven an effective 'tool of democracy'. In fact, given Cuba's relative success at liberalization, and the promise that it holds for future growth, the

US embargo against Cuba has reached the point of diminishing returns. On 16 July 1996, [and again on 3 January 1997,] President Clinton delayed the enforcement of Helms–Burton's Title III, thereby averting a wave of retaliatory legislation from its allies over the right of US citizens to sue foreign companies and individuals trafficking in confiscated assets. Instead, Clinton held out the threat of its use in the future to persuade foreign nations to adhere to the US embargo. However, the President would be well advised to consider an approach which is mindful of European and Canadian sovereignty as well as those countries' policies of engagement. In light of the deleterious effects of Helms–Burton on US influence in the international community, it is difficult to assess whether the Act will prove more harmful to Cuba or the United States. But it is certain that the continued pursuit of a punitive 'secondary boycott' will compromise more US interests than it will promote.

NO

Alberto J. Mora

STATEMENT OF ALBERTO J. MORA

Thank you, Mr. Chairman, and other distinguished members of the Committee. I am honored by the invitation to testify before you today on the Cuban Liberty and Democratic Solidarity (LIBERTAD) Act, a bill whose enactment represents a watershed event both in the advancement of the international law on expropriation and the effort to encourage and assist the transition to democracy in Cuba....

The Helms-Burton Act is a novel and complex piece of legislation that seeks to accomplish a variety of interlaced remedial and foreign policy objectives using multiple tools. Yet the bill was conceived and gestated in controversy. Indeed, its very passage was in doubt until the Cuban regime's cold-hearted and unjustified destruction of two unarmed civilian aircraft and four human rights activists, three of them U.S. citizens, consolidated national support behind the bill. Following its enactment and the administration's early enforcement efforts, Helms-Burton generated acute international opposition, including threats of legal reprisals, even among close allies such as Canada and the European Community. Some nations have already adopted countermeasures. Challenges as to the bill's compliance with international law are commonly heard. So too are questions as to the wisdom of its central policy assumption that tighter sanctions, not the normalization of commercial ties, are the surest path to Cuban democracy.

Much of the international controversy that surrounds Helms-Burton appears to stem from a fundamental misunderstanding as to what the Act is and does. Even policy statements issued by foreign governments criticizing the Act—which one would presume would contain a measure of sophistication—ascribe to Helms-Burton characteristics that it does not have or, alternatively, recite conclusory statements that are unsupported by analysis. Regrettably, these misguided criticisms can now be said to have coalesced overseas into a type of conventional wisdom that Helms-Burton constitutes an impermissible attempt by the United States to extend its extraterritorial jurisdiction.

These hearings are therefore timely. More than four months after the enactment of the Act, it is time to take stock, to engage the critics, and to clear up

From U.S. Senate. Committee on Foreign Relations. *The Libertad Act: Implementation and International Law.* Hearing, July 30, 1996. Washington, DC: Government Printing Office, 1996. (S.Hrg 104-564.) Notes omitted.

any misunderstandings. We should ask ourselves: has Helms-Burton advanced its remedial and foreign policy objectives? Is the Act good law or, as some allege, unlawful under international law as an unwarranted extension of U.S. jurisdiction? Does it provide an effective remedy for those U.S. citizens who lost property as a result of confiscations by the Cuban regime but received no compensation? Does it advance the cause of Cuban democracy? Lastly, does the international opposition to the Act annul its hoped-for benefits?

I have concluded that Helms-Burton is achieving the legal and foreign policy objectives that its proponents intended. Moreover:

- The Helms-Burton Act is consistent with international law;
- The Act represents a new standard for state practice in response to international violations of property rights. Thus, it could help shape the development of customary international law in a direction that is more protective of such rights;
- The Act establishes effective and desirable remedies—but not cure-alls—for those U.S. citizens who suffered uncompensated expropriations at the hands of the Cuban regime. Fewer claimants than expected will actually recover compensation from traffickers as a result of Title III actions, while more than anticipated could benefit from the cumulative effect of the Act's other sanctions and, in addition, from post-transition property settlements with a democratic Cuban Government;
- The Act is and will continue to be effective in reducing trafficking in confiscated property, and thus will both put pressure on the Cuban regime to liberalize its economy and will facilitate the settlement of U.S. property claims in the post-Castro era; and
- Notwithstanding the international opposition to the Act (which is serious and should not be taken lightly), the Helms-Burton Act should cause foreign governments to reexamine policies that for too long have operated oblivious to the Cuban regime's widespread violations of property and human rights, and thus could lead to greater and more effective international pressure for change in Cuba.

Each of these five conclusions is discussed in greater detail below.

Helms-Burton Complies With International Law

At the risk of oversimplification, what the Helms-Burton Act does is to provide U.S. nationals whose property in Cuba was confiscated without payment of appropriate compensation with a series of remedies against those who traffic in the property and who are found within the jurisdiction of the United States. It is not to be confused, as it apparently frequently is, as an effort by the U.S. Government to interdict commerce with Cuba that has no linkage to the confiscated property. The Act —including Title III, which permits claimants to bring civil lawsuits against traffickers in the U.S. District Courts—is in full conformity with international law.

In my view, many who take the contrary view fail to understand the true target of Helms-Burton—which is to block commerce (or trafficking) in stolen property, rather than block otherwise lawful trade with or investment in Cuba—and fail to grasp the jurisdictional underpinnings of the Act. A review of Helms-Burton's target and its jurisdictional basis should help establish its legality under international law.

Trafficking in stolen property. The Cuban regime's wholesale confiscation of property belonging to U.S. nationals and Cuban citizens (some of whom are now U.S. nationals) without payment of compensation violated, depending on the circumstances, international law, Cuban domestic law, and human rights norms. The property which Helms-Burton addresses is, therefore, stolen. Under principles of jurisprudence common in most countries throughout the world, those who with intent aid and abet the unlawful taking away of someone else's property are guilty of larceny, as are those who knowingly receive the stolen property. Generally accepted principles of jurisprudence also provide that theft cannot divest the owner of title to the property.

Indeed, the remedial measures adopted by the Act, in particular the private cause of action created by Title III, merely facilitate the assertion of commonplace claims, such as conversion and trespass, that could have been asserted in court against traffickers under the common law even without Helms-Burton. With the possible additional exception of the treble damages provision, perhaps the most significant effect of Title III was... to neutralize the act of state doctrine as a potential defense to claims brought under the Act.

That U.S nationals who suffered uncompensated expropriations at the hands of the Cuban regime should thus have rights which they may be interested in asserting against those responsible for their losses, including traffickers, should

be cause for neither objection nor surprise, particularly on the part of traffickers with prior notice. And, indeed, the right of the U.S. claimants to obtain compensation appears to be widely accepted. With the claimants' right to compensation thus established, the only remaining issue is whether the remedies fashioned by Helms-Burton to obtain this compensation are appropriate as applied to non-U.S. nationals under international law. This becomes an issue of jurisdiction.

The jurisdictional underpinnings of Helms-Burton. Most of the international criticism of Helms-Burton appears to conclude that the Act is unlawful under international law because it constitutes an excessive exercise of "extraterritorial" jurisdiction by the United States. This criticism is misplaced and reflects a misunderstanding of what Helms-Burton provides or its jurisdictional bases or both. In point of fact, Helms-Burton has a solid jurisdictional base under three jurisdictional doctrines: territorial sovereignty, the "effects" doctrine, and protective jurisdiction.

Of these three jurisdictional bases, the extent to which the territorial is perhaps the principal jurisdictional basis for the Helms-Burton Act deserves to be better understood. Although the Act clearly vests subject matter jurisdiction over trafficking cases in U.S. district courts, it is arguably silent as the extent to which personal jurisdiction is to be extended or not extended over potential defendants. Such silence has been interpreted to create a presumption against the extraterritorial application of statutes, a presumption that is perhaps also strengthened by the Supreme Court's stated policy of exercising "great care and reserve" when extending U.S. notions of personal jurisdiction into the international field.

As a result, the judicial exercise of personal jurisdiction over any Helms-Burton defendant is forbidden unless the requirements of the Due Process Clauses of the United States Constitution —which in fact are intended to guard against excessive exercises of jurisdiction —are met. As established by the Supreme Court in the seminal *International Shoe* case:

> [D]ue process requires only that in order to subject a defendant to a judgment *in personam*, if he be not present within the territory of the forum, he have certain minimum contacts with it such that the maintenance of the suit does not offend "traditional notions of fair play and substantial justice."

The court further refined this holding in *Hanson* v. *Denckla*, one of the many subsequent cases to develop the "minimum contacts" test, when it stated that it was "essential" in each case "that there be some act by which the defendant purposefully avails itself of the privilege of conducting activities within the forum state, thus invoking the benefits and protections of its laws."

Although this due process analysis could be extended much further, it is sufficient for purposes of answering those critics of Helms-Burton who assert that the Act constitutes an unwarranted "extraterritorial" assertion of U.S. jurisdiction to point out that, in fact, due process safeguards will require that there be evidence of minimum contacts with the United States and purposeful acts that "invok[e] the benefits and protections" of U.S. laws. Such requirements will shift the jurisdictional basis of Helms-Burton much closer to the territorial concept. In addition, since it can be presumed that many traffickers do not have the requisite minimum contacts with the United States—or, in some cases, any contacts— they will also probably result in a significant reduction in the number of potential defendants who run the risk of Title III liability.

Helms-Burton Is Helping International Law Develop into a More Effective Instrument to Protect Property Rights

International law develops through the practices and behavior of states over time; state practice which becomes accepted and emulated such that it becomes normative gradually attains the status of law. Although, as noted above, the protection of the property rights of citizens and aliens is enshrined in international law and human rights principles, the failure of the international system to respond effectively to Cuba's violation of the property rights of U.S. nationals demonstrates how ineffective the mechanism to enforce those rights can be.

Helms-Burton, as an example of pathbreaking state practice, can help bring about a better system. The Act empowers victims of property rights violations with the tools to assert and protect their claims while at the same time reinforcing the efforts of individual claimants through meaningful state sanctions against those who would profit from the illegally-confiscated property. Two other historical examples help illustrate why Helms-Burton, and subsequent Helms-Burton models as appropriately modified, should gain broader acceptance to protect property and human rights.

The first example was the systematic dispossession of property suffered by Jews during the Holocaust. The conscience recoils both at the magnitude of the injustice perpetrated through the Nazi expropriation decrees and the notion that traffickers in the expropriated property could be benefiting from the fruits of this historic crime. Yet the injustice continues unresolved despite some efforts on the part of individual nations to address the wrong.

In a more contemporary setting, we can easily imagine the perpetrators of "ethnic cleansing" in the former Yugoslavia, both individuals and nations, seeking to profit by the possession or sale of property acquired through this barbaric practice. Legislation and norms of international law based on the Helms-Burton model could be effective in helping protect the property and human rights of the victims as well as in helping dissuade others who might be tempted to engage in the practice from believing that they could profit from it.

Helms-Burton's Remedial Measures Are Effective in Advancing the Property Interests of U.S. Nationals Who Suffered Confiscations in Cuba

With respect to individual claimants, Helms-Burton's remedial measures are designed to do two things: to obtain compensation for losses through Title III and, in the event compensation is unavailable, to position the claimant in a more favorable position to assert a property claim in a democratic Cuba by helping eliminate clouds on title. Although it is somewhat premature to draw a final conclusion, it appears that Helms-Burton is succeeding on both counts. This is less so, however, in obtaining compensation than in providing greater protection for the rights of U.S. nationals in post–Castro Cuba.

The Helms-Burton Act's effectiveness stems not only or even primarily from Title III (although its *in terrorem* effect is considerable), but from its entire body of interrelated remedial measures and sanctions. In my view, the amount of litigation filed as the result of Title III is likely to be quite small, more on the order of a few hundreds of cases (if that), rather than the thousands or even hundreds of thousands of cases that some have fancifully predicted.

Title III will not generate the volume of litigation predicted because claimants will not select litigation as the initial or preferred recovery strategy given the availability of other Helms-Burton weapons. In addition, they are aware or will soon become aware that in Title III litigation they will encounter the difficulties common to all transnational litigation, difficulties which are certain to be compounded by the fact that Cuba, a hostile nation, has the closest relationship to the subject matter of the litigation. These difficulties will be encountered in attempting to: obtain initial information to identify trafficking and the traffickers involved; obtain personal jurisdiction over many of the traffickers; obtain the evidence necessary to establish the unlawful trafficking; identify defendant's assets and collect upon judgments, if the assets are overseas; and the expense, delay, and risk associated with litigation generally. In addition to these hurdles, one can also anticipate as additional difficulties the enactment of legislation which various nations have announced in response to Helms-Burton, including blocking and clawback statutes and other types of retaliatory legislation. As a result, it can be forecast that entities at highest risk from Title III actions will be the large multinational entities engaged in visible, high-value projects in Cuba and also operating in the United States. For other types of companies or ventures, the litigation risk could drop sharply.

That there should be less recourse to Title III litigation than initially anticipated does not detract from the effectiveness of the Act's remedial measures. Indeed, it would appear from anecdotal evidence that traffickers or potential traffickers come to regard the Act's other measures—potential identification as a Cuban trading partner, the threat to relationships with U.S. financial institutions if U.S. financing is used in trafficking; and, in particular, possible Title IV exclusion from the United States—as sanctions which may be sufficient independent of Title III to dissuade engagement in trafficking.

Claimants are also aware, of course, of these other non-Title III measures. One can anticipate, therefore, that most claimants will seek the path of least resistance and risk in attempting to assert their property rights. A claimant is thus likely to start the bidding by dispatching to the trafficker a notification of his claim coupled with a demand for entry into immediate settlement negotiations. If the threat (or application) of non-Title III sanctions are insufficient to induce a satisfactory settlement, Title IV always remains as the remedy of last resort.

Although there are no reports yet of any Helms-Burton settlements, the logic of Helms-Burton and the uncertainties surrounding post-transition disposition of property claims in Cuba suggest that entry into settlements could have significant advantages for both claimants and at least certain classes of traffickers. Those traffickers which have investments in Cuba, particularly in real property, understand that they have two hurdles to surmount before being assured of a long-term presence in Cuba: (1) Helms-Burton and (2) post–Castro property claims. By entering into settlements, traffickers can structure agreements that can eliminate the Helms-Burton risk and greatly minimize post-transition uncertainties.

Helms-Burton Is Effective in Promoting Democratic Change in Cuba

In addition to creating its remedial measures. Helms-Burton can also be said to constitute a foreign policy initiative in that it seeks to advance two long-standing U.S. objectives regarding Cuba: to promote democratic change and to hamper the regime's exercise of totalitarian control over the Cuban population. I believe that Helms-Burton is achieving these objectives as well.

The 37 years of the Castro regime provide ample evidence by which to judge its nature and to predict its future policies. As the regime creaks towards extinction—and its longevity is likely to be exactly congruent with the span of Castro's life—it behaves as it always has and always will, dedicated only and to no higher principle than to the obsession of ensuring its continued grip on power at whatever cost to the Cuban people. Unfazed and unembarrassed by the demise of its putative model, the Soviet Union, or of its organizing ideology, marxism, the regime stands naked in its simple determination to adopt only such economic "reforms" as economic circumstances force it to adopt and proudly declares its intent to dispense with them as soon as circumstances might permit.

Competent only at its own perpetuation, the Castro regime otherwise boasts a record of economic achievement that could only be considered as spectacularly incompetent were the improvement in the living standard of the population an objective, which it does not appear to be. Once the second richest nation in all of Latin America, Cuba is now well into its fourth decade of food rationing and has a standard of living hovering near Haiti's; its housing and infrastructure are returning to the state of nature through neglect and lack of maintenance; and the growth of its tourism sector depends in no small measure upon Cuba's reputation as the sexual tourism (i.e., prostitution) capital of the Western Hemisphere.

None of this is the fault of the United States. Cuba's devastated condition is not the function of U.S. foreign policy, but of Castro's own war against the Cuban people. It is not as if the formula for prosperity were a mystery. In the 18th century Adam Smith observed that "little else is requisite to carry a state to the highest degree of opulence from the lowest barbarism, but peace, easy taxes, and tolerable administration of justice." Castro, of course, has chosen contrary policies. Rather than peace, war: class struggle, foreign adventures, near constant military mobilization. Rather than easy taxes, implying the encouragement of a vibrant private sector, socialization: the near total confiscation of all property and the implacable effort to destroy private enterprise. Rather than justice and the rule of law, its destruction and replacement by the arbitrary rule of (one) man: himself.

Nothing in the history of the Castro regime, either before or after the demise of the Soviet Union, suggests that allowing the regime access to Western trade, investment, or tourism has had the slightest effect in prompting reform or weakening the regime's despotic rule. Certainly no claim to this effect has ever, to my knowledge, been advanced by the countries of the European Community despite their unbroken trade and investment relations with Cuba. If there is an historical analogy to be found it is to Ceausescu's Romania, which was for a long time believed to have been influenced to adopt moderate domestic and international policies by access to Western trade and credits. After Ceausescu's overthrow it was determined that the contrary had occurred: rather than moderating the dictator's behavior (which turned out to be among the most brutal in Eastern Europe), the additional resources obtained from Western sources only strengthened the regime's despotism.

So it is and will be with the Castro regime. With our without trade and investment from the United States and the other democratic nations, Castro will continue to steer the same circular course he plotted for himself and his nation decades ago. By enacting Helms-Burton the United States signals that it will not—as other countries have—abandon principle to align itself with his despotism and adopts measures that, by complicating Castro's governance problems, loosen his grip on the tiller of power. To that extent at least, the Act encourages the development of democracy on the island. At a minimum, Helms-Burton will facilitate as well the consolidation of democracy by simplifying the post-transition property claims of U.S. nationals.

Helms-Burton Is Effective in Compelling a Reexamination of International Tolerance for the Castro Regime

Out of the international furor surrounding the enactment of Helms-Burton, it is becoming increasingly apparent that

Helms-Burton could produce an additional, if initially unintended, effect: the reexamination by many nations of "hear no evil, see no evil, and speak no evil" diplomatic and commercial policies that treat Cuba, however perversely, as if it were a normal country, that is, as if the regime's continued existence did not depend—as it does—on systematic repression, the denial of human rights, and the control of property that was obtained unlawfully.

This effect will now be accelerated and, one hopes, pursued systematically as the result of the administration's announcement that it would work with the international community on a series of steps to promote democracy in Cuba, including:

Increasing pressure on the regime to open up politically and economically; supporting forces for change on the island; withholding foreign assistance to Cuba; and promoting business practices that will help bring democracy to the Cuban workplace.

As long as these measures—another direct result from Helms-Burton's enactments—are pursued energetically and the filing of Title III law suits remains a possibility, the temporary suspension of the right to file a Title III action can be considered to be an acceptable cost to pay in return for a significant potential return. In addition, the suspension does not materially affect, at least for a time, the ability of U.S. nationals to pursue their rights through direct negotiations with traffickers or the Act's deterrent effect on trafficking.

CONCLUSION

In conclusion, the Helms-Burton Act is consistent with international law, is effective in protecting the property rights of U.S. nationals which were violated by the Cuban regime, and directly or indirectly has triggered actions that could facilitate the development of democracy in Cuba.

POSTSCRIPT

Should Sanctions Against Cuba Under the Helms-Burton Act Be Abandoned?

The Clinton administration at first made tentative moves toward easing, perhaps eliminating, U.S. economic sanctions against Cuba, but American outrage at the downing of two unarmed aircraft in early 1996, and the fact that it was a presidential election year, persuaded Clinton to sign the Helms-Burton Act. Many other countries consider the U.S. position anachronistic. However, residual anticommunism and the existence of a strong, anti-Castro Cuban American community in Florida and elsewhere have thwarted most efforts to ease sanctions and helped lead to the passing of the Helms-Burton Act. According to both the act and long-standing U.S. policy, a fundamental requirement to end the sanctions is that Castro allow free elections and restore democracy. On this issue, see Carollee Bengelsdorf, *The Problem of Democracy in Cuba* (Oxford University Press, 1994). For a discussion of the value of sanctions as a diplomatic tool, consult David Cortright and George A. Lopez, eds., *Economic Sanctions: Panacea or Peacebuilding in a Post–Cold War World?* (Westview Press, 1996).

It is also important to remember that the Helms-Burton Act has much wider implications than merely its impact on Cuba. Similar laws have applied sanctions to Iran, Libya, and other countries that the United States does not like. This raises a number of issues. One is whether or not the United States is in violation of the General Agreement on Tariffs and Trade (GATT). Several European countries have threatened to bring a complaint before the judicial arm of GATT's administrative body, the World Trade Organization (WTO). So far that has been avoided because the Helms-Burton Act gave the president the ability to suspend penalties against foreign countries and nationals if he thinks it is not in the U.S. national interest to enforce penalties. President Clinton has repeatedly taken this action, and other countries have not pressed the WTO to take up the case as long as the waiver continues. A number of countries and the EU also enacted measures to retaliate against the United States. For example, because one aspect of the Helms-Burton Act allows Americans to sue foreign companies that have acquired property in Cuba expropriated from (now) Cuban Americans, the Canadian government introduced legislation that would allow Canadian companies to countersue U.S. companies in Canadian courts if the U.S. companies sued the Canadian companies in U.S. courts. Said one of the Canadian bill's sponsors, "The idea is to point out that if you're going to use domestic law to interfere with business relations with foreign states, other people can do the same thing."

ISSUE 8

Is the Current Trend Toward Global Economic Integration Desirable?

YES: Murray Weidenbaum, from "American Isolationism Versus the Global Economy: The Ability to Identify With Change," *Vital Speeches of the Day* (January 15, 1996)

NO: Gregory Albo, from "The World Economy, Market Imperatives and Alternatives," *Monthly Review* (December 1996)

ISSUE SUMMARY

YES: Business professor Murray Weidenbaum argues that the integration of the American economy with the world is both inevitable and desirable.

NO: Professor of political science Gregory Albo maintains that globalization is neither irreversible nor, in its present form, desirable.

One of the important political and economic changes during the twentieth century has been the rapid growth of economic interdependence between countries. The impact of international economics on domestic societies has expanded rapidly as world industrial and financial structures have become increasingly intertwined. Foreign trade wins and loses jobs; Americans depend on petroleum and other imported resources to fuel cars, homes, and industries; inexpensive imports help keep inflation down and the standard of living up; the very shirts on our backs and the televisions we watch were probably made in another country. Global exports grew from $53 billion in 1948 to $5.2 trillion in 1995.

The world's largest trader is the United States, which in 1995 exported $784 billion in goods and services and imported $894 billion in goods and services. Export production that year employed approximately 17.5 million Americans, about one of every eight U.S. workers.

In addition to trade, the trend toward globalization also includes factors such as the growth of multinational corporations (MNCs), the flow of international investment capital, and the increased importance of international exchange rates. There are now at least 40,000 MNCs that conduct business (beyond just sales) in more than one country. Of these, just the 500 largest global corporations in 1995 had assets of $32.1 trillion, produced $11.4 trillion in goods and services, and employed over 35 million workers.

Foreign investment is also immense. Americans alone own over $1.7 trillion in foreign stocks and bonds, and foreigners own over $1.2 billion in U.S. stocks and bonds. Such holdings are often seen as the province of the rich, but, in reality, an ever-increasing number of less wealthy people are involved in overseas investment through their pension plans and mutual funds.

The issue here is whether this economic globalization and integration is a positive or negative trend. For more than 50 years, the United States has been at the center of the drive to open international commerce. The push to reduce trade barriers that occurred during and after World War II was designed to prevent a recurrence of the global economic collapse of the 1930s and the war of the 1940s. Policymakers believed that protectionism had caused the Great Depression; that the ensuing human desperation had provided fertile ground for the rise of dictators who blamed scapegoats for what had occurred and who promised national salvation; and that the spawning of fascism had set off World War II. In sum, policymakers thought that protectionism caused economic depression, which caused dictators, which caused war. Free trade, by contrast, would promote prosperity, democracy, and peace.

Based on these political and economic theories, American policymakers took the lead in establishing a new international economic system. As the world's dominant superpower, the United States played the leading role at the end of World War II in establishing, among other things, the International Monetary Fund (IMF), the World Bank, and the General Agreement on Tariffs and Trade (GATT). The latest GATT revision talks were completed and signed by 124 countries (including the United States) in April 1994. Among the outcomes was the establishment of a new coordinating body, the World Trade Organization (WTO).

The movement during the entire latter half of this century toward economic globalization has been strong, and there have been few influential voices opposing it. Most national leaders, business leaders, and other elites continue to support economic interdependence. The people in various countries have largely followed the path set by their leaders.

More recently, the idea that globalization is either inevitable or necessarily beneficial have come under increasing scrutiny. Some analysts question how widely the benefits are distributed in a society. What is the morality of buying products manufactured by MNCs in other countries where businesses are free to pay workers almost nothing, give them no benefits, and perhaps even use child labor? Is there a benefit if MNCs avoid environmental laws by moving to a country with less strict requirements? If global warming is really a threat, does it make any difference whether the industrial emissions come from the United States or Zimbabwe?

Murray Weidenbaum and Gregory Albo take up the issue in the following two selections. Weidenbaum maintains that the world is on the globalization track, which is going in a positive direction. Albo argues that it is wrong to assume that history is on the side of a tired, destructive economic system that values profit over human and ecological needs.

YES

Murray Weidenbaum

AMERICAN ISOLATIONISM VERSUS THE GLOBAL ECONOMY

Delivered to the Fourteenth Annual Monetary and Trade Conference in Philadelphia, Pennsylvania, November 13, 1995

A growing paradox faces the United States. It is the simultaneous rise of a new spirit of isolationism amid the increasing globalization of business and economic activity. Viewed independently, each of the two trends possesses a certain logic. In juxtaposition, however, isolationism amid globalization is simply unachievable. Some explanation may help.

The end of the Cold War brought on a widespread expectation that the United States could safely and substantially cut back its military establishment. The threat from a powerful Soviet Union was a fear of the past. Moreover, government leaders could shift their attention from foreign policy to the host of domestic problems that face the American people. Surely, there is no shortage of urgent national issues to occupy our attention, and they are all inwardly oriented—welfare reform, health care, immigration, environmental cleanup, crime control, deficit reduction, and tax reform. The isolationist tendency is visible and apparent.

But, in a far less dramatic way, it is also becoming clear that the rest of the world is not content with going its separate way. Overseas forces, institutions, and people increasingly affect the workers and managers of America's business and their families. The global marketplace has rapidly shifted from just being a simple minded buzzword to complex reality. International trade is growing far more rapidly than domestic production. That's true all around the globe. It is hardly a matter of a company or an investor deciding to participate or not. The days of agonizing over whether to go global are over. Eight basic points illustrate the changing external environment for public sector and private sector decisionmakers.

From Murray Weidenbaum, "American Isolationism Versus the Global Economy: The Ability to Identify With Change," *Vital Speeches of the Day* (January 15, 1996). Copyright © 1996 by Murray Weidenbaum. Reprinted by permission.

1. Americans do not have to do anything or change anything to be part of the global marketplace. Even if a business does not export a thing and has no overseas locations, its owners, managers, and employees are still part of the world economy. The same goes for the many companies and individuals that supply it with goods and services. The issue has been decided by technology. The combination of fax machines, universal telephone service (including cellular), low-cost, high-speed copiers and computers, and speedy jet airline service enables money, goods, services, and people to cross most borders rapidly and often instantly. And that goes especially for what is the most strategic resource—information.

A dramatic example of the ease of business crossing national borders occurred during the Gulf War. On the first day of the Iraqi attack on Kuwait, a savvy Kuwaiti bank manager began faxing his key records to his subsidiary in Bahrain. Every once in a while the shooting got close and transmission was interrupted. By the end of the day, however, all of the key records had been transferred out of Kuwait. The next morning, the bank opened as a Bahraini institution, beyond the reach of the Iraqis—and also not subject to the U.S. freeze on Kuwaiti assets. Literally, a bank was moved from one country to another via a fax machine.

No American business of any consequence remains insulated from foreign producers because of vast distances. Every American is subject to competition from overseas. If that force has not hit a region yet, it probably is on its way.

2. Employees, customers, suppliers, and investors in U.S. companies are increasingly participating in the international economy. That is not just a matter of sales or even earnings originating from foreign operations. Increasingly, U.S. firms are establishing factories, warehouses, laboratories, and offices in other countries. As a result, one-half of Xerox's employees work on foreign soil. The pharmaceutical firm Pfizer is exceedingly blunt on this subject:

> Pfizer does not have a choice about whether to manufacture in the EC [European Community] or not.
>
> If we are going to sell to Europe, we have to manufacture there.

Surprisingly large numbers of American companies have already deployed a majority of their assets overseas. Here are a few important examples: Citicorp (51 percent), Bankers Trust (52 percent), Chevron (55 percent), Exxon (56 percent), Digital Equipment (61 percent), Mobil (63 percent), Gillette (66 percent), and Manpower Inc. (72 percent). To underscore the point, a recent Conference Board survey of American manufacturing companies shows that becoming an internationally oriented company usually pays off. Sales by firms with foreign activities grow at twice the rate of those with no foreign operations. Firms with international activities grow faster in every industry —and profits are higher. Geographic diversification is especially important for profitability. Companies with factories in North America, Europe, and the Asian rim outperform companies that stay in one region.

3. The transnational enterprise is on the rise. It is far more than merely a matter of which country to choose to locate a manufacturing or marketing operation. For the dominant companies, the locus of executive decision-making is shifting. "Think global but act local" is not just a slogan. It is a competitive necessity. The larger business firms operating in several regions of the world have been setting up multiple locations for decision-making. For those domestic firms that sell goods or services to other American companies, increasingly their customers are located in one or more decentralized divisions, some of which are now based overseas. That works two ways for Americans. DuPont has shifted the headquarters of its electronic operation to Japan. Germany's Siemens has moved its ultrasound equipment division to the United States.

Moreover, cross-border alliances have become commonplace. It is the rare business of any considerable size that has not entered into some form of cooperative arrangement with one or more companies located overseas—companies that they still often compete against in many markets. The concept of strategic alliances has moved from the classroom to the boardroom. A new set of international business relationships has arisen: joint ventures, production sharing, cross-licensing agreements, technology swaps, and joint research projects.

Increasingly, the successful business looks upon its entire operation in a global context. It hires people, buys inputs, and locates production, marketing, and decision-making centers worldwide. An example helps to convert theory to reality. Here is a shipping label used by an American electronics company:

> Made in one or more of the following countries: Korea, Hong Kong, Malaysia, Singapore, Taiwan, Mauritius, Thailand, Indonesia, Mexico, Philippines. The exact country of origin is unknown.

Any comprehensive and balanced analysis also tells us that not every aspect of the international economy has a positive impact on Americans. Of course, a similar warning applies to the business environment here at home.

4. Some overseas markets are more profitable than domestic sales, but high risk and high rewards tend to go together. The attraction of overseas locations is increasing. Southeast Asia is the faster growing part of the world. Any observant visitor to Hong Kong, Singapore, Malaysia, or Thailand will see that the 8 percent real growth they have been reporting is no statistical mirage. Each of those economies is booming. Mainland China has been experiencing double-digit expansion year after year. Only the most modest slowdown is in sight. Of course, starting off from a small base makes it easier to achieve large percentage gains than is the case for an advanced industrialized country like the United States. But far more than that is involved.

Government policy in each of those countries welcomes foreign investment. With the inevitable exceptions, they encourage the formation of new private enterprises. The contrast with the United States is striking—and ironic. While these present or former communist and totalitarian countries are moving toward capitalism and trying to reduce the role of the public sector, we have been moving in the opposite direction. Despite efforts by the House of Representatives, the United States is still expanding government regulation of business. The result is to make it more difficult and certainly more costly for private enterprise to prosper. Under these circumstances, it is not surprising that so many American companies are doing their expansion overseas.

Take the energy company that explores in faraway Kazakhstan, or the mining enterprise that moves to Bolivia, or the medical devices firm that sets up a laboratory in the Netherlands, or the manufacturing corporation that builds a new factory in Guangdong. To a very considerable extent, these companies are responding to adverse domestic policies as much as to the attractions of overseas markets. The villains of the piece are the government officials in the United States who lock up much of the nation's natural and labor resources in fear that somebody somewhere may make a profit.

Nevertheless, the risks overseas may be great. Over the years, many companies have suffered the expropriation of their foreign assets. You do not have to go farther than Mexico to recall a vivid, although not recent, instance. Iran furnishes a more current and dramatic example. The dangers are not just political. Wars and insurrections are more likely in the regions of the world with less strongly established political institutions. There is no shortage of examples —Croatia, Bosnia, Armenia, Azerbaijan and Chechnya currently make the headlines. Civil wars and large scale violence occurred in recent decades in Indonesia, Malaysia, Thailand, Sri Lanka (Ceylon), and Myanmar (Burma).

Less dramatic but still noteworthy are the difficulties experienced by some Western enterprises in collecting on their debts in China. Moreover, many companies operating in that region report that the special expenses of doing business there make it difficult to convert sales into profits. One large American law firm expects to show its first profit only after six years of doing business on the mainland.

The special risks are numerous. Differences in language, culture, and business practices are pervasive. Our notions of personal honesty are not exactly universal. My purpose is not to scare anyone away from foreign markets, but to emphasize the often painfully close relationship between high profits and high risk. But there is a new positive side to all this.

5. *The rise of the global market place provides vast new opportunity for Americans to diversify their investments and—of course —to broaden business risk.* The last half dozen years provide a cogent example in terms of the global business cycle. At first, the AngloSaxon economies lost momentum. Remember when our friends in continental Europe needled us about the odd phenomenon of an English-speaking recession? That was the time when the economies of the United States, the United Kingdom, Canada, Australia, and New Zealand all were in decline simultaneously.

But, as we were coming out of recession, Japan and most of Western Europe started to experience slowdowns and then downturns in their economies. The American economy has been coming off a cyclical peak and is now slowing down. At the same time, Western Europe has turned the corner and is on an expansion path once again.

In the case of the developing countries, it is hazardous to forecast which one of them will get unglued. There is no certainty that any of them will. But the odds are that at least one of those rapidly growing nations will be derailed from the path of continued progress. Military coups and domestic insurrections do occur. The biggest uncertainties are what will happen to China [now that Deng Xiaoping has died] and how well... the integration of Hong Kong [is going].

6. *The rise of China and Southeast Asia is a new and durable force in the world economy that Americans will have to recognize.* Depending how you measure national economies, China is in the top 10 or top

three, or top two. That is an interesting range of variation.

Even the most experienced Asia experts candidly tell you that they do not know what will happen [in the post-Deng era]. There is already considerable pressure in China to reverse course, to move back to a more authoritarian society with less opportunity for private ownership. China also has a history of internal dissension, of splitting up into several regions each of which is the size of several major Western European countries. So far, the ability of the economic reforms to create tremendous amounts of income and wealth is the best guarantee of their being continued. But, the many misunderstandings between China and the United States constitute a very real dark cloud on the political as well as economic horizon.

The economies of several other countries in Southeast Asia are also growing rapidly at about 8 percent a year, compared to China's 10–12 percent. They seem to be welcoming American and other Western businesses with more enthusiasm than the Chinese.

Malaysia is a good example of a fairly stable nation with a sound economic policy, notably a balanced budget—and an 8 percent overall growth rate. Other opportunities for geographic diversification exist in Thailand, Indonesia, and now the Philippines, whose economy has turned around. To the surprise of some, Vietnam welcomes American businesses as well as tourists.

A decade from now, Southeast Asia will be one of the major economic regions of the globe—along with Japan, North America, and Western Europe. Americans must face the fact that the economies of Southeast Asia are potentially both customers and competitors for our companies. To think of that area as just low-cost labor is misleading. The level of technology is high in Taiwan, Singapore, and Malaysia. The amount of education is also impressive. Intelligent and productive work forces are available in substantial quantities—and they also constitute a substantial and rapidly rising consumer base.

The $1^1/_2$ billion people in Southeast Asia constitute the major new market area of the world. A noteworthy although not particularly welcome trend is for the nations of Southeast Asia increasingly to trade with each other. That is not surprising when you examine the investment patterns. Who are the major investors in China, Malaysia, Indonesia, Thailand, and Vietnam? The answer is neither the United States nor Western Europe. It is Hong Kong, Taiwan, South Korea, and Japan.

As a result, the major sources of imports into Southeast Asia are Hong Kong, Taiwan, South Korea, and Japan. Likewise, those same four nations are the major markets for Southeast Asia's products. As Southeast Asia continues to grow rapidly, it will be a major challenge to Western businesses to participate in that key market.

7. Despite the military and political issues that divide Western Europe, the economic unification is continuing full bore. With a minimum of fanfare, Sweden, Finland, and Austria are entering the European Union. Note the successive changes in terminology as the nations of Western Europe move closer together while increasing their membership. The six-nation European Common Market became the 12-nation European Community. Now we have the 15 member European Union.

As in every major change, there are winners and losers—for Americans as well as for Europeans. With the elimination of internal trade barriers, the stronger European companies can now compete in a continent-wide market. They enjoy considerable economies of scale. American companies well established in Western Europe—such as Ford —are included in that category. The losers are the high-cost European producers who were accustomed to the protections afforded by a restricted national market. The loser category also contains those American producers who have been taken by surprise by the reinvigorated European competition.

Fifteen member nations are not going to be the end of the line for the European Union. The entrance of Austria is a strategic move because Vienna is a major gateway to Eastern Europe. Hungary, Poland, and the Czech Republic are anxious to develop closer economic and business relations with Western Europe.* They can become low-cost suppliers or low-cost competitors—likely both.

Perhaps the most important positive development in that continent in the coming decade will be the new economic strength of the largest member, Germany. It is taking more time than expected to fully consummate the integration of the "new provinces" (neuer Under), as East Germany is now referred to. Any visitor is struck by the substantial amount of physical investment that the national government is making in the East. That is bound to result in a strong and newly competitive region. All in all, we should not forget Europe in our attention to the Orient.

*[Hungary, Poland, and the Czech Republic were invited to join in the North Atlantic Treaty Organization in 1997.—Ed.]

Let us end on an upbeat and realistic note.

8. The American economy is still the strongest in the world and our prospects are impressive. We are not a weak or declining nation in the world marketplace. Legislation and political pressures to "buy local" may be popular, but they fly in the face of economic reality.

Our concern for the losers in the domestic marketplace requires a constructive response; make the United States a more attractive place to hire people and to do business.

After all, in a great many important industries, American firms are still the leaders. U.S. firms rank number one (in sales volume) in 13 major industries— aerospace, apparel, beverages, chemicals, computers, food products, motor vehicles, paper products, petroleum, pharmaceuticals, photographic and scientific equipment, soap and cosmetics, and tobacco.

What about the future? Recall that the first of these eight points began with an illustration of the awesome power of technology. Nobody can forecast which specific technologies will succeed in the coming decade. But the prospects for American companies being in the lead are very bright. There is a special reason for optimism.

Although in the 1990s, America will be benefiting from the upsurge of industrial research and development (R&D) during the 1980s. A key but undramatic crossover occurred in the early 1980s. For the first time in over a half century, the magnitude of company-sponsored R&D exceeded the total of government-financed R&D. That primary reliance on private R&D continues to this day.

Few people appreciate the long-term impact of that strategic crossover. The new and continued dominance of the private sector in the choice of investments in advanced technology makes it more likely that there will be an accelerated flow of new and improved civilian products and production processes in the years ahead. A progression of innovation may be forthcoming comparable to the advent of missiles and space vehicles following the massive growth of military R&D in the 1950s and 1960s. Just consider how the fax machine has altered our customary work practices.

There is a positive macroeconomic aspect to continued technological progress. When the persistent trade deficit of the United States is disaggregated, we find some surprisingly good news: our exports of high-tech products steadily exceed our high-tech imports. We more than hold our own. This country does indeed enjoy a comparative advantage in the production and sales of goods and services that embody large proportions of new technology.

Of course, these are not laurels to rest on. The point is that there is no need to take the low road of economic isolationism—which is protectionism—to deal with foreign competition. We should take the necessary actions, in both the public and private sectors, which make American business and labor more productive and hence more competitive in what is increasingly a globalized marketplace. The ingredients are well known—tax reform, regulatory reform, and a modern labor policy.

Perhaps the most basic development since the end of the Cold War has been missed by all observers and analysts because it is so subtle. During the Cold War, the two military superpowers dominated the world stage. It is currently fashionable to say that in the post–Cold War period, three economic superpowers have taken their place—the United States, Japan, and Germany. That is technically accurate but very misleading.

During the Cold War, government was the pace-setting player on the global stage. Governments made the strategic decisions. Businesses were important, but they were responding to government orders, supplying armaments to the superpowers. In the process, of course, business created substantial economic wealth. But the shift from military to economic competition is fundamental. It means that the business firm is now the key to global economic competition. Governments, to be sure, can help or hinder, and in a major way. But they are supporting players, at best.

The basic initiative in the global marketplace has shifted to private enterprise. Individual entrepreneurs and individual business firms now make the key decisions that will determine the size, composition, and growth of the international economy. That makes for an extremely challenging external environment for the competitive American enterprise of the 1990s. It also requires greater degrees of understanding and forbearance on the part of U.S. public policymakers.

The rapidly growing business-oriented global marketplace is a source of great actual and potential benefit to American entrepreneurs, workers, and consumers. Because the international economy is changing so rapidly, Americans face both threats and opportunities.

Those who identify with the change are likely to be the winners; those who resist will be among the losers.

History tells us that trying to shut ourselves off from these "foreign" influences just does not work. When imperial China tried to do that some 500 years ago, it fairly quickly went from being the world's most advanced and powerful nation to becoming a very poor backwater of the globe.

One thing is certain; it is futile to say, "Stop the world, I want to get off!"

NO

Gregory Albo

THE WORLD ECONOMY, MARKET IMPERATIVES AND ALTERNATIVES

In the crisis after 1974, social democratic governments like Sweden's and technologically ascendant countries such as Germany seemed to be moving in very different directions from other capitalist countries. Today, these divergent economic paths seem to be only alternate routes converging in neoliberalism. The world economy in the 1990s, everyone now seems to agree, accommodates only one model of development: export-oriented production based on flexible labor markets, lower real and social wages, less environmental regulation and freer trade. Neoliberal economic strategies are proposed for conditions as vastly different as those faced by the new ANC government in South Africa, the transitional economies of Eastern Europe, and the new center-Left coalition in Italy.

The Right, of course, has greeted these developments triumphantly. The Left has responded less with triumph than with resignation, but it still accepts them as inevitable. A stalwart American Liberal such as [Secretary of Labor] Robert Reich baldly concludes that "as almost every factor of production... moves effortlessly across borders, the very idea of an American economy is becoming meaningless." Fritz Scharpf, a leading strategist of the German SDP [Social Democratic Party], voices what is often a convention on the Left, that "unlike the situation of the first three postwar decades, there is now no economically plausible Keynesian strategy that would permit the full realization of social democratic goals within a national context without violating the functional imperatives of a capitalist economy. Social democracy must rethink its traditional goals to accommodate the new imperatives. And from outside the traditions of social democracy, [one analyst] despondently reports that "the future belongs to the set of [capitalist] forces that are overtaking the nation-state."

Across a broad political spectrum, then, economic strategies have come to be based on the common premise that "there is no alternative," that "globalization is irreversible," and that economic success depends upon encouraging and enhancing this process. Neoliberals have fostered the movement to freer trade and deregulation of labor markets, arguing that overcoming the constraint of limited markets is the means to increase growth, remedy trade imbalances, and lower unemployment. The state needs to be forced to comply with the "laws" of the market. Social democrats differ from neoliberals only in their belief that there are specific constraints on the market that need to be surmounted—for instance, the constraints imposed by an insufficiently skilled workforce, which can be surmounted by training policies—to allow the harvest of globalization to be reaped.

On empirical grounds alone it is quite clear that the result of policies which advance globalization has been a series of economic failures, particularly increasing trade imbalances and mass unemployment. But the various proposals for correcting these failures and imbalances are deeply flawed not only empirically but also in their theoretical foundations —from neoliberal assumptions about the market, to Keynesian conceptions of market regulation, and social democratic variations on the theme of "shaped advantage." The problems of neoliberal theories are well known after two decades of these policies. The flaws in social democratic proposals have been less widely discussed. I want first to outline the theoretical flaws in the social democratic version of market regulation and then to argue that there are, in fact, alternatives for socialists even in capitalist societies.

The common view that there is no alternative, that we must submit to the market and that the autonomous agency of the state has been diminished, is really based on circular reasoning. It is true only if we begin by accepting the social property and power relations that impose global market imperatives

in the first place. But if we challenge this presumption, there are alternatives even within the existing social relations of power in capitalism.

THE ILLUSION OF SOCIAL DEMOCRACY

Economic processes occur in real historical time, not in the timeless space of neoliberal equilibrium models. These models assume that, for every economic imbalance, there is an immediate correction that will bring the economy back into balance. But in the real world, capitalist techniques and workers wage demands do not change instantly, as soon as there is excess labor supply; and a change in the value of currency does not necessarily bring about greater export demand or cause expenditures to be shifted from exports to domestic industry.

If Left economists generally acknowledge these flaws in the equilibrium model, beyond this very general agreement various stands of the Left part company. For Marxists these market instabilities arise from the inherent contradictions of capitalism, and they can be resolved only by transitional strategies of disengagement from market relations. Social democratic Keynesians on the other hand, believe that the market simply needs to be regulated to remove certain *specific* constraints which present capitalism from reaching the volumes of output associated with full employment.

If economic openness is irreversible and trade expansion is a foundation for prosperity, as the new conventional wisdom insists, social democratic economic policy is left with only one central question: how should national (or regional) competitiveness be created and maintained? Everything else—from macroeconomic policies to strategies for training and welfare—flows from this question.

Since markets are not perfect, social democratic theorists argue that the economy cannot be left to work itself out through free trade: states can and must help "shape advantage" to improve trade balances and competitiveness. New industries, for example, often require protection before they can face import competition. Early entry into the market and increasing economies of scale can "lock in" market share before rivals gain a chance to develop. In this way, the technically superior BETA recorders lost out in the capitalist marketplace to the less capable VHS in the early 1980s.

In the social democratic view, then, it is imperative to have a strategic trade policy to get new products developed and into markets as quickly as possible. Since technological change is a continual process of building up technical skills, capacity, and entrepreneurship, a "technological dynamism" needs to be nourished. Countries that lose technological capacity suffer the economic misfortunes vividly exemplified by Britain's fall in world standing. In this case, every attempt to expand demand, instead of raising domestic output, has simply sucked in imports, and the economy has been forced to slow down in order to avert a balance-of-payments crisis. The result has been a vicious stop-go cycle, and this has discouraged investment, which requires stable growth. As a result, in the absence of new technical capacities, competitiveness has increasingly come to depend upon low cost production. In contrast, stronger competitors can continue to keep investment high in new techniques, thereby enhancing output capacity and competitive advantage.

The social democratic case for an industrial policy of shaped advantage has found particularly strong advocates in the economically declining powers of Britain, Canada, and the United States, as with popular writers like Will Hutton, Jim Laxer, Lester Thurow, and Robert Reich. In their view, a world economy of ever-increasing trade volumes affords ample market opportunities if the industrial successes of Japan, Germany, and Sweden can be replicated (and their failures ignored). Shaped advantage can resolve the problems of external trade imbalances and create a stable capitalism.

There are several competing social democratic positions—though to some extent they complement each other—on how shaped advantage can also resolve the internal imbalances of employment. The "progressive competitiveness" strategy emphasizes the effects of *external* constraints imposed by globalization. In a globalized market, what distinguishes one economy from another is the skills of its labor force and the nature of workplace relations. Training policies should, therefore, be the central component of a jobs and welfare strategy, while relationships of "trust" and co-operation should be fostered within enterprises.

The "shared austerity" strategy stresses the *internal* constraint of distribution relations. Full employment requires severe restraint on workers pay and consumption to keep exports competitive, investment high, and the state budget under control. Incomes policy has a role to play in spreading work through wage restraint and keeping unit labor costs down for exports.

Finally, the "international Keynesian" view maintains that removing constraints on the market simply requires the *political will* to shift expansionary policies from the national to the supranational level, where leakages to exports and capital outflows would be irrelevant. What is needed, according to this view, is international co-ordination of economic policy; and a "cosmopolitan democracy" imposed on global governance structures would legitimate that kind of international co-ordination.

All these variants of social democratic Keynesianism avoid the neoliberal illusion that free trade and deregulation of labor markets will resolve trade and employment imbalances. But they also have in common the conviction that constraints on the market are not general barriers to capital accumulation but just specific problems that can be resolved by judicious policy. This conviction is simply unsustainable for several reasons and cannot be the basis of an economic strategy for socialists.

THE MARKET IN THE REAL WORLD

First, let us consider the problem of "internal" balance, the growing reserve army of the unemployed. Unemployment is regarded as a result of the relation between competitive capacity and the level of demand: the more "competitive" an economy becomes by improving its technical capacities, specifically by means of labor-saving technology, the less labor it needs to meet the same demand. So shaping advantage to improve technical capacity will *create* unemployment, unless there is an increase in total income—and hence an increase in demand—which would create a need for increasing total hours of work; yet unemployment itself tends to reduce total income and hence reduces demand. The strategy of "shaping advantage" to maintain high employment depends on increasing external trade in relation to domestic output, in order to make up for shortfalls in domestic demand by seeking markets elsewhere, so that employment can be created to meet these external demands. And as technological change continues, trade must continue to grow at an accelerating rate to generate a given level of employment and hours of work.

This strategy therefore requires some very delicate maneuvering, but such "knife-edge" balance becomes difficult to maintain when the strategy must be implemented in real historical conditions and in real historical time. Even in a stable world economy it would be quite fanciful to expect it all to work out. In a capitalism that is exhibiting the trade asymmetries and currency instability that exist today, it is quite impossible. Shaped trade advantage is no substitute for national and local employment policies that would constrain the capitalist market to deal with the unemployment crisis.

Second, it is just as unrealistic to assume that shaped advantage can resolve *external* imbalances. Indeed, the reliance on market adjustment may well make matters worse. Countries that succeed in maintaining export-led growth may be able to sustain the necessary balance between technological advance, external demand, and internal growth in employment. But deficit countries will have listless investment and faltering technological capacity. They will be forced to rely on "competitive" wages in order to try to resolve their trade imbalance. The pressures to compete by lowering labor costs are obvious in countries such as Britain and the United States, which have been suffering from structural deficits; but they also have become increasingly visible in cases like Germany and Japan which have enjoyed relatively constant trade surpluses. In Germany, for instance, the relatively "uncompetitive" costs of labor have in recent years been accompanied by unusually high levels of unemployment. In other words, uneven development and trade imbalances can be expected to persist. Countries (or regions) in this kind of competitive world economy must inevitably enter into an ever more intense battle over unit labor costs and employment.

Third, if shaped advantage has drawbacks for individual national economies, there are even greater contradictions in the system as a whole. As Marxists have often insisted, capitalism must be evaluated as a total system, not just by the relative success of some piece of the system which succeeds at the expense of others. Shaped advantage relies on export-led growth. Trading partners must leave their economies open while the country engaging in policies of shaped advantage improves its competitive position. An immediate problem arises: if the country whose market is to be penetrated responds with protectionism or its own shaped advantage policies, any trade and employment gains are wiped out.

If the actions of a single trading partner can create problems for the theory of shaped advantage, a world of many, if not all, countries seeking to shape advantage makes a shambles of social democratic economic policy. It is obvious that not all countries can have successful export-led economic strategies. As all countries cannot run trade surpluses to improve employment: some must incur deficits. Trade imbalances and unemployment will necessarily co-exist. Indeed, this has been the norm for the world economy over the economic history of capitalism. This is, in effect, what happened in the great crisis of the 1930s.

As the strategy of shaped advantage is pursued over time, and more countries are forced to adopt it or face balance-of-payments problems, everyone can be left worse off. Indeed, as trade imbalances persist, there is every incentive for competition over unit labor costs to spread from improving productivity to more general austerity programs, *even* in technologically leading countries. Technological laggards must compete by means of lower wages to reduce unit costs or face a growing trade deficit. Paradoxically, this tends to undermine the foundations on which the successful policies of the *leading* economies are based: lower incomes in other countries deprive successful economies of growing markets, while their capacity to produce more output is increasing because of their technical advances and growing productivity. This means that technological leaders are eventually obliged to follow the losers or they will lose their own surpluses and suffer increased unemployment.

So even technologically advanced countries with an explicit policy of shaping advantage like Japan and Germany begin to feel the sting of "competitive austerity," while peripheral economies such as Ghana and Newfoundland eventually buckle and collapse from the exhaustion of a never-ending competitive spiral. The only possible winners are the fortunate few capitalists in societies which can combine cheap labor with technological capacity so that rates of exploitation can be maintained. But social democrats would concede that Korea and Malaysia are not particularly desirable economic models. For the capitalist system as a whole, therefore, the social democratic strategy of unplanned external trade based on shaped advantage policies is not much better than neoliberal free trade, and equally capable of increasing economic instability.

Fourth, if we add the real world condition of massive capital mobility, the social democratic case for shaped advantage is weakened even further. Shaped advantage requires long-term planning and thus what social democrats call "patient capital." Yet the more global the economy becomes, the greater will be the uncertainty and risk of investment, so financial capital in a global market is increasingly driven by short-term demands for profit and liquid assets as a hedge against risk. Global financial markets therefore pose an obstacle to industrial policy. If there is instability and thus increasing risk and uncertainty, financial capital will be even less willing to be tied to the long-term investments necessary to increase capacity in export industries.

Keynesian economics has always acknowledged that there is a mismatch between the time horizons of financial and industrial capital: where the latter requires long-term investment, the former thrives on short-term profit. Capital mobility and floating exchange rates in a world economy raise this problem to an entirely new level. So the traditional socialist argument that democratizing financial capital is a necessary condition for political alternatives is now more important than ever.

But something more, and different, is needed than the "democratic" structures of international governance advocated by social democrats of the "international Keynesian" variety. These structures would not go to the heart of the problem. They are not, for example, designed to restrict capital mobility. More democratic international institutions of the kind envisaged by international

Keynesians would do little more than confer a greater political legitimacy on the existing global economy formed by internationalized capital movements. To do more than that would require giving up the very assumptions on which the social democratic strategy of shaped advantage is based. It would require abandoning the consensus that globalization is irreversible and that the capitalist market is essentially efficient.

Similarly, international Keynesianism must assume that the world market suffers only from a specific, and soluble, problem of adequate demand. Yet stimulating global demand to reduce unused capacity is likely only to compound existing trade imbalances. It will do nothing to clear these imbalances. Neither will it reverse unemployment in economically declining regions such as Atlantic Canada which lack industrial capacity (or whose advantage in natural resources has already been wiped out by the competitive game, as in the Atlantic fishery), nor reverse the cheap labor strategies adopted in, say, Alabama.

Moreover, the capitalist market imperatives of competition prevent the co-operation necessary for international relations. How do you encourage co-operation when it is always possible to achieve better trade balances and rates of employment by cheating—through import restraints, cheap currency, or austerity—before your competitor does? The world can stand only so many Swedens of competitive devaluations, Japans of import controls, or Germanys of austerity shaping advantage to prop up export surpluses and employment.

If economic efficiencies can be achieved by industrial policy, it can only be by means of trade regimes that plan trade and control capital mobility. Social democratic economic policy for national competitiveness through shaped advantage simply rests on the indefensible assumption that globalization is irreversible, that market imperatives require the global economy to be maintained as it is, and that, even if the planet is ravaged by endless economic growth, there is no other way of sustaining employment. These assumptions cannot be the basis of a socialist economic strategy.

THE MYTHS OF GLOBALIZATION

The internationalization of capitalism no doubt accentuates the imperatives of the market and places certain limits on socialist economic policy. Yet the only thing that obliges us to conclude that there is no alternative to international competitiveness is the *a priori* (and unexamined) assumption that existing social property relations—and hence the structural political power sustained by these relations—are sacrosanct.

Even *The Economist* seems to concede this point. This highly respected mouthpiece of neoliberal dogma has said that the "powerless state" in the global economy is simply a "myth" and that governments have "about as many economic powers as they ever had." The notion that the nation-state at one time, before globalization, acted as the center of social power and the regulator of economic activity, and that it is no longer capable of doing so today, is fundamentally misleading. The process of world market formation together with the "international constitutionalism of neoliberalism has taken place through the agency of states."

This does not mean that the imperatives of competition in a world market have not lessened the autonomous agency of individual capitalists or states. The NAFTA [North American Free Trade Agreement], Maastricht, and WTO [World Trade Organization] agreements all have restricted the capacity of nation-states (or regions) to follow their own national (or local) development strategies. It does mean, however, that the limits on state policy are to a significant extent self-imposed. Market imperatives certainly place limits on state policy, but there is no obligation to accept those imperatives. If we are prepared to question the social property and power relations that imposed global market imperatives in the first place, the scope of state action increases and there are indeed alternatives.

Globalization has to be considered not just as an economic regime but as a system of social relations, rooted in the specific capitalist form of social power, which is concentrated in private capital and the nation-state. What globalization basically means is that the market has become increasingly universal as an economic regulator; and as the scope of the market widens, the scope of democratic power narrows: whatever is controlled by the market is not subject to democratic accountability. The more universal the market becomes as an economic regulator, the more democracy is confined to certain purely "formal" rights, at best the right occasionally to elect our rulers; and this right becomes less and less important as the domain of political action is taken over by market imperatives. So the more globalized the economy becomes, the less possible it is for socialists just to tinker with economic policies. The more global the economy, the less possible it is for socialist *economic* policy to avoid *political* contestation over the social property relations of capitalism.

Finding an alternative to globalization, then, is as much a question of democracy in opposition to the imperatives of the market as it is of alternate development models. The alternative to globalization is democracy, not just in the sense of civil liberties or the right to vote but also the capacity to deliberate collectively as social equals about societal organization and production, and to develop self-management in workplaces and communities. Democracy in this sense is both a form of political organization and an alternative to the market as an economic regulator.

The geographic expansion of production prompts, then, challenging questions for socialists about the space and scale of both economic activity and democracy. The replacement of market imperatives by democratic regulation means more than just the "democratization" of institutions like the EC [European Community], NAFTA or even the IMF [International Monetary Fund]. It is quite clear that the "rational interest" of workers, peasants, and ecologists, North and South, entails taking a stand against globalization as it actually exists: globalization is an internationalism only of the capitalist class which is disrupting local communities and environments at a breathtaking pace. Progressives who call for international strategies to remedy the democratic deficits of existing international economic institutions have yet to demonstrate how this could possibly be anything but productivist and socially polarizing if the market itself is untouched.

Indeed, the imperatives of a capitalist market at the global level makes such an outcome inevitable *unless* the spatial expansion of democracy is matched by capital controls which more firmly embed production in national and local economies. How, then, can we plan production or begin a process of transition to democratic organizational forms at the global level?

SOCIALIST ALTERNATIVES: EXPANDING DEMOCRACY, CONTROLLING PRODUCTION

The answer may be a dual, and somewhat paradoxical, strategy: expanding the scale of democracy while reducing the scale of production. Expanding the scale of democracy means changing the governance and policy structures of international agencies and fora, but also of extending the basis for democratic administration and self-management nationally and locally. Let us be clear here. Expanding the scale of democracy in any meaningful sense will entail a challenge to the social property relations of capitalism. To make collective decisions implies some democratic capacity, backed by the coercive sanctions of the state, to direct capital allocation and thus to establish control over the economic surplus. The point is to enhance, with material supports, the capacities of democratic movements (which will vary tremendously according to the class relations and struggles in specific places), at every level, from local organizations to communities up to the nation-state—so as to challenge the power of capital.

Reducing the scale of production means shifting towards more inward-oriented economic strategies, but also forming new economic relations of cooperation and control internationally. The logic of the capitalist market creates a need for large-scale production, an obsession with quantity and size, to which all other considerations—of quality, of social need, and so on—are subordinated. The general objective of socialist policy should be to reduce the scale of production runs as the central economic objective putting other social considerations before quantity and size. Of course the massive material inequalities between nations mean that the general principle of reducing the scale of production will have to vary between developed and developing countries. Certain major industrial sectors necessary to produce adequate levels of welfare will obviously need to be put in place. Scale economies will also be important in some sectors to achieve the most efficient plant size, to reduce inputs and environmentally damaging outputs. But the reduction of scale should remain the general guiding principle, in keeping with the socialist conviction that production should above all meet basic needs, foster self-management capacities, and adopt more labor-intensive techniques when capital-intensive ones, like chemicalized agriculture, have large negative environmental consequences. The present desperate levels of economic insecurity, the volume of contamination and resource use, and degradation of local ecologies in the developed countries have surely made clear that economic growth cannot be equated with human welfare in any simple manner.

This implies that socialist economic policy must take a strong stand in support of those institutional structures at the level of the world economy which favor alternative development models. There is a sound basis for this approach. The postwar period displayed a variety of models of economic development, in the diversity of Fordism in the North, import-substitution industrialization in the South, and the various "socialist experiments." Even the attempt to impose a neoliberal homogeneity of development confirms that there is no single economic path: there is now a diversity of disasters across the North, the East, and the South. It is impossible for socialists to put forward alternatives unless it is insisted that there are variable ways of organizing economic and ecological relations, if only we create the political space for them.

The objective of such a solidaristic economic policy can be summed up like this: to maximize the capacity of different national collectivities democratically to choose alternate development paths (socialist or capitalist) that do not impose externalities (such as environmental damage) on other countries, by re-embedding financial capital and production relations from global to national and local economic spaces.

Such an objective would entail, broadly speaking, control of open trade and diversity of inward-oriented economic policies. This strategy obviously does not do away with international fora or the need to democratize them. But democracy at this level would not be just a place where more accountable elected representatives meet to enlarge the space of the market. Instead, the purpose of international bodies would be to constrain capitalist social property relations and widen the space for democratic organizational forms and capacities.

For example, it is quite easy to envision these democratized agencies being mandated to co-ordinate and plan the institutional and material supports for alternate development models, planned trade, control of capital, and enforcement of ecological standards. This cannot be accomplished by some kind of "international civil society" or a "cosmopolitan democracy"—as some currently fashionable and rather vague formulations of the Left suggest. It can only be the result of specific national and local struggles for democratic control of space, solidaristically supported by international movements.

Alternate development equally requires a coherence between tax and welfare policies, collective agreements, the enforcement of environmental regulations and, to the maximum extent possible for ecological reasons, the maintenance of bio-regional zones. Neoliberalism and globalization have seriously damaged the internal coherence of virtually all national and local economies and ecologies. This is the madness in which mono-culture crops for export flourish while peasants starve and the bio-diversity of plant life is lost; national exports of computers attain record volumes but local schools cannot afford them; and long-established cultural institutions lack resources while global advertising budgets flourish.

Socialist economic policy has always been—or ought to have been—redistributive not just in apportioning incomes among social classes but also in sharing out political power, the democratic capacity to direct sustainable economic activity. It is possible here, too, to identify strategies that re-orient institutions and resources against market imperatives. The redistribution of work simply to expand demand will neither absorb the unemployed nor be ecologically sound. A socialist policy should be directed at productivity advances that take the form of reducing work-time, spreading work, and equalizing incomes; a tax regime that will expand democratically controlled and egalitarian services where most job growth will occur; an industrial policy that expands employment on the basis of increased worker input and quality products; and market-modifying policies that control capital movements and plan capital allocation. The radical reduction of work-time, for example, might enhance ecological health and spread work within the existing power relations of capitalism. But if some of that reduced worktime is allocated to the administrative work of self-management it will also contribute to the long revolution toward socialism.

UTOPIAN CAPITALISM, REALISTIC SOCIALISM

This is a long way from where we are now. The configuration of the world economy that has evolved since the end of the postwar boom remains unstable: the structural asymmetries in the world payments system, the debt burden weighing down governments North and South, the uncertainty of currency markets, the strengthened hand of speculative rentier interests over state policies, and marginalization of large geographic zones form the ruined economic landscape of the 1990s. The policy of restraint adopted by OECD [Organization for Economic Co-operation and Development] governments in the 1970s, in the initial response to the economic crisis, was meant to be only a minor period of correction in a quick return to a high-growth path; and the Volcker-Reagan shocks of the 1980s were supposed to inflict the short-term pain of adjustment in exchange for long-term gains of jobs and income. Now, under governments of varied political stripe, the long-term pain of austerity will only yield more long-term pain of austerity.

The market imperatives in the world economy to compete or join the marginalized—for individuals, companies, state governments and, indeed, nation-states—have not yet led to depression and war like the "beggar-thy-neighbor" policies of the 1930s; that was how the last appearance of an unregulated world market ended. The multilateral trade agreements at least prevent this disaster from unfolding today. Yet the same competitive dynamic is being transferred to the "beggar-thy-working-class" cost-cutting policies that are actively being pursued by virtually all governments.

The imperative of "competitive austerity" leaves the world economy stagnant and, as every quiver of the stock exchange reveals, full of potential for rapid deflation. This imperative is what lies behind the spread of the North American model of development, with its income-splitting, insecure jobs, longer hours of work, and impoverishment of the public sector. It also means that the post-Fordism of the Japanese, Swedish, or German models advocated by social democrats are little more than intellectual phantoms.

In Raymond Williams's novel, *The Fight for Manod*, one of the characters grapples with the question of political alternatives to social decay, and decries the impasse which he presents as a specifically British disease but which today seems universal:

> The whole of public policy is an attempt to reconstitute a culture, a social system, an economic order, that have in fact reached their end, reached their limits of viability. And then I sit here and look at this double inevitability: that this imperial, exporting, divided order is ending, and that all its residual forces, all its political formations, will fight to the end to reconstruct it, to re-establish it, moving deeper all the time through crisis after crisis in an impossible attempt to regain a familiar world. So then a double inevitability: that they will fail, and that they will try nothing else.

In just this way, neoliberal and social democratic economic polices are today utopian in the bad sense of the word: attempting to fashion an unregulated laissez-faire capitalism at the world level on the one hand, or trying to recapture the human side of capitalism of the postwar period on the other. The only alternative that is realistic, in the good sense of the word, is to try something else that begins with the actual social relations of power in capitalism while challenging them from within. History can hardly be on the side of an old tired social order which still imposes the imperatives of the market against all other needs, human and ecological.

POSTSCRIPT

Is the Current Trend Toward Global Economic Integration Desirable?

The latest strengthening of free trade and investment under GATT and the creation of the WTO in 1994 was just one of many significant steps toward globalization in recent years. In the short term, the forces of economic integration carried the day. Regional economic organizations are also rapidly growing. The European Union has expanded and is set to create a single currency. The North American Free Trade Agreement will eventually commingle the American, Canadian, and Mexican economies; by the year 2005 the Free Trade Agreement of the Americas (FTAA) will include virtually all countries in the Western Hemisphere. The Association of Southeast Asian Nations (SEAN) is adding new members. For an overall view of modern international trade, see Bruce E. Moon, *Dilemmas of International Trade* (Westview Press, 1996) and Ralph Pettman, ed., *Understanding International Political Economy, With Readings for the Fatigued* (Lynne Rienner Press, 1996).

Now, however, an increasing number of voices are being raised against the trend toward integration. Countries may lose their ability to control their own economies and may even become strategically vulnerable. Japan, for example, worries about being flooded with cheap agricultural imports and losing the ability to feed itself independently. There is also something of a strange alliance between those on the right wing and left wing based on the sovereignty issue. Among Americans, for example, the right wing takes the nationalist view that the United States should not surrender its unilateral decision-making ability to the WTO or any other international organization. The left worries that the United States can no longer restrict the sale of imported products that are produced by child labor, produced in ways that damage the environment, or produced in some other socially unacceptable way.

It is important to avoid being too concerned about the labels of those who favor or oppose free economic exchange. Albo writes against free economic interchange from a socialist perspective, but you should think about his arguments regardless of the perspective he takes. For further investigation, read William Greider, *The Manic Logic of Global Capitalism* (Simon & Schuster, 1997). Greider's views in shorter form can be found in his "Global Warning: Curbing the Free-Trade Freefall," *The Nation* (January 13–20, 1997). Also explore the various claims made for and against free trade. For example, the idea that free trade will promote peace is addressed in Katherine Barbeieri, "Economic Interdependence: A Path to Peace or a Source of Interstate Conflict?" *Journal of Peace Research* (vol. 33, no. 1, 1996).

ISSUE 9

Should the Developed North Increase Aid to the Less Developed South?

YES: James P. Grant, from "Jumpstarting Development," *Foreign Policy* (Summer 1993)

NO: Editors of *The Economist,* from "The Kindness of Strangers," *The Economist* (May 7, 1994)

ISSUE SUMMARY

YES: James P. Grant, executive director of the United Nations Children's Fund (UNICEF), contends that many world problems stem from the impoverished conditions found throughout much of the world and that one way to jump-start solutions to these problems is to extend more assistance to the poor countries.

NO: The editors of the *Economist,* a well-known British publication, suggest that the way that aid is typically given and spent makes it a waste of resources and may even have a negative impact on the recipients.

One stark characteristic of the world system is that it is divided into two economic classes of countries. There is the North, which is industrialized and relatively prosperous. Then there is the South, which is mostly nonindustrial and relatively, and sometimes absolutely, impoverished. The countries that comprise the South are also called the less developed countries (LDCs) or the developing countries and were once known in a cold war context as the Third World. By whatever name they are known, however, LDCs have social conditions that are unacceptable. At a macroeconomic level, approximately three-quarters of the world's people live in the LDCs, yet they possess only about one-seventh of the world's wealth (measured in gross national products, or GNPs). On a more personal level, if you compare the lives of the average citizens of Japan and the average citizens of Nigeria, the Nigerians die 27 years earlier, earn an income that is 88 times smaller, are half as likely to be literate, are 53 times more likely to die during childbirth, and will find it 82 times more difficult to find a physician for medical help.

Despite the rhetoric of the North about the LDCs' plight, the countries of the North do relatively little to help. For example, U.S. economic foreign aid in 1994 was approximately $15 billion, which amounted to only about half of what Americans spent annually in retail liquor stores. Canada's foreign aid, about $2.8 billion, is equivalent to only about one-third of what its citizens spent in 1994 on tobacco. Foreign investment in the LDCs is also extremely limited, and what increases there are go to the relatively few countries, such as South Korea, that have been able join the ranks of what are called newly industrializing countries (NICs). Furthermore, loans to the LDCs have declined, and repayment of existing loans is draining much-needed capital away from many less developed countries. Trade earnings are another possible source of development capital, but the raw materials produced and exported by most LDCs earn them little compared to the cost of importing the more expensive finished products manufactured by the North.

There are a number of ways of approaching this issue of greater aid by the North for the South. One approach focuses on morality. Are we morally obligated to help less fortunate humans? A second approach explores more aid as a means of promoting the North's own self-interest; some analysts contend that a fully developed world would mean greater prosperity for everyone and would be more stable politically. A third avenue pursues the causes for the LDCs' poverty and lack of development in order to assess who or what is responsible.

It is possible to divide views on the origins and continuance of the North-South gap into three groups. One believes that the uneven (but unintended) spread of the Industrial Revolution resulted in unequal economic development. From this point of view, the answer to the question "Who is at fault?" is, "Nobody; it just happened." A second group finds the LDCs responsible for much of their continuing poverty. Advocates of this view charge the LDCs with failure to control their populations, with lack of political stability, with poor economic planning, and with a variety of other ill-conceived practices that impede development. This group believes that foreign aid is wasteful and is destructive of the policies needed to spur economic development.

A third group maintains that the North bears much of the responsibility for the South's condition and, therefore, is obligated to help the LDCs. Those who hold this view contend that the colonization of the LDCs, especially during the 1800s, when the Industrial Revolution rapidly took hold in the North, destroyed the indigenous economic, social, and political organizations needed for development. These powers then kept their colonial dependencies underdeveloped in order to ensure a supply of cheap raw materials. Even though virtually all former colonies are now independent, this view persists; the developed countries continue to follow political and economic strategies designed to keep the LDCs underdeveloped and dependent.

In the following selections, James P. Grant takes the position that, notwithstanding the poor media image of the LDCs as a lost cause, there is real momentum for change. He recommends focusing on the children of the LDCs—that if educated, kept healthy, and given other basic advantages, they can be the force for rapid positive change in the LDCs. The editors of the *Economist* argue that aid is ill-managed today and that, even if aid were vastly increased and managed well, it is not certain that the recipient countries would do much better.

YES
James P. Grant

JUMPSTARTING DEVELOPMENT

Anyone who thought, amidst the euphoria of dizzying change starting in 1989, that the end of the Cold War would usher in an age of global harmony and easy solutions has long since been disabused of the notion. Every day we open our newspapers to dark headlines confirming that the world is still a very dangerous place—in some ways more dangerous than before. We are confronted with a host of problems, both old and new, that are reaching crisis proportions. Is there a way of "jumpstarting" solutions to many of those problems? In fact, there is.

To many, it may not seem so. Ethnic conflict, religious hatred, failed states, economic devastation in Eastern Europe and the former Soviet Union, AIDS, and environmental degradation all seem intractable problems. Meanwhile, the number of poor in the world continues to increase at about the same rate as the world's population. The World Bank put their number at 1.1 billion in 1990. A fifth of the world's population is living on less than one dollar a day, and during the 1980s the poor actually lost ground. The 1990s show little evidence that the world economy will return anytime soon to a high growth trajectory.

The negative trends have even begun to afflict the rich. In the last decade, poverty increased in a number of industrialized countries, most notably in the United States and the United Kingdom and, of course, in the former communist countries of Europe. In most of those countries, children bore the brunt of the reversal. In America today, one in five children is poor, the highest level of child poverty in a quarter century in the world's richest country. In both the United Kingdom and the United States, child poverty has nearly doubled in a decade.

Small wonder that the lead article in this journal's spring issue contended that "all the trends" are in the wrong direction and that the world "appears to be at the beginning, not of a new order, but of a new nightmare." Such pessimism, however, can be misplaced. The world is in fact on the threshold of being able to make vastly greater progress on many problems that have long seemed intractable. Rather than merely reacting to situations after they have become critical, as in Somalia, the world has an opportunity in the 1990s to make an effective—and efficient—social investment to convert despair into hope and go a long way toward preventing future crises and building healthy societies.

The situation today may be analogous to that of Asia in the mid 1960s, when population growth seemed set to outrun the food supply. Many predicted widespread famine, chaos, and instability for the last third of this century. But then, quite suddenly, within four or five years, the Green Revolution took hold in Asia, extending from the Philippines through South Asia to Turkey. In country after country, wheat and rice production increased at annual rates unprecedented in the West. The immediate cause was not so much a scientific breakthrough—strains of the miracle wheats had been around for as many as 15 years—as a political and organizational one. Only by the mid 1960s had fertilizer, pesticides, and controlled irrigation become widely used, thanks in large part to earlier aid programs. At the same time, the combination of Asian drought and increasing awareness of the population explosion created the political will to drastically restructure price levels for grains and agro-inputs, and to mobilize the multiple sectors of society—rural credit, marketing, transport, foreign exchange allocations, media—required for success. U.S. president Lyndon Johnson deserves credit for his leadership contribution to that effort, though his deep personal involvement remains a largely untold story.

We may be in a similar position today, but on a much broader front—poised for advances in primary health care, basic education, water supply and sanitation, family planning, and gender equity, as well as food production—and covering a much wider geographical area, including Africa and Latin America as well as Asia. With an earnest effort from the major powers, the 1990s could witness a second green revolution—extending, this time, beyond agriculture to human development.

Frequent illness, malnutrition, poor growth, illiteracy, high birth rates, and gender bias are among poverty's worst symptoms. They are also some of poverty's most fundamental causes. We could anticipate, therefore, that overcoming some of the worst symptoms and causes of poverty would have far-reaching repercussions on the national and global level. The recent experiences of such diverse societies as China, Costa Rica, the Indian state of Kerala, Sri Lanka, and the Asian newly industrializing countries (NICs) suggest that high population growth rates, which wrap the cycle of poverty ever tighter, can be reduced dramatically. Reducing poverty would give a major boost to the fragile new efforts at democratization that will survive only if they tangibly improve the lives of the bottom half of society. As we know from the experience of Singapore, South Korea, Taiwan, and the other Asian NICs, such progress would in turn accelerate economic growth. By breaking the "inner cycle" of poverty, we would increase the capacity of the development process to assault poverty's many external causes, rooted in such diverse factors as geography, climate, land tenure, debt, business cycles, governance, and unjust economic relations.

We are uniquely positioned to succeed in the 1990s. Recent scientific and technological advances—and the revolutionary new capacity to communicate with and mobilize large numbers of people—have provided us with a host of new tools. The world's leaders can now use them together to produce dramatic, even unprecedented, results.

For example, the universal child immunization effort—the largest peacetime international collaboration in world history—has since the mid 1980s established systems that now reach virtually every hamlet in the developing world and are saving the lives of more than 8,000 children a day—some 3 million a year. Here, too, the technology was not new; vaccines had been available for some 20–30 years. Success has been the result of applying new communication and mobilization techniques to the immunization effort, often led personally by heads of state, making use of television and radio advertisements, and supported by a wide range of local leaders. School teachers, priests, imams, local government officials, nongovernmental organization (NGO) workers, and health personnel all joined the effort. By 1990, more than 80 per cent of the developing world's children were being brought in four or five times for vaccinations even before their first birthdays. As a result, Calcutta, Lagos, and Mexico City today have far higher levels of immunization of children at ages one and two than do New York City, Washington, D.C., or even the United States as a whole.

A similar effort is now being made to spread the use of oral rehydration therapy (ORT) to combat the single greatest historical killer of children, diarrhea, which takes the lives of some 8,000 children every day, down from 11,000 daily a decade ago. ORT was invented in the late 1960s, but only recently have leaders mobilized to use this lifesaver on a national scale. Every year it now saves the lives of more than 1 million children, a figure that could easily more than double by 1995 with increased national and international leadership.

The arsenal is now well stocked with other new technologies and rediscovered practices that can bring tremendous benefits with inspired leadership and only modest funding. Thus, the simple iodization of salt—at a cost of five cents annually per consumer—would prevent the world's single largest cause of mental retardation and of goiter, which affect more than 200 million people today as a result of iodine deficiency. Universal access to vitamin A through low-cost capsules or vegetables would remove the greatest single cause—about 700 cases per day—of blindness while reducing child deaths by up to a third in many parts of the developing world. The scientific rediscovery of the miracles of mother's milk means that more than a million children would not have died last year if only they had been effectively breast-fed for the first months of their lives, instead of being fed on more-costly infant formula. In such diverse countries as Bangladesh, Colombia, Senegal, and Zimbabwe, it has proven possible to get poor children, including girls, through primary education at very little cost. Recent advances have shown how to halve the costs of bringing sanitation and safe water to poor communities, to less than $30 per capita. New varieties of high-yield crops—from cassava to corn—are now ready to be promoted on a national scale in sub-Saharan Africa.

Meanwhile, with such tools in hand, the new capacity to communicate—to inform and motivate—empowers families, communities, and governments to give all children a better chance to lead productive lives. In short, we are now learning to "outsmart" poverty at the outset of each new life by providing a "bubble of protection" around a child's first vulnerable months and years. Strong international leadership and cooperation—facilitated enormously by the end of the Cold War and the expansion of democracy—could leverage that new capacity into wide-ranging social progress.

A CHILDREN'S REVOLUTION

Notwithstanding the media image of the Third World as a lost cause, there is real momentum there for change. In fact, for all the difficulties and setbacks, more progress has been made in developing countries in the last 40 years than was made in the previous 2,000, progress achieved while much of the world freed itself from colonialism and while respect for human and political rights expanded dramatically. Life expectancy has lengthened from 53 in 1960 to 65 today, and continues to increase at a rate of 9.5 hours per day. Thirty years ago, approximately three out of four children born in the developing countries survived to their fifth birthdays; today, some nine out of ten survive.

At the same time, the birth rates in countries as disparate as Brazil, China, Colombia, Cuba, Korea, Mexico, Sri Lanka, Thailand, and Tunisia have been more than halved, dramatically slowing population growth and the inherent strains it places on limited natural resources and social programs. Among the factors that have helped contain population growth, improving children's health is undoubtedly the least well-known and appreciated. As the United Nations Population Division puts it, "Improvements in child survival, which increase the predictability of the family building process, trigger the transition from natural to controlled fertility behavior. This in turn generates the need for family planning." While they are important priorities themselves, reductions in child mortality, basic education of women, and the availability of family planning make a strong synergistic contribution to solving what Yale historian Paul Kennedy calls, in *Preparing for the Twenty-First Century* (1992), the "impending demographic disaster." As population specialist Sharon Camp noted in the Spring 1993 issue of FOREIGN POLICY:

> Measures like quality reproductive health care, greater educational and economic opportunities for women, and reductions in infant and child death rates can and will bring about rapid birthrate declines. If all developing countries were to emulate the most effective policies and programs and if donor governments such as the United States were to provide adequate levels of assistance, the population problem could be resolved in the lifetime of today's children.

In fact, a children's revolution is already under way in the developing world, often led by those in power. Developing country leaders took the lead in seeking history's first truly global summit—the 1990 World Summit for Children—with an unprecedented 71 heads of state and government participating. They also pressed for early action on the Convention on the Rights of the Child, which was adopted by the [UN] General Assembly in November 1989 and which has since been signed or ratified in record time by more than 150 countries—with the United States now being the only major exception.

The experience of the past decade showed it possible—even during the darkest days of the Cold War and amid the Third World economic crisis of the 1980s—to mobilize societies and the international community around a package of low-cost interventions and services, building a sustainable momentum of human progress. The United Nations Children's Fund (UNICEF) and NGOs called it the Child Survival and Development Revolution, and as a result more than 20 million children are alive today who would not otherwise be; tens of millions are healthier, stronger, and less of a burden upon their mothers and families; and birth rates are falling.

Leaders are learning that productive things can be done for families and children at relatively low cost, and that it can be good politics for them to do so and bad politics to resist. More than 130 countries have issued or are actively working on National Programmes of Action to implement the goals set by the World Summit for Children, all of which were incorporated into Agenda 21 at the June 1992 Earth Summit in Rio de Janeiro. Those ambitious goals—to be met by the year 2000—include controlling the major childhood diseases; cutting child malnutrition in half; reducing death rates for children under five by one-third; cutting in half maternal mortality rates; providing safe water and sanitation for all communities; and making family planning services and basic education universally available. In 1992, most regions of the developing world took the process a step further by selecting a core of targets for 1995, when the first World Social Summit will review children's progress within the broader development process. For the first time since the dawn of history, humankind is making long-term plans for improving the lives of the young.

In part, that new concern has its roots in the communications revolution that brings daily pictures of large-scale famine or violence into our homes. At the same time, the new communications capacity has permitted deprived populations everywhere to see how much better people can live, firing grassroots movements for reform and democracy. But most of the Third World's suffering remains invisible. Of the 35,000 children under age five who die every day in the developing countries, more than 32,000 succumb to largely preventable hunger and illness. No earthquake, no flood, no war has taken the lives of a quarter million children in a single week; but that is the weekly death toll of the invisible emergencies resulting from poverty and underdevelopment. In 1992, 500,000 children under the age of five died in the kind of dramatic emergencies that attract media attention, but that is a small portion of the nearly 13 million children under five who are killed every year by grinding poverty and gross underdevelopment. The tragic deaths of 1,000 children per day in Somalia last year captured far more public attention than those of the 8,000 children around the world who die every day from the dehydration caused by ordinary diarrhea, which is so easily treated and prevented.

As the international community assumes greater responsibility for proliferating civil strife and other emergencies, it must come to terms with the realities of limited resources. How many operations to rescue failed states like Somalia can the international community afford? It is estimated that the U.S. component of the Somalia operation alone will cost more than $750 million for just four months' involvement, nearly comparable to UNICEF's average annual global budget of recent years, much of which is used to prevent future crises. There are now 48 civil and ethnic conflicts in progress around the globe. The United Nations is involved in 14 peacekeeping operations on five continents. Last year, those operations cost more than $3 billion, about four times higher than the previous record. Those operations are the most expensive way to relieve suffering, and it is clearly time to invest far more in *preventing* emergencies and conflicts, and in buttressing the new democracies, even as we put out the world's fires. As U.N. secretary-general Boutros Boutros-Ghali argues in his *Agenda for Peace,* prevention can prove far less costly—and produce far greater results—than relying on expensive and sometimes ineffective rescue operations.

As the international community shifts toward prevention—as it must—it makes the most sense to focus on eradicating poverty's worst manifestations early in the lives of children, breaking the cycle of poverty from generation to generation. At the World Summit for Children, the international community identified the basic package of high-impact, low-cost interventions that can make a difference in the short and medium term, while helping to build long-term development. Now it has only to make them work, albeit on a massive scale.

The overall price tag for reaching all the year 2000 goals for children and women, which would overcome most of the worst aspects of poverty, would be an extra $25 billion per year. The developing countries themselves are trying to come up with two-thirds of that amount by reordering their domestic priorities and budgets, while the remaining third—slightly more than $8 billion per year—should come from the industrialized world in the form of increased or reallocated official development assistance (ODA) and debt relief. That is a small price for meeting the basic needs of virtually every man, woman, and child in the developing world in nutrition, basic health, basic education, water and sanitation, and family planning within this decade.

In Russia and the other former Soviet republics, such aid could produce rapid grassroots results at an affordable cost, easing pain and helping to buy time until democratic and macroeconomic reforms show concrete progress. Plans for restoring democracy to Cambodia, Haiti, and Mozambique will need to alleviate suffering among the poor quickly; and targeting the essential needs of children and women can produce the biggest impact at the lowest cost. International relief programs for Somalia must rapidly give way to assistance that constitutes an investment in human development, and no such investment has been found to be more cost-effective than primary health care, nutrition, and basic education for children and women. The road to power for many of the world's extremist movements—whether based in religion or political ideology—is paved with the unmet needs of the poor.

Sadly, the U.S. has stagnated or regressed over the past decade with respect to children, even while much of the developing world has been making impressive progress. The United States has provided little leadership for that progress, except for that provided by the bipartisanship of Congress, which actively encouraged U.S. support to child survival and development programs abroad. But by increasing investment in American children and strengthening American families, and by reordering foreign assistance to reflect that new priority, the United States, the world's sole superpower, could once more set the global standard and give a major boost to human development and economic growth.

First, few actions would have more immediate impact than the signature and ratification this year of the historic Convention on the Rights of the Child. President Bill Clinton's signature of the convention and its submission to the U.S. Senate for early ratification (as has been urged by bipartisan leadership) would send an important message to the world, bringing the rights of children close to becoming humanity's first universal law.

Second, the United States needs to demonstrate a new culture of caring for its own children. The much-needed reordering of priorities for American children, women, and families is already under way, with initiatives on Head Start, universal immunization, parental leave, family planning, and health services for all. A "Culture of Caring," the American plan in response to the World Summit for Children that was issued at the end of the Bush administration—in January 1993 —provides a useful base for bipartisan action.

Third, the United States needs "20/20 vision." It should support the May 1991 proposal of the United Nations Development Programme, which had two components: It called on developing countries to devote at least 20 per cent of their budgets to directly meeting the basic human needs of their people, roughly double current average levels. It also argued that 20 per cent of all international development aid should go to meet those same basic needs: primary health care, nutrition, basic education, family planning, and safe water and sanitation. Today, on average, less than 10 per cent of already inadequate levels of ODA are devoted to that purpose. Different ways of defining and reporting social sector allocations within national and ODA budgets make precise quantification of those proportions somewhat difficult, and efforts are therefore underway to achieve a common form of reporting. But even if subsequent research changes the target percentages, the "20/20 vision" concept underscores the importance of restructuring both sets of budgets in line with the priorities established at the World Summit for Children, which may require—on average—a doubling of existing allocations.

On the ODA side, the United States today devotes less than $1 billion to basic human needs. Of the projected $25 billion extra annually that will be required globally by mid-decade to meet the World Summit year 2000 goals, the U.S. share would be $2 billion. The roughly $3 billion total would then still be less than 20 per cent of all U.S. foreign and military assistance. It is a small price to pay for jumpstarting solutions to so many of the overwhelming problems of population, democracy, and the worst aspects of poverty, to say nothing about saving tens of millions of young lives this decade. The additional funds can be obtained from reductions in the military and security component of the U.S. international affairs budget.

Fourth, the new spirit of democratic change and economic reform in Africa will not survive if its creditors do not give it some debt relief: Together, the sub-Saharan African countries pay $1 billion in debt service to foreign creditors every month, and its debt is now proportionally three or four times heavier than that of Latin America. At the November 1992 Organization of African Unity–sponsored International Conference on Assistance to African Children, donor countries and lending agencies alike pledged to promote more debt relief while expanding or restructuring ODA in order to help Africa protect and nurture its children. Here again the

United States could help lead the way, preventing Africa from deteriorating into a continent of Somalias. The G-7 Summit in Tokyo in July 1993 should make a definitive commitment to debt relief, with much of the local currency proceeds going to accelerate programs for children, women, and the environment through a variety of debt-swapping mechanisms. With the right mixture of domestic and international support, and with apartheid ending in South Africa, we could see dramatic progress in most of Africa by the year 2000. That could include a food revolution every bit as green as Asia's—but African countries will need help. The alternative could be a return to authoritarian rule, corruption, and conflict throughout large parts of the continent.

Fifth, the United States must actively support multilateral cooperation. With human development and poverty alleviation increasingly accepted as the focus for development cooperation in the 1990s, the United States has an opportunity to transform rhetoric into reality. Active U.S. support and leadership along those lines in the World Bank, the International Monetary Fund, the regional banks, and throughout the U.N. system will go a long way toward overcoming, in our time, the worst aspects of poverty in the South, where it is most acute. Land-mark U.N. conferences have been scheduled on human rights (1993), population (1994), and women (1995); U.S. leadership at those conferences and at the U.N. summit on social development in 1995 will strengthen their impact. The U.S. role will also be critical in reducing poverty in the North and in the transitional societies of Eastern Europe and the former Soviet Union.

Finally, the United States must strengthen its commitment to the United Nations. The new administration's initiative to seek restoration of U.S. funding for the United Nations Population Fund is a welcome step—a step that Congress should rapidly implement. That and a decision to rejoin the United Nations Educational, Scientific, and Cultural Organization (UNESCO) would not only give an important boost to family planning and global education, but—together with full payment of its U.N. arrears—it would signal long-term U.S. commitment to the United Nations as the global village's central vehicle for development cooperation and safeguarding the peace.

Focusing on children as a means of attacking the worst aspects of poverty will not solve all the world's problems, but it would make a historic contribution—at this all-too-brief juncture of opportunity —to the better world we all seek. It could change the course of history.

NO

THE KINDNESS OF STRANGERS

The old jibe about aid—"poor people in rich countries helping rich
people in poor countries"—has plenty of truth in it. Donors need to
learn from past mistakes if they want to help poor countries grow.

Anybody who tried to see the case for aid by looking merely at the way it is
allotted would quickly give up in despair. The richest 40% of the developing
world gets about twice as much per head as the poorest 40%. Big military
spenders get about twice as much per head as do the less belligerent. El
Salvador gets five times as much aid as Bangladesh, even though Bangladesh
has 24 times as many people and is five times poorer than El Salvador.

Since 1960, about $1.4 trillion (in 1988 dollars) has been transferred in aid
from rich countries to poor ones. Yet relatively little is known about what
that process has achieved. Has it relieved poverty? Has it stimulated growth
in the recipient countries? Has it helped the countries which give it? Such
questions become more pressing as donor governments try harder to curb
public spending. This year, two of the biggest players in the international aid
business are looking afresh at their aims and priorities.

Brian Atwood, appointed by the Clinton administration to run America's
Agency for International Development (AID), inherited an organisation en-
cumbered over the years with 33 official goals by a Congress that loved using
aid money to buy third-world adherence to its pet ideas. Now, faced with a
sharp budget cut, Mr Atwood is trying to pare down to just four goals: building democracy, protecting the environment, fostering sustainable economic
development and encouraging population control. Not, however, anything
as basic as the relief of poverty.

A few blocks away from Mr Atwood's Washington office, the World Bank
is going through a similar exercise. Set up in 1946, the Bank has become the
most powerful of all the multilateral development organisations. But a critical
internal report recently accused the Bank of caring more about pushing out
loans than about monitoring how well the money was spent. Now the Bank
hopes to improve the quality of its lending. It is also wondering about its
future. Some of its past borrowers in East Asia are now rich enough to turn
lenders themselves. More should follow. The Bank is trying to move into new

areas, such as cleaning up the environment and setting up social-welfare systems. But some people wonder how long it will really be needed.

AID and the World Bank are unusual (although their critics rarely admit as much) in their openness and in the rigour with which they try to evaluate what they do. But other donors will also have to think about which kinds of aid to abandon as their budgets stop expanding. In the 1980s the official development assistance[1] (ODA) disbursed by members of the OECD's [Organization for Economic Cooperation and Development's] Development Assistance Committee (DAC)—21 rich countries plus the European Commission—increased by about a quarter in real terms; but between 1991 and 1992, the DAC's disbursements rose by just 0.5%. Development Initiatives, an independent British ginger group [a driving force within a larger group], believes "the end of an era" may have come; it reckons that aid budgets around the world are ceasing to grow at all. Almost the only exception is Japan, which provides a fifth of DAC aid and plans a substantial increase over the next five years.

Most multilateral donors, such as the UN agencies, also have budgets frozen. A rare exception is the European Development Fund [EDF], the aid arm of the European Union, which is taking a rapidly rising share of member-states' aid budgets. The EDF's secrecy and its mediocre reputation with recipient countries make some bilateral donors unhappy. "British officials are concerned about having to devote increasing quantities of their aid, which they regard as successful, to the European programme," reports Robert Cassen, a British aid expert.

Figure 1

More from the Market: Net Resource Flows to Developing Countries [in] $bn, Constant 1991 Prices and Exchange Rates

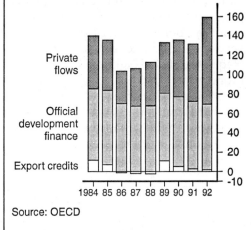

Source: OECD

NEEDED: A CASE FOR GIVING

Some developing countries—mainly the faster-growing ones perceived as "emerging markets"—have found the international capital markets to be increasingly willing suppliers of finance (see Figure 1). But demands for ODA are still appearing in new forms and from new sources. Astute third-world countries are giving old projects a green tinge to profit from fashionable enthusiasm for the environment. The countries of Eastern Europe and the former Soviet Union are competing with the third world for help. And the proportion of aid spent on relieving disasters has soared from 2% five years ago to around 7% today.

But with the clamour for more money goes increasing uncertainty about what aid is for and what it has achieved. The naive taxpayer might imagine that aid's main purpose was to relieve poverty. Yet only relatively small amounts of ODA go to the poorest of countries or to projects that benefit mainly the poorest of people. A study of America's aid programme conducted by the Overseas Development Council (ODC), a Washington, DC, think-tank, found that more than $250 per person went to relatively high-income countries, but less than $1 per person to very low-income countries. Mahbub ul Haq of the United Nations Development Programme (UNDP), a fierce critic of aid's failure to reach the poorest, points out that the ten countries that are home to two-thirds of the world's poorest people receive only one-third of world aid.

NOT HELPING THE POOR

Within poor countries, too, aid is rarely concentrated on the services that benefit the poorest. The World Bank reckons that, of all the aid going to low-income countries in 1988, a mere 2% went on primary health care and 1% on population programmes. Even the aid that is spent on health and education tends to go to services that benefit disproportionately the better-off. Aid for health care goes disproportionately to hospitals (in 1988–89, for instance, 33% of Japan's bilateral aid for health went on building hospitals); aid for education, to universities. In sub-Saharan Africa in the 1980s, only $1 of ODA went on each primary pupil; $11 on each secondary pupil; and $575 on each university student.

Such spending patterns often reflect the priorities of the recipient governments. Some donors have tried to persuade governments to distribute aid differently. They have had mixed success —not surprisingly, for their own motives in aid-giving often override the goal of poverty relief.

One such motive, powerful even since the end of the cold war, is the pursuit of national security. Most governments are coy about the role that national security plays in their aid budgets, but the biggest donor of all, the United States, is blatant: roughly a quarter of its $21 billion foreign-aid budget takes the form of military assistance, and roughly a quarter of the total budget goes to Israel and Egypt alone. "The United States has spent a lot less money on development than on advancing political and military goals," says John Sewell of the ODC. This year, America's aid budget protects the shares of Israel and Egypt. America also sees aid to Eastern Europe and to the countries of the former Soviet Union primarily in strategic terms.

"National security" is also now being used as an argument for giving more weight to all sorts of other goals in the drawing-up of aid budgets. Environmentalists claim that some types of environmental damage, such as global warming and the thinning of the ozone layer, may be worsened by poor-country growth, and they argue that rich-country aid donors should in their own interests take special care to minimise such risks. Others say aid should be used to parry the threats to rich countries posed by the trade in illegal drugs, by population growth and by third-world poverty.

If the goal of national security can conflict with that of poverty relief, then the commercial interests of aid donors can do so even more. Japan's approach has at least the merit of simplicity: its development assistance goes mainly to countries that are most likely to become its future customers. All DAC countries tie some aid—the average is about a quarter—to the purchase of their own goods and services. One problem with tying is that it forces countries to pay over the odds for imports: on average, some estimates suggest, recipients pay 15% more than prevailing prices. Another is that it often distorts development priorities. It is easier to tie aid to a large item of capital spending, such as a dam, road or hospital, than to a small rural project that may do more good. Not surprisingly, tying is especially common in transport, power generation and telecommunications projects.

Aid recorded as tied has been falling as a proportion of bilateral ODA, according to the OECD, which monitors the practice. That may be partly because of the rise in spending on disaster relief. It may also reflect an international agreement on guidelines for tied aid. But governments are clever at finding ways to use aid to promote exports. It has, for example, taken two official investigations to uncover some of the links between British aid to Malaysia and British arms sales to that country.

Some kinds of ODA are given in the sure knowledge that the money will be spent mainly in the donor country, but without explicit tying. One example is technical assistance. Of the $12 billion or so which goes each year to buy advice, training and project design, over 90% is spent on foreign consultants. Half of all technical assistance goes to Africa —which, observes UNDP's Mr Haq, "has perhaps received more bad advice per capita than any other continent". Most thoughtful people in the aid business regard technical assistance as one of the least effective ways to foster development.

Stung by the claims of their aid lobbies that too little help goes to the poor, some governments are trying to steer more money through voluntary bodies, such as charities and church groups. Such bodies, known in the trade as non-governmental organisations or NGOs, have proliferated at astonishing speed in both the rich and poor worlds. The OECD counted 2,542 NGOs in its 24 member countries in 1990, compared with 1,603 in 1980. The growth in the south may have been faster still. Roger Riddell, of the Overseas Development Institute in London, who has made a special study of NGOs and development, talks of a "veritable explosion" in their numbers; he mentions 25,000 grass-roots organisations in the Indian state of Tamil Nadu alone. The public and private money dispensed by NGOs amounted to 13% of total net ODA flows in 1990, and the share has been creeping up.

NGOs may be better than central governments at handling small projects and more sensitive to what local people really need. But even NGOs, according to Mr Riddell, usually fail to help the very poorest. "If government and official aid programmes fail to reach the bottom 20% of income groups, most NGO interventions probably miss the bottom 5–10%," he guesses. And, as more aid is channelled through NGOs, some groups may find it harder to retain the element of local participation which is their most obvious strength. More searching questions might be asked about whether they are efficiently run, or achieve their purported goals: a study of projects supported by the Ford Foundation in Africa in the late 1980s found "very few successes to talk about, especially in terms of post-intervention sustainability".

AND WHAT ABOUT GROWTH?

When the modern panoply of official aid institutions grew up after the second world war, the intention was not to relieve poverty as such but to promote economic growth in poor countries. Aid was seen as a transitional device to help countries reach a point from which their economies would take off of their own accord. Its use was to remove shortages of capital and foreign exchange, boosting investment to a point at which growth could become self-sustaining.

In their baldest form, such views sit oddly beside the fact that, in many of the countries that have received the most aid and have the highest levels of capital investment, growth has been negligible. For at least 47 countries, aid represented more than 5% of GNP [gross national product] in 1988. Many of those countries were in sub-Saharan Africa, where GDP [gross domestic product] per head has been virtually flat for a quarter of a century. Yet, as David Lindauer and Michael Roemer of the Harvard Institute for International Development point out in a recent study, some of them were investing a share of GDP almost as large as that of much faster growing South-East Asian countries: Cameroon, Côte d'Ivoire, Kenya, Tanzania and Zambia all invested at least 20% of GDP, a figure comparable with that for Indonesia or Thailand.

Such rough comparisons may prove little, but they draw attention to an awkward point. Some third-world countries have enjoyed fast economic growth with relatively little aid per head. In particular, some Asian success stories, such as China and Vietnam, had little or no aid at a time when donors were pouring money into Africa (although China is now the World Bank's largest single customer). If some countries can achieve economic growth with little aid, while other countries which get a great deal of aid do not

grow at all, what if anything is aid good for?

One way to try to answer that question is to review the experience of individual countries and aid projects. In the late 1980s there were two valiant attempts to do just this: one conducted by a team led by Mr Cassen, the other on a more modest scale by Mr Riddell. Mr Cassen's team argued that "the majority of aid is successful in terms of its own objectives", but added that "a significant proportion does not succeed." Aid had worked badly in Africa; better in South Asia. Where aid did not work, the reason was sometimes that donors failed to learn from their mistakes or the mistakes of other donors; and sometimes that a recipient country failed to make the most of what was offered to it.

As for the impact of aid on economic growth, Mr Cassen concluded cautiously that one could not say that aid failed to help. In some countries, indeed, he found evidence that it did increase growth. Mr Riddell was similarly tentative. Aid, he concluded, "can assist in the alleviation of poverty, directly and indirectly" and "the available evidence... fails to convince that, as a general rule, alternative strategies which exclude aid lead in theory or have led in practice to more rapid improvements in the living standards of the poor than have been achieved with aid."

These are hardly ringing endorsements. But these evaluations of individual aid programmes and projects are more positive in their findings than attempts to establish broader links between aid and growth, which have usually failed entirely. Plenty of economists have picked holes in the original idea that aid would boost investment: why should it, some ask, when governments may simply use income from aid as an excuse to spend tax revenues in other, less productive ways?

Other economists, such as Howard White of the Institute of Social Studies at The Hague, who has reviewed many of the economic studies of the effects of aid on growth, point to the difficulties of generalising. Given the various transfers that count as "aid", the many conditions that donors attach, the differing importance of aid in national economies and the complexity of economic growth, there are simply too many variables to say much that is useful.

THIRD-WORLD DUTCH DISEASE

Since the start of the 1980s, many donors have come to believe that the quality of a country's economic management will do most to determine whether aid will do some good. Aid in the 1980s was frequently used, especially by the World Bank, as a prod to encourage countries to begin "structural adjustment" programmes. In some cases, the economic performance of these countries did improve—Ghana is one of the Bank's favourite examples. In other cases, it did not. A review by the IMF [International Monetary Fund] of 19 low-income countries which had undergone structural adjustment found that their current-account deficits averaged 12.3% of GDP before adjustment and 16.8% in the most recent year; and that their external debt had grown from 451% of exports to 482%.

Why was this? Were countries encouraged to adopt the wrong policies? Did they ignore the advice they were given? Or did the aid itself do some damage? Stefan de Vylder, a Swedish economist, argued for the last of these explanations at a conference in Stockholm in March.

Figure 2

Friends in Need: Aid* as % of GDP, 1992

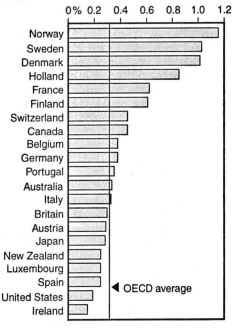

*Net official development assistance
Source: OECD

He argued that large volumes of aid (such as those associated with structural adjustment programmes) could damage an economy's international competitiveness; and countries where export performance was especially bad tended to be "rewarded" with low-interest loans and grants.

The damage to competitiveness, Mr de Vylder believes, is a version of "Dutch disease". This was the term coined in the 1970s to describe how Holland's exports of natural gas boosted its real exchange rate and thereby harmed its export competitiveness. Mr White thinks something similar happened in Sri Lanka between 1974 and 1988, when a sharp increase in aid contributed to a divergence between the nominal and real exchange rates; this hurt the growth of the country's manufactured exports.

Mr de Vylder also worries about the tendency of aid to compensate for failure rather than to reward success. Bilateral donors have increasingly found that much of the aid they give to some countries goes towards paying back money unwisely lent by international financial institutions. Take Zambia as an example. Between 1974 and 1987, Zambia had entered into seven stand-by or structural agreements with the IMF—one every two years. Each was broken by the Zambian government. When, in 1987, Mr de Vylder visited Zambia to assess the latest bout of economic disaster, he asked a minister how seriously the government was worried at being lambasted by every aid donor. "Concerned?" mused the minister, seeming somewhat surprised. Then: "Oh no. They always come back." The minister was right, says Mr de Vylder. Shortly afterwards, the international financial institutions were again knocking on the door, asking for a new agreement.

It is easy, with aid, to find examples of individual projects that do some good. Most of those who criticise aid argue that if the quality were better—if donors tried harder to learn from each other's mistakes, if they were less keen to reap commercial gain, if they concentrated harder on meeting basic human needs— then there would be far fewer failures. All that is true; but—other things being equal —there would also be much less aid. Will poor countries do worse, over the next 30 years, if rich countries decline to give or lend them another $1.4 trillion? At that price, the answer should be "Yes". Given the way that aid works at present, it is only "Maybe".

NOTES

1. Defined as aid administered with the promotion of economic development and welfare as the main objective; concessional in character; and with a grant element of at least 25%.

POSTSCRIPT

Should the Developed North Increase Aid to the Less Developed South?

There can be no argument that most of the people in most of the countries of the South live in circumstances that citizens in the developed countries of the North would find unacceptable. There is also no question that most of the LDCs were subjugated and held in colonial bondage by the developed countries. Apart from these points, there is little agreement on the causes and the solutions to the plight of the South.

Many LDC specialists blame colonialism for the LDCs' lack of development, past and present. This view is held in many of the LDCs and is also represented widely in Western scholarly opinion. Johan Galtung's "A Structural Theory of Imperialism," *Journal of Peace Research* (1971) is a classic statement from this perspective. This belief has led to the LDCs' demand for a New International Economic Order (NIEO), in which there would be a greater sharing of wealth and economic power between the North and the South. More on the common views and efforts of the LDCs can be found in Darryl C. Thomas, *The Theory and Practice of Third World Solidarity* (Praeger, 1994). It is also possible to argue that continued poverty in the LDCs, especially amid the general prosperity of the economically developed countries, will increase anger among the people of the economically less developed countries, decrease global stability, and have a variety of other negative consequences. For a discussion of the growing military capabilities of the LDCs, consult Donald M. Snow, *Distant Thunder: Third World Conflict and the New International Order* (St. Martin's Press, 1993).

Other analysts argue that colonialism actually benefited many dependencies by introducing modern economic techniques and that those former colonies that have remained close to the industrialized countries have done the best. Still others have charged that some LDCs have followed policies that have short-circuited their own development. This point of view sees calls for an NIEO as little more than an attempt by the South to increase their power and to reorder the international system. Steven D. Krasner's *Structural Conflict: The Third World Against Global Liberalism* (University of California Press, 1985) is written from this point of view.

There are also disagreements about how much the North should aid the South, irrespective of who has caused their problems. Humanitarian concerns, as well as a sense that all the world's people will eventually be more prosperous if the 80 percent who live in poverty in the South can develop, argue for greater aid, a view represented in David Aronson, "Why Africa Stays Poor and Why It Doesn't Have To," *The Humanist* (March/April 1993).

On the Internet . . .

Arms Control and Nonproliferation: The Clinton Administration Record
This is a fact sheet released by the Office of the Press Secretary for The White House, Washington, D.C., September 23, 1996.
http://www.state.gov/www/global/arms/fs_arms.html

PeaceNet
This large PeaceNet site offers information on the areas of peace, social and economic justice, human rights, and the struggle against racism.
http://www.igc.org/igc/peacenet/

United Nations Peace-keeping Operations: OSCE Field Activities
This UN site provides access to descriptions of current and past peacekeeping operations, a survey of operations, and Security Council and security system pages.
http://www.fib.ethz.ch/fib/pko/intro.html

U.S. Information Service Israel
This site has been created to promote mutual understanding between the United States and Israel. It offers press releases, resource centers, and search capabilities.
http://www.usis-israel.org.il/

PART 3

International Security

Whatever we may wish, war, terrorism, and other forms of physical coercion are still important elements of international politics. Countries calculate both how to use the instruments of force and how to implement national security. There can be little doubt, however, that significant changes are under way in this realm as part of the changing world system. Strong pressures exist to expand the mission and strengthen the security capabilities of international organizations and to reduce or eliminate nuclear weapons worldwide. This section examines how countries in the international system are addressing these issues.

■ Does the World Need to Have Nuclear Weapons at All?

■ Should a Permanent UN Military Force Be Established?

ISSUE 10

Does the World Need to Have Nuclear Weapons at All?

YES: Tom Bethell, from "No Nukes America," *American Spectator* (December 1996)

NO: George Lee Butler, from "Eliminating Weapons of Mass Destruction: The Scourge of Nuclear Weapons," *Vital Speeches of the Day* (February 1, 1997)

ISSUE SUMMARY

YES: Tom Bethell, Washington correspondent for the *American Spectator*, contends that the drive toward denuclearization is likely to leave the United States exposed to its enemies.

NO: George Lee Butler, a retired U.S. Air Force general and former commander of the Strategic Air Command, advocates the elimination of all nuclear weapons.

Efforts to control weapons of war go back to nearly the beginning of written history. Although progress was rarely made, it can be argued that the limited killing power of weapons made arms control agreements seem a low priority. That changed rapidly as the destructive capability of weapons grew exponentially during the industrial and then the technological ages. The first, albeit ineffective, multilateral arms negotiations were the Hague Conferences (1899, 1907). The awful toll and fearsome weapons of World War I prompted renewed arms control efforts. Conferences in Washington and London set limits to battleship tonnage among the world's leading naval powers.

The arms control efforts were spurred yet again by the horror of World War II and then by the existence—and use on Hiroshima and Nagasaki, Japan, in 1945—of atomic weapons that had the potential to end civilization. In January 1946 the UN established the International Atomic Energy Agency to try to limit the use of nuclear technology to peaceful purposes. Later that year, the UN also called for the "general regulation and reduction of armaments and armed forces" and established a Commission for Conventional Armaments.

Still, for almost 20 years nuclear weapons building and testing mushroomed unimpeded. Then, in 1963, the first major nuclear arms control agreement was signed, and by its terms most countries agreed to cease testing nuclear weapons in the atmosphere. Arms control efforts strengthened in the 1970s and continued to speed up. The cost of weaponry; the huge arsenals that each superpower had; the ever-increasing speed, power, and accuracy of those weapons; and the moderation of the cold war all prompted this acceleration.

Several of the arms control agreements are worth noting: the two Strategic Arms Limitation Talks treaties (SALT I and II, 1972 and 1979); the Intermediate-range Nuclear Forces (INF) Treaty (1987); and the two Strategic Arms Reduction Talks treaties (START I and II, 1991 and 1993). The SALT treaties limited the number of weapons systems that each superpower could possess. The INF Treaty eliminated an entire type of missile—those missiles with an intermediate range (500–5,500 km). It was the first step toward actually reducing the number of nuclear weapons. The START treaties took up the abolition of the intercontinental-range (over 5,500 km) U.S. and Soviet weapons, now all held by Russia. Like the INF Treaty, the START treaties pledged the signatories to reduce their nuclear arsenals. Unlike the INF Treaty, the reductions agreed to are substantial.

Under START II, which superseded START I, Russia will possess all the former Soviet intercontinental-range nuclear weapons delivery systems (missiles, bombers) and their associated weapons (warheads, bombs). Arsenals will be slashed to 3,500 weapons for the United States and 2,997 for Russia by the year 2003. The two sides agreed to eliminate all multiple-warhead land-based missiles. The treaty has been ratified by the United States but not, to date, by Russia.

The question before us here is, If the two nuclear behemoths can slim down their nuclear systems by approximately 75 percent, as they did comparing the SALT II and START II limits, then why not reduce the two sides' weapons (including both long-range weapons and the still-formidable short-range systems of bombs and artillery shells) to zero? Before we move to that debate, it is important to note that the closer one comes to zero, the more important others' nuclear arsenals become. Three countries (and their number of weapons) that have substantial arsenals are China (284), France (534), and Great Britain (200). Israel, India, Pakistan, and perhaps North Korea also have nuclear weapons.

The following selections carry the debate over nuclear weapons into the future. Tom Bethell outlines a number of reasons why it would not be wise for the United States to take the lead in eliminating nuclear weapons in the foreseeable future. George Lee Butler contends that attaining a nuclear-free world is neither wishful thinking nor a perilous path but, rather, attainable and desirable.

YES

Tom Bethell

NO NUKES AMERICA

Over a period of several decades, the weapons in the U.S. nuclear arsenal were assembled at the Pantex plant, a few miles northeast of Amarillo, Texas. The components were fabricated elsewhere—at Rocky Flats, near Denver; at Hanford reservation, in Washington state; at the Savannah River reactor in South Carolina—but they were finally all put together at Pantex, 16,000 acres of parched scrub surrounded by steel fences and coils of razor wire. The plant is dotted with infrared motion detectors and armed guards in desert camouflage.

Today, the entire U.S. nuclear weapons assembly line is running in reverse. All the nuclear-weapons production facilities are closed down, and the bombs themselves, having been retrieved from silos and Air Force bases, are being brought back to the same Pantex plant at a rate of about 35 or 40 a week. They are transported across U.S. highways in unmarked, heavily guarded tractor-trailers; at Pantex they are disassembled, and their plutonium "pits" stored in bunkers. State officials have expressed concern that Pantex is fast becoming "an unlicensed plutonium dump." The U.S. is said to be dismantling its arsenal at a rate of about 2,000 weapons a year.

The planned final size of the arsenal is secret, but some say the total may be no more than 1,000 weapons. Anti-nuke groups stationed outside the Pantex gates monitored the trucks as the completed weapons left the plant, and they continue to monitor them as they return.

In the postwar period, the U.S. produced some 70,000 nuclear weapons, of about 75 different types. Annual production rates in the early 1960's reached about 5,000 a year, and a maximum stockpile of over 32,000 warheads was reached in 1967. Information provided by Boris Yeltsin and Mikhail Gorbachev implied that the Soviets' arsenal at its peak exceeded 40,000 warheads. France today has about 480 nukes, China about 450, Britain 200, Israel "probably 100 plus devices," India 60-odd, and Pakistan 15–25, according to a guide published by the Carnegie Endowment for International Peace, *Tracking Nuclear Proliferation.*

It seems undeniable that the quantity of Soviet and U.S. nukes at their peak defied logic on both sides. Misleading "perceptions," inter-service rivalry,

From Tom Bethell, "No Nukes America," *American Spectator* (December 1996). Copyright © 1996 by *American Spectator.* Reprinted by permission.

and the skewed incentives of government agencies contributed to a build-up that was vastly in excess of whatever could have been used. The elimination of superfluous arsenals by definition does not jeopardize security, and there is much to be said for the current "build down." But it also has its disquieting aspects. Above all, it will be difficult to reverse the present course. In an emergency it could be done, but by then it would be too late, in view of the time required to build or re-start the industrial infrastructure. It is safe to say that the existing atomic-weapons production facilities will never be reopened. The enduring superstition surrounding all things nuclear will see to that: Not in my back yard, or anyone else's.

* * *

As the Cold War was coming to an end, the environmentalists gained a crucial and little remarked ascendancy over the military in the ordering of government priorities. It helped that George Bush was president when this happened, for he was willing to do almost anything to ward off accusation from environmentalists. Weapons plants were stigmatized as contaminated sites, "hot spots," sources of hazardous waste. All of the major nuclear weapons facilities have since then been included on the Environmental Protection Agency's "Superfund" National Priorities List of the worst contaminated sites in America. "In preparing to fight a nuclear war with the former Soviet Union," according to the Center for Defense Information's *Defense Monitor*, "America succeeded in 'nuking' itself." It is an irony, surely, that the plants that arguably yielded a 50-year stretch of domestic peace rarely enjoyed by any nation should in the end have been so condemned.

The symbolic moment came in June, 1989, when Rocky Flats was raided by FBI agents. The nation's only source of purified plutonium for nuclear weapons, Rocky Flats manufactured the softball-sized plutonium cores at the heart of the weapon. The raid came as a surprise to the Department of Energy, which has responsibility for the production and maintenance of nuclear weapons. Until the mid 1980's the department successfully argued that the practices of weapons-plant contractors were exempt from federal environmental laws. But by 1992 it had in effect become a loyal subsidiary of the Environmental Protection Agency. In that year, Rockwell International, the Rocky Flats contractor, pleaded guilty to charges that it had violated hazardous waste and clean-water laws. The company was fined $18.5 million. Today, according to the General Accounting Office, nuclear weapons facilities all across the country are closed "for environmental, health and safety reasons." The Department of Energy has estimated that cleaning up these sites will cost $300 billion—more than the annual defense budget.

In order to gain insight into future nuclear-weapons policy, it is worth studying the tracts of the anti-nukes, the bulletins of atomic scientists, and the pug-wash of "responsible" physicists and physicians. Their goal is unmistakable: America as a nuclear-free zone. The present deconstruction of America's nukes was prescribed in their earlier manifestos. But abolition is the goal. In 1992 the *Bulletin of the Atomic Scientists* published its "Agenda 2001." Among the contributors was Daniel Ellsberg of Harvard Medical School, earlier the publicist of the *Pentagon Papers*. It is fair to say that the present (anti) nuclear policies of the U.S., if not of the other nuclear states, are currently in line with his recommendations: No nukes are being built, production facilities are shut tight, the current arsenal is being deconstructed, and the U.S. has signed the Comprehensive Test Ban Treaty.

If ridding the whole world of nukes cannot quite be achieved, eliminating America's may be manageable. At the signing ceremony for the United Nations test-ban treaty this September, Clinton expressed the hope that the "role" of nuclear weapons could be "ultimately eliminated." Signatories include the *declared* nuclear powers (the U.S., Russia, China, France, Britain). The treaty has not taken effect, one reason being that India has refused to sign. (Gandhi must be turning in his sainted grave.) But the U.S. will respect its own signature and abide by its own gentleman's agreement. The effect will be to deny the benefits of modernization to just those countries that can be most trusted with nuclear weapons. Only those countries whose diplomats believe in the efficacy of such mantras as "trust but verify" will in the end sign on the dotted line.

The modernization of weapons without testing them is still permitted, and the U.S. is doing so. Innards are being removed, and old technology is being replaced by modern electronics. But the bombs can no longer be detonated, whether under the ground or above it, and so computer simulations must replace explosions. Will the new mechanisms actually work as intended? Nuclear weapons have a stockpile life of twenty years, and the U.S. arsenal is aging rapidly. Former Defense and Energy Secretary James Schlesinger says that the Clinton administration is hiding the reality that "with an end to testing, confidence in the nuclear stockpile must decline." He adds that if we are determined not to "design, test, manufacture or stockpile nuclear weapons," then perhaps shutting down our production facilities "makes logical sense."

* * *

Bill Clinton adopted a policy of no more testing against the advice of the director of the Los Alamos National Laboratory, Sigfried Hecker. In May 1993, he told Clinton that testing was the best way to maintain a reliable deterrent. Two months later, Clinton nonetheless ordered an end to testing. When China proceeded with an atmospheric test a few weeks later, U.S. policymakers chose to pay no attention. (Why make trouble with the big boys?) Russia is reliably reported to be maintaining its production lines, perhaps assembling as many nuclear weapons a year as we are disassembling. Even the humble Brits continue with a slow but active weapons production cycle to keep their hand in. But the U.S. has produced no weapons since 1990.

Tritium, a hydrogen isotope that is an essential ingredient of all American nukes, has not been produced anywhere in the U.S. since 1988, when the Savannah River reactor was shut down. With a half life of 12.6 years, most of the installed tritium will have vanished into thin air by the year 2015. At that point the U.S. arsenal will have a short half-life indeed. Tritium could be manufactured by electricity-generating nuclear reactors, but here we encounter the popular ignorance that has been both nurtured and exploited by the anti-nukes. Tritium-production would expose power plants to the charge that they are "hydrogen bomb plants." A recent editorial in *Science* suggested that maybe we could buy some tritium from Canada. Or, er, the Russians. That would "improve our relations" with them, and, in case you hadn't thought of it, "help alleviate their need for hard currency."

The main concern of those who are responsible for maintaining the nuclear arsenal today is that the needed human capital, experience, and knowledge will dwindle away along with the tritium. Automobile mechanics who know how to rebuild a 1933 Jaguar S-type sports coupe are difficult to find today. The refusal to allow further testing ensures that nuclear weapons technology will become increasingly outdated. It will require the expertise of those who understand and know how to maintain the nuclear equivalent of cathode ray tubes. The best minds will not be attracted by the prospects of working with museum technology in a dying industry.

The blueprints of nuclear weapons are now widely diffused throughout the world, and the knowledge they embody can never be eradicated from human consciousness. Because crude bombs can be assembled without the need for testing—the Hiroshima bomb was of a type that had not been tested—an end to testing enhances global security only in the minds of those who think the U.S. is the great threat to it. The main constraint on proliferation is the difficulty of obtaining weapons-grade fissile material: highly enriched uranium and plutonium. Neither occurs in nature —the main reason why all things nuclear are regarded with dread and horror by *homo sapiens*-hating enviros—and both depend for their production upon an advanced industrial capacity that itself has not yet proliferated much beyond the Western world.

The uncomfortable fact is that the U.S. has pursued its undeclared policy of unilateral denuclearization at just the time when this material has become more available than ever before, thanks to the breakup of the former Soviet Union. More than 100 cases of smuggling of weapons grade material have been detected, and it seems only a matter of time before a sufficient quantity of it finds its way into the hands of people who pay only lip service to the sleep-inducing diplomatic formulae. Will we feel more secure, let us say ten years from now, when more countries have acquired nuclear weapons, and it sinks in that our own dwindling arsenal is untested and of questionable reliability?

NO

George Lee Butler

ELIMINATING WEAPONS OF
MASS DESTRUCTION

Delivered to the Stimson Center Award Remarks, Washington, D.C., January 8, 1997.

Permit me to quote briefly from a memorandum that many of you will find familiar. It is from Secretary [Stimson] to President Truman, dated September 11, 1945:

"If the atomic bomb were merely another, though more devastating, military weapon to be assimilated into our pattern of international relations, it would be one thing. We could then follow the old custom of secrecy and military superiority relying on international caution to prescribe the future use of the weapon, but I think the bomb instead constitutes merely a first step in a new control by man over the forces of nature too revolutionary and dangerous to fit into the old concepts. I think it really caps the climax of the race between man's growing technical power for destructiveness and his psychological power of self-control, his moral power."

This prescient insight gives perfect expression to the growing sense of alarm, which over the course of my long experience in the nuclear arena, evolved ultimately to a singular goal: to bend every effort, within my power and authority, to promote the conditions and attitudes which might someday free mankind from the scourge of nuclear weapons.

To my utter astonishment and profound gratitude, the opportunity to advance that agenda came in the form of two wholly unanticipated and unlikely eventualities. One, of historic consequence, was the end of the Cold War; the other, of little moment, was my appointment as the commander of America's strategic nuclear forces. I was electrified by the prospects presented by the sudden shattering of the Cold War paradigm. And on entering my new office, I was seized by the opportunity to promote fundamental changes in nuclear weapons policy, force structure, planning and operational practice.

Two days after taking the helm of Strategic Air Command, I called together my senior staff of 20 generals and one admiral, and over the course of what I am sure for all of them was a mystifying and deeply unsettling discussion,

I presented my case that with the end of the Cold War, SAC's mission was effectively complete. I began to prepare them for a dramatic shift in strategic direction, to think in terms of less rather than more, to argue for smaller forces, fewer targets, reduced alert postures and accelerated arms control agreements. This was a wrenching readjustment. It prompted angry debate, bruised feelings and the early termination of a dozen promising careers. But in the final analysis, I could have not been prouder of a staff that over the course of a few short months endorsed the cancellation of $40 billion of strategic nuclear force modernization programs; that supported my recommendations to convert the B-2 to a primarily conventional role and to stand the entire bomber force down from 30 years of alert; that did pioneering analysis in developing national nuclear war plans numbering down to hundreds of targets; and perhaps most notably, unanimously supported my decision to recommend that Strategic Air Command itself be dis-established after 46 years at the nuclear ramparts.

This was an extraordinary period, a promising start to a wholesale realignment of America's national security policy and practice. And in the ensuing months there has been much to record and to applaud, thanks to a host of agencies and initiatives. Conversely, there is yet no cause for celebration nor satisfaction. The harsh truth is that six years after the end of the Cold War we are still prisoner to its psychology of distrust, still enmeshed in the vocabulary of mutual assured destruction, still in the thrall of the nuclear era. Worse, strategists persist in conjuring worlds which spiral towards chaos, and concocting threats which they assert can only be discouraged or ex-

punged by the existence or employment of nuclear weapons.

It is well that Secretary Stimson did not survive to witness this folly. I can readily imagine his dismay at witnessing mankind's miraculous reprieve from nuclear disaster only to risk losing the race between self-destructiveness and self-control, or seeing technological prowess and mistrust triumph over morality and the rule of law. For my own part, I find it unconscionable, and for that reason I felt increasingly the moral imperative to reenter the public arena.

That resolve was crystallized by an invitation from the Government of Australia in late 1995 to join the Canberra Commission on the Elimination of Nuclear Weapons. I was deeply moved by Prime Minister Keating's forceful condemnation of the resumption of French nuclear testing, and his courageous effort to bring focus to the ensuing international outcry.

I come away from the Canberra Commission experience with decidedly mixed feeling. On the one hand, I was enormously enriched by this year-long association with men and women of such great stature. I was equally gratified by the unanimity of view and the forceful logic of our report. It captured in measured, balanced, and reasoned terms the essence of my own conclusions about the risks and penalties associated with nuclear weapons. Most importantly, it set forth a practical, realistic blueprint for working toward their elimination.

... I can discern the makings of an emerging global consensus that the risks posed by nuclear weapons far outweigh their presumed benefits.

[I am d]isappointed, thus far, by the quality of the debate, by those pundits who simply sniffed imperiously at the goal of elimination, aired their stock Cold War rhetoric, hurled a personal epithet or two, and settled smugly back into their world of exaggerated threats and bygone enemies. [I am also disappointed] by critics who attacked my views by misrepresenting them, such as suggesting that I am proposing unilateral disarmament or a pace of reduction that would jeopardize the security of the nuclear weapon states.

And finally, [I am] dismayed that even among more serious commentators the lessons of fifty years at the nuclear brink can still be so grievously misread; that the assertions and assumptions underpinning an era of desperate threats and risks prevail unchallenged; that a handful of nations cling to the impossible notion that the power of nuclear weapons is so immense their use can be threatened with impunity, yet their proliferation contained.

Albert Einstein recognized this hazardous but very human tendency many years ago, when he warned that "the unleashed power of the atom has changed everything save our modes of thinking, and thus we drift toward unparalleled catastrophe."

How else to explain the assertion that nuclear weapons will infallibly deter major war, in a world that survived the Cuban Missile Crisis no thanks to deterrence, but only by the grace of God? How else to accept the proposition that any civilized nation would respond to the act of a madman by adopting his methods? How otherwise to fathom a historical view that can witness the collapse of communism but fail to imagine a world rid of nuclear weapons? Or finally, to account for the assumption that because we are condemned to live with the knowledge of how to fabricate nuclear weapons, we are powerless to mount a global framework of verification and sanctions which will greatly reduce the likelihood or adequately deal with the consequences of cheating in a world free of nuclear weapons.

Many well meaning friends have counseled me that by championing elimination I risk setting the bar too high, providing an easy target for the cynical and diverting attention from the more immediately achievable. My response is that elimination is the only defensible goal and that goal matters enormously. First and foremost, all of the declared nuclear weapon states are formally committed to nuclear abolition in the letter and the spirit of the nonproliferation treaty. Every President of the United States since Dwight Eisenhower has publicly endorsed elimination. A clear and unequivocal commitment to elimination, sustained by concrete policy and measurable milestones, is essential to give credibility and substance to this long-standing declaratory position. Such a commitment goes far beyond simply seizing the moral high ground. It focuses analysis on a precise end state; all force postures above zero simply become way points along a path leading toward elimination. It shifts the locus of policy attention from numbers to the security climate essential to permit successive reductions. It conditions government at all levels to create and respond to every opportunity for shrinking arsenals, cutting infrastructure and curtailing modernization. It sets the stage for rigorous enforcement of nonproliferation regimes and unrelenting pressures to reduce nuclear arsenals on a global basis. I say again, the goal matters enormously and the only defensible goal is elimination.

But hear me say clearly, and unreservedly, that no one is more conscious than am I that realistic prospects for elimination will evolve over many years. I was in the public arena for too long ever to make the perfect the enemy of the good. I hasten to add, however, my strong conviction that we are far too timorous in imagining the good, we are still too rigidly conditioned by an arms control mentality deeply rooted in the Cold War. We fall too readily into the intellectual trap of judging the goal of elimination against current political conditions. We forget too quickly how seemingly intractable conflicts can suddenly yield under the weight of reason or with a change of leadership. We have lost sight too soon that in the blink of a historical eye the world we knew for a traumatic half-century has been utterly transformed.

How better then, you may well ask, to proceed. As I noted earlier, my own prescription is carefully detailed in the report of the Canberra Commission. It begins not with a call for greater reductions, but rather to initiate immediate, multilteral negotiations toward ending the most regrettable and risk-laden operational practice of the Cold War era: land and sea-based ballistic missiles standing nuclear alert. Why is it that five years after removing bombers, the most stable element of the nuclear triad, from alert, we keep missiles, with their 30-minute flight time, on effectively hair-trigger postures? What possibly can justify this continuing exposure to the associated operational and logistical risks? What could be more corrosive to building and sustaining security relationships built on trust? What could undercut more overtly the credibility of our leadership in advancing a nonproliferation treaty premised on a solemn obligation to eliminate nuclear arsenals?

There are a host of other measures outlined in the Canberra Commission report which should also be given immediate consideration. But this is not the time nor place to debate alternative agendas, although thoughtful debate is both urgent and essential. What matters more is the much larger and defining question upon which the debate must ultimately turn: above all nations, how should the United States see its responsibility for dealing with the conflicted moral legacy of the Cold War? Russia, with its history of authoritarian rule and a staggering burden of social transformation, is ill-equipped to lead on this issue. It falls unavoidably to us to work painfully back through the tangled moral web of this frightful 50-year gauntlet, born of the hellish confluence of two unprecedented historical currents: the bi-polar collision of ideology, and the unleashing of the power of the atom.

As a democracy, the consequences of these cataclysmic forces confronted us with a tortuous and seemingly inextricable dilemma: how to put at the service of our national survival, a weapon whose sheer destructiveness was antithetical to the very values upon which our society was based. Over time, as arsenals multiplied on both sides and the rhetoric of mutual annihilation grew more heated, we were forced to think about the unthinkable, justify the unjustifiable, rationalize the irrational. Ultimately, we contrived a new and desperate theology to ease our moral anguish, and we called it deterrence.

I spent much of my military career serving the ends of deterrence, as did millions of others. I want very much to believe that in the end that it was the nuclear force that I and others commanded and operated that prevented World War

III and created the conditions leading to the collapse of the Soviet Empire. But, in truth, I do not and I cannot know that. It will be decades before the hideously complex era of the Cold War is adequately understood, with its bewildering interactions of human fears and inhuman technology. Nor would it much matter that informed assessments are still well beyond our intellectual reach, except for the crucial and alarming fact that, forgetting the desperate circumstances which gave it birth, and long after their miraculous resolution, we continue to espouse deterrence as if it were now an infallible panacea. And worse, others are listening, have converted to our theology, are building their arsenals, are poised to rekindle the nuclear arms race, and to rewaken the specter of nuclear war.

What a stunning, perverse turn of events. In the words of my friend, Jonathan Schell, we face the dismal prospect that:

"The Cold War was not the apogee of the age of nuclear weapons, to be succeeded by an age of nuclear disarmament. Instead, it may well prove to have simply been a period of initiation, in which not only Americans and Russians, but Indians and Pakistanis, Israelis and Iraqis, were adapting to the horror of threatening the deaths of millions of people, were learning to think about the unthinkable. If this is so, will history judge that the Cold War proved only a sort of modern day Trojan Horse, whereby nuclear weapons were smuggled into the life of the world, made an acceptable part of the way the world works? Surely not, surely we still comprehend that to threaten the deaths of tens of hundreds of millions of people presages an atrocity beyond anything in the record of mankind? Or have we, in a silent and incomprehensible moral revolution, come to regard such threats as ordinary, as normal and proper policy for any self-respecting nation."

This cannot be the moral legacy of the Cold War. And it is our responsibility to ensure that it will not be. We have won, through Herculean courage and sacrifice, the opportunity to reset mankind's moral compass, to renew belief in a world free from fear and deprivation, to win global affirmation for the sanctity of life, the right of liberty, and the opportunity to pursue a joyous existence.

Winston Churchill once remarked about the nuclear era that, "the stone age may return on the gleaming wings of science."

POSTSCRIPT

Does the World Need to Have Nuclear Weapons at All?

Do arms, nuclear or otherwise, provoke war or provide security? For a general review of arms control, read Jeffrey A. Larsen and Gregory J. Rattray, eds., *Arms Control: Toward the Twenty-First Century* (Lynne Rienner Press, 1996). There is no doubt that arms make war possible and also sometimes help to create the tensions that are fertile ground for war. But the relationship is complex. Arms may be amassed *because* of war-producing tension. Many analysts argue that weapons are necessary for survival in a predatory world. As political scientist Hans Morgenthau once put it, "Men do not fight because they have arms. They have arms because they . . . fight." This logic suspects that disarmament would actually increase the likelihood of war or domination by tempting aggressors to cheat and spring their weapons on an unsuspecting and defenseless victim. For a study of the relationship between arms control and political tension, see Vally Koubi, "Military Buildups and Arms Control Agreements," *International Studies Quarterly* (1994).

The power of nuclear weapons makes the relationship between weapons and war particularly important. The contention that nuclear arms are dangerous and that they decrease security is the prevailing view among political leaders, scholars, and others. But it is not a universally accepted view. British prime minister Winston Churchill once suggested that nuclear weapons may have rendered nuclear war and even large-scale conventional war between nuclear powers too dangerous to fight. Some would point to the absence of a U.S.–USSR war during decades of overt confrontation as proof that nuclear arms do provide security. Secretary of State James A. Baker III made this point in 1991, declaring, "I am not prepared to walk away from the concept of nuclear deterrence that has kept the peace for more than 40 years."

The decision whether or not to eliminate all nuclear weapons is a cosmic roll of the dice. If, as Churchill and Baker suggest, nuclear weapons have eliminated war between major powers, then such weapons are a force for peace, however scary they may be. That view is supported by some scholars, including Paul K. Huth, Christopher Gelpi, and D. Scott Bennett, in "The Escalation of Great Power Militarized Disputes," *American Political Science Review* (1994). If Churchill and Baker are wrong, and war has not occurred for other reasons, and if nuclear war is possible by inadvertence or conscious decision, then they are gravely mistaken by advocating the retention of the vehicles of Armageddon. For a view that the risk is not worth it, read Barry M. Blechman and Cathleen S. Fisher, "Phase Out the Bomb," *Foreign Policy* (Winter 1994–1995).

ISSUE 11

Should a Permanent UN Military Force Be Established?

YES: Joseph E. Schwartzberg, from "A New Perspective on Peacekeeping: Lessons from Bosnia and Elsewhere," *Global Governance* (vol. 3, no. 1, 1997)

NO: John F. Hillen III, from "Policing the New World Order: The Operational Utility of a Permanent U.N. Army," *Strategic Review* (Spring 1994)

ISSUE SUMMARY

YES: Joseph E. Schwartzberg, a professor of geography, proposes a standing UN Peace Corps military force of international volunteers to better enable the UN to meet its peacekeeping mission.

NO: John F. Hillen III, a lieutenant in the U.S. Army and a doctoral student in international relations, criticizes the ideal of a permanent UN army on several grounds and concludes that such a force is unworkable.

The United Nations seeks to maintain and restore peace through a variety of methods. These include creating norms against violence, providing a forum to debate questions as an alternative to war, making efforts to prevent the proliferation of weapons, diplomatic intervention (such as mediation), and the placing of diplomatic and economic sanctions. Additionally, and at the heart of the issue here, the UN can dispatch troops under its banner or authorize member countries to use their forces to carry out UN mandates.

UN forces involving a substantial number of military or police personnel have been used more than two dozen times in the organization's nearly 50-year history and have involved troops and police from more than 75 countries. There is, therefore, a significant history of UN forces. Nevertheless, recent events and attitude changes have engendered renewed debate over the military role of the UN.

The increased number of UN operations is one factor contributing to the debate. Of all UN operations throughout history, about half are currently active. Furthermore, several of the recent missions, including the UN presence in Bosnia, Somalia, and Rwanda, have included large numbers of troops and, thus, have been very costly. Increased calls for UN peacekeeping operations and the sometimes sizable nature of those operations has increased the UN's annual peacekeeping budget from $235 million in 1987 to approximately $1.3 billion in fiscal year (FY) 1997.

A second factor that has sparked controversy about UN forces are the successes and failures of their missions. Often UN forces have played an important part in the peace process; other times they have been unsuccessful. The limited mandate (role, instructions) and strength (personnel, armaments) of UN forces has frequently left them as helpless bystanders.

A third shift that has raised concerns about UN forces is the change in the international system. With the cold war ended, some people are trying to promote a new world order. This new world order would require countries to live up to the mandate of the UN charter that they only use force unilaterally for immediate self-defense or unless they are authorized to use force by the UN or a regional organization (such as the Organization of American States). This means that collective action under UN auspices is becoming more normal, unilateral action by a country more the exception. The UN-authorized war against Iraq in 1991 is an example of this trend.

Two potential changes in the operation of UN forces apply to the issue here. The first is to increase the scope of the mission of UN forces. To date, UN forces have operated according to two concepts: *collective security* and *peacekeeping*. Collective security is the idea that aggression against anyone is a threat to everyone. Therefore, the collective body should cooperate to prevent and, if necessary, defeat aggression. The second, long-standing UN role of peacekeeping usually involves acting as a buffer between two sides to provide an atmosphere that will allow them to settle their differences, or at least to not fight. Neither collective security nor peacekeeping, however, precisely apply to situations such as domestic civil wars, in which there is no international aggressor and/or clearly identifiable aggressor. Some people consider this a gap in what the UN does to prevent the scourge of war and, therefore, would augment the UN's role to include *peacemaking*. This would involve intervening in either international or civil wars, with or without the consent of any of the participants, to force the warring parties to desist.

The second potential change for UN forces relates to proposals to create, at maximum, a standing UN army or, at least, a ready reserve of troops. These troops would remain with the forces of their home countries, but would train for UN operations and be instantly available to the UN.

The immediate background to the issue debated here began with a January 1992 summit meeting of the leaders of the 15 countries with seats on the Security Council. The leaders called on the UN secretary-general Boutros Boutros-Ghali (1991–1996) to report on ways to enhance UN ability "for preventative diplomacy, for peacemaking, and for peacekeeping." In response, the secretary-general issued a report entitled *An Agenda for Peace,* in which he recommended the establishment of a 100,000-soldier UN rapid deployment force and other strategies to enhance UN peacekeeping. In the following selections, Joseph E. Schwartzberg supports the idea of a permanent UN Peace Corps to pave the way to lasting international peace and security. John F. Hillen III argues that the secretary-general's recommendations and other such proposals are mostly ill-conceived and should not be supported.

YES
Joseph E. Schwartzberg

A NEW PERSPECTIVE ON PEACEKEEPING: LESSONS FROM BOSNIA AND ELSEWHERE

The threat to use force is neither credible nor effective if there is no ability or preparedness to actually use it.

—The Commission on Global Governance, 1995

The cited passage, made with specific reference to the Bosnian peacekeeping fiasco, offers a lesson that the international community can ignore only at its peril. A corollary is that the stronger and more credible a peacekeeping force is and the sooner the willingness to apply it is made clear, the less likely will be the necessity of actually employing it in an overt combat role. It follows, then, that the willingness to invest substantially in peacekeeping, though seemingly expensive in the short term, is likely to prove exceedingly economical in the longer term. One is reminded in this context of the admonition "If you think education is expensive, just try ignorance." Similarly, one might observe, "If you think peacekeeping is expensive, try anarchy."

Regrettably, as recent experience has demonstrated, the international community—despite the painful lessons of Bosnia, Somalia, Rwanda, and, I would argue, Iraq—has yet to learn that an ounce of prevention is worth a pound of cure. As surely as the lack of preventive health measures with respect to the human body or the lack of timely preventive maintenance for an automobile engine will exact a future penalty, so too will continued failure to fund and empower effectively UN peacekeeping efforts. In recognition of that simple truth, this essay sets forth a proposal for a cost-effective UN Peace Corps. It discusses the increasing need for such an entity, specifies the functions that such a corps could perform in both peacetime and emergency situations, indicates the means by which the corps may be recruited and trained, outlines the essential elements for its command and control, estimates its likely costs and benefits, and suggests the transitional arrangements that would smooth the way from the present ad hoc mode of peacekeeping to a more efficient and dependable system.

From Joseph E. Schwartzberg, "A New Perspective on Peacekeeping: Lessons from Bosnia and Elsewhere," *Global Governance: A Review of Multilateralism and International Organizations*, vol. 3, no. 1 (1997). Copyright © 1997 by Lynne Rienner Publishers, Inc. Reprinted by permission of the publisher. Notes omitted.

THE GROWING NEED

While falling short of the recommendations set forth in this essay, a number of thoughtful recent calls have been made to establish a standing all-volunteer force of peacekeepers, directly under UN command. Such a force, it is asserted, would be able to provide a needed rapid response in situations of grave threat to the peace and function until such time as nationally recruited standby contingents could be brought to bear to help stabilize the situation and prevent either new outbreaks of hostilities or the expansion of armed conflicts already under way. Had even a small, elite, rapid-reaction force been available in the case of Rwanda, there can be little doubt that it would have averted the slaughter of hundreds of thousands of innocent civilians in the genocidal orgy of 1994. As the commander of UNAMIR (the UN Assistance Mission for Rwanda), Maj. Gen. Roméo Dallaire, observed: "In Rwanda, the international community's inaction... contributed to the Hutu extremists' belief that they could carry out their genocide.... UNAMIR could have saved the lives of hundreds of thousands of people.... A force of 5,000 personnel rapidly deployed could have prevented the massacres... that did not commence in earnest until early May, nearly a month after the start of the war."

Similarly, timely intervention of a small interpositionary force of UN peacekeepers might have dissuaded Saddam Hussein's 1991 invasion of Kuwait. It is also likely, though by no means certain, that had such a peacekeeping force been available early in 1992, the Bosnian cataclysm might somehow have been prevented. But it does seem clear that the presence of a small UN interpositionary force in Macedonia has been among the factors that have prevented the Balkan conflict from spilling southward into that republic and that have averted, thus far, the anticipated Serbian crackdown on Albanian separatists in the neighboring, formerly autonomous, area of Kosovo.

As matters transpired, the forces introduced into Bosnia and other republics of the former Yugoslavia were too few and too late; they lacked funding, logistical support, and a clear mandate to prevent several waves of "ethnic cleansing," other massive violations of human rights, and untold destruction of property. Because of those initial inadequacies, the subsequent infusion into Bosnia of an additional relatively small UN peacekeeping force, no matter how well trained and commanded it might have been, would not have sufficed to restore peace to the region. Moreover, the Bosnian Serbs' successful defiance (for a time) of UN peacekeepers in Bosnia led to the ultimate withdrawal of all UN forces (similar to the case with U.S. forces in the Somali UN operation once the going got rough). These facts point to two important conclusions. The first is that the required scale of future UN peacekeeping missions will often exceed what would have been necessary for the success of comparable missions in the past. The second is the need to put future UN missions under direct and exclusive UN command and to staff them with volunteer soldiers who are not subject to unpredictable recall by the leaders of individual UN member nations responding to domestic political pressures.

Although operations such as the one currently being mounted by NATO in Bosnia may appear to be a feasible alternative to UN peacekeeping in certain contexts, one can hardly expect NATO to take on the role of the world's police force.

The legitimacy of its doing so would surely be called into question, especially when a single power, the United States, occupies so prominent a position within NATO. Moreover, as we shall see, most of the many future conflicts that seem likely to call for UN intervention lie outside the area of NATO's concern.

In the brief period since the dismantling of the Berlin Wall and the ending of the Cold War, several dozen new conflicts have erupted around the planet. Most of these are civil wars pitting repressed ethnic minorities against dominant national groups; but many of the conflicts threaten to involve neighboring nations in which most or a substantial part of the population identifies strongly with one or another party in the struggle. As of 1990, I had enumerated some 321 linguistic minorities in the world—mainly in Africa, Asia, and Eastern Europe—with populations of half a million or more, most of whom had ample reason to be dissatisfied with the system of governance under which they were living. In addition to the potential disputes relating to linguistic minorities are those that involve scores of religious and racial minorities. These figures suggest hundreds of wars waiting to happen. The downfall of repressive regimes in many parts of the world, the easing of restraints formerly imposed by the United States and the Soviet Union on the political behavior of their client states, the spread of the notion of representative democracy and of the idea of national self-determination, and the power of the telecommunications revolution jointly conduce to a greater likelihood of ethnic conflict in the foreseeable future than at any time in the past. While many potential conflicts will undoubtedly be averted—because of continuing repression or, less frequently, through enlightened statesmanship (as in the former Czechoslovakia)—many others will not. And more than a few of the potential conflicts seem likely to become sufficiently serious to call for various forms of international intervention, in some instances by regional organizations such as the OAS, but—given the meager resources of most such organizations—more often by the UN. Ideally, this intervention will be mediatory and not entail the use of armed peacekeepers, but experience suggests that resort to peacekeeping and to the use of interpositionary forces to prevent the eruption or spread of armed conflict will, from time to time, be necessary.

Apart from ethnic and religious struggles, there are in the world scores of other potential conflict situations involving territorial disputes. In addition to traditional disputes over boundaries on land, there are literally hundreds of new maritime boundaries that have yet to be determined because of the coming-into-force of the UN Comprehensive Law of the Sea Treaty; and many of these sea boundaries, especially with regard to the newly established "exclusive economic zones," are even now (as in the South China Sea) being hotly contested. Finally, in a world of burgeoning populations and dwindling resources, the likelihood of strife with respect to such vital needs as arable land, fresh water, and petroleum is certain to increase. Thus, there can be little doubt that the post–Cold War period, far from having ushered in a new era of peace, remains fraught with danger.

For these reasons, a strong case can be made that the world increasingly requires a globally recruited, all-volunteer, elite, highly trained, multipurpose UN Peace Corps (UNPC) larger than any such force proposed to date. Admittedly, the problems to be solved in establishing a

UNPC are dauntingly complex. The cost of such a body would obviously be high, with annual expenditures substantially greater than those allocated for current UN peacekeeping operations. Further, given the present reluctance (especially in the United States) to fund existing UN commitments, it would be unrealistic to anticipate widespread early support for the far-reaching recommendations set forth in this essay. Nevertheless, I make the case that the ultimate benefits would enormously outweigh the costs, not merely with respect to conflicts and destruction averted, but also in the vast reductions in national military expenditures that the proposed new force would permit. I also indicate numerous other realizable benefits of a nonmilitary nature. If the arguments I set forth prove persuasive, the support that now seems unattainable may yet be forthcoming, and a planned sequence of steps toward the establishment of the envisaged UNPC might soon be initiated.

None of the recommendations I propose should be taken to imply that the application of military force is the preferred means of dealing with international or intranational conflict. Much more desirable is the whole range of preventive diplomacy and peacemaking measures spelled out in Boutros Boutros-Ghali's *Agenda for Peace,* and it is obviously potentially more fruitful to refine the tools for effective mediation than to develop measures for dealing with armed strife after preventive diplomacy fails. However, in the foreseeable future, failures will at times occur, and the international community must be ready and able to deal with them.

It is also important to stress at the outset that for military missions to be lastingly effective, decisions by the Security Council to sanction them must be perceived as legitimate and not made primarily in the interests of only one or a small coterie of the council's most powerful states. While legitimacy alone provides no guarantee of a mission's success, it seems obvious that compliance with the actions of a legitimately empowered force is more likely than with those of one whose legitimacy is open to question. Hence, the establishment of a more democratic Security Council, better representing the world's people than does the present council, will significantly enhance the probability of success of whatever missions it may order.

FUNCTIONS OF THE UNPC

The more numerous and worthwhile the tasks the proposed UNPC can perform, the greater will be the willingness to provide it with political and financial support. Thus, rather than thinking solely in terms of being able to respond rapidly to pressing military emergencies, one should also consider a multiplicity of additional functions the corps might appropriately perform, many of which could keep units productively occupied during the (one hopes) long periods during which they are not required to play an active, specifically military role.

In the relatively narrow military mode are such functions as patrolling ceasefire lines and monitoring violations, protecting civilian populations in zones of conflict and overseeing the evacuation of refugees from areas of danger, guarding emergency relief supplies to war-affected areas, establishing interpositionary forces to prevent conflicts from spreading to countries under palpable threat of invasion (the first such example of this is the UN force in Macedonia), and—when the Security Council deems it necessary—engaging in peace-enforcing operations under Chapter VII of the UN Charter. Distinctively different functions would be to restore, in concert with civilian specialists, some semblance of normalcy in failed states or in situations in which sovereignty is being transferred from one state to another. (The recent experiences in Cambodia and Somalia provide useful lessons in the former regard and those in West New Guinea/Iran Barat, in 1962–1963, in the latter.) Other vital functions, more likely to be undertaken following the conclusion of conflict than in times of open combat, are clearing minefields, disposing of ordnance, and dismantling selected military installations and/or weapons-making plants (for example, with respect to operations following the Gulf War).

There is no reason why units of the UNPC, when not actively engaged in military activities, should not be employed, in cooperation with other agencies, in a broad range of peace-building projects of a developmental and humanitarian nature. These might include constructing or upgrading roads, airports, and other components of the infrastructure of host countries; establishing projects to improve local drinking-water supplies, sanitation, and other aspects of public health; participating in training activities that would enhance the skills of the local citizenry; responding globally to urgent needs in times of famine, earthquakes, flooding, and other natural catastrophes; providing logistic support to nongovernmental organizations (NGOs) and specialized UN agencies dealing with such catastrophes; and creating and maintaining strategically situated supply depots to facilitate the provision of emergency disaster relief. Finally, election monitoring presents yet another potential task.

Admittedly, all these functions are already being performed on a limited scale by the UN Development Program or, as in the case of election monitoring, through various teams established by the UN on an ad hoc basis; but the scope for enhancing such worthy efforts through the participation of the UNPC would be enormous. Cost-sharing arrangements for such activities would have to be worked out through contracts involving host governments, various agencies within the UN system, NGOs, and others.

The UNPC would provide additional benefits in the training of its internationally recruited male and female volunteers, especially for the many who are likely to come from developing countries. Apart from the valuable technical skills the volunteers would be taught, one must consider the habits of discipline and devotion to duty and the esprit de corps that a well-run, elite military unit would impart. Such intangible benefits have enormous potential to contribute to nation building and social development once the volunteers complete their terms of service and return to their countries of origin. Service in the corps would, as a rule, provide a badge of honor and respect for its veterans and enhance their ability to later function as effective development agents in their home settings. (The experience of veterans of Gurkha units recruited to both the British and the Indian armies is instructive in this regard.) Moreover, the service would bring the elite of different countries into close working contact with one another and thereby help break down negative cultural and gender stereotypes and establish enduring bonds of international amity. The service would also greatly enhance the ability of many volunteers to communicate in one or more new languages, the economic and social benefits of which should be obvious. Apart from the benefits from work-related activities are those that would stem from recreational pastimes, such as organized sporting events (including matches between UNPC and host-country teams), cultural activities within the host country, and foreign travel during periods of paid leave. Finally, the establishment of a corps of men and women inspired with an ethos of global service and common allegiance to humanity, rather than to specific countries, would help forge a new, much-needed planetary consciousness.

RECRUITMENT AND TRAINING

Service in the UNPC would be open equally to qualified men and women from all parts of the world. This presupposes the establishment of offices for the screening, testing, and selection of would-be volunteers. Most of these offices could be permanently attached to those of the already existing network of UN country coordinators, while others would operate perhaps for only one or two months per year, at a sufficiently well distributed set of localities so as to make the option of enlisting a practicable one in areas where the costs of travel are high in relation to average income levels. The physical, mental, and moral requirements for eligibility at all ranks should be sufficiently high to ensure that the corps would be an elite body. Establishing the requisite physical, mental, and behavioral standards and the means to ensure that they were faithfully adhered to would be the task of a specially appointed subcommission of those powers entrusted with drawing up the interim arrangements leading up to the establishment of the UNPC (as will be discussed in the final section of this essay).

All recruits would undergo an initial period of rigorous basic training, the length of which would vary depending on whether preliminary language instruction was necessary.... Terms of service, following the successful completion of basic training, would be four additional years for all noncommissioned ranks, which could be renewed only once; a few exceptions could be made for needed specialists. This stricture would preclude the creation of a large body of career soldiers.... To ensure continuity of command, training, and operational functions, however, the length of permissible service for officers and a small cadre of key noncommissioned officers should be longer than for lower ranks.

On pragmatic grounds, the number of operating languages within the corps would have to be limited. For an initial period, English, French, and Spanish would best serve, given their global distribution and their status as either official or auxiliary languages in a substantial majority of the world's countries. Moreover, while not all recruits would initially be proficient in any of those three tongues, those whose native language was close to one of the UNPC languages would be able to learn the new language well enough to use it effectively within six months or so following recruitment.... Within each command (to be discussed below), a single language would be selected for training and for most operational purposes....

Compensation, in terms of salaries and other benefits, would be generous. In addition to the usual provision of uniforms, food, billeting, other necessities, and paid leave time, all personnel would receive a salary appropriate for the area in which they served and a supplemental amount deposited in a home-country bank account would become available to them on honorable conclusion of their period of service. A system of postservice educational benefits (comparable to the remarkably successful GI Bill of Rights for veterans of the armed forces of the United States) should also be instituted. Service, therefore, would be regarded not merely as a job, but as a hard-won privilege. This would be essential to maintain high morale and to create a healthy esprit de corps. It would also greatly enhance the respect accorded to the UNPC wherever it may be called on to serve.

COMMAND AND CONTROL

Largely following the 1989 recommendations of the Norwegian Commission of Experts, the chain of command for the UNPC would run from the Security Council through the secretary-general and an International Military Staff Committee within the Secretariat to a UN Central Command and thence to three regional commands. Taking into consideration numerous geographical, logistical, and political factors, the following division of responsibilities is suggested: a Western Command for the Americas, the operating language for which would be Spanish; a dual Central Command for Europe, Africa, and the Middle East, one component of which would use French and the other English; and an Eastern Command for the balance of Asia and Oceania, the operating language for which would be English. There could be some units within each command, however, using languages other than the official command language. . . .

The subordination of English within the Western Command structure and the lack of Russian- and Chinese-speaking commands may appear to some to be significant shortcomings. But, as a practical matter, one must recognize that in the foreseeable future the UNPC is unlikely to be called upon to intervene in crises originating in or involving the United States, Russia, or China, or, for that matter, any other veto-wielding permanent member of either the present or an expanded future Security Council. Nor, in all likelihood, would the UNPC be asked to intervene in the areas of a substantial number of other states (e.g., Canada or the Scandinavian countries) whose commitment to peace appears firm. Should any of the world's larger powers become guilty in the near future of armed aggression, that would represent a threat to world peace of such a magnitude that it is not likely that armed intervention, even by the UNPC, would be particularly efficacious. Other ad hoc mechanisms for dealing with the issue would have to be devised. Ultimately, elimination of the veto in the Security Council would go a long way toward remedying this admitted limitation of the present proposal (as well as of all others that call for standing UN peacekeeping forces); but an even more fundamental requisite is an essentially disarmed world. The achievement of that worthy goal, however, will necessitate overcoming a host of political obstacles that cannot be addressed within the scope of this brief essay.

Normally, troops from only one regional command would be used in a specific military mission; and one would hope that the size of the force at its disposal would suffice to carry out effectively whatever task it might be assigned. Nevertheless, one must anticipate instances when obdurate military resistance to a given UNPC intervention would be of such a magnitude that it would become necessary to draw on forces from other commands. Thus, each command would provide, in effect, a strategic reserve for the others. It is further conceivable that an occasion might arise when available units from the combined UNPC commands would be unequal to a specific military assignment. In such a case, the UNPC would still form the nucleus and spearhead of the force assigned by the Security Council to meet the threat; but it would have to be supplemented by additional units provided by individual member states (as originally envisaged in Chapter VII of the UN Charter). In such a case, a resolute mustering of the necessary military would be essential.…

The headquarters of each regional command, along with a substantial part of the staff, should be placed on bases leased from reasonably stable countries with relatively democratic regimes within the regions where they are likely to be needed. The countries selected should offer adequate facilities for logistical support by both sea and air from powers capable of providing such support. If the system were currently in place, suitable candidates might be Costa Rica or Ecuador for the Western Command; Morocco or Senegal for the French-speaking component of the Central Command and Egypt or South Africa for the English-speaking component; and the Philippines or Malaysia for the Eastern Command. A limited number of additional bases, including supply depots, could be established at appropriate leased sites in each of the three commands. Preference would be given in all cases to sites in countries with democratic regimes, thereby providing an incentive for maintaining such governments.…

In its initial phase, the UNPC would rely on the larger powers for naval and air support, using leased vessels and aircraft in much the same way as in present UN peacekeeping missions. In time, however, there is no reason in principle why the UNPC should not acquire its own ships, aircraft, and personnel.

A final, but crucial, requirement with respect to the UNPC command and control is that the criteria for intervention and the rules of engagement once intervention is sanctioned by the Security Council must be clearly specified.

COSTS AND BENEFITS

As noted, the costs of establishing and maintaining the proposed UNPC would be great. Annual expenditures would undoubtedly be substantially greater than that of the combined ongoing UN peacekeeping operations. Such peacekeeping costs peaked at more than $3.5 billion in 1994; but, because of severe budgetary constraints requiring the termination or curtailment of a number of missions, the figure has since fallen to roughly $1.6 billion in 1996.

At present, the annual cost per man/woman in uniform in the world's major armed forces (including land, sea, and air forces) varies over a remarkably wide range. Sample figures, calculated to the nearest $1,000 [range from] India $4,000… to the United States $173,000. For the countries toward the upper end of this spectrum, however, a very large part of the expenses indicated derives from the high costs of sophisticated equipment, especially for offensive weapons systems for the air force and navy.… However, relatively little in the way of high-tech lethal ordnance would be appropriate for the UNPC. In light of these considerations, it seems reasonable to suggest a cost per soldier in the neighborhood of $40,000 per year.

If, then, we assume a total force of three hundred thousand in all three commands once the UNPC attains full strength, and average annual maintenance costs of $40,000 per soldier, ... that would yield a total of $12 billion when the UNPC is functioning in a nonmilitary mode. Actual military operations would, of course, add significantly to this sum, especially with respect to the leasing of needed ships and aircraft for logistic support. In the initial years of the UNPC, costs would obviously be different from what they would be once the commands were brought to full strength. On the one hand, there would be substantial start-up costs for recruiting and for building and stocking military bases (though significant savings might be realized in this regard by utilizing UNPC cadres themselves for much of the work). On the other hand, the number of personnel initially involved would be substantially less than the full complement, and the costs for postservice benefits would, for some years, be negligible.

While the anticipated expenses of the UNPC may at first appear prohibitively large, they pale in comparison to the world's national military expenditures, which in 1992 totaled $815 billion, or to the Clinton administration's budgeted $1,302 billion for military expenditures over the period 1995–1999 for the United States alone. One should also compare the likely costs of the UNPC with the vastly greater costs of the wars it could avert. For example, while reliable figures for the Gulf War are hard to come by, it is estimated to have cost the victorious allies more than $100 billion, not to mention the incalculable losses to Iraq, Kuwait, and other countries (with respect to lives lost, destruction of property and military equipment, damaged economic infrastructure, and massive environmental degradation) and the subsequent expenses—to both victor and vanquished—of maintaining UN-mandated sanctions against Iraq. On a much more modest scale, we may consider the comparably tragic costs of the UN's recent involvement in Rwanda, where the needed funding and rapid deployment capability was so conspicuously lacking.

> During the slow process of creating UNAMIR, the Security Council made it clear that it wanted the operation conducted at minimal expense. Only a fraction of the US$200 million estimated cost of the operation was ever received by the UN. Only a portion of the troops required to implement UNAMIR's mandate ever arrived in the theatre. The lack of funding and material support for UNAMIR stands in sharp contrast to the money spent by the international community in aid and human resource support once the crisis attracted the attention of the international media. The United States alone provided US$350 million in aid in the first six weeks of the Goma tragedy.

How many more Rwandas will it take for the global community to liberate itself from its self-defeating, penny-wise and pound-foolish mode of response to looming threats of genocide, aggression, and other catastrophic events?

While nobody can accurately foretell the future, it is nevertheless in order to indulge in a bit of plausible economic speculation. Let us suppose that, in some future year X, the costs of the UNPC, including those of actual military operations, total $20 billion (roughly five times the UN expenditures on peacekeeping in 1994). Let us also suppose that the sense of heightened regional and global security generated by the UNPC's capacity to contain conflicts before they get out of control (contrary to what happened, for example, in the former Yugoslavia) will induce the world's nations to reduce annual military expenditures by roughly a fourth, say by $200 billion. If these hypothetical figures are accepted (though there is no compelling reason to suppose that the savings in national military expenditures could not be much greater), they alone would yield a cost-benefit ratio of 10:1, making the UNPC an incredibly good investment. One should also consider the enormous additional savings that would accrue from the many instances in which the very existence of a UNPC will have averted destructive wars —or the imputed value of preventing even a single campaign of genocide on the scale of the one recently witnessed in Rwanda. Finally, one must consider the numerous tangible and intangible benefits that would flow from the UNPC's manifold nonmilitary functions. Though those anticipated benefits are admittedly largely unquantifiable, they alone might more than compensate for the UNPC's cost. Thus, unless the foregoing assumptions are deemed incredibly wide of the mark, by any reasonable economic or political calculus the UNPC would clearly warrant implementation.

Since the anticipated costs of the UNPC substantially exceed the present costs of the entire UN system, one might reasonably consider how such an undertaking could best be financed. Although many creative proposals for enhancing UN revenues have been put forward, the one that appears most appropriate with respect to the UNPC would be a proportional and progressive levy on the defense expenditures and/or on international arms sales of all UN member nations. Apart from their inherent logic, such levies would provide a significant inducement for disarmament. Regrettably, however, while numerous workable ideas have been advanced, they are yet to be accompanied by the requisite will to effect the needed systemic change. What is now necessary is for enough governments to overcome their myopia and distrust with respect to financing and empowering the UN and to recognize the magnitude of the savings and other benefits that would very rapidly accrue from prudent investment in bold peacekeeping initiatives.

TRANSITIONAL ARRANGEMENTS

What has been provided here is a general outline, not a plan capable of being effected in the short term. To get from where we are at present to the proposed UNPC, the UN should first enhance its capability for timely reaction to crises. This will require the establishment of a rapid deployment force of relatively modest size, backed up by standby national contingents capable of responding swiftly and credibly to future threats to the peace up to a level significantly greater than those faced in the former Yugoslavia. Even that reasonable and limited goal, however, will not be reached without a clear determination on the part of the international community, and especially its leading powers, to take effective, timely, and credible military action to prevent future aggression, genocide, and other flagrant abuses of human rights.

As future peacekeeping successes are achieved, and as the recognition spreads that there are indeed reliable international mechanisms for preventing or containing violence, the justification for maintaining large national military establishments will diminish. Then, given popular pressure for reducing tax burdens, nations should be increasingly willing to divert portions of their military budgets away from their individual defense establishments and toward supporting a UNPC....

Well-thought-out plans to meet widely sensed and urgent needs are likely to elicit the needed popular and diplomatic support. This would be true even if only the purely military needs for a UNPC were being considered. But as has been indicated, numerous and substantial nonmilitary, developmental, and humanitarian benefits—many of the latter in situations calling for a rapid-response capability—would also result from the establishment of a multipurpose UNPC. Such ongoing benefits, in addition to the narrower military raison d'être for such a force, should go far toward making it internationally acceptable.

NO

John F. Hillen III

POLICING THE NEW WORLD ORDER: THE OPERATIONAL UTILITY OF A PERMANENT U.N. ARMY

Proposals to create a U.N. Army are not new. They are designed to provide a mechanism and structure that will allow the U.N. to exercise its mandate while circumventing the problem that usually hobbles U.N. operations: the lack of a common political will. Political obstacles aside, there are operational reasons for rejecting a standing U.N. Army. The most important reason for this rejection is that such a force is redundant if employed at the lower end of the U.N. military operations spectrum (observation missions and first generation peacekeeping) but incapable of having any real impact at the upper end (second generation peacekeeping and enforcement).

In the three years immediately following the end of the Cold War, there was a heady optimism about the renewed capacity of the United Nations to enforce resolutions concerning international peace and security. Now, due to the apparent impotency of United Nations forces in Bosnia and Somalia, the mood has swung back toward the pessimism characteristic of the Cold War era. This has not stopped debate about mechanisms that the U.N. can use to enforce its resolutions, including an idea that never quite seems to go away for long: a permanent U.N. Army. Proponents say that such a force could rise above the ebb and flow of national interests and provide a genuinely useful security tool for the United Nations. However, what many of these observers fail to realize is that the limited operational capabilities of a permanent U.N. Army would rarely allow it to influence situations like Bosnia and Somalia. In some respects, it is a worthwhile idea, but it is self-defeating in that the force could make little impact on the very problems it was created to alleviate....

A RECURRING THEME

The idea of a permanent force for the U.N. is not envisaged by the U.N. Charter: it is in fact a concept that seeks to rectify a weakness in the Charter.

Article 43 of the U.N. Charter was intended to create for the U.N. continued access to the massive forces of the victorious World War II alliance. Even the most modest of proposals for U.N. forces constituted under Article 43 visualized 12 Army divisions, 900 combat aircraft, and almost 50 capital warships. The charter structure for using these forces visualized a fairly consistent process. The Security Council could determine a threat to international peace and security (Article 39), order action to redress such a threat by land, sea, and air forces under U.N. authority (Article 42), and call said forces to its service through the agreements reached according to Article 43. However, this security structure was doomed from the start because the critical agreements of Article 43 never materialized.

Thus, all proposals for a permanent U.N. Army have a common goal: to provide the U.N. with the mechanism and structure necessary to exercise its mandate: to maintain international peace and security....

[C]urrent proposals for a permanent U.N. Army are fueled by the desire for a tool that the U.N. can employ without being buffeted by the tides of a fickle international community. This most recent revival of the call for a permanent U.N. force does not seek to harness international consensus for the United Nations... but to institutionalize a security mechanism for the U.N. that does not rely on that consensus. The contemporary rationale for a permanent U.N. force is that it can circumvent the lack of political resolve in such situations as Bosnia.

THE SPECTRUM OF U.N. MILITARY OPERATIONS

Operations involving military personnel conducted under the auspices of the United Nations or its mandates span a broad operational spectrum. This spectrum ranges from unarmed peace observation missions to the conduct of war against an intransigent state. The operational nature of a U.N. military mission can be determined by many different factors, most of which can be subsumed under two categories: 1) the environment in which the force operates; and 2) the level of military effort or force used.

The environment in which the operation takes place could range from completely benign to very hostile. This important factor in the planning of U.N. military missions largely determines the size, nature, and composition of the U.N. force and its tasks. The level of military effort and the force employed reflects the environment and/or opposing forces as well as the nature of the tasks to be performed. By measuring these factors in all U.N. military operations, one can actually plot the spectrum of operations. While it is a continuous spectrum, there are discernible mission subsets: 1) Observation Missions; 2) First Generation Peacekeeping; 3) Second Generation Peacekeeping; and 4) Enforcement Actions.

The first two sets of U.N. military operations share many of the same operational characteristics. These are largely derived from the "principles of peacekeeping" which were recently articulated by the Under Secretary-General for peacekeeping operations.

1. They are United Nations operations. The forces are formed by the U.N. at the outset, commanded in the field

by a U.N.-appointed general, under the ultimate authority of the U.N. Secretary-General, and financed by member states collectively.

2. Peacekeeping forces are deployed with the consent of all the parties involved and only after a political settlement had been reached between warring factions.

3. The forces are committed to strict impartiality. Military observers and peacekeepers can in no way take sides with or against a party to the conflict.

4. Troops are provided by member states on a voluntary basis. During the Cold War era, the superpowers or even "big five" [the permanent members of the Security Council—China, France, Great Britain, the Soviet Union (now Russia), and the United States] rarely participated in these missions, and the majority of troops were supplied by the so-called "middle nations" to reinforce the concept of neutrality.

5. These units operate under rules of engagement that stress the absolute minimum use of force in accomplishing their objectives. This is usually limited to the use of force in self-defense only, but some missions have used force in "situations in which peacekeepers were being prevented by armed persons from fulfilling their mandate."

These five principles are especially applied in earnest in *observation missions.* There have been fifteen of these missions to date, and they represent the low end of the operational spectrum....

FIRST GENERATION PEACEKEEPING

Another class of U.N. military operations guided by the "principles of peacekeep-ing" are first generation peacekeeping missions. These operations were all initiated during the Cold War era, as an improvised response to "the failure of collective security and the success of early U.N. peace observation missions." There were seven operations of this kind.... Three are still operational: Cyprus, the Golan Heights, and Lebanon, in their 29th, 19th and 15th years respectively. These operations share the salient feature of observation missions. Because peacekeeping forces are deployed after a political settlement and because they must remain strictly neutral, they rely on the goodwill and cooperation of the belligerents to accomplish their mission.

These forces differ from observation missions in that they are made up of entire military units from U.N. member states. These units are organically equipped, organized, trained, and armed (albeit lightly) for combat. They therefore possess some modicum of offensive capability and a credible defensive capacity. First generation peacekeeping forces have usually been deployed in a "buffer" role, physically occupying and controlling neutral territory between belligerents. These missions have focused primarily on ensuring the continued separation of the previously warring factions.

First generation peacekeeping missions do not generally have ambitious tasks: missions are derived from political objectives. The main objective is to contain the armed conflict in order to provide a stable atmosphere in which the conflict can be politically resolved. First generation peacekeeping missions (with the exception of parts of the U.N. intervention in the Congo) have no mandate or capacity to impose a political solution on the belligerents. After all, if deployed in accordance with the "principles of peacekeeping" there should be no need for forceful action in an atmosphere of cooperation. However, the operational environment has generally been more bellicose than that experienced by observation missions and there have been over 750 U.N. peacekeepers killed in these seven missions. That environment, and the more complicated military tasks involved for these combat units place these operations higher on the operational spectrum.

SECOND GENERATION PEACEKEEPING

Second generation peacekeeping missions share some operational characteristics with their Cold War predecessors but transcend the "principles of peacekeeping." The U.N. has initiated five of these operations since the relaxation of the superpower confrontation in 1987–1989: in Namibia, Cambodia, the former Yugoslavia, Somalia and Mozambique. In the main these operations are far more ambitious in their objectives, which include disarming the warring factions, maintaining law and order, restoring civil government and its associated functions, setting up and supervising elections, and delivering humanitarian aid. What makes these second generation tasks so challenging is that they very often take place in an atmosphere of continued fighting between factions, civil turmoil, and general chaos. The rate of U.N. fatalities in these missions is climbing.

There are considerable differences between these missions and those of the first two classes. While second generation peacekeeping forces are formed and deployed with unprecedented Security Council consensus, the warring parties often do not want them. Unlike first generation peacekeeping, a cease-fire is not a *sine qua non* [essential] for U.N. deployment. The U.N. forces involved in these operations face the prospect of having little or no cooperation from the factions on the ground, since second generation peacekeeping missions often consist of heavily armed combat units possessing considerable offensive capability, frequently contributed by the major powers.

The large and combat-heavy force structure of second generation peacekeeping forces means that they are able not only to protect themselves and other U.N. personnel, but also to attempt to impose an agreement on unwilling belligerents. The risks inherent in this have been most graphically portrayed in Bosnia and Somalia. In each case, military force has been employed against particular parties in the conflict. In Bosnia, it has mainly consisted of an enforced flight ban against the Serbs and the low level use of force to protect the delivery of humanitarian aid and keep supply lines open. In Somalia, the U.N. authorized the capture by force of Mohammed Aideed, again clearly taking sides in the attempt to impose a political solution. The offensive use of military force in these missions has not produced great dividends for the "peacekeepers" as yet.

The operational characteristics of most second generation peacekeeping missions bear little resemblance to the five "principles of peacekeeping." 1) While they are U.N. operations, they sometimes must rely nonetheless on other organizations or member states for complex operational capabilities that the U.N. does not possess. The use of NATO to enforce the Bosnian flight ban and a U.S. military task force to initially intervene in Somalia are two examples of this. 2) There has been no concrete political settlement in some cases and there is hardly an environment of consent for a U.N. presence. 3) As mentioned above, the doctrine of strict neutrality has not been followed. 4) The forces of the permanent members of the Security Council are often heavily involved. 5) The rules of engagement have been enlarged substantially to allow second generation peacekeepers the capacity to impose a solution on the local parties through the use of force.

In most respects, these missions are only one step short of full-scale enforcement operations. The U.N. has recognized that, considering the innocuous forces and methods employed, traditional peacekeeping can only succeed under favorable political conditions. But second generation peacekeeping military forces are caught on the horns of a prickly dilemma. While lesser operations are governed by the principles of peacekeeping and higher operations are governed by the principles of war, second generation peacekeeping operations are quite simply ungoverned by doctrine of any kind.

ENFORCEMENT

Enforcement actions represent the high end of the operational spectrum, taking place in a bellicose and adversarial environment that necessitates the use of large-scale military force. The operational characteristics of these campaigns are those of war. The role of military forces in this enterprise is obviously more clear cut than the somewhat ambiguous parameters of action in peacekeeping missions. There is no cooperation from the enemy and therefore no need for impartiality. The forces can use purely military doctrine to calculate the force needed to impose the dictates of the U.N. resolution on the aggressor. From a military point of view, this is the only type of U.N. operation where the force can actually create the environment it needs to guarantee success. The only two examples of U.N. collective security operations of this type are Korea in 1950–1953 and Kuwait in 1990–1991.

Each of these situations presented a unique set of circumstances for the exercise of collective security under the auspices of the U.N. In each case the command and control of the operation and the majority of forces were provided by the United States, leading many to dismiss these operations as American wars. However, both were multinational operations authorized by the legislative bodies of the U.N. The fact that the U.N. was essentially following the U.S. lead in both cases illustrates an important characteristic of large-scale enforcement actions. They must have the wholesale participation of a great power in order to bring about the huge resources, sacrifices, and political will required to wage modern war against an intransigent state. Only a few states or groups of states can provide the complex infrastructure and large forces necessary to undertake complicated military enterprises like Operation Desert Storm.

THE PERMANENT U.N. ARMY

Having described the types of military operations in which a U.N. force operates, we must now briefly address the different types of permanent U.N. force proposed. This paper will not consider Article 43-type proposals which would create, on paper, a huge force available to the U.N. for any operation up to major enforcement actions. The main reason for this is that there appears to be no chance that an Article 43 agreement will be signed in the foreseeable future. This is the main reason that [U.N. Secretary-General Boutros] Boutros-Ghali's *An Agenda for Peace* calls for the mobilization of a large force separate from Article 43 agreements. It is an effort to bypass the perpetual deadlock surrounding that luckless article.

Boutros-Ghali proposes "units that would be available on call and would consist of troops that have volunteered for such service." This plan would identify units from member states that could be called upon to build a U.N. force "package" when the Security Council authorizes a mission. Communications units, logistics units, transportation units, medical units, and other expensive sophisticated support elements would be earmarked by member states for U.N. service as well as the traditional light infantry units. These units would have to concentrate the majority of their training on U.N. duties and it has been recommended that their deployments be financed through national defense budgets. Needless to say, the response to these proposals from member states has been tepid at best. "Such modeling assumes that there will be major cuts in national armies as a result of diminishing East-West tensions and that this reduction could be matched by a growth in U.N. military capabilities." That assumption has proved to be naive in the extreme.

The proposal addressed here calls for a supra-national force of U.N. volunteers. Much like the civilian bureaucrats and officials employed by the U.N., these soldiers would be international civil (military) servants. They would be volunteers for international service and would not be under military obligation to any member state: only to the United Nations. They would be recruited, trained, equipped, and paid by the United Nations. The force proposed is usually infantry brigade-size, five to six thousand troops, with organic support and transportation capabilities. There are countless practical difficulties associated with forming such a force, but let us for the moment assume that it can be formed, trained, and deployed by the U.N.

THE UTILITY OF A U.N. ARMY

Naturally, even the most enthusiastic proponents of this small U.N. force recognize that its utility is limited by its size and capabilities. The most important advantage of this force is its rapid reaction capability. Since it is not drawn from member states, with all the attendant difficulties of that process, it can be deployed at the discretion of the Secretary-General on very short notice. The key element contributing to its success would be timeliness. "Clearly, a timely intervention by a relatively small but highly trained force, willing and authorized to take combat risks and representing the will of the international community, could make a decisive difference in the early stages of a crisis." This force would be akin to a small kitchen fire extinguisher, whose greatest utility is in the very earliest stages of a possible fire.

But operationally, we must ask where such a force could really enhance the credibility of the U.N. It is not needed for observation missions, as they are composed of experienced individual military observers. In addition, these missions are formed to observe a previously concluded political settlement. An unarmed observation mission would never be undertaken in a situation where dangerous tensions are at the boiling point and the rapid deployment of combat troops is needed.

Would timely and rapid intervention by such a small force make any difference in first generation peacekeeping missions? As these are also only initiated in response to a completed political agreement, would a rapid deployment force greatly increase the efficiency of the peacekeepers on the ground? "Even a full contingent of peacekeeping troops cannot prevent renewal of hostilities by a determined party. Maintenance of the cease-fire ultimately depends on the willingness of the parties to refrain from fighting." On the other hand, rapid deployment can have a favorable impact. In the case of Cyprus, "Canadian troops arrived... within twenty-four hours of UNFICYP's [U.N. force in Cyprus's] approval. A symbolic presence is perhaps all that is needed in the first days of a cease-fire anyway."

Surprisingly, it is in the conduct of second generation peacekeeping missions that U.N. Army enthusiasts foresee the greatest utility for such a permanent force, despite the bellicose environment frequently associated with these missions. To use this force in such a mission would mean that the U.N. would continue its selective abandonment of its "principles of peacekeeping" which it articulated to define success. In fact, the force is targeted for these difficult missions because "few, if any, governments are willing to commit their own troops to a forceful ground role in a situation which does not threaten their own security and which may well prove to be both violent and open ended."

Thus the paradox of using a permanent U.N. force in these operations is exposed. On the one hand it is proposed as a mechanism to circumvent the unwillingness of member states to get involved in difficult missions such as those of the second generation of peacekeeping. It will replace the ground troops which were never committed by reluctant member states. On the other hand, it is acknowledged that this small and symbolic force would be deployed to impose a solution on an armed party which has not accepted a solution through diplomatic channels. It is genuinely hard to imagine how the timely intervention of such a force could have forced a different outcome in Bosnia or Somalia.

In Bosnia, without the conclusion of a political settlement, any U.N. force in limited numbers operating under peacekeeping rather than enforcement rules of engagement is bound to be hostage to its environment. Because the lack of consensus among member states keeps the mandate and size of the force small and innocuous, any U.N. force is powerless to influence the environment in which it operates. Therefore, dozens of U.N. resolutions on the conflict go unenforced. Rapid reaction by a U.N. military force would not have changed this. Neither unarmed observers nor light infantry with soft-skinned armored vehicles can impose or enforce action in a bellicose combat environment. In both cases, the force is merely a tripwire and its operating imperative is almost solely based on its moral strength as a symbol.

In Somalia, the dilemma stems from the fact that "the basic distinction between peacekeeping and enforcement action... has been blurred. The forceful measures taken by U.S. troops to disarm warring factions, while fully within the mandate of UNOSOM II [U.N. force in Somalia], have highlighted the particular risks of attempting to combine the coercive use of force with peacekeeping objectives." Once again, the basic question is how to use the force to effect the political objectives. Any permanent U.N. force would be faced with exactly the same question no matter when it arrived. Only it might get to face that dilemma a bit sooner.

Naturally, a small, permanent U.N. force would have no great utility in enforcement action either. The fact that large-scale enforcement actions are taking place means that diplomacy or previous intervention has failed. The only scenario in which a permanent U.N. force could be involved at this end of the spectrum was if it was deployed, came under heavy attack, or suffered a similar failure to pacify a volatile environment, and withdrew prior to large scale intervention authorized by an Article 42 resolution.

The only outstanding use of such a force would be in preventative deployments, of which Macedonia is the only current example. In this case, the force does not seek to exercise any sort of operational capability other than limited observation and patrolling. It is a human tripwire, a symbol of the will of the international community. Any violent actions directed against this force (or the peace it seeks to keep) will have to be met with a U.N. response that transcends the organic capacity of this very small and lightly armed force. The soldiers involved are in an unenviable position, as they are powerless to influence their own environment. Their fate rests on the goodwill of the belligerents and the credibility of the United Nations in the eyes of the opposing factions. That bluff has been called in the past and the casualty lists are fast approaching 1000.

OPERATIONAL QUESTIONS

In short, preventative deployment by a permanent U.N. force begs a whole series of operational questions:

1. Under what circumstances will the force be deployed? Guidelines for intervention must be clearly defined. After all, "demand for U.N. peacekeeping since early 1992 has begun to outstrip the supply, whether that supply is measured in money or in national political will." Resources ultimately come from the member states, and are limited no matter what form they take. It is easy to imagine the small force being called upon for almost every potential conflict.
2. Will the U.N. force be governed by the "principles of peacekeeping" or will it be expected to enforce or impose solutions on belligerent factions? If the time-consuming negotiations necessary to obtain the consent of all parties are still underway, the rapid deployment capabilities of this force will have little utility.
3. What explicit mechanisms would be needed to determine the composition and missions of follow-on forces to relieve the rapid reaction force? There must be an organized process by which the crisis is evaluated, and intervention is either continued, upgraded, or abandoned. The involvement of a permanent U.N. force in an open-ended commitment would completely negate its utility.

While such guidelines are necessary, in some cases they will be inadequate to address the *sui generis* [unique] conflicts of the post–Cold War era. On the one hand, doctrine governing the use of a U.N. force must be stringent enough to provide real direction. On the other hand, that same doctrine will rule out intervention in many pressing crises. The doctrine guiding the use of U.N. force must cover a bewildering myriad of crises. It must also have a mechanism which forces decisionmakers to evaluate its immediate utility in a timely manner.

The deployment of a permanent U.N. rapid reaction force would catapult issues onto the U.N. agenda which member states are not ready to address. It could quite easily upset a natural control measure in an organization made up of nation-states. "States may well prefer a situation in which the provision of military force for U.N. activities is managed in an *ad hoc* manner, thereby giving them a greater degree of control over events."

There have been situations where the U.N. Security Council has called for troops to staff operations and the member states have simply failed to comply (Somalia 1992, Georgia 1993). It is reasonable to assume that these same member states would not support the deployment of a force controlled by the Secretary-General, which would require them to provide quick reinforcements. The reaction of member states to calls for collective operations are an important barometer of their willingness to act in common with others. A mechanism which forces or circumvents that common ground could backfire.

CONCLUSION

Even when one completely ignores these attendant political difficulties discussed briefly, it is still obvious that the operational utility of a permanent U.N. force is extremely limited. The value of such a force lies in its preventative role. Other

than that role, it does not fit naturally into the spectrum of U.N. military operations conducted since 1948. Even in a preventative role, its small size, limited operational capabilities, and constrained mandate would limit its effectiveness to operations at the low end of the spectrum.

And at this end of the spectrum, there is not only little need for rapid deployments, but little need for forces other than those constituted by traditional means. When acting as a tripwire and in a symbolic role, an *ad hoc* blue-helmet force or an expensive permanent U.N. Army are scarcely different in terms of operational effectiveness or political viability. The past approach to staffing U.N. operations at the low end of the spectrum has always been adequate, has never been seen as responsible for mission failures, and is an important mechanism for involving states in the maintenance of international peace and security. The strategic utility of such a force is marginal when compared with the current system for staffing U.N. operations at the low end of the spectrum.

Many supporters want the U.N. force to solve problems in operations at the upper end of the operational spectrum. This force could never have the complex operational infrastructure and capabilities to make a difference in missions which entail even modest enforcement operations. The whole issue of staffing and directing U.N. operations at the high end of the spectrum needs much greater attention. Second generation peacekeeping and enforcement missions are quite obviously much more reliant on the vigorous political backing of powerful member states. Beyond the politics involved, these missions require the leadership of a major power for two reasons: 1) large-scale enforcement against an intransigent party is an immensely complicated and expensive enterprise; and 2) only a very few member states have the actual military capability to command and control such a campaign. A small force only under the control of the Secretary-General cannot affect these types of situations.

This dilemma stems from the nature of the post–Cold War world and the attendant difficulties of military intervention. It cannot be solved by the implementation of a single mechanism whose operational utility is very limited.

POSTSCRIPT

Should a Permanent UN Military Force Be Established?

The increase in the use of UN peacekeeping forces is partly a result of the changes from the cold war to the post–cold war era, which can be explored in Karen A. Mingst and Margaret P. Karns, *The United Nations in the Post–Cold War Era* (Westview Press, 1995). Within this larger context, the debate over creating a potentially permanent international police force, perhaps even an army, is being seriously debated in many forums. A good place to begin more reading is with the report issued by Boutros Boutros-Ghali, *An Agenda for Peace: Preventive Diplomacy, Peacemaking, and Peacekeeping* (United Nations, 1992). For more on the debate from a broad perspective, read James S. Sutterlin, *The United Nations and the Maintenance of International Security* (Praeger, 1995). There are some who advocate even stronger measures than those that Schwartzberg recommends, including arming UN forces with nuclear weapons, as is evident in Kosta Tsipis and Philip Morrison, "Arming for Peace," *The Bulletin of the Atomic Scientists* (March/April 1994).

Other analysts are skeptical of the possibility or wisdom of a standing UN force and its possible uses. Some of these concerns are based on such narrow factors as cost. The entire cost of UN peacekeeping for FY 1997, however, is less than what it cost to keep the entire U.S. military operating for two days. More substantively, there are worries that a more powerful, proactive UN might undermine the sovereignty of the less developed countries (LDCs), with the UN Security Council serving as a tool of the five big powers that control the council through their veto. This concern has prompted a drive to revise how the Security Council operates. It is important to recognize that these reservations are not necessarily unfounded. Laura Neack, in "UN Peace-Keeping: In the Interest of Community of Self?" *Journal of Peace Research* (1995), finds that an analysis of the record from 1945 to 1990 reveals that the "interests that have been served by UN peacekeeping are those of the Western states whose interests are served by the status quo and a few non-Western states that lay claim to some prestige in international affairs through their UN activities." This use of the UN, Neack continues, may "amount to Western interventionist foreign policy bordering on imperialism." The recent expansion of UN peacekeeping activities may indeed signal an era in which sovereignty is eroded, but only for non-Western states. There is also concern about the ethics of humanitarian intervention even by the UN and other outside forces. This is expressed by David Fisher in "The Ethics of Intervention," *Survival* (Winter 1994).

On the Internet ...

Amnesty International
Information about the current state of human rights throughout the world is available at this Web site. The 1997 Amnesty International report that documents acts of violence in 151 countries is also available. *http://www.amnesty.org/*

Canada-U.S. Human Rights Information and Documentation Network
This site was developed to facilitate the exchange of ideas and information among human rights organizations, including exchanges with information and documentation networks in other parts of the world. *http://www.aaas.org/spp/dspp/shr/cushrid.htm*

Country Reports on Human Rights Practices for 1996
These are reports released by the Bureau of Democracy, Human Rights, and Labor. The site offers a search capability. *http://www.usis.usemb.se/human/index.html*

Information Office of State Council of People's Republic of China
This official site of China's government contains policy statements by the government related to human rights. *http://www.cityu.edu.hk/HumanRights/index.htm*

PART 4

Values and International Relations

In this era of increasing global interdependence, the state of relations among countries will become an ever more vital concern to all the world's people. This section examines issues of global concern and issues related to the values that affect relations and policy making among nations.

- Should Foreign Policymakers Minimize Human Rights Concerns?

- Does the Spread of Democracy Promote World Peace?

- Should China Be Condemned as a Violator of Human Rights?

ISSUE 12

Should Foreign Policymakers Minimize Human Rights Concerns?

YES: Alan Tonelson, from "Jettison the Policy," *Foreign Policy* (Winter 1994/1995)

NO: Michael Posner, from "Rally Round Human Rights," *Foreign Policy* (Winter 1994/1995)

ISSUE SUMMARY

YES: Alan Tonelson, a fellow of the Economic Strategy Institute in Washington, D.C., contends that the United States' human rights policy has collapsed and ought to be jettisoned.

NO: Michael Posner, executive director of the Lawyers Committee for Human Rights, maintains that Tonelson's argument is flawed and that the United States should continue to incorporate human rights concerns into its foreign policy decisions.

This debate on the role of human rights and other moral issues in determining foreign policy is one over which realists and idealists disagree strongly.

Realists are averse to applying moral standards to foreign policy. When Adolf Hitler's Nazi Germany invaded Joseph Stalin's communist Soviet Union, Sir Winston Churchill, the prime minister of democratic Great Britain, offered aid to Stalin. When a critic in Parliament challenged the decision of the prime minister, he replied: "If Hitler had invaded Hell, ... [I would] make favorable reference to the devil." It is not that realists are amoral. Instead, they agree with the view of Secretary of State George Shultz (1982–1989) that "we ... have ... to accept that our passionate commitment to moral principles [cannot] be a substitute for sound foreign policy in a world of hard realities and complex choices." This is true, he argues, because "moral impulse, noble as it might be, [can] lead either to futile and perhaps dangerous global crusades, on the one hand, or to escapism and isolationism, equally dangerous, on the other." Similarly, Hans Morgenthau, one of the founders of the academic realists' school, argued that it is unconscionable as well as risky for a state to abandon realpolitik in favor of moralism. He contended that "while the individual has a moral right to sacrifice himself" in defense of a moral principle, "the state has no right to let its moral disapprobation ... get in the way of successful political action, itself inspired by the moral principle of national survival."

Idealists, in contrast, believe that it is both right and wise to consider human rights when making foreign policy decisions. Richard Falk, a leading idealist scholar, criticizes realists for their "tendency to discount... the normative aspirations of society." Some policymakers agree with this view. President Jimmy Carter declared during a speech marking the 30th anniversary of the Universal Declaration of Human Rights of 1948 that Americans should be "proud that our nation stands for more than military might or political might," that "our pursuit of human rights is part of a broad effort to use our great power and our tremendous influence in the service of creating a better world in which human beings can live," and that "human rights is the soul of our foreign policy." Idealists also reject the realists' contention that a country will be at a disadvantage if it applies moral standards to foreign policy making in a dangerous world. Secretary of State Cyrus Vance (1977–1980) once commented that it is a "dangerous illusion" to believe that "pursuing values such as human rights... is incompatible with pursuing U.S. national interests" because we can "never be secure in a world where freedom was threatened everywhere else."

The end of the cold war has, in many ways, made the issue of human rights more acute. During the cold war the human rights abuses of friendly regimes were often ignored in the interests of solidarity as the West faced the threat from the Soviet-led communists. That threat has ended, of course, and with it has died the easy standard that an anticommunist dictator is better than no anticommunist government at all. Idealists now argue that we act on our principles without the fear that we are empowering an enemy. Realists rejoin that the end of the cold war did not mean the end of power politics.

The debate over whether or not to incorporate human rights standards into foreign policy making is not simply a matter of intellectual speculation. The controversy also involves important policy choices. If democracy truly does promote peace, then perhaps the United States, Canada, and other democracies should pressure, even force if possible, other nondemocratic regimes to change. The United States, backed by the United Nations, did that in Haiti. Should the same standard apply to friendly nondemocratic regimes such as Saudi Arabia, which is ruled by a feudal monarchy? Also, what should a country do when the dictates of realpolitik point in one direction and human rights concerns point in another?

YES
Alan Tonelson

JETTISON THE POLICY

President Bill Clinton's team-up with the Haitian military and his [recent] acknowledgment that trade sanctions would not hasten democracy's development in China are only the latest signs that America's human rights policy has collapsed. The signs of America's failure to achieve the policy's objectives appear everywhere: from the halls of power in defiant Beijing to the streets of Port-au-Prince, from the mountains of Bosnia to the tenant farms of rebellious Chiapas in southern Mexico. At least as important, the policy has antagonized or simply turned off numerous democratic countries, as well as endangered a broad range of U.S. strategic and economic interests in key regions around the world.

No one can fairly blame U.S. policy for the world's continuing—and in many respects worsening—human rights situation. But Washington has been so ineffective in combating human rights violations in so many places for so long, and so many of its efforts at promoting democracy—especially their unilateral elements—have entailed such high costs, that the usual explanations seem inadequate.

Rather than blame Secretary of State Warren Christopher's alleged incompetence and Clinton's allegedly naive campaign promises, or struggle to better "balance" human rights concerns with other major U.S. interests, Americans might instead begin asking a fundamental question: Does any government-centered human rights policy make sense in the post–Cold War era? All the evidence indicates that such policies, however morally compelling, are obsolete—swamped, ironically, by the very forces that only yesterday inspired such bipartisan optimism in a new age of human rights progress. The immense tides of information, technology, goods, and capital that now flow so effortlessly across borders have turned Washington's efforts into Cold War relics, as antiquated as fallout shelters—and, in their own way, as falsely comforting.

Since the Cold War spawned U.S. human rights policy, its post–Cold War collapse should come as no surprise. American leaders have spoken out against oppression abroad throughout U.S. history, and the American people fought two global hot wars as well as a cold war against imperialist adversaries. But a systematic, dedicated policy to promote greater respect worldwide for human rights dates back only to the 1970s. Unfortunately, the policy was never rooted in a rigorous critique of prevailing American approaches to world affairs, or in a careful search for alternatives, but in a politically inspired temper tantrum by foreign policy professionals of the Left and Right.

Of course, as left-of-center human rights advocates argued, Washington's Cold War alliances with anticommunist dictators sometimes backfired. Of course, as right-of-center human rights advocates argued, American leaders episodically kept quiet about communist oppression whenever they pursued détente-like policies. And, of course, there was much heartfelt concern at the grassroots level about the moral tone and impact of American foreign policy. But the high-profile politicians and activists across the political spectrum who created and debated official human rights policies were, at bottom, simply venting frustrations over the compromises with evil that no foreign policy in an imperfect, anarchic world can avoid, and using human rights debates to push broader, more questionable agendas.

Liberals and other left-wing opponents of the Vietnam War used the human rights issue to push the broader view that millennial change was sweeping over world affairs, and that the United States could abandon the use of force and power-politicking altogether. They asserted that America's essential foreign policy objectives could be secured with more morally and aesthetically pleasing tools like foreign aid, diplomacy, and acceding to the (usually legitimate) interests of even hostile powers. The political Right used the human rights issue to attack détente with the Soviet Union and the larger belief that peaceful coexistence with other nuclear superpowers not only was necessary, but also could improve national security by reducing tensions and even produce mutually beneficial agreements.

Not surprisingly, given such political and polemical origins, human rights policy rarely advanced U.S. national interests in the 1970s. Relations with both allies and adversaries worsened (including West European countries that criticized the policy's heavy-handed treatment of the former Soviet Union), dictatorial friends were often weakened without generating better replacements (as in Iran and Nicaragua), and equally dictatorial foes remained securely in power (throughout the communist bloc and much of the developing world).

More surprisingly, prominent human rights advocates rarely sounded troubled when their policies failed to significantly improve human rights practices worldwide. Did U.S. policy simply help replace a friendly autocrat with an equally ruthless and hostile successor, as in Iran and Nicaragua? Did American initiatives lead a target regime to crack down on dissenters or aspiring emigrants, as in the Soviet Union? Was America aiming at countries where it had no influence at all, as in Vietnam or Ethiopia?

When advocates did try to answer such questions, their responses spoke volumes about their real priorities. Symbolism was critical. Consistency was essential—never mind that the objects of human rights policy were countries that differed completely in their level of social and economic development, their significance to the United States, and their political relations with America. The United States had to go on record. Americans had to do "what they could"—implying, of course, that salving American consciences was the main point.

For those reasons, moderate critics of the policies were missing the point entirely when they labored mightily to reconcile human rights positions with American strategic and economic interests. U.S. efforts did score limited successes—securing the release of numerous political prisoners during the 1970s (especially in Latin America) and joining in rare global economic sanctions that did advance the cause of reform in South Africa—although how those successes made the United States appreciably more secure or more prosperous was never explained. But human rights activism was never primarily about enhancing national security and welfare, or even alleviating suffering abroad. It was an exercise in therapy. The bottom line, as Jimmy Carter made clear, was to give Americans a foreign policy they could feel good about.

By the early 1980s, human rights policy became bogged down in sterile debates over the relative merits of left- and right-wing dictators, or the relative importance of the more traditional political rights such as free expression and the vote versus social and economic rights (to a job or education). Advancing the national interest or achieving concrete results receded further into the background. Pushing one's left- or right-wing sympathies and elegantly rationalizing them became higher priorities.

HUMAN RIGHTS IN THE AGE OF CLINTON

The end of the Cold War generated broad optimism that human rights would take center stage, not only in U.S. foreign policy, but in world politics as a whole. Economic and trade issues aside, human rights dominated Clinton's intermittent foreign policy rhetoric during the 1992 campaign, as he and other Democrats repeatedly blasted George Bush's alleged indifference to human rights horrors in Tiananmen Square [China], Iraq, and the former Yugoslavia.

And so far—again, leaving economics aside—human rights issues have dominated Clinton's intermittent foreign policy making as president. His inaugural address promised to use American power if necessary whenever "the will and conscience of the international community is defied." His national security adviser Anthony Lake has made the "enlargement" of the world's roster of democratic countries one of America's top foreign policy priorities. And human rights considerations permeate the U.S. foreign policy agenda from Russia to China to Somalia to Bosnia to Haiti.

Clinton's priorities clearly reflected a rapidly emerging bipartisan conventional wisdom. The reasons for optimism were obvious to conservatives and liberals alike—although they disagreed sharply on what some of them were. Both were thrilled by the prospect of an America no longer forced to back dictators for anti-Soviet reasons. Both expected the collapse of Soviet power and Soviet stooges around the world to bring the blessings of national self-determination to numerous captive peoples. And both assumed that the global revolutions in communications and commerce would inevitably carry democratic political ideas and liberal economic practices into even the most repressive and backward societies.

But conservatives were more taken with the role that America, as the last superpower, could play unilaterally in fostering democracy and capitalism. Some even urged the United States to launch a global crusade to help the process along and create a worldwide Pax Democratica shaped by American political principles and by Reaganomics.

Liberals focused on multilateral approaches, churning out blueprints for creating a U.N. that could oust repressive regimes through sanctions or force of arms. As demonstrated most dramatically in 1991 by the establishment of safe havens for Iraq's Kurds, the international community, they argued, was acquiring the right to intervene in sovereign states' internal affairs when rights violations threatened international security or passed some unspecified threshold of savagery.

Yet none of the countries that the president or the world community has focused on have become significantly freer or more democratic places since Clinton's inauguration or since the Soviet Union's demise. In other areas of American concern, notably Russia and its "Near Abroad," the situation has arguably worsened in recent months. Bleaker still is the human rights outlook in those regions that have so far eluded either the administration's or the media's focus—from sub-Saharan Africa to suddenly shaky Mexico to the Arab world.

Even in Western Europe, democracy is deeply troubled as high unemployment and burgeoning immigrant populations have strengthened xenophobic politicians in many countries. And writers such as Jean-François Revel argue convincingly that the rampant corruption of social democratic systems in Italy and France has undermined the public trust in government that is crucial to the survival of democracy.

However, success stories are by no means unknown. So far, they include Taiwan, South Korea, and Chile, and even economically troubled countries such as Argentina, the Czech Republic, and the Baltic states. Nor can prospects for near-term improvement be written off completely in Russia and Mexico.

Still, one of the most comprehensive annual studies of the global human rights picture—the traditionally optimistic Freedom House's *Comparative Survey of Freedom*—concluded at the end of last year that "freedom around the world is in retreat while violence, repression and state control are on the increase." Of course, recent U.S. policy is not exclusively, largely, or even significantly responsible for that. But it is not apparent that official efforts have achieved many durable gains, either.

Even more disturbing has been the global reaction to U.S. human rights policies, especially their unilateral elements. Not a single major power, for example, emulated Washington's linkage of trade relations with human rights progress in China. Some of America's staunchest regional allies, such as Japan and Australia, openly criticized that strategy from the start. Other allies, principally the West Europeans, quietly worked overtime to cut deals with a booming economy that is already the world's third largest.

Furthermore, many East Asian governments—and many Asian voices outside government—have openly challenged U.S. human rights initiatives as arrogant efforts to impose Western values on proud, ancient societies that are doing quite well economically and socially, thank you. Similar resentments are widely expressed in the Arab world and other Islamic countries.

But the best evidence of failure is the administration's zig-zag record on numerous human rights fronts. Human rights issues are a large part of the president's most embarrassing retreats from campaign promises. Clinton has decided to follow the Bush administration's approach to China, finally agreeing that continued economic engagement is the best way to advance America's human rights and broader agendas with the world's most populous country. Even before his inauguration, the president had to endorse his predecessor's policy of returning Haiti's boat people, and in September 1994 he acquiesced in an agreement negotiated mainly by former president Jimmy Carter for joint U.S. administration of Haiti's democratic transition with the very military leaders he had condemned as murderers and rapists the week before. Moreover, bitter experiences in Somalia and Haiti in 1993 have so far led to a lowering of America's peacekeeping goals.

DECLINE IN PUBLIC SUPPORT

In part, U.S. human rights policies are failing because their consistently shaky strategic foundations have crumbled. During the Cold War, a plausible case could be made for denying an ideologically hostile rival superpower targets of opportunity by fostering democratic practices abroad. But in the absence of such a rival, the state of human rights around the world does not have, and has never had, any demonstrable effect on U.S. national security. America's rise to global prominence occurred primarily in periods when democracies were few and far between, and a combination of geography, power, wealth, and social cohesion will continue to be the country's best guarantees of security in a turbulent world.

In the wake of the Cold War, both liberal and conservative human rights advocates (including the president) have argued that democracies rarely fight each other—hence the more there are, the merrier and safer America will be. Yet the jury is still out: Significant numbers of democracies have existed together only in the last 50 years. Furthermore, U.S. leaders obviously have never bought the argument themselves—otherwise, they would not continue to be terrified by the prospect of democratic Germany and Japan carrying out independent foreign policies or going nuclear.

Moreover, strong domestic support for an active human rights policy has been difficult to detect. Although Americans often endorse vigorous human rights policies when talking with pollsters, they have not recently acted or voted as if they cared much about them. Carter made human rights a top foreign policy priority and was rewarded with early retirement —because he let the economy deteriorate and seemed ineffective in dealing with the Soviets. His 1980 opponent, Ronald Reagan, promised to uphold American values against an evil Soviet empire, but his most politically popular foreign policy position was his stand against the military threat he saw emanating from Moscow. And what happened when the greatest White House communicator since Franklin Roosevelt tried to mobilize public support for his Reagan Doctrine policies of arming "freedom fighters" combating pro-Soviet Third World regimes? He failed everywhere except in Afghanistan, where the Soviet occupation arguably threatened the oil-rich Persian Gulf.

What politicians and pundits do not understand—and may not want to understand—is that unlike their leaders, the American people evidently have learned from past mistakes. Vietnam has happened. The Iran hostage crisis has happened. As the 1992 election and its aftermath showed, when voters care deeply about issues—from the economy to [U.S. attorney general nominee] Zoe Baird's nanny problem—they are not shy about making their feelings known. And just as they never filled the streets or flooded Washington's phone banks protesting oppression around the world during the 1970s and 1980s, they have not been demanding the denial of tariff breaks to China or intervention in basket-case countries in the 1990s. If the American people retain any significant missionary impulse, or much optimism that the world craves American guidance on human rights issues, they are hiding their feelings well.

To a depressing degree, however, U.S. human rights policy grinds on along the same well-worn tracks. Despite the China trade decision, another China-like struggle over linking trade relations with human rights practices may be unfolding with Indonesia, and yet another looms with Vietnam. Both controversies have scary implications for America's economic position in rapidly growing Asia (where establishing long-term relationships and, consequently, a reputation for reliability are keys to business success) and other emerging markets.

And as during the 1970s and 1980s, today's human rights skeptics unwittingly play along, accepting the basic assumptions driving human rights policy but pleading for moderation, perspective, and "balancing" human rights considerations with America's strategic and economic objectives.

In the process, critics have periodically aired stronger objections, calling human rights policy arrogant, naive, inconsistent —a juvenile protest against life's built-in imperfections. They are largely correct. Yet two even greater obstacles to a successful government-led U.S. human rights policy are embedded in the very nature of the post–Cold War world.

The first concerns the phenomenon of failed states that has been exposed by the retreat of Soviet power in Eastern Europe and by the end of Cold War confrontation in much of the Third World—in Bosnia, Georgia, Haiti, Somalia, Rwanda, and elsewhere. The often horrendous general conditions and specific outrages that have resulted from the breakdown of governments in those regions are usually described as "human rights violations," but the phrase trivializes the problem. At worst, they are endemic features of deep-rooted ethnic conflicts. At best, they are symptoms of a monumental struggle over issues not of liberalization or democratization, but of minimal coherence or further fragmentation. Welcome to the dark side of national self-determination, as Colonel E. M. House warned Woodrow Wilson nearly 75 years ago.

Outside Western Europe, North America, and East Asia, most "countries" around the world simply do not deserve that label. They may have the trappings of statehood—postage stamps, U.N. membership—but their populations lack a sense of mutual loyalty and obligation, and their politics lack strong institutions, a commitment to the rule of law, and even a tradition of public service as anything more than an opportunity for theft and vengeance. They are straining to reach minimal viability not even as nation-states but as societies. The conceit behind the idea that even the best designed policies, or a few billion dollars' worth of foreign aid, or "how to" democracy courses can make a real difference is, to put it kindly, immense.

As for U.S. human rights policies toward more advanced repressive countries, they are swamped by a similar problem—by the very global economic and cultural interaction responsible for much of the optimism of human rights advocates. Precisely because ideas and capital and technology—and, to a somewhat lesser extent, people—can cross borders so easily, official rhetoric and even sanctions get lost in the shuffle. Government words and deeds form merely one small breeze in the gales of commerce and culture blowing around the world today. Western and American values will not be the only seeds dropped by those winds. But if we consider their spread and growth to be essential, then we are better advised to lead from strength—to energetically add to America's already vast commercial, cultural, and ideological influence around the world, rather than seek to replace it with legislation or executive orders or official oratory.

Leave aside for the moment the op-ed level arguments that dominated the China most-favored-nation debate—for example, over which country has the most leverage, over whether economic relations with America strengthen the Chinese government's economic base and help pacify the population, over whether other countries will rush in to replace American suppliers and investors. Say Americans were to start from scratch on an imaginary campaign to reform China. What would the most promising tools be? "Sense of the Congress" resolutions? Cutbacks in the numbers of American

companies that the Chinese can work for or do business with, and that pay Chinese employees higher wages and provide safer working conditions than do China's state-owned enterprises? Or would America send as many businesspeople to China as quickly as it could? The answer should be obvious even to those who do not believe in business-created utopias.

The China issue, however, along with [the recent] controversy over the North American Free Trade Agreement, does bring up one bona fide human rights issue where more effective U.S. government action is needed: the question of how most of America's workforce can benefit from trade with countries that repress labor rights. American workers are already exposed to strong competition from hundreds of millions of workers in developing countries who are highly educated, highly productive, and organized by the world's leading multinational corporations, but who are paid a fraction of what their U.S. counterparts earn and who are systematically denied the right to form independent unions and bargain collectively for wages that bear some relationship to productivity increases, for decent workplaces, and for nonwage benefits—rights and conditions until recently taken for granted in North America and Western Europe. Many more such workers will soon be coming into the world economy from China's interior (as opposed to its already booming coastal regions), from South and Southeast Asia, and, farther down the road, from Russia and Eastern Europe.

Even if all of them work for politically and socially progressive American companies, which they will not, the capacity of those workers to export will exceed by orders of magnitude their capacity to consume. Lack of labor rights is hardly the only reason, but it can create major competitive advantages. As Labor Secretary Robert Reich noted in an April 1994 speech, the problem is part and parcel of the inherent difficulties of commerce between countries at greatly differing levels of economic and social development in an age of highly mobile capital and technology.

Unlike other human rights issues, moreover, labor rights controversies and their resolutions are already having concrete effects on the lives of millions of Americans. But they are best seen not as human rights issues at all, but as challenges in managing interdependence —in ensuring that the great integrative forces shaping the world economy work for the long-term benefit of the great majority of the American people, not against it.

Nor can labor rights controversies be successfully resolved by acting out the stylized morality plays that make up human rights policy today—by issuing the same threats and voluminous reports, by trotting out the same dissidents in front of the press, by fasting, or by any other attempts to dictate the social and economic priorities of other countries. Instead, labor rights problems require a raft of new trade, technology, foreign investment, and other policies designed to increase America's economic power.

A vibrant industrial base that creates millions of new high-wage jobs can give America the economic leverage needed to negotiate beneficial economic agreements with the rest of the world. A prosperous America can generate enough markets, capital, and technology to give other countries powerful incentives to conform to U.S. labor, environmental, and other standards voluntarily—not as acknowledgements of American moral superiority or as acts of surrender, but simply as the price of access.

As Americans will discover in many foreign policy fields, crusades to bring about utopian change around the world will rarely achieve their goals. The best bets lie in measures that enable the country to survive, flourish, and bargain successfully in the deeply flawed world that we will remain stuck with for many decades. Americans wishing their government to act in moral ways might consider focusing on their own country —which suffers its share of problems and moral outrages, but is also blessed with the institutions and social cohesion to make serious reform more than a pipe dream.

NO

Michael Posner

RALLY ROUND HUMAN RIGHTS

Alan Tonelson has written a provocative but premature obituary to international human rights. He asserts that the tragedies in Bosnia, Somalia, and Haiti prove that it is no longer useful or productive for the U.S. government to challenge state-sponsored murder and torture in other countries and to emphasize human rights as an element of its foreign policy.

Tonelson's postmortem is flawed in at least four basic assumptions: In a relatively short space, he manages to misrepresent the origins of human rights, its scope and objectives, reasonable measures to judge the effectiveness of U.S. human rights policy, and the view of key U.S. allies with respect to this policy.

According to Tonelson, the emphasis on human rights was a product of the Cold War, designed principally to challenge the Soviet Union. From his perspective, the starting point for the discussion was the 1970s. He is wrong, both about the purpose and the timing. Contrary to Tonelson's narrow world view, attention to international human rights has evolved steadily over the last five decades.

The international community in fact began to focus on human rights immediately after World War II. Shaken by the Holocaust and determined to make amends for their slow and inadequate response to the murder of millions of innocent victims, the United States and its allies sought to take steps to prevent similar future occurrences. The United Nations Charter, adopted in 1945, made human rights a central purpose of that new organization. Governments pledged to take joint and separate actions to encourage a more just, humane world.

A year later, the U.N. created its own Commission on Human Rights, with former first lady Eleanor Roosevelt serving as its first chair. Under her stewardship, the commission moved quickly to draft a body of human rights principles—the Universal Declaration of Human Rights, adopted by the U.N. General Assembly in 1948. Working closely with the U.S. Department of State, Roosevelt helped develop two other key treaties, the International Covenant on Civil and Political Rights and the International Covenant on Economic, Social and Cultural Rights. Many other countries participated in those early

From Michael Posner, "Rally Round Human Rights," *Foreign Policy* (Winter 1994/1995).

developments and many more, including virtually all key American allies, now view the treaties as the basis for international consideration of those rights.

Official U.S. attention to those issues increased significantly in the 1970s with congressional efforts like the Jackson-Vanik Amendment, which linked trade with the Soviet Union to its willingness to allow emigration by Soviet Jews. As president, Jimmy Carter greatly expanded U.S. initiatives in the area and gave human rights a much higher profile.

Nongovernmental organizations also came of age at that time. Amnesty International was awarded the 1977 Nobel Peace Prize in recognition of its unique role in human rights advocacy. Several key U.S.-based human rights organizations, including Helsinki Watch (now part of Human Rights Watch) and the Lawyers Committee for Human Rights, were also founded during that period. Thus, over the past 50 years, significant progress has been made in developing human rights law and in setting practical objectives for its implementation.

SCOPE AND OBJECTIVES

Tonelson offers a confusing and sometimes contradictory view of the scope and objectives of U.S. human rights policy. On one hand, he criticizes politicians and activists for using human rights "to push broader, more questionable agendas." On the other hand, he urges that we pursue labor rights, not because it is the right thing to do, but to protect the economic well-being of "millions of Americans."

Tonelson also builds straw men, only to tear them down. He refers repeatedly to "human rights advocates," a term he never defines. Using that broad rubric, he notes that conservatives are using

human rights to foster "democracy and capitalism." He then accuses liberals of using human rights to advocate using U.N. sanctions or military force "to oust repressive regimes." While some have indeed used the language of human rights to pursue these broad political objectives, in doing so they are going beyond the core meaning of human rights, which is to challenge governments when they mistreat their own people.

Human rights advocates such as Amnesty International and hundreds of national rights advocacy groups around the world rely on international human rights standards that set minimum requirements for governments. States that ratify international treaties make a pledge to abide by those core legal principles, which include commitments not to torture their own people, subject them to slavery, or engage in political murder. Tonelson blithely dismisses efforts by human rights groups and others to challenge such violations as "an exercise in therapy." On the contrary, human rights advocacy has evolved into a worldwide movement aimed at exposing and combating official misconduct and alleviating suffering. There is now ample evidence that by exposing violations and challenging the violators, lives are being saved.

The international treaties provide a foundation for such efforts, but set forth only broad basic principles. The civil and political covenant, for example, requires governments to allow for a free press, for the right to hold public meetings, and for the right to speak freely. It also requires popular participation in choosing a government. But it neither spells out how that should be accomplished, nor suggests a specific political structure or system. Those who seek to wrap broader economic and political agendas in the flag of human rights, including some in the Clinton administration, are overloading the system.

The treaties are also silent on the sanctions that may be imposed on governments that systematically violate basic human rights. Although there is nothing to prevent the U.N. Security Council from invoking the language of human rights to help justify military action, there is nothing in the treaties that compels it, or even suggests that it should do so.

Some governments, including that of the United States, have linked their provision of bilateral aid and trade privileges to human rights. In the last 20 years, the United States has occasionally withheld or delayed the provision of bilateral aid—particularly military aid— in situations where a sustained pattern of violations was occurring. The connection to military aid is the most direct, given the possibility that the weapons being provided will be used to commit further violations.

It is much more difficult to impose trade sanctions, in part because there is much less agreement on the usefulness of trade restrictions as an instrument of leverage. The Jackson-Vanik Amendment, which restricted trade to the former Soviet Union, was an exception for two reasons: U.S. economic opportunities in the USSR were limited, and such sanctions had bipartisan support in the broader effort to challenge Soviet influence worldwide.

The recent controversy over the linkage between trade and human rights in China was not surprising, given the economic opportunities at stake. Yet the Clinton administration's decision to de-link the two issues by renewing China's most-favored-nation trading status does not mean that future human rights initiatives should be avoided, or that long-term international pressure on the human rights front will be ineffective.

MEASURES OF EFFECTIVENESS

Tonelson's sole criterion for measuring human rights progress appears to be whether U.S. strategic interests are being advanced. That is the wrong place to start. While governments that respect human rights are likely to be more stable and reliable strategic allies, the protection and promotion of basic rights worldwide is important in itself. Consistent with our values and traditions, the U.S. government should promote international initiatives designed to alleviate suffering and to challenge governments that deny basic freedoms to their own people.

Tonelson argues that since human rights are being violated all around the world, the human rights policy must be failing, and therefore should be abandoned. That is akin to arguing that since thousands of businesses go bankrupt each year, we must abandon the free market system. While progress on human rights cannot be evaluated with the precision of a profit and loss statement, there are several useful measures of effectiveness.

The first measure is public attention to and awareness of human rights issues. Twenty years ago it was rare to see any reference to international human rights in the news media. By contrast, in any newspaper today one is likely to see several articles, often including one or more front-page stories, where human rights issues are featured prominently. While growing awareness does not automatically lead to greater respect for human rights, it is an important step toward that goal. Most governments are surprisingly thin-skinned on these issues and will go out of their way to avoid being stigmatized by a broad public spotlight.

A second measure of progress is the extent to which indigenous human rights activists are raising the issue in their own countries. Apparently Tonelson does not see such activists from his perch in Washington, since he makes no reference to the proliferation of national advocates and organizations. In the 1970s there were perhaps a few dozen human rights organizations around the world. Today, there are hundreds of such organizations operating in countries throughout the world. Every day the groups are busy documenting abuses, filing lawsuits, and challenging their own governments when they violate basic human rights. Most of the groups are underfunded and work in very difficult circumstances. Those who participate in such activism frequently do so at personal risk. But they carry on, often relying on international diplomatic pressure from the U.S. government and influential parties to protect them and help reinforce the legitimacy of their efforts.

Many of the Asian governments, like those of China and Singapore, that are most critical of U.S. human rights policy and seek to characterize it as Western-based and culturally biased are among the declining number of regimes that absolutely prevent any independent human rights groups from operating. Their claims of cultural relativism can only be sustained if they can continue to prevent their own people from raising human rights issues. But they are fighting a losing battle. Recent experience in countries as diverse as Chile, Kuwait, Nigeria, South Africa, and Sri Lanka leave no doubt that where people are allowed to organize and advocate their own human rights, they will do so. The common denominators in this area are much stronger than the cultural divisions.

Finally, look around the world and note that progress continues to be made on human rights issues. Contrast the Latin America today with the one of 15 years ago. Tonelson's own criteria also lead him to assert that none of the countries on which Washington has focused its attention since 1991 have become any freer or more democratic. On that he is simply wrong. A great majority of South Africans, among others, would undoubtedly disagree with him.

Even in the many places where governments do continue to commit serious violations, Tonelson offers no viable alternative to challenging the violators. His suggestion that the United States abandon ship rather than risk the embarrassment of future failure adds little more than a rhetorical flourish to his argument.

The fourth broad mistake in Tonelson's analysis is his assertion that U.S. human rights policy is a failure because it has "antagonized or simply turned off numerous democratic countries." To support his proposition, he notes that not a single "major power" followed the Clinton administration's lead in linking human rights and trade in China. He also notes that some of America's strongest allies in the region, such as Australia and Japan, were openly critical of the policy.

While Tonelson is correct in identifying discomfort and in some cases opposition to the U.S. approach, his analysis is incomplete and therefore misleading. A number of key U.S. allies—Canada, Great Britain, the Netherlands, Sweden, Australia—include human rights as a component in their own foreign policies. But they often prefer to pursue those concerns on a multilateral rather than a bilateral basis. Historically, the U.S. government has disdained multilateral institutions, viewing U.N. debates as an exercise in damage control. In the 1980s, U.S. representatives to the U.N. repeatedly opposed resolutions that called for the appointment of special experts to investigate and report on the situations in Guatemala, Haiti, and El Salvador, among others—preferring to address those situations in a less-confrontational manner.

Tonelson also misses another important point, which is the declining U.S. ability to act unilaterally. During the Cold War, the United States invested billions of dollars in bilateral military and economic aid. Most of the money went to the support of strategic allies in the geopolitical confrontation with the Soviet bloc. A number of governments, such as those in El Salvador, Haiti, Indonesia, Liberia, the Philippines, and Zaire, were committing serious human rights violations. In those situations, the United States had enormous influence and could threaten to cut off aid as a means of ultimate leverage. Following the collapse of the Soviet Union, however, Congress drastically reduced foreign aid—particularly military aid—and, concomitantly, U.S. influence and ability to act unilaterally.

To date, both the Clinton administration and the human rights community have been slow to accept the new reality. The real failure of Clinton's China policy was not that he tried to link trade and human rights, but that he tried to do it alone. American companies quickly mobilized when they realized that not only would they be shut out of a huge market, but that their overseas competitors would jump in to fill the void. So while it remains an open question whether linking trade to human rights is a politically viable option for advancing the cause of human rights, in China or elsewhere, it is clear that whatever America's tactical approach is, it can no longer act alone if it is going to be effective.

Concern for human rights is far from obsolete—either as a set of U.N. principles or as an element of U.S. foreign policy. In looking to the future, these issues are likely to loom more prominently than ever before, particularly in those societies that are in transition, such as China, India, Mexico, Nigeria, and Russia. To be effective, U.S. policymakers and activists need to rethink strategies while working more in concert with others who regard human rights as a vital international concern.

POSTSCRIPT

Should Foreign Policymakers Minimize Human Rights Concerns?

The debate over morality and politics is both ancient and continuing. For recent general works on the topic, consult Mervyn Frost, *Ethics in International Relations* (Cambridge University Press, 1996) and Cathal J. Nolan, *Ethics and Statecraft* (Greenwood Press, 1995). There are times when promoting human rights standards and the realpolitik pursuit of the national interest can both be furthered by the same policy choice. Defeating dangerously militaristic and unconscionably evil Nazi Germany is one clear example. At other times, the degree to which human rights and realpolitik point in the same direction are less clear. The juncture between national interest and human rights was the focus of President Bill Clinton's November 1995 address to the nation. He asked Americans to support the deployment of U.S. troops to Bosnia on the grounds that "it's in our interest to do so and because it's the right thing to do." Clinton argued that it was in U.S. national interest to intervene "because problems that start beyond our borders can quickly become problems within them." Among other potential evils, he cited terrorism, the spread of weapons of mass destruction, and the possibility that continued violence in Bosnia "could spread like a poison throughout the region, eat away at Europe's stability, and erode our partnership with our European allies." The humanitarian concern, Clinton said, was the "quarter of a million men, women, and children who have been shelled, shot, and tortured to death." There are yet other times when decision makers are reluctant to press other countries on human rights and, instead, follow a realpolitik policy. China is one such case.

To study the divergent realist and idealist approaches to morality in foreign policy, begin with Hans Morgenthau's classic *Politics Among Nations* (Alfred A. Knopf, 1985) and the review of the book by leading idealist scholar Stanley Hoffmann in the *Atlantic Monthly* (November 1985). A more recent exposition of U.S. policy from the realist point of view is diplomat and scholar George F. Kennan's "On American Principles," *Foreign Affairs* (March/April 1995). For the idealist perspective, see Walter Russell Mead, "Lucid Stars: The American Foreign Policy Tradition," *World Policy Journal* (Winter 1995). From a practitioner's point of view, there are numerous, predominantly realist memoirs by former presidents and secretaries of state. The most recent of these is James A. Baker III, *The Politics of Diplomacy* (G. P. Putnam's Sons, 1995). An idealist orientation can be found in Cyrus Vance, *Hard Choices* (Simon & Schuster, 1982).

ISSUE 13

Does the Spread of Democracy Promote World Peace?

YES: James Lee Ray, from "The Democratic Path to Peace," *Journal of Democracy* (April 1997)

NO: Mary Caprioli, from "Why Democracy?" An Original Essay Written for this Volume (1997)

ISSUE SUMMARY

YES: James Lee Ray, a professor of political science at Vanderbilt University, contends that the evidence shows that the democratization of all the world's countries would promote peace.

NO: Mary Caprioli, a doctoral candidate at the University of Connecticut, argues that there is no conclusive evidence that global democratization will result in world peace.

The practice of democracy (from the Greek *demos*—citizenry) dates back 2,500 years to the ancient Greek city-states. For most of the interim, however, democracies were few and usually short-lived. The gradual rise of English democracy, and then the American and French Revolutions, began the slow growth of modern democratization. In recent years, Latin American has become mostly democratic, democracy has spread in Asia and Africa, and Eastern Europe and Russia and the other former Soviet republics have moved toward democracy. When they occurred, these changes persuaded some observers that the world was about to enter an era in which Western-style democracy would become the global norm.

Whether or not this prediction was true, the wave of democratization led to renewed scholarly interest in an old theory. In 1795 German philosopher Immanuel Kant wrote in *Perpetual Peace* that the spread of democracy would change the world by eliminating war because "if the consent of the citizens is required in order to decide that war should be declared ... nothing is more natural than that they would be very cautious in commencing such a poor game, decreeing for themselves all the calamities of war." Contemporary scholars, including James Lee Ray and Mary Caprioli, are now trying to determine whether or not Kant was correct by evaluating whether or not democratic regimes are more peaceful, especially with one another.

Using empirical methods, some scholars have found evidence that democracies seldom fight with each other. One study that analyzed 30 wars that occurred between 1816 and 1988 involving democracies on one or both sides found that at least 90 percent of the conflicts were clear democracy-versus-nondemocracy wars. Another study examined countries that share borders (and, thus, are most likely to go to war) and concluded that of various possible combinations (democracy-democracy, democracy-nondemocracy, nondemocracy-nondemocracy), contiguous democracies were the least likely to go to war.

Why would democracies be less bellicose than autocracies? Some scholars believe that the range of opinions that characterize democracy restrain decision makers and lessen the chance of war. A second view is that democracies are less likely to fight one another because they share similar values. Third, it may be that societies that are used to settling domestic differences peacefully are also more likely to do so internationally.

Not all scholars agree with the theory of democratic peace. Some analysts are skeptical that the absence of war between democracies is anything more than a statistical or historical anomaly that may not persist in the future. Other analysts contend that although democracies are somewhat less aggressive, their behavior becomes more aggressive under certain internal conditions, such as economic hardship.

There are also important disagreements among scholars about how to measure such basic factors as *democracy*. What is a democracy? What is not? It is important not to dismiss these matters as mere quibbling. One cannot know if democracies are more peaceful without first agreeing on which countries are democratic and which are not.

For example, one issue rests on the standards of *procedural democracy* versus *substantive democracy*. Americans, for one, tend to equate democracy with procedure. If citizens periodically choose among competing candidates and follow other such procedures, then there is democracy. Many other cultures in the world view democracy as a substantive product associated with equality. This view suggests that you do not have a democracy if, despite meeting procedural requisites, your system of government produces a perpetual racial, ethnic, or gender socioeconomic underclass. It can be argued that this is true in the United States.

A second confounding set of standards is *individualism* and *communitarianism*. Individualists are prone to arguing that democracy rests on the rights and liberties of the individual being paramount. American political culture is strongly individualistic. Communitarian political cultures, found widely in Asia and elsewhere, lean toward favoring the welfare of the collective (the community, the society) over those of any one individual.

Ray and Caprioli take up the debate over the relationship of democracy and peace in the following two selections. Ray concludes that the scholarly evidence shows that there is a strong positive connection between the two concepts. Caprioli disagrees and suggests that sufficient evidence exists to bring the validity of the democratic peace thesis into serious question.

YES
James Lee Ray

THE DEMOCRATIC PATH TO PEACE

The idea that democracy has an important pacifying impact on relationships among states is an old one. In recent years, nevertheless, it has resurfaced as if it were a new idea. Why? What are its origins? How persuasive is the evidence in favor of the proposition that democratic states have not, and are not likely to, engage in international wars against each other? Let us deal with each of these questions in turn.

Academic research on the democratic peace idea may be said to have established itself as a full-fledged, undeniably important phenomenon with the appearance [since 1993 of articles and books] devoted to the topic. . . . In addition, U.S. deputy assistant secretary of defense Joseph Kruzel acknowledged in 1994 that "the notion that democracies do not go to war with each other . . . has had a substantial impact on public policy. . . . There are very few propositions in international relations that can be articulated this clearly and simply, but when you have one, you can really cut through the clutter of the bureaucratic process and make an impact."

There is a clue to the timing of the current focus on the democratic peace proposition in the fate of somewhat earlier work on that proposition, appearing from the late 1970s to the early 1980s. Starting in the early 1970s, R. J. Rummel began work on five volumes, the fourth of which, published in 1979, stated the central conclusion of his massive research effort: "Violence does not occur between free societies." A couple of years after the appearance of the last of these five volumes, two articles by Michael Doyle developed in detail the . . . origins of the idea that democratic states will deal peacefully with one another.

Except for a couple of articles that refuted Rummel's contention that democratic states are more peaceful in general (and not just in their relationships with each other), the five volumes by Rummel and the elegant philosophical arguments by Doyle were largely ignored. Certainly compared with the flurry of interest that later work on democratic peace received as the 1980s turned into the 1990s, the earlier work by Rummel and Doyle languished in obscurity.

From James Lee Ray, "The Democratic Path to Peace," *Journal of Democracy*, vol. 8, no. 2 (April 1997), pp. 49–62. Copyright © 1997 by The National Endowment for Democracy and Johns Hopkins University Press. Reprinted by permission. Notes omitted.

These contrasting reactions become easier to understand when one recalls that the earlier work appeared at a time when the Cold War was being reborn, while the later work was published while the Cold War was ending. The Cold War's rebirth made the earlier work look like ideologically inspired, partisan cheerleading, at least to many academic specialists, The Cold War's end, in contrast, made democracy less controversial, ideologically speaking, and also made it possible to envision a largely democratic world, at least among the major powers. This was fertile ground, in turn, for the idea that a largely democratic world might be a far different and better place than one which had been marked by such brutal and costly conflicts between democratic and autocratic states as the First World War, the Second World War, and the Cold War.

THE ORIGINS OF AN IDEA

Standard answers to the question regarding the origins of the idea that democratic states will have peaceful relationships with one another point to [German philosopher] Immanuel Kant's 1795 essay "Perpetual Peace." Such standard answers, however, are usually wrong, or at least highly debatable.

Woodrow Wilson has almost certainly had a greater impact on current work regarding the democratic peace proposition than Kant or any of his contemporaries. Wilson characterized the First World War as an effort to make the world safe for democracy: after that war, his arguments "dominated the new utopian discipline of international relations." Henry Kissinger argues that "Woodrow Wilson originated... what

would become the dominant intellectual school of American foreign policy."

But no discussion of the origins of the contemporary flurry of interest in the democratic peace proposition would be complete without at least a mention of a source rather more obscure than President Wilson. In 1972, an associate research scientist at the New York State Narcotic Addiction Control Commission named Dean Babst published an article in the journal *Industrial Research* which concluded that "no wars have been fought between independent nations with elective governments between 1789 and 1941." ... An article published in *Industrial Research* is not likely to be noticed by scholars in the field of international politics, but it was cited by Melvin Small and J. David Singer, two scholars associated with the well-known Correlates of War Project at the University of Michigan, in an article published in 1976. Even though the major point made by Small and Singer was that Babst's thesis regarding the pacifying force of democracy was probably not valid, they did concede that with only unimportant and marginal exceptions, his observation that democratic states do not fight wars against each other was essentially accurate.

Small and Singer attempted to explain away the lack of wars between democracies, and in so doing may have emphasized a distinction that was a key, on both the psychological and logical levels, to the burgeoning interest in the democratic peace proposition some 15 years later. Everyone in academic and policy circles has long been aware of the idea that democracy is an important pacifying force. But most have until recently also been consciously or subconsciously convinced that its hoary status, the fact that

Hitler became chancellor of Germany through a largely constitutional process, the inflammatory character of the idea in the context of the Cold War, and the aggressive behavior by democratic states during the period of colonialism (in the Spanish-American War, in Vietnam, and so on), made the idea mostly uninteresting. What has seemed new to many attracted to the democratic peace proposition in its contemporary form is its emphasis on relationships between democratic states.

I believe that it is the stunning simplicity of the democratic peace proposition, and the equally impressive simple evidence that supports it, which account in large measure for the attention it has attracted....

[T]he evidence in favor of virtually every other proposition in international politics about how to avoid international war is, when compared with the evidence for the democratic peace proposition, relatively subtle, complex, and difficult to interpret. In contrast, the best—or at least the psychologically most impressive—evidence in support of the democratic peace proposition is that no dispute or crisis between states has ever escalated into an international war unless at least one of the states involved in that dispute or crisis was *not* democratic.

Of course, even that evidence is not so simple and straightforward as to be beyond dispute. The validity of the assertion that no two democracies have ever fought a war against each other depends heavily on definitions of the key terms "war" and "democracy," and the second term is especially well known for its ambiguous, and some would say essentially contentious, nature.

Even definitions of "war" can create disputes. But advocates of the idea that democracies have not fought "wars" against each other have tended to rely on the definition most widely used in academic research on the causes of war in the last two or three decades. According to that definition, "no hostility... qualified as an interstate war unless it led to a minimum of 1,000 battle fatalities among all the system members involved." The 1,000-battle-death threshold has the advantage of excluding small incidents that might result from the whims of local commanders in faraway places (rather than decisions by governments), and it turns out that there are relatively few historical incidents that cluster around that threshold. Thus it minimizes the number of cases that can never be categorized with confidence. In any case, there are not numerous incidents having just below 1,000 battle deaths that would otherwise qualify as wars between democratic states.

THE PROBLEM OF DEFINITION

A "truly" democratic government, according to the definition that most people who care about such things carry around in their heads, must accurately reflect the wishes, hopes, and desires of the governed. A large number of processes—including, for example, dictatorships of the proletariat—can be imagined to fulfill this fundamental requirement. And conversely, competitive elections are inherently incapable, in the view of some, of "truly" reflecting the will of "the people."

Fortunately, the debate about the democratic peace proposition need not resolve the philosophical debate about which regimes are "truly" democratic. The theory, as well as the research efforts relevant to the evaluation of the pacifying effect of democracy, utilizes a notion of liberal democracy involving the presence of competitive elections, civil liberties, wide or universal suffrage, and the like. Whether or not these criteria successfully identify governments that "truly" reflect the political preferences of "the people" is not ultimately crucial. The vital question is, rather: Do regimes characterized by competitive elections, a free press, civil liberties, wide suffrage, and the like behave differently, especially in their relationships with one another?

Even so, it is far from trivial to determine which governments for which years should be counted as "democratic" when evaluating the assertion that democratic governments never (or only rarely) fight wars against one another. Most of the recent research on the relationship between regime type and international conflict has utilized a data set in which virtually every country in the world is assigned a number from 0 to 10 for every year since 1800, depending on how democratic it is. "Democracy" is assumed to be reflected in such governmental characteristics as competitive elections, selection of governmental executives by election, the openness of executive recruitment, and parity between the legislative and executive branches of government. Each of these dimensions is rather complex. The final democracy score is derived by adding up the scores on these separate dimensions.

... This [point system] is problematic on at least two important counts. First, democracy is clearly a characteristic that states exhibit in greater or lesser degrees.... Second, since states can achieve [scores] on the democracy index in a fairly large number of ways, with a conceptually bewildering array of combinations of scores on the different dimensions, the score itself has no clear meaning....

I have suggested that [instead of using points] states can be categorized as "sufficiently" democratic for the purpose of evaluating the validity of the democratic peace proposition by focusing on whether or not the political leaders in the legislative and executive branches of a government achieve this position in a process based on fair, competitive elections. Competitive elections can be defined as those in which at least two formally independent political parties offer candidates. Whether or not an election is "fair" is a complex question. Let us stipulate for the sake of argument that the electoral process in a given state is "fair" if at least 50 percent of the adult population is allowed to vote, and if it has produced at least one peaceful transfer of executive power from one independent political party to another.

The basic rationale of such a threshold is that it will isolate a set of states that will be sufficiently democratic so as to avoid fighting wars against one another. It will accomplish this because in states whose governments meet these criteria, political leaders will face a distinct possibility that they can be defeated in an election, and lose power because of that defeat. The possibility that such a loss of power can take place in an election-based process is a key factor (or an indicator of the presence of a key factor) in virtually all of the most important theoretical defenses of the democratic peace proposition.

Exposure to the democratic peace idea almost always evokes a search through historical memories for exceptions to the "rule" that democratic states do not fight wars against one another. Perhaps the most common example produced by such searches is the War of 1812 between the

United States and Great Britain. The potential exception to emerge most prominently out of current writing on the subject is probably the Spanish-American War. Other important examples commonly cited include the American Civil War, the Boer War, the First World War (Germany did have an elected parliament with important democratic characteristics), and democratic Finland's participation in the Second World War, which pitted it officially against such democratic states as Great Britain, the United States, and France. Space restrictions preclude any detailed discussion of these examples. Suffice it to say that if it is stipulated that states are categorized as "democratic" (or sufficiently democratic) only if the national legislative and executive leaders assume power in a process based on fair, competitive elections, then none of these wars will qualify as a war between democratic states.

ARE THERE EXCEPTIONS?

The debates about these putative exceptions to the rule that democratic states do not fight wars against one another are important for a couple of reasons. If it turns out, upon examination of the historical record, that there have been even a handful of wars between democratic states, then the democratic peace proposition becomes rather less glamorous, dramatic, and attention-getting. In that case, the proposition would be reduced to an assertion that there is a statistical, probabilistic—not to mention technical and relatively boring—relationship between regime type and conflict.

The debate about possible exceptions to the rule about peaceful relationships among democratic states is also important because it would only take a few exceptions to wipe out entirely the distinction between the incidence of warfare among pairs of states that are not jointly democratic and those that are. Wars have been far too common, it is true, but statistically, they are rather rare. In most years, at least 99 percent of all the pairs of states in the world experience only peace between the members of the pairs. In other words, there are always lots of peaceful pairs. In recent decades, when the world has had about 150 states (there are now almost 200), there have been around 11,175 pairs of states. Each year, around 11,170 (at least) of these pairs consist of states that are at peace with each other. (Admittedly, most pairs, like Bolivia and Burma or Mali and Malaysia, comprise states that have little or nothing to do with each other.)

Even though war is so rare... research discussed earlier... has established that the rate of warfare among democratic states, either in the entire time from 1816 to the present, or just since the Second World War, is "significantly" different from the rate of warfare among those pairs of states consisting of at least one undemocratic state.

Admittedly, there are technical reasons to doubt this conclusion. Perhaps the most important of these involve questions regarding the significance or meaning of repeated observations of the same pairs of states. In all of these analyses, for example, each year that the United States and Great Britain do not fight a war (and are jointly democratic) is counted as a statistical victory of sorts for the democratic peace proposition—as, perhaps, each should be. The statistical techniques relied upon, however, cannot distinguish between several observations of the same states year after year, and observations of different pairs of states. Clearly, observations of different pairs of states provide more information than repeated observations of the same states. Nevertheless, even analyses that combine annual observations into one category, and count peace between the United States and Great Britain after the Second World War as just one observation in favor of the democratic peace proposition (rather than, say, 40 annual observations), show that while the rate of warfare for pairs of states that are not democratic is generally low, that for democratic pairs of states is significantly lower—in fact, zero.

Yet even if we assume that states are accurately categorized as democratic or not in these analyses, and that technical statistical problems do not invalidate the conclusion that democratic states have been visibly different from other kinds of states in their historical propensity to fight wars against one another, the conclusion that it is democracy per se that has an important pacifying impact would still be debatable. Correlation does not prove causation. Other factors might bring about this correlation between democracy and peace, so that democracy would be only coincidentally or spuriously or misleadingly associated with peace, without in any important way being a cause or a condition without which the peace would be eliminated.

[Many scholars] have anticipated this objection. Thus they statistically controlled for the possibility that such factors as wealth, alliance ties, geographic proximity, and economic factors (like trade links) might conjure up a relationship between democracy and peace that is merely statistical, and not substantively significant. Their analyses do not reveal that the relationship between democracy and peace is misleading or spurious, which bolsters confidence in the idea that

democracy does have an important and independent pacifying impact on relations among states.

Among the confounding factors that might produce a statistically systematic yet substantively meaningless relationship between democracy and peace, one of the most important is the presence of alliance ties. Democratic states have existed in significant numbers only since the end of the Second World War and the beginning of the Cold War, which came to a close only recently. The Cold War produced common interests as well as formal alliance ties among significant numbers of those democratic states. Keeping this in mind, a fair-minded analyst might understandably conclude that democratic states did not fight wars with one another during the Cold War because they had common enemies—their communist opponents—who fostered unity and peace among them. Of course, this analyst might conclude, the democratic states allied with one another during the Cold War (which is to say most of the democratic states that have existed over the last century or two) did not fight wars among themselves; they would have been too concerned about the threat from their communist enemies to allocate time and effort to such wars and disputes....

As plausible as this critique is, it ultimately is not entirely persuasive. First, the previously mentioned research ... reveals that statistical controls for the presence of alliance ties between states (an intuitively plausible operational indicator of "common interests") do not eliminate the relationship between democracy and peace. In addition, some of this research focuses on historical epochs extending well beyond the Cold War era.

On a more intuitive level, it would seem that if having a Cold War enemy is sufficient to produce peaceful relationships among states, then having as formidable enemies the bloc of rich, powerful, democratic (and capitalist) states in the world should have produced solid tranquility among the states in the socialist (and autocratic) camp. Instead, however, we see that during the Cold War the Soviet Union attacked Hungary and Czechoslovakia, not to mention Afghanistan, and became involved in serious border clashes with China as well. In addition, Vietnam attacked and partially occupied Cambodia, and then became in turn the target of an attack by mainland China. Meanwhile, relationships among states in the "free world" were not always models of tranquility, either. El Salvador fought a war with Honduras in 1969, Turkey and Greece fought over Cyprus in 1974, and Great Britain fought with Argentina over the Falkland (or Malvinas) Islands in 1982. It is not an accident, from the point of view of a theorist about democratic peace, that each of these wars on the noncommunist side of the Cold War involved at least one undemocratic state.

SOME SPECIFIC CASES

Abstract theoretical arguments and complex statistical analyses of large numbers of cases are of limited appeal to some people that is one reason that the simplicity of the assertion that democratic states have never (or only rarely) fought international wars against one another is such an important element of its general appeal. Also, many analysts are predisposed for reasons of personal taste and training to be more impressed by the close analysis of individual cases than by theoretical generalizations or statistical patterns. Indeed, most analysts would agree that

general theoretical arguments and statistical analyses of many cases will ideally be complemented by evidence based on individual cases. For that reason, analyses of individual cases are accumulating; their authors hope to demonstrate that democracy can have the pacifying effect claimed for it, or, alternatively, that individual examples of peaceful relationships that might appear to have causal origins traceable to democracy have actually been brought about by other factors.

Obviously this is not the place to try to sort out arguments about individual cases (like the Fashoda Crisis of 1898, or the Spanish-American War, or a "cod war" over fishing rights between Great Britain and Iceland). Let me instead make two general points about the relevance and interpretation of such cases. First, there is an assumption by some analysts that if a case is to be counted as containing evidence in favor of the democratic peace proposition, then an analysis of the historical record must show that decision makers involved in a crisis (say, between two democracies) that is ultimately resolved peacefully must have been aware of the pacifying impact of democracy, and must have also commented on that impact specifically and explicitly. In short, some analysts, unless they find historical accounts revealing that decision makers involved in a given crisis thought and said something like, "Well, we are a democracy and they are a democracy, and democracies shouldn't fight wars against one another," would conclude that democracy did not have a pacifying effect on that crisis.

This is an unwarranted assumption. Human beings are not always aware of, nor do they consistently discuss, factors that may have profound effects on their behavior. Voters quizzed in exit polls about their decisions, for example, will explain their votes in terms of their opinions about issues, news events, or a host of other factors of which they are most conscious. Few if any will account for their behavior by referring to the way in which their parents socialized them. Yet that does not mean that their parents had no important impact on their voting behavior.

Furthermore, it should he noted that democracy may have its most powerful pacifying impact by moderating day-to-day relationships between democratic states and preventing them from becoming involved in serious disputes or militarized crises in the first place, rather than by allowing such disputes or crises to be resolved peacefully. Thus the assertion that evidence of a causal connection between democracy and peace must he demonstrated within the confines of individual cases is misguided; it amounts to a demand that "noncrises" resulting in "nonwars" must somehow be identified and analyzed. But evidence of the pacifying effect of democracy that keeps democratic states out of crises as well as wars with one another must necessarily rely on analyses of rates of involvement in crises and wars by democracies compared with those for other kinds of states. Only analyses of relatively large numbers of observations can reveal such differences in rates of crisis or war involvement.

TWO MYTHS

Let us turn to two persistent myths that occur with amazing consistency in much of the writing and discussion of the democratic peace proposition. The first such myth is that, although it may be true that democratic states have not fought wars against one another, they are just as war-prone as autocratic states in general in their relationships with other kinds of states. The other myth is that although it may be true that democratic states do not fight wars against one another, this is an empirical regularity or pattern which up to this point is entirely bereft of any convincing theoretical explanation. It has been reported almost endlessly for years now that "nobody knows," or has convincingly demonstrated, why democracies do not fight wars against one another.

Despite what appears in some ways to be a nearly universal consensus that democratic states, while relating to one another in a universally peaceful manner, are just as war-prone as other states in general, the evidence on this point is surprisingly mixed. There are numerous flaws in the body of evidence which supports the consensus that democratic states are not more peaceful, in general, than autocratic states. It has recently been demonstrated, for example, that one of the oft-cited pillars of evidence in support of that consensus actually is based on data which, if analyzed with statistical techniques more appropriate for dealing with its peculiarities, reveal that democracies are less warlike *in general*, and not just in their relationships with one another. Evidence confirming this point can in fact be found in many of the standard, widely recognized works on the democratic peace proposition, as well as in many more recent attempts to address the question. In short, the evidence regarding the war-proneness and conflict behavior of democratic states in general is too complicated (to choose a term that is perhaps excessively conciliatory) to warrant much confidence in the widely asserted proposition that democratic states are no less conflict-prone than autocratic states.

The widespread opinion that the absence of war between democratic states is merely an empirical observation with no basis in a well-developed or convincing theoretical explanation is insufficiently cognizant, it seems to me, of an extensive body of theoretical work on the question. For example, [one study] ... develops a "cultural" or normative explanation of the democratic peace idea into a set of nine specific, interrelated propositions. These focus on the impact of norms of conflict resolution that will be developed in democracies in bargaining about internal conflicts, and how these are likely to affect interactions between democratic states. [This study] also provides a detailed exposition of a "structural/institutional model" that focuses on the impact of checks and balances present in most democracies, as well as the effects of decentralized power and the need for public support on bargaining among democratic states.

In addition, [another study] has recently provided an excellent summary of theoretical work regarding the democratic peace proposition.... [The study] points out that democracy has pacifying effects on relationships between states with democratic regimes because of their domestic legitimacy and accountability; their institutional checks and balances; the transparency of their political processes and the resulting lower costs of "regime" creation; the relative ease with which democratic states make credible commitments; and, finally, the relative sensitivity within democratic polities to the human and material costs of war.

Some of the most recent research focuses theoretical attention on the importance of trading ties and mutual member-ships in international organizations on relationships among democratic states. A new formal model regarding the connections between internal domestic politics and foreign policies as well as international relationships begins with the fundamental assumption that the highest priority of political leaders is to stay in power. This model highlights the impact of the size of the winning coalition in democracies, on the one hand, and in autocracies, on the other. Democratic leaders must satisfy relatively large winning coalitions. They cannot command a sufficiently large amount of resources to satisfy this coalition with private goods or individual payoffs. General policy successes or failures are relatively important to democratic leaders; autocratic leaders, by contrast, can retain power, even in the wake of significant policy failures, such as a loss in an international war, by paying off the members of their relatively small governing coalitions with tax breaks, receipts from official corruption, or other economic or political rewards. This makes democratic leaders more cautious about launching wars that they might lose. It also turns out that democratic states are particularly formidable opponents in international wars. They are, in short, more likely to win the wars in which they participate. Furthermore, democratic leaders are in fact more likely to lose power in the wake of a lost war than are autocratic leaders.

Democratic states, then, are probably quite likely to avoid wars against one another for reasons ultimately based on the desire of their elected leaders to keep themselves in power. It may also be the case that these kinds of structural constraints are particularly likely to exert their pacifying impact on those relatively rare occasions when serious conflicts and disputes do arise among democratic states, while the cultural or normative constraints exert their more profound impact by making it unlikely that such serious disputes or conflicts arise in the first place.

ABOUT THE FUTURE

One of the more prominent attacks against the democratic peace proposition, by Edward Mansfield and Jack Snyder, asserts that while stable democratic states may not have become engaged in wars against one another, states that are in the process of becoming more democratic are actually quite war-prone. They conclude that the tendency for democratizing states to be war-prone should dampen and perhaps eliminate altogether the idea that fostering democracy is a foreign policy that can be expected to make the world more peaceful.

In a way, this argument reinforces earlier points by... advocates of the democratic peace idea... [who have] acknowledged that democracy must be relatively firmly entrenched in a given state before it can be expected to exert a pacifying effect. But the critique in question goes further, for it implies not only that democracy will fail to have a pacifying effect unless it is firmly in place, but also that transitions to democracy are dangerous, and an important force for war.

... One comprehensive review of this issue reveals that while it is true that democratizing regimes are more war-prone than stable regimes, states involved in transitions to autocracy are *even more* war-prone. This [review] also finds that "democratizing" regimes that do get involved in conflict typically have not moved very far in the direction of democracy. In other words, they are still quite autocratic.

Another detailed analysis of this controversy finds, again, that transitions to autocracy are more consistently associated with conflict than are transitions to democracy. And even more to the point, this second analysis concludes that transitions to democracy are likely to be dangerous only within a particular context, that is, if the states undergoing such transitions are surrounded by or have important relationships with quite autocratic states....

Much of the energy devoted to the debate about the democratic peace proposition springs from the implication that democracy can potentially have a revolutionary impact on world politics, making international war obsolete. Democracy can only do this, obviously, if the world becomes uniformly democratic. And there are some signs that the "third wave" of democratization has begun to recede in recent years.

It is important first to note, however, that even if only "all major powers were to become democracies, then big wars could be consigned to humankind's barbarian past." Furthermore, recent (even post–Cold War) democratic success stories in such diverse places as Nicaragua, Malawi, Botswana, South Africa, Sierra Leone, Mongolia, Haiti, and even Russia indicate that democracy is not a cultural flower destined to bloom only in northwestern Europe and North America. An impressive accumulation of evidence suggests that democracy's spread could greatly reduce the incidence of war and violent interstate conflicts (not to mention maniacal campaigns of genocide launched against domestic populations by dictators). Such evidence should not be interpreted as a justification for heavy-handed or intrusive efforts to encourage the adoption of democratic forms of government. But the evidence is sufficiently robust to justify prudent efforts and policies designed to take advantage of the pacifying impact of democracy.

NO

Mary Caprioli

WHY DEMOCRACY?

As the international system changes, many scholars await the coming of peace as postulated by the democratic peace thesis. Various scholars and American politicians, alike, view the promotion of democracy as a replacement for the Cold War policy of containment and as the new direction for a successful foreign policy to ensure peace. The true nature of the democratic peace, however, must be understood before the spread of democracy can legitimately be hailed as a harbinger of international peace.

BACKGROUND

Our understanding of international relations and quest for peace seems to have taken root in the concept of democracy. Scholars have linked the origins of war to domestic politics and in particular, to regime type. The resultant theory is the democratic peace thesis.

Although no consensus exists, the democratic peace thesis has two major components: First, democratic nation-states do not go to war with other democratic nation-states. Numerous scholars, in fact, have confirmed Immanuel Kant's original prediction that democracies do not go to war with other democracies as presented in Kant's 1795 essay "Perpetual Peace." Second, even though democratic nation-states do not go to war with one another, they are just as likely to become involved in wars with non-democratic nation-states. In general, democracies are no less war-prone than are non-democracies.

But what is democracy? With few exceptions, scholars dichotomize regime type into two categories: democracies and non-democracies. The definition of democracy is based on the Western conception of procedural democracy —one example of which is political participation. On the surface, political participation seems to be a legitimate measure of procedural democracy. That is, until you take a second look.

Political participation is measured in the democratic peace research by such concepts as the non-exclusion of political opposition interest groups, a non-identified broad-based electorate, 10 percent male suffrage, and 30 percent male suffrage. The problem with these measures should be obvious, for all would code countries as democracies that deny voting rights to certain segments of society, most notably women and other minorities. Do these standards actually reflect true characteristics of democracy? By most standards, universal suffrage is a necessary requirement of democracy. Yet, research supporting the democratic peace thesis fails to account for universal suffrage.

Even when democratic rights are universally guaranteed by law, measures of procedural democracy do not adequately reflect domestic reality, for they fail to capture the extent to which democratic rights are enforced. For example, a democracy with extensive laws protecting the civil rights of all citizens may unevenly enforce or implement those same laws, thereby undermining the tenets of democracy. Discrimination/inequalities can be masked under the guise of legal political freedoms that are not universally applied as is the case with political access. In democracies, for example, why are legislators and executives predominantly Caucasian males? Of course, there may be several reasons for this phenomenon: women and other minorities avoid politics by nature, an unlikely and unproven presumption; women and other minorities are denied access by convention; or women and other minorities are prevented from gaining access.

Democratic law and domestic reality may diverge in many ways other than limited political participation, voting rights. Is the potential political strength of minority groups minimized by arbitrary voting districts? Does everyone have equal access to the voting centers, or does getting to the voting center place an undue burden on those who live in outlying areas without transportation? If, for example, a person has no transportation to the voting centers, then legal voting rights lose their meaning—in reality the poor are denied voting rights. None of these realities are captured in legally espoused, procedural measures of democracy. Undeniably, these concepts are hard if not impossible to measure. Measures of democracy, however, must truly reflect the actual political environment of citizens, because much of the explanation for the democratic peace thesis is based on norms/socialization as discussed below.

Certainly, the current measures of procedural democracy are inadequate. The democratic peace thesis is based on a concept of democracy that is not well defined and may not even capture real democratic factors. It is not valid to place countries into one of two categories: democracies and non-democracies. There are many gray areas in which a country is certainly not autocratic but on the other hand, is not truly a democracy. A primary example of which would be Switzerland, which has been consistently considered a democracy even though the majority of women did not gain voting rights until 1971, and true universal suffrage was not granted until 1991.

EXPLANATION

The literature surrounding the democratic peace thesis relies on the idea that domestic political reality is reflected in international behavior. Such a foundation requires, or *should* require an inquiry into the democratic peace thesis that actually measures political reality. A domestic facade of democracy, a situation in which there might be legal rights but no enforcement of those rights, would surely result in the same undemocratic international behavior.

Scholars explain the democratic peace thesis using either a structural or a cultural approach. Structural arguments emphasize two characteristics of domestic politics: 1) the restraining effect of public opinion on political leaders' ability both to mobilize support and maintain political legitimacy; and 2) the constraints of democratic constitutions on decision makers.

If structural restraints on democratic regimes exist, the structural restraints would always be present and would serve as a defining characteristic of democracy. Domestic structural restraints on the use of force is an internal characteristic, independent from the regime type of other nation-states with whom a democracy might become involved in an international dispute. The structural restraints cannot, by definition, be dependent on external factors. For instance, a democracy cannot be structurally constrained only from going to war only with other democracies but must also be structurally constrained from going to war with any type of nation-state. According to the structural explanation, a democratic nation-state should, in most cases, be structurally constrained from going to war.

If a democracy is constrained by structural domestic forces from using violence in international disputes, we can then say that democracies are inherently peaceful. We know, however, that democracies are no less war-prone than are other regime types and may well rely on force that falls short of war in relations with other democracies. Structural restraints, therefore, are not defining characteristics of democracies and cannot be used to determine the war-proneness of a country.

Furthermore, are these structural restraints unique to democracies? Undoubtedly, broad-based public opinion is only of consequence to elected officials. A military junta, for example, has no immediate worry about its level of popular support. A military junta is, however, dependent on the support of the military or some other elite, whose favor serves to keep it in power. Most, if not all, regime types have structural constraints. These constraints may not be written into a formal constitution but are no less real. The important question is the nature of the structural constraints. Do structural constraints in democracies predispose democracies toward peaceful conflict resolution? According to research, the answer is a resounding no, because democracies are no less war-prone than are non-democracies.

We must now turn to an examination of the cultural explanation of the democratic peace thesis. The cultural explanation stresses the overriding influence of democratic norms on foreign policy decisions. According to this explanation, domestic political behavior in democracies emphasizes peaceful conflict resolution, and this norm of peaceful conflict resolution is reflected in foreign policy. According to the cultural theorists, shared beliefs among democracies and an emphasis on law, human rights, and peaceful conflict resolution explain the absence of war among democracies, with the greatest emphasis placed on peaceful conflict resolution.

First, can we accept that the norm of peaceful conflict resolution characterizes domestic behavior between a democratic government and its citizens? The answer would have to be relative to so-called non-democratic societies. Notwithstanding the colonial era, civil war, Kent State,

Waco, Texas, and police brutality, the answer is yes. Generally, citizens in democracies are not arbitrarily picked up on the street and either jailed or killed. And, citizens in democracies, when they do break the law, are theoretically guaranteed due process. Although the system may not be without violence or prejudice, it is rather peaceful compared with other regime types.

We can confidently say that peaceful conflict resolution pervades domestic interaction. But, is it valid to say that the norm of peaceful conflict resolution pervades democratic international interaction? The real area of scrutiny should be an analysis of democracy-democracy and democracy/non-democracy international interaction. In the event of an international dispute, what are the characteristics of the victor in this type of interaction, and what is the method employed in achieving those objectives? This analysis would reveal whether democracy-democracy interaction is truly based on peaceful conflict resolution or on bullying tactics, the threat to use force, or other tools of coercive statecraft. Do the wealthy democracies always win? Who makes the greatest concessions, or takes the biggest loss? Who stands the most to lose in the interaction? Unfortunately, there has been little if any analysis in this area. From a non-Western perspective, a Western democracy would not seem very peaceful to a non-Western democracy that is essentially bullied into compliance.

According to recent research, the cultural explanation is, perhaps, the more important factor in explaining the democratic peace. Many scholars rely on the socializing effect of democracy on citizens to translate into peaceful international relations. Citizens of democracies are socialized to act in a manner consistent with the environment in which they were raised. The hypothesized socialization effect of democracies is that people believe in equal rights and that human rights, law, and peaceful conflict resolution should be held paramount. A country that is considered a democracy as measured by procedural factors may, however, be based on exclusion thus instilling a very different socialization effect than the one hypothesized.

Some inadequacies of procedural measures of democracy such as political participation and voting rights were discussed above. We can use, as an illustration of socialization, the hypothetical standard James Lee Ray offers as an example of a valid measure of democracy in his 1997 article "The Democratic Path to Peace" in *The Journal of Democracy*. In the article, Ray states that if 50 percent of the adult population can vote, then a country passes one standard of democracy: it has a fair electoral process. If 50 percent of the adult population can vote, however, then 50 percent of the adult population *cannot* vote. In such a society, a social hierarchy would exist with certain segments of the population necessarily deemed inferior as evidenced by their being denied voting rights. Only some segments of the population would be considered worthy of equal treatment—the lesson learned: some people are better than others.

We must explore what effect this might have on international relations. Are only some countries worthy of equal treatment, and what standards might be used to pass judgment? Is wealth a criteria; is race? Psychological research has shown that children learn what they live/experience not what they are told is true. The old adage "Do what I say, not what I do" has no lasting impact on a child's future behavior. A child is socialized through example. A country that has legal rules of action based on democratic values but whose citizens experience a different reality does not socialize its citizens according to the theoretical values but according to its actions, the actual experience of citizens. The ramifications of this line of inquiry go far beyond the scope of this essay. Suffice to say, that any socializing effect of democracy can neither be assumed nor used as a definitive explanation supporting the democratic peace thesis when the concept of democracy is inadequately measured.

If peaceful conflict resolution is the predominant norm characterizing foreign and domestic policies of democracies, then we need to question why democracies go to war with non-democracies. What happens to the norm of peaceful conflict resolution when a democracy has an international dispute with a non-democracy? At the most basic, norms are rules of conduct, standards. By definition, a norm cannot be sporadically applied. Yet, the norm of peaceful conflict resolution seems to lay dormant when a democracy interacts with a non-democracy.

Perhaps the cultural explanation for the democratic peace needs a qualifying statement: democracies operate according to the norm of peaceful conflict resolution only when interacting internationally with another democracy. This may be feasible, for in no country do all citizens enjoy equality in their everyday lives—hierarchies exist in all countries. The socializing effect of democracies was discussed above and can be applied to this situation. Perhaps democracies view other democracies as equals and treat them accordingly, but non-democracies are not equal and are not treated equally.

This is a tenuous basis at best. If true, perceived equality may be based on many different arbitrary factors. If all countries were to become democratic, that is if democracy is even an important factor, would another basis be used to judge equality? Of course, this is supposition as is much of the research used to support the democratic peace.

DEFINITIONS

The definitional problems surrounding democracy were previously discussed, yet there are more definitional problems. For example, how are war and peace defined? This is not merely an exercise in semantics. We saw how crucial the definition of democracy is to the democratic peace thesis. The definitions of war and peace are no less important, for they determine the validity of the democratic peace thesis and the avocation of the spread of democracy as a foreign policy to ensure peace.

The democratic peace thesis is confirmed by analyzing the occurrence of war among democracies. All scholars recognize that war is a rare occurrence, thus making it difficult to study. Within the democratic peace literature, war is defined as 1,000 or more total battle deaths as established by Melvin Small and J. David Singer's 1982 book, *Resort to Arms: International and Civil Wars 1816–1980.*

Defining a war based on the number of dead seems ludicrous. Force may be used without even one person dying. Within traditional political science conflict studies, peace is broadly defined as the absence of violence, with violence defined as war. As Johan Galtung argues in his 1990 essay "Violence and Peace,"... peace cannot be measured merely by the absence of war. Other scholars have also questioned the validity of current definitions of war as being too narrow by excluding, for example, covert military actions. If we are to argue that the spread of democracy yields peace, then we need to understand the concept of peace.

Is peace purely the absence of an officially declared war involving fewer than 1,000 battle deaths? How are covert military operations, unwelcome peacekeeping and peacemaking operations, and the covert support of military groups within another country defined? These operations are not considered war, yet their existence does not exactly conjure up images of peaceful coexistence.

Scholars often modify definitions of both war and democracy so that the following events are not considered wars between democracies: the War of 1812, the Spanish-American War, the American Civil War, the Boer War, Germany's role in WWI, and Finland's role in WWII. If we must manipulate the very definitions that constitute the democratic peace thesis, then our theory must surely be weak. The first step in creating a solid theory is to create a hypothesis, define the relevant terms, and then, to test the theory. A scholar cannot first create and test a hypothesis, and then at the end, offer definitions that will strengthen the theory.

OTHER VARIABLES

Some scholars criticize the democratic peace thesis as being valid only during certain time periods, all of which are after World War II. Henry S. Farber and Joanne Gowa, in their 1995... article "Polities and Peace," find that the occurrence of war and serious disputes is only lower between democratic states than between other pairs of states after 1945.

In order for the democratic peace thesis to be confirmed, it should be valid throughout history, not simply during the Cold War era. Otherwise, we can only confidently state that democracies did not fight other democracies during the Cold War. This is a critical issue when the spread of democracy is recommended as a foreign policy to bring world peace. The international system is in transition—will the democratic peace thesis apply in this new era?

There is yet another unanswered question about the democratic peace thesis. Even if it is proven that certain types of nation-states do not go to war with similar types of nation-states, is regime type one of the more important factors in predicting international conflict involvement? Scholars have shown that geographic contiguity and wealth, among others, all play an important role in a nation-state's propensity for war. Indeed, scholars have consistently shown that these two factors have a greater level of statistical significance than does regime type. Geographic contiguity and wealth are more important than democracy. Yet, these same scholars continue to argue that democracy is the key factor.

If wealth is so important, why not advocate a foreign policy that shares the wealth? Ridiculous you say? Why? It is easier for Westerners to believe that their type of government is supreme—it validates their way of life. Spreading the wealth goes against our capitalist values/our interests, and as such, cannot possibly be the basis of our foreign policy. In fact, Farber and Gowa... argue that it is precisely the protection of interests that guides foreign policy, and this explanation warrants examination.

Interests may refer to either leaders' interests or the interest of the population as a whole. In democracies, the interests of the populace and of the leaders are likely to converge to a greater extent than in non-democracies, thus limiting the propensity for war. For example, a crazed dictator out for vengeance can lead his country to war; whereas, the leader of a democracy might want vengeance but is constrained by both a constitution and popular support. Structural constraints may simply help curb interests, which would also be determined by societal norms. As argued by Farber and Gowa, . . . peaceful conflict resolution may serve the interests of both the leaders and the people in democracies. After all, war is financially costly, and the ire of an unhappy electorate against a government that uses force is politically costly.

Speaking of costs, what is one of the most important tenets of capitalism?— profit. Perhaps it is capitalism and not democracy that results in an emphasis on peaceful conflict resolution. Measures of capitalism are quite different from trade relations among states, which leave scholars in two well defined camps: extensive trade relations increases the propensity for war; and extensive trade decreases the propensity for war. Capitalist countries would seek to maximize profit, which is rarely achieved by force or with enemies. A capitalist country would be friendly toward a country with a large, untapped potential market, as well as countries that supply needed raw materials and primary goods. This concept fits well with Farber and Gowa's idea of interests, with profit as the interest. Non-capitalist countries may well be the target of aggressive foreign policy as those countries would not offer economic opportunities to the capitalist countries, because industry is controlled

by the government and restrictive trading policies would likely be in effect. Plus, non-capitalist countries tend to be less wealthy, thus further reducing the opportunity for profit.

On the other hand, gender might be the important variable. Some scholars theorize that the inclusion of women in foreign policy analyses would lead to a diminished emphasis on the use of violence. Thus far, feminist scholars have concentrated on measuring gender differences in public opinion. Most of the research testing for the existence of a gender gap focuses on the difference between the level of female and male support for war and willingness to use force. If women are less likely to support the use of force, the inclusion of women as equal members of society, with equal political, social, and economic access, would impact foreign policy. This implies that the higher a nation-state's level of gender equality, the more peaceful that nation-state is likely to be.

Additionally, some scholars have found a correlation between a state's level of militarism and sexism, measured by women's inequality in relation to that of men. Other scholars have linked masculinity with militarism. The hypothesized link between masculinity and militarism is maintained by men's higher social status in relation to that of women. According to these theories, a nation-state's level of militarism and use of military force in foreign policy would decrease in conjunction with increased gender equality.

According to this literature, gender, not democracy, may be the important variable explaining a country's emphasis on peaceful conflict resolution. In the event that gender is the critical variable, one could easily understand the confusion with democracy. In democracies, women have greater equality than in non-democracies. A precursory analysis would mistake democracy as the important variable, thereby overlooking the role of gender.

CONCLUSION

Many of the critiques of the democratic peace thesis cited above are speculative. There are many areas of inquiry that remain unexplored. Sufficient evidence exists, however, to bring the validity of the democratic peace thesis into serious question. At the most fundamental level, there remain definitional problems with democracy, war, and peace that seriously undermine the validity of the democratic peace thesis. The questions raised throughout this essay warrant further research before democracy can be hailed as a harbinger of peace. Perhaps all we can confidently state is that two nation-states each with a mutual emphasis on peaceful conflict resolution will not go to war. What still needs to be answered is why a nation-state might emphasize peaceful conflict resolution.

Scholars may have identified a common characteristic of nation-states that do not go to war with one another—

democracy. For Westerners, the conclusion is that democracy is the supreme form of government that leads to international peace, excuses crimes/war committed in the name of democracy and redeems, especially American, foreign policy over the years. How wonderful to discover that Kant was correct.

But, why democracy? It seems scholars may have fallen into the trap of identifying a non-causal characteristic of nation-states that do not go to war with one another. An example of which is the following: on hot days more ice-cream is sold and eaten; on hot days the number of rapes increase; therefore, ice-cream causes the number of rapes to increase. In actuality, hot weather is the real cause of the increased number of rapes, which have nothing to do with the ice-cream. With such a simple example, it is easy to identify the problem with the logic of the explanation. Perhaps it is not democracy that prevents nation-states from going to war with each other. Are we missing the logic in identifying democracy as the important characteristic of nation-states that do not go to war with one another and/or are our explanations incorrect? Once again, we must ask: Why democracy?

POSTSCRIPT

Does the Spread of Democracy Promote World Peace?

The debate over the degree to which a democratic country is also a peaceful country is more than just a matter of scholarly interest. It also has policy implications. There is an assumption held by many leaders and others that there is a connection between a government that is democratic and one that is stable and friendly. President Bill Clinton has commented, "We ought to be promoting the democratic impulses around the world. Democracies are our partners. They don't go to war with each other. They're reliable friends in the future." Applying that belief, Clinton advocated giving financial and other support to the government of Russian president Boris Yeltsin on the grounds that "our own security... lie[s] with Russian reformers like Boris Yeltsin." Clinton also justified the U.S. intervention in Haiti on the grounds that "history has taught us that preserving democracy in our own hemisphere strengthens American security."

The debate over whether or not democracy can be equated with international peace is far from over, and there are numerous articles and books that address the subject. A general review can be found in Michael E. Brown, Sean Lynn-Jones, and Steven E. Miller, eds., *Debating the Democratic Peace* (MIT Press, 1996). For a longer exposition of Ray's views, see his *Democracy and International Conflict* (University of South Carolina Press, 1995). The issue is also well debated by Henry S. Farber and Joanne Gowa, who argue that democracy and peacefulness are not inherently connected, in "Polities and Peace," *International Security* (Fall 1995).

One answer to the ongoing dispute is that democracy may be just one of several factors that promote peace. Among other things, it is the case that no magic line exists to separate democracies from autocracies. Instead, there is a range of governance between absolute despotism and unfettered democracy. In even relatively democratic countries, like the United States, some groups are denied an equal voice in determining who governs (in practice, more than by law). Women, African Americans, Latinos, and others are all underrepresented. Insofar as the evidence shows that women are less likely to favor war than are men, it may be that a society in which women have a greater voice is one that is less likely to be bellicose. Arie M. Kacowicz, in "Explaining Zones of Peace: Democracies as Satisfied Powers," *Journal of Peace Research* (1995), finds that the likelihood of war is most predictable when levels of democracy or autocracy are combined with other factors, such as the degree of trade interdependence or the degree to which countries are satisfied with the territorial status quo.

ISSUE 14

Should China Be Condemned as a Violator of Human Rights?

YES: Bureau of Democracy, Human Rights, and Labor, from *China Country Report on Human Rights Practices for 1996,* U.S. Department of State (January 30, 1997)

NO: Information Office of the State Council of the People's Republic of China, from "Another U.S. Attempt to Use Human Rights to Create Confrontation," *Beijing Review* (April 7–13, 1997)

ISSUE SUMMARY

YES: A report by the U.S. Department of State's Bureau of Democracy, Human Rights, and Labor contends that China violates the human rights of its people in a variety of ways.

NO: The State Council of the People's Republic of China maintains that the report condemning China is culturally biased, inaccurate, and violates China's sovereignty.

Ask your friends if they are in favor of human rights, a concept that includes both civil rights (such as freedom from torture or discrimination) and civil liberties (such as freedom of speech, assembly, and press). Few, if any, of the people you asked would come out solidly against human rights. If you then asked whether or not those individuals and countries that violate human rights should be condemned, the majority in favor of backing human rights might narrow. You might well even lose the majority if you asked a third question: Should diplomatic or economic sanctions be applied to the violator? A fourth question that probed the willingness to use military force to intervene and end the human rights violations would almost certainly win the support of only a minority of people.

On a scale ranging from condemnation to military intervention, the reasons that people might give to support human rights would fall into two groups. *Cultural relativism* is one group. Accusations of human rights violations may be, to a degree, matters of perception and culture. It may be that practices that we sometimes condemn in others are not abuses. Rather, they may be practices that we disapprove of because of our cultural biases.

Pragmatism is the second group. Some people argue that condemning human rights abuses is unlikely to help the oppressed and only serves to antagonize the government that is being accused. What is worse pragmatically is that the accused government may retaliate by denying access to their markets, for example. Certainly, there would be retribution and other costs if a government applies sanctions or intervenes militarily. A pragmatic concern with sovereignty would fall into this group.

These two groups of concerns very much affect the issue of whether or not we should condemn alleged violations of human rights by China and whether or not the United States should take tangible actions against China. There can be little doubt that China's human rights practices are very different from those found in the United States and other countries. This has long been true, but there has been a focus on human rights since protesters in Tiananmen Square and elsewhere in China were attacked and killed by government troops in 1989. The Chinese government contended that the students' rights did not extend to trying to undermine the socialist movement, which had done much to benefit Chinese society.

Many people in China and elsewhere see American-style democracy as divisive, even dangerous. Chinese officials argue that the country faces so many huge problems that it cannot afford the luxury of what they see as the interminable debate and political gridlock of Western democracies. Instead, as communists, they believe in what they call *democratic centralism*. This means that since the government is supported by the mass, then it is democratic and has the authority to make decisions centrally, which the mass is then obligated to follow. According to Wu Jianmin, a spokesman for the government of China, Western criticisms of China's style of democracy "arise largely from the fact that East and West have different conceptions of human rights."

Then there is the matter of pragmatics. There have been various attempts in the United States since 1989 to impose sanctions on China, mostly by revoking its status as a normal trading partner. This status, extended to almost all countries, is called most-favored-nation (MFN) status. Efforts to revoke China's MFN status have been unsuccessful because former president George Bush and President Bill Clinton have regularly resisted imposing sanctions. Both presidents have reasoned that China is a strategically important country, has a veto in the UN Security Council, is an important market for U.S. exports and capital investment, and otherwise is a critical country that the United States does not wish to antagonize unnecessarily.

The sense of sovereignty also comes into play in that China strongly rejects the right of the United States or anyone else to comment on human rights in China. The Chinese view of the calls for human rights reform was depicted by President Jiang in a speech before the UN General Assembly in 1995 as part of a neoimperial plan by "certain big powers for encroaching on the sovereignty of others under the pretext of promoting human rights and democracy."

Congress has mandated that the U.S. State Department review and report on the human rights records of all countries. In the first of the following selections, the report issued in 1997 condemns China's human rights record. The State Council of the People's Republic of China, the counterpart of the U.S. president's cabinet, replies that the accusations are not justified.

YES

**Bureau of Democracy,
Human Rights, and Labor**

CHINA COUNTRY REPORT ON HUMAN RIGHTS PRACTICES FOR 1996

CHINA

The People's Republic of China (PRC) is an authoritarian state in which the Chinese Communist Party (CCP) is the paramount source of power. At the national and regional levels, party members hold almost all top civilian, police, and military positions. Ultimate authority rests with the members of the Politburo, who often consult with still-influential past members of that body on major decisions. These leaders stress the need to maintain stability and social order and are committed to perpetuating rule of the CCP and its hierarchy. Citizens lack the freedom to peacefully express opposition to the party-led political system and the right to change their national leaders or form of government. Socialism continues to provide the theoretical underpinning of Chinese politics, but Marxist ideology has given way to economic pragmatism in recent years. Economic decentralization has increased the authority of regional officials. The party's authority rests primarily on the success of economic reform, its ability to maintain stability, appeals to patriotism, and control of the security apparatus.

The security apparatus comprises the Ministries of State Security and Public Security, the People's Armed Police, the People's Liberation Army and the state judicial, procuratorial, and penal systems. Security policy and personnel were responsible for numerous human rights abuses.

China has a mixed economy that is expanding rapidly. Economic reforms are raising living standards for many, strengthening entrepreneurs, diminishing central control over the economy, and creating new economic opportunities. Although there are problems in the state sector, individual economic opportunities continue to expand rapidly with increased freedom of employment and mobility. As the Government continues to adopt market-based policies, both state-owned and nonstate enterprises are benefiting from increased freedom to compete in domestic and overseas markets. As economic opportunities grow, however, income disparities between coastal and inland

From U.S. Department of State, Bureau of Democracy, Human Rights, and Labor, *China Country Report on Human Rights Practices for 1996*, January 30, 1997 (Government Printing Office, 1997).

areas continue to widen. The number of citizens living in absolute poverty continues to decline, although estimates of those in poverty range from official figures of 65 million to estimates as high as 350 million out of a total population of 1.2 billion. Tens of millions of peasants have left their homes in search of better jobs and living conditions. According to estimates, as many as 100 million people make up this "floating population," with many major cities counting 1 million or more such people. Urban areas are also coping with workers idled by industrial reforms. An estimated 10 million state workers have been laid off, or not paid. Millions more have been idled on partial wages.

The Government [has] continued to commit widespread and well-documented human rights abuses, in violation of internationally accepted norms, stemming from the authorities' intolerance of dissent, fear of unrest, and the absence or inadequacy of laws protecting basic freedoms. The Constitution and laws provide for fundamental human rights, but they are often ignored in practice. Abuses included torture and mistreatment of prisoners, forced confessions, and arbitrary and lengthy incommunicado detention. Prison conditions remained harsh. The Government continued severe restrictions on freedom of speech, the press, assembly, association, religion, privacy, and worker rights. Some restrictions remained on freedom of movement. In many cases, the judicial system denies criminal defendants basic legal safeguards and due process because authorities attach higher priority to maintaining public order and suppressing political opposition than to enforcing legal norms.

Although the Government denies that it holds political prisoners, the number of persons detained or serving sentences for "counterrevolutionary crimes" or "crimes against the state," or for peaceful political or religious activities are believed to number in the thousands. Persons detained during 1996 included activists arrested for issuing petitions or open letters calling for reforms and greater democracy.

Overall in 1996, the authorities stepped up efforts to cut off expressions of protest or criticism. All public dissent against the party and government was effectively silenced by intimidation, exile, the imposition of prison terms, administrative detention, or house arrest. No dissidents were known to be active at year's end. Even those released from prison were kept under tight surveillance and often prevented from taking employment or otherwise resuming a normal life. Nonapproved religious groups, including Protestant and Catholic groups, also experienced intensified repression as the Government enforced 1994 regulations that require all such groups to be registered with government religious affairs bureaus and come under the supervision of official "patriotic" religious organizations. Discrimination against women, minorities, and the disabled, violence against women, and the abuse of children remain problems. Serious human rights abuses persist in minority areas, including Tibet, Xinjiang, and Inner Mongolia. Controls on religion and on other fundamental freedoms in these areas have also intensified.

During 1996 the National Peoples' Congress (NPC) passed new laws designed to reform criminal procedures and the legal profession. The Government's village elections program conducted closely supervised multicandidate elections in villages inhabited by hundreds of millions of rural citizens. Although these offer some opportunity for local clans and other groups to work out differences democratically, they are tightly controlled and do not threaten the leading role of the Communist Party....

In many respects, Chinese society continued to open further. Greater disposable income, looser ideological controls, and freer access to outside sources of information led to greater room for individual choice, more diversity in cultural life, and increased media reporting. Although the sale and use of satellite dishes are tightly regulated, satellite television broadcasts are widely available, particularly in coastal areas. Increasing numbers of citizens have access to the Internet although the Government closed down some World Wide Web sites, including Chinese-language sites in Hong Kong and Taiwan, those of Western news organizations, and attempted to control the political and social content of the material available through the Internet. Controls on reporting economic information imposed in 1995 continued, and the Government placed new restrictions on the news media.

RESPECT FOR HUMAN RIGHTS

Section 1. Respect for the Integrity of the Person

a. Extrajudicial Killings

There were reports of extrajudicial killings, including some carried in the Chinese press. There is, however, no reliable information about the number of such killings or the adequacy of the government response. There have been numerous executions carried out immediately after mass summary trials. Often these "trials" occur under circumstances where the lack of basic due process protections borders on extrajudicial killing....

b. Disappearance

In January [1997] the United Nations Working Group on Enforced or Involuntary Disappearances reported on three new cases of disappearances that allegedly occurred in 1995. Most of the 56 cases which the Working Group has under review occurred between 1988–90. The majority were Tibetans, the others were political activists. The Government still has not provided a comprehensive, credible public accounting of all those missing or detained in connection with the suppression of the 1989 Tiananmen demonstrations. Long incommunicado detentions continued (see Section 1.d.).

c. Torture and Other Cruel, Inhuman, or Degrading Treatment or Punishment

The law prohibits torture, however, both official Chinese sources and international human rights groups continued to report many cases in which police and other elements of the security apparatus employed torture and degrading treatment in dealing with detained and imprisoned persons. Former detainees have credibly reported that officials used cattle prods, electrodes, thumb cuffs, prolonged periods of solitary confinement and incommunicado detention, beating, shackles, and other forms of abuse against detained men and women. Persons detained pending trial were particularly at risk as a result of government failure to correct obvious systemic weaknesses in design and operation of pretrial detention. These weaknesses include a reliance on confessions as a basis for convictions and the lack of access to prisoners by legal counsel and family members until after authorities file formal charges, a step that often takes months....

In April a Chinese delegate to the United Nations Commission on Human Rights stated that "the Chinese judiciary deals with every complaint of torture promptly after it is filed, and those found guilty are punished according to law." The Government also claimed in its report to the United Nations Committee against Torture that "the State, taking an extremely serious view of any incident of torture, has adopted commensurate measures through administrative and judicial means to punish by law anyone guilty of such an act." However, because prisoners remain inaccessible to international humanitarian organizations, such as the International Committee of the Red Cross (ICRC), these claims are impossible to verify independently....

China does not permit independent monitoring of prisons or reeducation-through-labor camps. The Procuratorate is charged with law enforcement in the corrections system. The official press reported in July that 50,000 reprimands were issued to prison personnel during the first 5 months of 1996 for inappropriate conduct. Negotiations with the ICRC regarding access to prisoners have not been resumed since the Government suspended discussions in March 1995.

d. Arbitrary Arrest, Detention, or Exile
Under the Criminal Procedure Law, officials may hold detainees for up to 10 days before the Procuratorate must approve a formal arrest warrant. In theory, the Administrative Procedure Law permits a detainee to challenge the legality of his detention. In practice, however, lack of access to legal counsel inhibits the effective use of this law to obtain prompt judicial decisions on the issue. In known cases involving political dissidents, authorities have interpreted the law in the Government's favor and strictly against detainees.

Activist Wang Dan was held in incommunicado detention for 17 months in connection with the issuance of a prodemocracy petition before being charged, tried, and sentenced in October to 11 years in prison. He is appealing his sentence to the Supreme Court, having lost a lower level appeal.

There is no system of bail, but at the discretion of public security officials some detainees can be released pending further investigation. The authorities must notify the detainee's family or work unit of his detention within 24 hours; in practice, however, authorities seldom give timely notification. Under a sweeping exception to the law, officials need not provide notification if it would "hinder the investigation" of a case. The Government held dissident Liu Nianchun incommunicado for more than a year without charges before his wife was notified of his whereabouts and permitted to visit him.... His suit contesting his detention was initially dismissed in mid-1996 for reasons that included the fact that his legal papers were written with a ballpoint pen, a minor detail usually overlooked in Chinese courts....

Authorities detained political and labor activists without cause at "sensitive" times during the year and also used parole regulations to control their activities. Guangzhou authorities detained dissident Wang Xizhe for 15 days in June, ostensibly because he violated his parole by attending a family dinner in an area outside of Guangzhou City. (Wang fled the country in October.) Wang's arrest coincided with the anniversary of the 1989 Tiananmen demonstrations....

e. Denial of Fair Public Trial

According to the Constitution, the court system is equal in authority to the State Council and the Central Military Commission, the two most important government institutions. All three organs are nominally under the supervision of the NPC. Officials state that China's judiciary is independent but acknowledge that it is subject to the Communist Party's policy guidance. All of these state organs are given policy direction by the high-level Party Political and Legal Commission. Party and government leaders use a variety of means to direct the courts on verdicts and sentences. Corruption and conflicts of interest also affect judicial decision making....

Officials often ignore the due process provisions of the law and of the Constitution. Both before and after trial, authorities subject prisoners to severe psychological pressure to confess. Defendants who fail to "show the right attitude" by confessing their crimes are typically sentenced more harshly. Criminal trials remain essentially sentencing hearings, despite official denials. Confessions without corroborating evidence are insufficient for a conviction under law, but coerced confessions are frequently introduced into evidence. International observers were especially concerned that the Government's "strike hard" anticrime campaign, which extended throughout most of the year, further encouraged law enforcement personnel to arrest, convict, and punish suspects without according full due process rights.

Under the 1979 Criminal Procedure Law, ... the authorities give accused persons virtually no opportunity to prepare an adequate defense while their cases are being investigated, the phase during which the question of guilt or innocence is essentially decided. The law provides that defense lawyers may be retained no earlier than 7 days before the trial. However, in some cases even this brief period is shortened under regulations issued in 1983 to accelerate the adjudication of certain serious criminal cases. Under the law, there is no requirement that the court appoint a defense attorney for the defendant unless the defendant is hearing impaired or a minor, although the court may appoint defense counsel if it feels an attorney is necessary. When attorneys do appear, they have little time to prepare a defense and rarely contest guilt; their function is generally confined to requesting clemency. The conviction rate is over 90 percent. The court's permission is required before the accused or his representative can interrogate witnesses, produce new witnesses, or review evidence.

The Criminal Procedure Law requires that all trials be held in public, except those involving state secrets, juveniles, or "personal secrets." Under this provision, details of cases involving "counterrevolutionary" charges have frequently been kept secret, even from defendants' relatives.... There is an appeals process, but appeals generally do not reverse arbitrary or erroneous verdicts. Under the Criminal Procedure Law, persons "exempted from prosecution" by procurators may still be deemed to have a criminal record, despite the lack of a judicial determination of guilt. Such provisions can be applied in counterrevolutionary crimes as well as for ordinary criminal offenses....

The impact of the lack of due process is particularly egregious in death penalty cases. China's 1979 Criminal Code contained 26 crimes punishable by death; 1995 legislation raised this number to 65, including financial crimes such as counterfeiting currency, passing fake negotiable notes and letters of credit, and illegal "pooling" of funds. In May the Supreme Court called for wider use of capital punishment, including in the case of crimes that result in death. It stated that persons whose crimes result in death should be punished by death regardless of extenuating circumstances or lack of a prior criminal record. National figures on the number of executions are not available, but in 1996 it has been estimated that several thousand executions were carried out. The Chinese press confirms that large numbers of speedy executions were carried out in 1996 as part of the "Strike-Hard" national anticrime campaign. A high court nominally reviews all death sentences, but the time between arrest and execution is often a matter of days, and reviews have consistently resulted in a confirmation of sentence. In June the Jilin Provincial Court held a news conference to report that, during a crackdown on crime in the preceding month, provincial authorities held 46 public rallies to "sternly and rapidly" sentence serious criminals. Defendants sentenced included three persons who were caught, tried, and executed within 10 days after they allegedly looted a car, and within 7 days of their arrest....

Only courts can sentence prisoners to facilities managed by the criminal justice system. Justice Ministry statistics issued in January 1995 showed that China has imprisoned and released approximately 10 million prisoners since 1949; there were 1,285,000 prisoners in prisons or reform-through-labor camps at the end of 1994. Government authorities can, however, assign persons accused of "minor" public order offenses to reeducation-through-labor camps in an extrajudicial process. Terms of detention run from a normal minimum of 1 year to a maximum of 3 years. The labor reeducation committee, which determines the term of detention, may extend an inmate's sentence for an additional year. According to prison officials, 200,000 detainees were in reeducation-through-labor facilities at the end of 1995, up from 153,000 at the end of 1993. Other estimates of the number of such inmates are considerably higher.

Since 1990 defendants have been able to challenge reeducation-through-labor sentences under the Administrative Procedure Law. While some persons have gained a reduction in or suspension of their sentences after reconsideration or appeal, in practice these procedures are not widely used, and such problems as short appeal times and lack of access to lawyers weaken their effectiveness in preventing or reversing arbitrary decisions....

Government officials deny that China holds any political prisoners, asserting that authorities detain persons not for the political or religious views they hold, but because they have taken some action that violates the Criminal Law. However, the authorities continue to confine citizens for political reasons. Perhaps thousands of political prisoners remain imprisoned or detained....

f. Arbitrary Interference With Privacy, Family, Home, or Correspondence

Economic liberalization is creating diverse employment opportunities and introducing market forces into the economy, thus loosening governmental monitoring and regulation of personal and family life, particularly in rural areas. In urban areas, however, most people still depend on their government-linked work unit for housing, permission to have a child, approval to apply for a passport, and other aspects of ordinary life. The work unit, along with the neighborhood committee, are charged with monitoring activities and attitudes, although these institutions have become less important as means of social or political control in urban areas.

Although the law requires search warrants before security forces can search premises, this provision is often ignored in practice. In addition, the Public Security Bureau and the Procuratorate issue warrants on their own authority....

Authorities frequently monitor telephone conversations, fax transmissions, electronic mail, and Internet communications of foreign visitors, businessmen, diplomats, residents, and journalists as well as Chinese dissidents, activists, and others. Authorities also open and censor domestic and international mail.... Government security organs monitor and sometimes restrict contact between foreigners and citizens, particularly dissidents. Rules implementing the State Security Law define as a violation of the law "activities of individuals outside the country (including non-Chinese citizens resident in China) who disregard dissuasion and meet with personnel in the country who have endangered state security or who are seriously suspected of endangering state security."

The Government continued to implement comprehensive and highly intrusive one-child family planning policies first adopted in the late 1970's. The State Family Planning Commission formulates and implements government policies with assistance from the Family Planning Association, which has 83 million members in 1.02 million branches. China's population policy most heavily affects ethnic Han Chinese in urban areas. Urban couples seldom obtain permission to have a second child. Exceptions are allowed for many of the 70 percent of Han who live in rural areas, and ethnic minorities are subject to less stringent population controls. In special circumstances, minorities in some rural areas are permitted to have as many as four children.

Population control policy relies on education, propaganda, and economic incentives, as well as on more coercive measures, including psychological pressure and economic penalties. Rewards for couples who adhere to the policy include monthly stipends and preferential medical and educational benefits. Disciplinary measures against those who violate the policy include fines, withholding of social services, demotion, and other administrative punishments that sometimes result in loss of employment. Penalties for excess births can be levied against local officials and the mothers' work units providing multiple sources of pressure. Fines for giving birth without authorization vary, but they can be a formidable disincentive. In Fujian, for example, the standard fine has been calculated to be twice a family's gross annual income or twice the calculated average income of rural families with no quantifiable cash income; additional, unauthorized births incur fines assessed in increments of 50 percent per child.... Unpaid fines have sometimes resulted in confiscation or destruction of personal property. There were also reports that teams of village officials expelled women and their families from their homes and then destroyed the houses....

Section 2. Respect for Civil Liberties, Including:

a. Freedom of Speech and Press

Although the Constitution states that freedom of speech and freedom of the press are fundamental rights enjoyed by all citizens, the Government interprets the Communist Party's "leading role" as circumscribing these rights. It does not permit citizens to publish or broadcast criticism of senior leaders or opinions that contradict basic Communist Party doctrine providing for a Socialist state under the party's leadership. During the year the Government and party further intensified control over expression of unauthorized political views. The formal charges brought against dissident and prodemocracy advocate Wang Dan were based on public criticisms of the Government. These criticisms together with his publication of articles and his activities in support of democracy advocates resulted in his November conviction and sentence to 11 years in prison, a much harsher sentence than he received for his prodemocracy activities in 1989....

The party and the Government continue to control print and broadcast media and compel them to propagate the current ideological line. All media employees are under explicit, public orders to follow CCP directives, and to "guide public opinion" as directed by political authorities. This greatly restricts the freedom of newspapers and broadcast journalists to report the news. Both formal and informal press guidelines continued to require reporters to avoid coverage of sensitive subjects and to protect "state secrets." Under the State Security Law, state secrets are broadly defined, and interpretation of the law is left to the Ministries of State Security and Public Security....

A Western press report stated that 38 newspapers have been shut down since 1994 either due to poor management or "political problems." According to reports other papers and magazines have been shut down for publishing sensitive articles on the plight of state farms, the cultural revolution, and debates on Deng Xiaoping's reform program.

Articles published by foreign journalists are monitored. The Government has withheld visas from journalists who have written stories critical of China. Foreign journalists working in China have also been subjected to surveillance and, on occasion, harassment....

The Government has continued to impose heavy ideological controls on political discourse at colleges, universities, and research institutes. In September, for example, authorities closed computer bulletin boards at universities in Beijing when students began using the Internet to urge government action in defense of Chinese sovereignty claims over the Diaoyu/Senkaku islands. As a result of official controls, many intellectuals and scholars, fearing that books or papers on political topics would be deemed too sensitive to be published, feel compelled to exercise self-censorship. In areas such as economic policy or legal reform, there was far greater official tolerance for comment and debate.

b. Freedom of Peaceful Assembly and Association

The Government severely restricts these rights.... Protests against the political system or its leaders are prohibited.

Authorities deny permits and quickly move to suppress demonstrations involving expression of dissident political views. On the June 4 anniversary of the 1989 Tiananmen crackdown, police arrested a woman who attempted to commemorate the event by leaving flowers at the Memorial to People's Heroes in Tiananmen Square....

The Communist Party organizes and controls most professional and social associations. Regulations require all organizations to be officially registered and approved. Authorities can detain violators for up to 15 days and impose fines up to $23 (RMB200). Ostensibly aimed at secret societies and criminal gangs, the regulations also deter the formation of unauthorized political, religious, or labor organizations. Political activists, including Liu Nianchun and Yang Zhou, were denied permission to register their labor and human rights associations....

c. Freedom of Religion

The Government seeks to restrict all religious practice to closely controlled and government-sanctioned religious organizations and registered places of worship. At the annual national religious affairs conference in January religious policy was "readjusted" to emphasize harder line aspects. During the year many religious groups were subjected to increased restrictions although the degree of restriction varied significantly in different regions of China....

The campaign to shut down unauthorized groups is in the hands of the police and religious affairs officials and is being conducted concurrently with other police actions against criminals and underground separatists, prodemocracy, and labor groups. The national goal for 1996 was to register or close down all unregistered religious groups.

Official Chinese media carried warnings of the "threat of religious infiltration." In August the Communist Party newspaper *People's Daily* said that "hostile international forces resort to ethnic and religious issues to 'Westernize' and 'split' Socialist countries and step up religious infiltration." The publication also quoted a senior Communist official as saying that religion had "interfered in government administration, judicial matters, education, and marriages." In November the People's Liberation Army *Daily's* report on military "spiritual civilization" stated that "it is necessary to conduct education in atheism so that they (the military) believe in science and oppose superstition. Participation in religious activities is forbidden."

d. Freedom of Movement Within the Country, Foreign Travel, Emigration, and Repatriation

The effectiveness of the Government's identification card system, used to control and restrict the location of individual residences within China, continued to erode. Estimates of the "floating population" of economic migrants leaving their home areas to seek work elsewhere in China range from tens of millions to as many as 100 million. This itinerant population enjoys increased economic opportunities but lacks official residence status which provides full access to social services and education. Unless they obtain resident status, they must pay a premium for these services....

Section 3. Respect for Political Rights: The Right of Citizens to Change Their Government

Citizens lack the means to change their government legally and cannot freely choose or change the laws and officials that govern them. Citizens vote directly only for party-reviewed candidates for delegate positions in county-level people's congresses and for village-level officials. People's congress delegates at the provincial level, however, are selected by county-level people's congresses, and in turn provincial-level people's congresses select delegates to the National People's Congress (NPC)....

The election and agenda of people's congresses at all levels remain under the firm control of the Communist Party, the paramount source of political authority in China. A number of small "democratic" parties that date from before the Communist takeover in 1949 play only a minor consultative role, and they pledge their allegiance to the Communist Party. The party retains a tight rein on political decisionmaking. Efforts to form new political parties are suppressed....

Direct elections for basic level or village government are legally sanctioned for all of China's approximately 1 million villages. Foreign observers estimate that more than 80 percent of these villages have already participated in elections for local leaders.... Many local observers do not, however, take village elections seriously. Political controls are tight, and village elections do not threaten to undermine implementation of unpopular central policies or endanger the leading role of the Communist Party.

The official requirement that associations register and be approved discourages independent interest groups from forming and affecting the system. Social organizations registered in recent years include groups promoting environmental protection, consumer rights, charitable work, and the rights of the disabled, but the Government monitors their ac-

tivities to ensure that they remain apolitical. Political activities are quickly suppressed. Liu Xiaobo, Wang Xizhe, and other activists submitted proreform petitions to government authorities. Liu was arrested in October and sentenced in a matter of hours to 3 years at a reeducation-through-labor camp. Shortly thereafter, Wang escaped China and is now living abroad.

Section 4. Governmental Attitude Regarding International and Nongovernmental Investigation of Alleged Violations of Human Rights

There are no independent Chinese organizations that publicly monitor or comment on human rights conditions in China.... The detention or incarceration of all active, prominent human rights activists confirms the Government's intolerance of such groups. For example, Wang Dan—the Tiananmen-era activist who announced in 1994 his intention to investigate China's human rights situation—was sentenced to 11 years' imprisonment in October after having been held in incommunicado detention for 17 months....

The Government remains reluctant to accept criticism of China's human rights situation by other nations or international organizations and often criticized reports by international human rights monitoring groups. To deflect attempts to discuss its human rights record, the Government strongly opposed and vigorously lobbied against a resolution on China's human rights record at the 1996 session of the U.N. Commission on Human Rights (UNHRC). The Government also introduced a procedural motion, as it has every year the resolution is introduced, to take no action on the resolution. The motion was passed by the Commission, and the resolution was not debated by the Commission.

TIBET

Because the Chinese Government strictly controls access to and information about Tibet, the scope of human rights abuses cannot be precisely determined. However, according to credible reports, during 1996 Chinese government authorities continued to commit widespread human rights abuses in Tibet, including instances of death in detention, torture, arbitrary arrest, detention without public trial, long detention of Tibetan nationalists for peacefully expressing their religious and political views, and intensified controls on religion and on freedom of speech and the press, particularly for ethnic Tibetans....

Those [traditional religious practices] seen as a vehicle for political dissent... are not tolerated and are promptly and forcibly suppressed. Individuals accused of political activism faced increased persecution during the year, as the Government moved to limit the power of religious persons and secular leaders who openly sympathized with the Dalai Lama. In February the Government issued orders to close all politically active monasteries, and during the year authorities increased repression, imprisonment, and abuse or torture of monks and nuns accused of political activism. According to authoritative Chinese press reports, in May Beijing launched a campaign to "limit criminal activity in the guise of religious practice." The crackdown appears to have three goals: To stop acts of defiance, to break the political power wielded by lamas, and to remove officials loyal to the Dalai Lama....

Discrimination against Tibetans is widespread, especially in the area of employment. In addition, ethnic Han and Hui immigrants from other parts of China, encouraged by government policies and new opportunities are competing with—and in some cases displacing—Tibetan enterprises and labor. Overall, government development policies have helped raise the economic living standards of many ethnic Tibetans. However, rapid and ecologically inappropriate growth has also disrupted traditional living patterns and thereby threatened traditional Tibetan culture.

The Dalai Lama continued to express concern that development projects and other central government policies encourage a massive influx of Han Chinese into Tibet, which has the effect of overwhelming Tibet's traditional culture and diluting Tibetan demographic dominance....

Economic development, fueled by central government subsidies, is modernizing parts of Tibetan society and changing traditional Tibetan ways of life. While the Government has made efforts in recent years to restore some of the physical structures and other aspects of Tibetan Buddhism and Tibetan culture damaged or destroyed during the Cultural Revolution, repressive social and political controls continue to limit the fundamental freedoms of ethnic Tibetans.

NO

Information Office of the State Council of the People's Republic of China

ANOTHER U.S. ATTEMPT TO USE HUMAN RIGHTS TO CREATE CONFRONTATION

On January 30, 1997, the US State Department released its *Country Reports on Human Rights Practices for 1996* (hereinafter referred to as Reports), in which it commented improperly on the human rights situation in 194 countries and regions, setting itself up as a "world human rights judge." The "China" part of the Reports continues to spread slanderous rumors against China in disregard of the Chinese people's strong opposition in past years, thus laying bare once again the attempt of the Reports to create confrontation and interfere in China's internal affairs by using the pretext of human rights.

PLAYING THE SAME OLD TRICK BY REPEATING FABRICATIONS

One of the major characteristics of the Reports is to repeat the old trick and continue to vilify China by making fabrications and distorting the facts.

The Reports attempts to mislead the public by using materials that were proven worthless long ago, and try to turn lies into truth by repetition.

For instance, the Reports, ignoring the fact that in 1996 China revised the Law Governing Criminal Procedures which was promulgated 1979, uses many words to attack the 1979 law, saying, "The law provides that defense lawyers may be retained no earlier than seven days before the trial;" "Under the law, there is no requirement that the court appoint a defense attorney for the defendant."

In fact, Article 110 of the revised law states that "as soon as a people's court decides to begin trial proceedings, it should send a copy of the indictment from the people's procuratorate to the accused no later than seven days before the trial, and should serve notice that the accused is able to seek counsel, or should appoint counsel for the accused if necessary."

Here, the "no later than seven days before the trial" is misquoted as "no earlier than seven days before the trial." The court is able to "appoint counsel for the accused" is misquoted as "there is no requirement that the court appoint a defense attorney for the defendant."

Although China has repeatedly pointed out that the materials, which charge China with "violating human rights," confound black and white and are contrary to facts, the Reports has used the materials year after year. This calls for more serious thought.

The Reports also cites some seemingly "new" materials and certain individual cases, but most are fabricated and contrary to the facts. For example, the Reports says that "Chinese authorities in Fujian refused in August to provide medical care for 76-year-old Catholic Bishop Zeng Jingmu, who had contracted pneumonia," and that "Zeng has been detained for holding illegal church services in his home."

The fact is that Zeng Jingmu, who is from Chongren County, Jiangxi Province, had been involved in illegal meetings in recent years that seriously disrupted the public order, and refused to stop in spite of repeated warnings.

In March 1996, a local re-education-through-labor commission, acting in accordance with the law, decided that he be subject to three years of re-education-through-labor. At present, Zeng is in good health and has not contracted pneumonia. The wording of having "contracted pneumonia" and "Chinese authorities ... refused ... to provide medical care" in the Reports is a fabrication and is unfounded.

The Reports says China "detained foreigners visiting Tibet, searched them ..." alleging that Ngawang Choephel, a foreign scholar visiting Tibet, was detained by Chinese authorities for making a documentary about Tibetan dancing arts, and was thus sentenced to 18 years in prison.

The fact is that the 30-year-old Ngawang Choephel, whose ancestral home is Zada County in Ngari Prefecture, Tibet, was a dance teacher with the song and dance ensemble of the "government in exile" of the 14th Dalai Lama before his arrest. Using funding and equipment provided by a foreign county, he entered China in July 1995 on order from the Dalai clique to engage in intelligence activities under the guise of collecting materials on Tibetan dances.

During his stay in Tibet, he conducted espionage activities in Lhasa, Shannan, Nyingchi and Xigaze by using methods conforming to the "information collection plan" he drafted before his visit.

Having gained sufficient evidence of Ngawang Choephel's espionage activities, China's public security departments arrested him in accordance with the law, and Ngawang Choephel made a full confession of his espionage activities. The Intermediate People's Court of the Xigaze Prefecture sentenced him to 18 years in prison on the charge of espionage, and deprived him of political rights for four years, also in accordance with the law.

After the first ruling, the defendant appealed to a higher court, and the second instance is now under way. With regard to such people who endanger a country's security and engage in espionage activities, any country that practices a legal system should punish them according to the law. It is a complete distortion of the facts when the Reports uses the term "visiting scholar" or "foreign tourist" to describe a spy.

The Reports also attacks China for arresting or detaining foreign businessmen at will, saying, "Austrialian businessman James Peng, whom Chinese public security officials kidnapped in Macao in 1994 and brought to China for trial, was sentenced to a lengthy prison term in September 1995."

The fact is that Peng Jiandong from Jiexi County in Guangdong Province became a naturalized Australian citizen in December 1991.

Acting as the general manager of the Shenzhen Yuangye Industrial Co. Ltd., Peng diverted HK$800,000 (US$103,000) of his corporation's investment remittances intended for the Sino-Australian Liupin Corp. in Australia to his own Kangya Co. in Hong Kong in March 1989.

When he became chairman of the board of Yuangye in November 1989, he embezzled 290,000 yuan (US$35,000) in funds from the corporation under the guise of borrowing money from its subsidiary, the Yuangye Materials Co., in February 1992.

Peng was arrested, according to law, for embezzlement and misappropriation of funds in October 1993. The Shenzhen Intermediate People's Court and the Guangdong Higher People's Court handled the case and sentenced him to 17 years in prison in addition to expulsion from China.

The Reports calls an economic criminal who violated China's law a "victim" of a kidnapping case; those writing it must have ulterior motives.

The Reports is full of flaws and contradictions, looking for justifications but failing to conceal its true intentions of making unwarranted accusations against China. For instance, on the one hand, the Reports says that "because the government tightly controls information, it is impossible to estimate accurately the total number of people subjected to new or continued arbitrary arrest or detention."

On the other hand, the Reports says, "Procurator General Zhang Siqing re-ported in March to the NPC that during 1995 the Supreme Procuratorate investigated 4,627 illegal detention cases."

Since the Chinese government "tightly controls information," how does the Reports account for the fact that the Supreme Procuratorate reported to the NPC the number of illegal detention cases?

And since the Supreme Procuratorate made the exact figure public, how can the Reports say that it is impossible to estimate accurately the total number of people subjected to arbitrary arrest or detention? Thus, the contradictory psychology of intending to attack China but failing to present any real evidence is evident.

For another example, the Reports says that the Chinese authorities fail to act in accordance with legal standards in an attempt to show China as a country without a legal system. But then, the Reports goes on to say that "the 1988 Law on State Secrets provides justification for denying a public trial. Details regarding cases falling under this provision are frequently kept secret."

That means when the Chinese legal departments work to implement the Law on State Secrets, they are "infringing on human rights." Such contradictions can be found throughout the Reports.

COOKING UP CHARGES BY HOOK OR BY CROOK

In order to cook up charges for China's "violations of human rights," the Reports refers to criminals and people who violate the law in China, or who harm national security and public order, "political dissidents," "political prisoners" and "defendants of conscience."

The Reports says that Wang Dan is a "political prisoner" who was sentenced to 11 years imprisonment in 1996 for "announcing his intention to investigate China's human rights situation in 1994."

The fact is that Wang was sentenced to four years imprisonment with one year deprivation of political rights in 1991 for working to subvert the Chinese government, in clear violation of the country's criminal code.

After he was released on parole on February 17, 1993, he contacted overseas anti-Chinese organizations in secret and became involved in a series of activities that were intended to overturn the Chinese government and harm national security. He was arrested in accordance with the law on October 3, 1996.

The No 1 Intermediate People's Court of Beijing began Wang Dan's trial, which was open to the public, on October 30, 1996, and sentenced him to 11 years imprisonment with two-year deprivation of political rights for conspiracy to overthrow the government.

Wang did not plead guilty and appealed the decision to the Beijing Higher People's Court, which heard the case in a public trial on November 5, 1996, but rejected his appeal, upholding the original sentence.

This demonstrates that Wang Dan was sentenced to prison not because he was a dissident who announced "his intention to investigate China's human rights situation," but because he violated the law by harming national security.

In fact, there are no "political prisoners" in China, and people do not violate the law merely by expressing their own ideology or opinions about public affairs. No one is punished by law just because he or she holds a different political view.

It is a groundless assertion for the Reports to refer to criminals who in fact harm national security and who would be sentenced in a court of law in any other country for such activities as "political prisoners," regardless of facts and international conventions.

The Reports slanders China by saying that "mental hospitals have reportedly been used on occasion to control political dissidents." The Reports claims that "dissident writer Wang Wanxing, who was arrested in 1992 for protesting in Tiananmen Square on the third anniversary of the 1989 demonstrations, was in good mental health but remained detained against his will at An Kang Psychiatric Hospital in Shanghai."

The fact is that Wang, who only had a middle school education, was found jeopardizing the social order in Tiananmen Square in June 1992. The police discovered that he had mental problems after they removed him from the square, and sent him to An Kang Hospital in Beijing, where doctors diagnosed him as suffering from paranoid delusions.

Doctors said his attempt to disturb the social order was the result of this problem and that he had difficulty in recognizing the normal state of things and was not responsible for his behavior. They decided he should hospitalized for treatment. The hospital reports Wang's health is better now.

This shows that the Reports' description of "in good mental health" but "detained against his will at the An Kang Psychiatric Hospital in Shanghai" is a groundless allegation.

It took a great deal of thought for the Reports to label a mental patient with the names of "writer" and "political dissident" in order to trump up charges against China for "violation of human rights."

The Reports accuses China of persecuting religious believers and encroaching on freedom of religion. To support its accusations, the Reports uses people who used religion to cover their criminal activity and who were therefore dealt with in accordance with the law, calling them "defendants of conscience."

The Reports says that "in 1996 police continued to put pressure on an underground evangelical sect called the 'Shouters'," and "its members have been repeatedly detained, fined, and imprisoned."

The fact is that the "Shouters," which is not regarded as orthodox by other Christian groups, was an evil religious organization engaged in anti-government, anti-social criminal activities against the law under the guise of religion. It was threatening to "organize all Christian sects to resist the government to the end" and getting its misguided followers to harass the government and government leaders, and was involved in criminal acts of rape and swindling people.

Some of the organization's leaders had raped or behaved indecently with more than 100 women and forcibly held more than 20 young female followers for a long period of time in the name of religion.

They were guilty of serious crimes and the Chinese government punished them in accordance with the law. This had nothing to do with religion. In fact, the Chinese government protects citizens' freedom of religion and their normal religious activities in accordance with the law. No one will be punished just for religious beliefs or for normal religious activities. At the same time, people cannot avoid penalties for criminal activity simply because they believe in religion or flaunt the banner of religion.

Evil religious organizations like the "Shouters" which use religion to cloak their law-breaking criminal activities have been dealt with by any government in the world in accordance with its laws.

It is ridiculous for the Reports to use China's methods of dealing with evil religious organizations and criminal activities, such as swindling or raping that violate social order, as evidence of its "violating human rights."

DISTORTING FREEDOM AND VILIFYING CHINA

In order to vilify China, the Reports uses a lot of space accusing it of having no freedom of speech, of the press or of information.

The Reports say that China encroaches upon the freedom of speech of its citizens because it "does not permit citizens to publish or broadcast criticism of senior leaders or opinions that contradict basic Communist Party doctrine, providing for a socialist state under the Party's leadership," that China invades freedom of the press by requiring reporters to guard "state secrets," and that China tampers with the freedom of information and communication by requiring Internet users "not to use the Internet to endanger security."

According to the logic of the Reports, it seems that China can conform to human rights only if it allows its citizens to deny legal state political power and the present political system, to endanger state security and to reveal state secrets. Otherwise, it will violate human rights. Obviously, this is a distortion of internationally recognized standards for human rights and freedom, and is utterly ridiculous.

It is common knowledge that there can be no freedom of speech, of the press or of information in the world, without some limits.

The 10th and 11th articles of the Declaration of the Rights of Man in France in 1789 state explicitly that freedom of speech and the press do not include "disturbing public order formed by the law," and that those who "abuse the freedom are required to shoulder the responsibilities" according the law.

According to the 19th article of the UN International Covenant on Civil and Political Rights, freedom of speech,which includes the right to seek, receive and impart information, "carries with it special duties and responsibilities." People are required to restrict their freedom of speech in order to "respect the rights or reputations of others," or "to protect national security, public order, public health, or morals" according to law. The 20th article stipulates that "any propaganda for war," or "any advocacy of national, racial or religious hatred that constitutes incitement to discrimination, hostility or violence shall be prohibited by law."

China's lawful limits to freedom of speech, the press, and information fully conform to the spirit of the international convention on human rights and to international practice.

In fact, US law limits the freedom of speech, the press and information in a more severe way than does the law of China. Statistics show that there are as many as 18 kinds of limits in general language in the United States. According to the interpretation of law cases in US federal courts, the application of freedom of speech should not go beyond the limit of not violating the stipulations of the US Constitution, and publications are not allowed to libel the government or attempt to overthrow the government.

The 2385th section, 18th article of the Public Laws of America says that whoever "advocates, abets, advises, or teaches the duty, necessity, desirability, or propriety of overthrowing or destroying the government of the United States," including "printing, publishing, editing, issuing, circulating, selling, distributing, or publicly displaying any written or printed matter" for that aim shall be sentenced to as much as 20 years in prison, or a fine of US$20,000, or both.

The 1717th section also stipulates that all "letters and writings containing matters advocating forcible resistance to any law of the United States as nonmailable" and their owners are to be punished according to the law. In addition, the United States is a country which exercises strict administration and control over the Internet.

Since US laws do not allow people to avail themselves of the freedom of speech, the press or of information to engage in activities of opposing the government and endangering national security, how can the Reports criticize China for observing the stipulations of the Constitution and laws and requiring citizens to "guard state secrets" and for prohibiting "going against the country's basic principles" or "engaging in activities which endanger national security?"

As a matter of fact, the Reports is not concerned about the question of whether Chinese citizens really enjoy freedom of speech, the press and information. Any politically unprejudiced person would not deny that the freedoms, including those of speech, the press and information, that the Chinese people enjoy today greatly surpass those of any other period in Chinese history.

In fact, the majority of Chinese people now have many more individual freedoms than ever before, Anthony Saich, representative of the Ford Foundation in charge of China affairs, said in February 1997.

Former US President George Bush said on February 24, 1997 that Chinese citizens today have more human rights and individual freedoms than at the time since he left the country. (Note: George Bush served as chief of the US Liason Office in China from 1974–1975.)

On the freedoms of speech, the press and information, the Reports itself has to admit that the Chinese society continues to open further, and "it has freer access to outside sources of information... satellite television broadcasts are widely available... increasing numbers of citizens have access to the Internet."

Why then does the Reports still accuse China of not having the freedom of speech, the press and information? In the words of the Reports, the real reason is that China does not permit citizens to deny "basic doctrine providing for a socialist state under the Communist Party's leadership," and that the freedoms the Chinese people enjoy are not enough to "endanger the leading role of the Communist Party." This clearly tells us that what the Reports calls for is not real freedom of speech, the press and information, but the "freedom" to oppose the socialist system and the ruling Communist Party. So long as China is still a socialist country where the Communist Party is at the helm of the state, no matter how democratic it is or how many freedoms its people really enjoy in speech, the press and information, for those who write the Reports it

is always "a country without freedoms." That is where the real problem lies.

COLD WAR MENTALITY AND RUNNING COUNTER TO HISTORICAL TRENDS

To reach its anti-Chinese, anti-Communist aims, the Reports ignores the facts and describes China, which is constantly developing, as a country with worsening human rights condition.

The fact is that in 1996, great improvements were made in China's human rights situation. China's economy achieved sustained, rapid and healthy growth, democratic and legislative construction was obviously enhanced, and people's rights to exist and develop and other human rights further improved.

According to statistics, in 1996, the national economy grew 9.7 percent in real terms over the previous year, and the per-capita income for urban residents reached 4,300 yuan (US$500), a 3.3 percent increase in real terms; the figure for rural residents reached 1,900 yuan, a 9 percent increase in real terms, the highest growth for the past several years.

Total bank savings deposits for both urban and rural residents reached 3,850 billion yuan (US$480 billion) in 1996, some 880 billion yuan more than in the previous year.

China has the fastest rate of poverty relief in the world. In 1996, as many as 7 million people in rural areas were helped out of poverty, bringing rural China's total number of the impoverished down from 250 million in 1978 to 58 million at the end of 1996, or less than a twentieth of the world's total compared to a fourth in the past.

In 1996, another 457 county-level administrative units in 26 provinces and autonomous regions realized their goal of eliminating illiteracy and achieving nine-year compulsory education for everyone. This benefited 190 million people, or 16.4 percent of the country's population.

Meanwhile, great achievements have been made in democratic construction at the grass-roots administrative body. More than 98 percent of the urban mini-districts established neighborhood committees or groups, 97 percent through direct election in 1996.

In 1996, China passed the Law on Protecting the Rights of the Elderly, the Law on Lawyers, the Law on Administrative Punishment and many other legal documents concerning human rights, and made significant amendments to the Criminal Law in an effort to protect human rights according to the law.

The amended Criminal Law in particular increased the participation of lawyers in criminal proceedings, provided those accused of crimes with greater rights protection, and standardized methods used in issuing summons, determining custody and other compulsory measures. These provide greater guarantees in dealing with criminals and in protecting innocent persons in legislative procedures. The facts show that human rights conditions in China continued to improve all around in 1996.

However, the Reports ignores all this, and chases after some so-called "individual cases." It even fabricates "facts" to show "China's violation of human rights" and draws a grim picture of China's human rights condition.

This shows that the authors of the Reports don't really want China to be strong, stable, and developing, nor do they want to see any improvement or development in human rights conditions for all Chinese people. What they really want to do is to use human rights as a tool with which to vilify China in the international community and sabotage China's stability and development.

It is not accidental that the Reports uses human rights to carry out a public opinion struggle against China. This is a full manifestation of the stubborn Cold War mentality of the United States.

As is known to all, the US State Department started to issue the human rights reports in the days of Cold War as part of its "human rights diplomacy" to meet Cold War political demands.

From their very beginning, they were a political tool US authorities used to put pressure on socialist and developing countries. After the end of the Cold War, the United States, to enhance its efforts in pursuing hegemonism and power politics, took socialist China, which persists in its own road of development, as its imaginary enemy, and frequently attacks China by using the issue of human rights.

The annual human rights reports of the US State Department have therefore become an important tool for opposing China, vilifying China and interfering in China's internal affairs.

However, just as motions advanced by the United States against China at the UN Commission on Human Rights have failed six times, the purpose of the US State Department's Human Rights Reports in opposing China will not be achieved.

China is a country whose civilization goes back 5,000 years and which is full of vitality and hope. In no way will the 1.2 billion Chinese, who have stood up, change their course of development because of foreign pressure.

The US State Department's reports openly interfere in the internal affairs of other countries and run counter to the spirit of the UN Charter and the trend of the times.

Item 3, Article 1 of the UN Charter clearly states that the fundamental approach to promoting human rights in the international community is to "promote international cooperation."

For a long time, however, human rights, under Cold War influences, have become a tool of big powers to stir up political conflicts, to practice hegemonism and to interfere in the internal affairs of other countries.

After the Cold War, people all over the world demanded that international human rights activities crawl out from under the shadow of the Cold War and take the healthy track of international cooperation and dialogue.

The Vienna Declaration and Program of Action adopted at the 1993 World Conference on Human Rights reiterated that improvements in human rights must be made in keeping with the aims and principles of the UN Charter, particularly with the United Nations' primary goal of international cooperation.

A resolution on increasing international cooperation in human rights, adopted at the 51st Session of the UN General Assembly in November 1996, again stressed that true and constructive dialogue based on mutual respect and equality is needed to promote international cooperation in human rights.

All this represents the trend in the present international community to demand cooperation and dialogue, and to oppose conflict and pressure in human rights.

The United States is neither a world government nor has it been vested with authority to act as one by any widely accepted international organization or conference. Nonetheless, it is trying in every way possible to pretend to be a "world judge of human rights," one that has issued reports year in and year out to make unwarranted charges against other countries. The move, which goes against the historical trend and man-made conflicts over human rights, runs utterly contrary to the spirit of the UN Charter and popular sentiment of the international community, and will necessarily meet with the opposition of more and more countries, including China.

POSTSCRIPT

Should China Be Condemned as a Violator of Human Rights?

What, if anything, should be done about China? Some of its practices are anathema to most Americans, but to what degree are these differences merely matters of cultural divergence? Also, to the extent that China is changing many of its laws to strengthen human rights, what should Americans' attitude be? In parts of the report not included here, the U.S. State Department concedes that China is attempting to change, but it argues that the changes are too slow—often even a sham—while the abuses continue in practice. Another defense of China's record, in this case by the chairman of the China Society for Human Rights Studies, is contained in the interview "Zhu Muzhi Addresses Human Rights," *Beijing Review* (February 17–March 3, 1997). What should the United States do if it is found that China is violating inherent human rights and that its reforms are largely meaningless? For an article that urges stronger action, see James Finn, "Limping Toward China: Clinton's Weak-Kneed Policy," *Commonweal* (April 25, 1997). Finally, if the U.S. government imposes sanctions for violations of civil rights and liberties, as has been done against Cuba and others, is it applying a double standard by doing nothing when equal or greater abuses are committed by powerful countries like China? Advocating this view is Aryeh Neier, "Human Rights: The New Double Standard," *Foreign Policy* (Winter 1996/1997).

The debate regarding relations with China continues in the United States and elsewhere. In 1997 some members of Congress attempted once again to end China's MFN status. House minority leader Richard A. Gephardt (D-Missouri) maintained that "this country is not about just business. This country is about an ideal, a moral belief that every human being in the world is created with liberty and freedom. If we don't stand for freedom in China, who will follow?" Clinton waged a furious campaign to defeat the move in Congress. In a June 1997 editorial, U.S. secretary of state Madeleine Albright replied to efforts to end China's MFN status by arguing that sanctions constituted a "wrecking ball" when a "scalpel" was needed and that "the administration is convinced [that] our interests are better served by a frank dialogue with China in which differences are aired and opportunities to establish common ground are explored." As has happened on several occasions before, with only the exact margins changing, the House defeated the effort to deny China MFN status by a vote of 259–173. For a review of U.S. views and actions, see Sidney Jones, "Asian Human Rights, Economic Growth, and United States Policy," *Current History* (December 1996) and John T. Rourke,

"United States–China Trade: Economic, Human Rights, and Strategic Issues," *In Depth* (1994).

China has also escaped unscathed at the international level. Each year since 1989, there have been attempts to condemn China in the United Nations Human Rights Commission (UNHRC). The 1997 resolution to condemn China was supported by the United States and some other countries. But China waged a strong and ultimately successful campaign against the resolution, even though it would have only been symbolic. The Chinese delegate termed the resolution "an outrageous distortion of China's reality" and "a Western attempt to dominate China." The delegate called on UNHRC members to choose "cooperation over confrontation." The Chinese also reportedly threatened economic retaliation against countries that voted for the resolution. This story was given credence by the Danish delegate who told reporters that "China conducted a rather aggressive campaign that has paid off. There were lots of threats." They certainly paid off. Only 17 countries voted for the resolution; 27 voted against. It was the widest defeat ever for the resolution.

On the Internet . . .

Association for the Study of Ethnicity and Nationalism (ASEN)
Founded in 1990 by research students and academics at the London School of Economics and Political Science, the Association for the Study of Ethnicity and Nationalism (ASEN) has established itself as the leading interdisciplinary, nonpolitical association for the study of ethnicity and nationalism.
http://158.143.104.181/depts/european/asen/

Global Warming: Understanding the Forecast
This site promotes the global warming exhibit on permanent display at Columbia University's Biosphere 2 Center near Tucson, Arizona. The site offers background information on global warming and a complete online, interactive version of the exhibit.
http://www.edf.org/pubs/Brochures/GlobalWarming/

The Migration Home Page
This site contains information on the International Organization for Migration (IOM) and migration-related information from around the world. *http://www.iom.ch/*

UN Development Programme (UNDP)
This United Nations Development Programme (UNDP) site offers publications and current information on world poverty, the UNDP's mission statement, information on the UN Development Fund for Women, and more. Be sure to see the "poverty clock." *http://www.undp.org/*

PART 5

Global Trends and International Relations

Many political analysts believe that the sovereignty of the state (country) is declining, that the political identification of people with the state is beginning to weaken, and that people are beginning to refocus their loyalties on their nationalities. This section takes up issues that relate to the movement of people from state to state and to the value and strength of nationalism.

■ Are UN-Sponsored World Conferences Beneficial?

■ Is Nationalism Destructive?

■ Should Immigration Be Restricted?

■ Is There a Global Population Crisis?

ISSUE 15

Are UN-Sponsored World Conferences Beneficial?

YES: Timothy Wirth, from Statement Before the Committee on Foreign Relations, U.S. Senate (June 4, 1996)

NO: Christine Vollmer, from Statement Before the Committe on Foreign Relations, U.S. Senate (June 4, 1996)

ISSUE SUMMARY

YES: Timothy Wirth, a U.S. assistant secretary of state, contends that UN-sponsored world conferences have helped shape a world that is more hospitable to American interests and values.

NO: Christine Vollmer, president of the Latin American Alliance for the Family, rejects what she sees as unwelcome policies being promoted by UN-sponsored conferences.

An increasing number of global conferences are being held, most of which are sponsored by the United Nations or by one of the UN's associated programs. These conferences are one indication of the growing awareness that protection of the environment, population control, women's rights, and other matters have global implications and, at least in part, require global solutions.

Just a partial recitation of these conferences helps to illuminate the range of issues they cover. Hunger has been addressed at the 1974 World Food Conference and the 1996 World Food Summit, both of which met at the (UN) Food and Agriculture Organization headquarters in Rome, Italy. Environmental issues have been taken up by the 1972 Conference on the Human Environment in Stockholm, Sweden; the 1990 World Climate Conference in Geneva, Switzerland; and the 1992 UN Conference on Environment and Development (UNCED) in Rio de Janeiro, Brazil. On a related subject, the World Summit on Social Development met in Copenhagen, Denmark, in 1995.

The UN has also conducted a series of conferences to focus world attention on the population issue. There have been three conferences, the first two of which met in Bucharest, Romania (1974), and in Mexico City, Mexico (1984). The most recent of these, the 1994 United Nations Conference on Population and Development (UNCPD) met in Cairo, Egypt.

Human rights have also been the subject of several conferences. These include the 1993 World Conference on Human Rights in Vienna, Austria, and the 1996 World Congress Against Commercial Sexual Exploitation of Children in Stockholm. There have been four UN world conferences on women. The most recent of these, the fourth World Conference on Women (WCW), convened in Beijing, China, in 1995.

Each of these conferences has come under the auspices of an international governmental organization (IGO), such as the UN. As such, the delegates to each of these conferences were appointed by the countries that are members of the IGO. In addition to the "official" IGO conference, however, there has been a growing trend to have a parallel, "unofficial" conference attended by representatives of nongovernmental organizations (NGOs). These NGOs are private organizations that have an interest in the subject of the conference. At least in sheer numbers, the unofficial conferences have become much larger than the official ones. The Rio Conference (UNCED) was attended by official delegates from 178 countries, and the parallel NGO conference drew 15,000 representatives of NGOs and national citizens' groups. In addition to the 3,000 national delegates from 180 countries at the 1995 WCW in Beijing, 30,000 delegates representing some 2,000 NGOs traveled to the parallel conference for NGOs at nearby Huairou.

What these conferences cannot do is to make laws or agreements that are legally binding on countries. The conferences do, however, have important impacts. They sometimes lead to the establishment of IGOs or divisions of IGOs to work on problems or to create international treaties that can legally bind signatories. The world conferences also focus global attention on an issue, and facilitate contact and cooperation among IGOs, NGOs, governments, and individuals with an interest in that issue. Less tangible, but still important, resolutions by the world conferences help establish a record of world opinion on an issue. This creation of values brings pressure, if slow and uncertain, on countries and individuals around the world to abide by certain standards.

Perhaps the single greatest testament to the importance of the world conferences is how much attention they are receiving. The Cairo Conference (UNCPD) on population and development, for example, set off a furious battle over such issues as women's reproductive rights. Most delegates to both the official and unofficial meetings tended to support a woman's right to choose abortion. There was also strong support in favor of encouraging family planning, including the use of artificial birth control measures. Not all agreed, however. Some Muslim countries and groups found these policies, especially abortion, repugnant.

Timothy Wirth and Christine Vollmer debate the value of world conferences. Wirth concludes that the conferences represent a good faith effort by the international community to work together on problems that cannot be solved without international cooperation. Vollmer condemns the conferences as conclaves dominated by those who do not represent world opinion and who wish to impose their views on the countries of the world.

YES

Timothy Wirth

STATEMENT OF TIMOTHY WIRTH

HISTORY

Let me begin by touching briefly on the history and origin of the major UN world conferences, dating back to 1972, when the Stockholm Conference on the Environment was convened in response to worldwide concern about a growing set of environmental challenges. Since then, 24 similar conferences have been held on a range of important and difficult long-term global challenges, from population growth and pollution to the plight of children and the fight against illiteracy.

The round of UN conferences mentioned in your letter of invitation, Mr. Chairman, have their origins in UN General Assembly or Economic and Social Council (ECOSOC) decisions that were taken in the period between 1989 and 1992. Under the Bush Administration, the United States joined consensus decisions at the United Nations authorizing these conferences to be held. Specifically, approval was given in the late 1980s and early 1990s for: the UN Conference on Environment and Development (UNCED) held in Rio de Janeiro; the World Conference on Human Rights held in Vienna; the International Conference on Population and Development held in Cairo; the World Summit on Social Development held in Copenhagen; the Fourth World Conference on Women held in Beijing; and the World Conference on Human Settlements... held ... in Istanbul, Turkey.

The responsibility for coordinating US substantive participation in these events has primarily rested with the Department of State. I have been pleased to have had the opportunity to personally participate in all but the latest of this series of meetings as a representative of the United States. In addition, during the Rio Conference, I participated as a member of the United States Senate's bipartisan observer delegation, which was chaired by then-Senator [Al] Gore and included several members of this Committee, including Senator Pell, one of the few individuals in the world to have attended both the Stockholm and Rio meetings.

From U.S. Senate. Committee on Foreign Relations. *United Nations World Conferences.* Hearing, June 4, 1996. Washington, DC: Government Printing Office, 1996.

ROLE AND FUNCTION

I want to begin this morning by offering some thoughts about the role and function of these conferences in shaping a world more hospitable to American interests and values.

During the past 30 years, the world has grown increasingly interdependent. As a result, the interests of the United States are more and more intertwined with peace and prosperity all over the world. With more than 5.7 billion people linked by advanced communications, travel and trade, it is ever more apparent that our geopolitical, economic and environmental interests are tied with those of the world. The prospects for jobs in Milwaukee, for example, has everything to do with the ability of Manila to import our goods and buy our services. Similarly, the health of our citizens is increasingly dependent on actions far beyond our boundaries, as evidenced in the destruction of the ozone layer or the spread of new and re-emerging infectious diseases.

In a world characterized by interdependence, American interests are served by engagement, not isolation. As the most successful society in the history of the globe, and the only nation capable of leading the entire world, we have a special responsibility to help show the way. For example, progress on stabilizing population and preventing environmental degradation helps reduce the pressure for migration around the world, and lessens explosive pressures on land and resources that have contributed to such tragedies as Rwanda. By encouraging cooperative efforts to prevent these pressures, we can save the need for hundreds of millions of dollars in humanitarian relief and promote a world of greater prosperity. The alternative is a world teeming with hundreds of millions more poor people, with little hope in their own countries, hopelessly damaged environments, and with no commitment or capability to staunch cross-border threats to the stability and the environment.

The Clinton Administration did not initiate the major conferences, but has participated in them to advance international action on these new and emerging global concerns that affect our own and the world's interests. By showcasing American accomplishments, we have demonstrated and gained broad acceptance for American values as a model for the rest of the world to follow. Specifically, we have sought to achieve a more peaceful and prosperous world by advancing core principles, including:

- The necessity and universality of human rights;
- The benefits of adherence to democratic decisionmaking processes;
- The imperative of free enterprise and open markets;
- The sovereign responsibilities of States;
- The importance of environmental protection for long-term economic progress;
- The need for equal rights for women.

Each of the recent conferences has offered the United States an opportunity to promote these ideas and encourage their adoption. The importance of these principles and the value of addressing them in a global forum is perhaps best reflected in the resistance they receive from repressive governments at each of these conferences.

We recognize that there are significant shortcomings associated with these conferences. Involving viewpoints and input from more than 170 nations, they are, by their nature, unwieldy. They require a good deal of time and money to put on and participate in. There are cultural and language barriers that are awkward and difficult to overcome. The documents are difficult to read and the debates all too often bogs down in arcane, least-common-denominator rhetoric. As with laws and sausage, the conference documents are not something you want to watch being made.

All these shortcomings, however, must be weighed against the advantages these conferences offer the United States and the international community to tackle matters of genuine relevance to the world we live in today, and we seek to shape for our children tomorrow.

First, these conferences reflect a creative effort on the part of the international community to address common, long-term, global challenges without setting elaborate programs or requiring enormous budgets. Each of the conferences we are discussing today has generated a comprehensive, non-binding "Program or Plan of Action" outlining steps that can be taken to achieve agreed goals for economic, social and environmental progress. When successful, the action plans developed at the major conference serve as a roadmap for nations, organizations and individuals to follow in subsequent months and years in the effort to implement carefully negotiated recommendations. The various Programs of Action that have emerged in recent years are of varying degrees of import and impact. Where the conference and associated action plan has broken new ground to define clear objectives and concrete steps for achieving those objectives (as in the case, for example, of the Rio and Cairo Conferences) they have resulted in a remarkable legacy of accomplishment.

Second, these conferences have enhanced government accountability. The global plans of action establish a kind of baseline on which the United States and the world can leverage adherence by governments to agreed upon standards. The nonbinding commitments that have emerged from recent documents are not recognized in the strict sense of international law, but they serve a valuable function in the court of public opinion. In this way, these agreements mobilize citizens around the world to work on behalf of their own and our interests—offering them a yardstick by which to measure the performance of their governments and a critical foothold for ensuring that their leadership follows through in implementing the commitments they helped negotiate and ultimately agreed upon. In short, these conferences have instilled a measure of accountability on reluctant nations for basic standards of human rights and decency, for free enterprise and the rule of law, for environmental protection and basic health.

Third, the development of these action plans has galvanized global attention in addressing newly recognized concerns —from global scale environmental challenges, to the exploitation of children and abuses of women that go far beyond cultural peculiarities and in fact fall into the realm of human rights violations.

Fourth, these conferences have brought together tens of thousands of citizens, organizations and business representatives to share insights and ideas in service of common objectives. As evidenced by the array of organizations and individuals participating, this opportunity is valued by NGOs [nongovernmental organizations] across the spectrum, both in terms of the subjects addressed and the points of view brought to bear. At the recent Women's Conference, for example, more than 30,000 women from all corners of the globe, including more than 7,000 Americans, traveled to Beijing to share experiences and ideas. These individuals have now returned to their communities, including scores here in the United States, dedicated to following up on the lessons they have learned and encouraging positive changes at the local level.

Fifth, the major world conferences have also served as a means for encouraging enhanced coordination among the various public and private entities involved in advancing solutions to the economic, environmental and social challenges that have been the subject of the respective world conferences. As a result of the extensive consultations and widespread attention associated with preparations, concrete steps have been taken by national governments, international organizations, the international financial institutions, non-governmental organizations and the private sector to work together in a more coordinated fashion on pragmatic strategies to advance the agreed goals that have been painstakingly negotiated.

RESULTS

Overall, I believe the United States delegations have had considerable influence in helping to defining agenda that are practical and consonant with American values. We have done so because we have marshaled the expertise and the will to work the unwieldy process that surrounds trying to reconcile diverse views. Forging consensus on difficult long-term challenges contributes, in ways that are not easy to measure

precisely, to a more peaceful and stable world. And where these conferences have been successful, the accomplishments are increasingly clear.

The Earth Summit, held in Rio in 1992, and the first in the recent string of world conferences, marked the largest gathering of heads of State ever in the world. Out of this remarkable gathering has come an equally remarkable set of accomplishments. Two international treaties were opened for signature—the Framework Convention on Climate Change and the Convention on Biological Diversity. Pursuant to understandings reached at Rio, international negotiations held after the conference have yielded agreements to combat desertification and to address the unique fishery challenges posed by straddling stocks and highly migratory species; as well as a successful negotiation of strategies for reducing land-based sources of marine pollution. And on the world's agenda for the future are important discussions about international flows of toxic waste, the elimination of lead from gasoline, worldwide protection from the most dangerous and persistent chemicals like DDT.

Institutionally, Rio led to creation of the Commission on Sustainable Development at the United Nations, a fledgling body that has initiated the development of national reports and measured progress by governments in fulfilling the agreements reached at Rio in each of the agreed priority areas. The CSD has emerged as a useful entity for promoting sustainable development—simultaneous economic, environmental and social progress—throughout the UN system.

At the national level, almost 100 nations, including the United States, have created national sustainable development councils to follow-up on UNCED. In the United States, the President's Council on Sustainable Development, comprised of government, business and non-governmental organization leaders, produced a comprehensive set of economic and environmental recommendations and presented them in March to the President.

The International Conference on Population and Development held in Cairo in late 1994 has also yielded a number of important results. At Cairo, 180 nations locked arms—North, South; rich, poor; Catholic, Muslim and Hindu; about the need to address the population challenge with sensitivity and urgency. The Cairo Conference resulted in a remarkable breakthrough in terms of recognizing that efforts to reduce rapid population growth must go beyond family planning to address the broader health and social context in which families make decisions about the number and spacing of their children. International population efforts must also involve coordinated efforts to address reproductive health needs; protect human rights by ensuring that voluntarism is the basis for all decisionmaking about family size; foster child and maternal health as part of a lifespan approach to primary health care; promote basic education, particularly for girls; advance the role of women around the world—economically, politically and socially; and encourage economic opportunity and progress.

Since the Cairo Conference, the international donor community has dedicated resources to these efforts and the overall challenge of encouraging simultaneously population stabilization and sustainable development. Specifically, Japan has pledged $3 billion for the comprehensive efforts agreed upon at Cairo over the next seven years; Germany has pledged $2.1 billion between now and the end of the century; the United Kingdom increased its [pledge] by 65 percent from pre-Cairo levels; the European Union has pledged a tenfold increase, to more than $400 million by 2000; Australia has increased by 50 percent; and the Netherlands has doubled its commitment. Complementing these efforts, a number of the recipient countries have formed an alliance—the South-South partnership—by which developing nations with successful population programs train leaders from other parts of the developing world.

Coupled with Cairo was the Fourth World Conference on Women, and together they laid the base for a number of important national actions. For example:

- In Botswana, the Government has begun the process of reviewing national legislation that discriminates against women;
- Namibia has passed a marriage-equality law, which gives married women the right to sign contracts, head up corporations and use the legal system;
- Uganda is stressing the education of girls from infancy through adulthood;
- Jordan has inaugurated a National Forum for Women to improve women's legal status and increase their participation in politics and the economy;
- A group of 100 women representing legal advice centers in Arab countries gathered in Amman to discuss strategy and improve contacts between organizations that serve victims of domestic violence;
- All over the world, efforts have been launched to address the abhorrent sexual exploitation of children, to

eliminate obstacles to credit and capital for women, and to counter persistent violence against women all over the world. These are important ideals, which we in the United States try to reflect in our policies and behavior, and for which we remain an important beacon for the rest of the world.

At the 1993 Vienna Human Rights Conference, the United States played a powerful role in defending the principle of universality of human rights and in urging action on the human rights challenges faced by women, further rooting this as a major theme for international attention. We obtained broad agreement on the proposition that underdevelopment and cultural differences are no excuse for violating basic human rights. Millions of people are better off, for example, because the United States stood up to those nations who tried to water down international human rights standards under the guise of cultural peculiarities. America once again championed the human rights enshrined in the UN Charter, which has served as the foundation for human rights since World War II. Vienna also led to the creation of a UN High Commissioner for Human Rights, and today the High Commissioner is playing a critical role—helping to deploy human rights monitors in Rwanda and contributing to civilian efforts in Bosnia.

DELEGATION SIZE

Before concluding, ... let me briefly discuss the size and cost of US delegations to these meetings. The Clinton Administration has been successful in keeping down the size of our delegations. By way of comparison, the official delegation to the Rio Conference included 49 US government officials and 10 private sector advisers. At Cairo, Copenhagen and Beijing, about 30 government officials and 10–15 private sector advisers were on our delegations; less than 20 government officials are on the delegation to Istanbul. We have been able to reduce the size of our delegations in part by utilizing private sector advisers, citizens with unique expertise who are in most cases planning to go to the conference anyway and therefore are able to pay their own way. In general, this practice has enabled us to ensure that US interests are represented and protected, while minimizing the need to spend scarce resources on official government travel. All told, delegations under the Clinton Administration are at least 25 percent smaller than the comparable delegation under the previous Administration.

MORATORIUM AND IMPLEMENTATION

The current series of major global conferences that began with Rio will come to an end when the World Conference on Human Settlements closes ... in Istanbul. The United States has made it clear that the UN must now build upon these conferences, to follow-up, solidify gains and implement the agreed upon programs of action.

Last year at the General Assembly, Secretary Christopher called for a moratorium on further world conferences and this remains our policy. The Secretary's decision to call for a moratorium was based on our sense that the world community needs to focus on implementing the mutually reinforcing commitments that have been agreed upon in the past four years, not on making new commitments. That is why our proposals for comprehensive reform in the UN system include a moratorium on these conferences and reliance instead on the General Assembly as a forum for debating major global issues. As just one example, we have successfully diverted a proposal to hold a global conference on narcotics into a tentative plan to dedicate a few days of discussion on this topic at a forthcoming meeting of the General Assembly.

... Taken together, flaws and all, these Conferences have represented a good faith effort by the international community to work together on problems that can't be solved without sustained, cooperative efforts. In the months and years ahead, we are committed to working with the Congress and the American people to ensure that our international partners implement the commitments that have been reached, in the interest of even greater peace and prosperity here at home and around the world.

NO

Christine Vollmer

STATEMENT OF CHRISTINE VOLLMER

I come from Venezuela, where I have occupied myself full-time with social work, mainly with unwed mothers, young people and handicapped children. I am President also of the Latin American Alliance for the Family, headquartered in my hometown of Caracas. I truly welcome the opportunity to give testimony at this hearing and thank the Senate Foreign Relations Committee for investigating the unwelcome things which are being decided for the future of our country under the guise of international agreements at the United Nations International Conferences, and which will most certainly worsen our social problems if enacted.

I have been attending these Conferences since 1990 and the General Assembly since 1989 as a member of the Holy See Delegation and in representation of the NGO [nongovernmental organizations] of which I am president, Latin American Alliance for the Family (ALAFA).

We are convinced that the American taxpayer has no idea that his/her hard-earned dollars are being used to undermine the Constitutions and values of other nations through legislation being promoted by this administration under the guise of "assisting" the underdeveloped world.

Permit me to explain here, to the best of my ability, the mechanisms to that effect that I have observed in my years of experience and some of the extraordinary elucidations discovered through the extensive reading I have done to try to understand what I have observed and experienced....

TIMOTHY WIRTH

Mr. Wirth is perceived in Latin America as an international proponent of abortion and a ruthless population controller, unashamed of coercive measures and disrespectful of religious and cultural values. His motivation seems to be fear of losing power to developing nations. To this effect he said in this Senate just [a few] years ago:

> "At the end of World War II, the developed countries accounted for almost 40 percent of world population. Today they hold about 20 percent, heading—if growth in the developing countries does not slow—toward as little as 12 percent.

From U.S. Senate. Committee on Foreign Relations. *United Nations World Conferences.* Hearing, June 4, 1996. Washington, DC: Government Printing Office, 1996. Notes and some references omitted.

Per capita resource consumption in the North is vastly greater than in the South. What are the prospects for long-term stability on a planet where about ten percent of the people consume more than 90 percent of the resources, a small island of wealth in a sea of greater poverty?

"For all these reasons, the cost of our population program is a fraction of not doing it."

In his speech at Prep Com II in May 1993, he announced that the United States was "back" as a world leader in population and laying out a "comprehensive and far-reaching new approach to international population issues." At that meeting he made clear the pro-abortion position of this administration. "Our position is to support reproductive choice, including access to safe abortion" (US Mission to the UN, 1993). After that, speeches by Wirth and other officials routinely included special mention of access to abortion. Sometimes the euphemism "access to reproductive health services" was used (defined by World Health Organization to included legal, safe abortion).

It is worth remembering that some years back, the then-President of Planned Parenthood, Dr. Alan Guttmacher, expressed a cynical new policy which became reality: "My own feeling is that we've got to pull out all the stops and involve the United Nation[s].... If you're going to curb population, it's extremely important not to have it done by the damned Yankee, but by the UN. Because the thing is, then it's not considered genocide.... If you can send in a colorful UN force, you've got much better leverage...."

Mr. Wirth chose no less than 22 members of Planned Parenthood, including its President, to be part of the US delegation. Planned Parenthood is in every country of our continent, actively undermining the moral, cultural and religious convictions of our people.

The population-connection between the Clinton administration and the UN is illustrated graphically by a booklet produced by the US Information Agency, which says it all. *Population, Development and the Role of Women,* was published for the Cairo Conference. It contains messages with photos of President Clinton, Vice President Al Gore and Timothy Wirth. This booklet makes clear that the position of this administration is in favor of abortion, as in the "Safe Motherhood Initiative" (SMI, defined as including abortion), and "safe services for terminating an unwanted pregnancy," "reproductive choice," sex education and contraceptives for teens. It delineates the need for a new "approach" (calling it "reproductive health"). Their anti-religious and pro-abortion philosophy is starkly stated: "To resist ethically mandated change because of long held beliefs or practices is a philosophical error." And "and the lack of access to safe, legal abortion are practices that cannot withstand critical ethical evaluation." ...

Issues Unacceptable to Our Peoples
It has been very disappointing and alarming for the countries of Latin America to see, rather than a commitment to assistance in real development, the totally immoral positions assumed by the United States of America's delegation, and the forcefulness with which they are imposing them on us. The position of the US delegation in reference to the Cairo document was inexplicably radical. By way of illustration, I will cite just the problems in Chapter 8 of the Cairo

document, because I happen to have my notes: the US—

- would not agree to this wording: "discourage un-safe sexual behavior and encourage responsible sexual behavior"
- would not agree to "spacing of births" even when more appropriate in the context than "family planning"
- argued in favor of such wording such as "eliminate all unwanted births
- insisted on wording to eliminate "un-safe" and "poorly performed" abortions, rather than "induced"
- would not agree to include the phrase: "Health providers must stress that the only known ways to eliminate the risk of HIV/AIDS include: sexual abstinence among the young and unmarried and monogamous relations within marriage, and avoidance of contaminated blood products and intravenous needles."

The US Delegation's Offensive Position

- "Reproductive choice, including access to safe abortion" in developing nations.
- "The US wants such choice as abortion to be available everywhere by 2000."
- "The US delegation will also be working for stronger language on the importance of access to abortion services..." etc.
- "Reproductive Rights," which for a time there was a great reticence to properly define, include abortion for adolescents.
- Access by adolescents to all methods of Family Planning and to "privacy."
- Parental rights were fought by the US delegation at every opportunity.
- The universal right to abortion. As there was considerable opposition to

this "right," the USA put "safe abortion" into every chapter.

- "Governments should respect the anonymity and confidentiality of adolescents who seek family planning services including abortion. Moreover, governments should try to waive any requirement that demands parental permission before adolescents can avail of such services."
- The US fixation with family planning and abortion was made evident by its inclusion even in chapters where it is not the subject. There was so callous a neglect of any other problems that the Ambassador of Benin finally asked "Why are we talking so much about abortion and reproductive health care, when the number one cause of death in the world is Malaria and nothing has been said about it?"
- Apart from these, the US position was totally against all mention of marriage, family values, and morality on sexual unions of all kinds, insisted on Confidentiality and Privacy for children, over and above the rights and responsibilities of the parents; abortion as a right, and all this in spite of all that had been agreed in former documents.

National Sovereignty

One of the issues that concern us the most is the elimination, in Beijing, of all the guarantees contained in former documents to the effect that national sovereignty would hold more authority than UN documents.

The chapter on principles of the Cairo document, and specifically its overarching first paragraph, reaffirmed "the sovereign right of each country to implement the recommendations in ways that are consistent with 'national laws and development priorities'" and with "full respect for the various religious and ethical values and cultural backgrounds of its people." Up through Cairo, every time conflictive language was inserted in the document, it was qualified by wording which said that it was subject to the local laws, and the cultural and ethical values of each country.

To understand the dangers of relinquishing our national sovereignty to an ever more powerful United Nations Organization, it is necessary not only to understand the philosophical, ideological and political ramifications of this decision, but in a purely practical way, to understand how the UN is run. It is necessary to take a good look at how countries are bribed, cajoled, and humiliatingly disregarded. It is necessary to face up to the fact that inasmuch as the UN is a "closed shop" operation, totally out of the sunshine, it makes free with an incredible jargon all its own, which enables it to be a law unto itself, answerable to no one.

The sentences allowing for respect of "cultural and ethical values" were firmly rooted out of the Beijing document. The elimination of this concept in Beijing is a typical, and extremely serious, example of the art of "building on" the previous Conference. Religious and cultural factors were all pulled out in favor of a benign and ineffectual mention, all by itself, of the benefits of religion to many women. (This paragraph is as favorable to Wicca as to Christianity.) This removal of what the US delegation, the Europeans and the UN do not like is what they call "building on Cairo." On the other hand to un-do wording which has caused difficulties in the countries, or that the delegates want to reject, that is called "re-opening Cairo," and is not allowed. The process of "building on," and never "re-opening" is all in one direction. Ever more progressive and ever more anti-family. This kind of stratagem would never pass in a democracy....

Covert US Policy?

In our nations of Latin America it has became known that the State Department *National Security Study Memo No. 200* was issued in 1974, and although classified for 16 years, has recently come to light. This NSSM 200 would appear to be the justification for Mr. Wirth's aggressive tactics. Mexico, Brazil, [and] Colombia are 3 of the 13 countries of "special US political and strategic interest" for population control named in NSSM 200. The report says Brazil "clearly dominates the continent demographically," and foresees a "growing power status for Brazil in Latin America and on the world scene over the next 25 years" if population programs were not successful at curbing fertility. "[P]opulation policy becomes relevant to resource supplies and to the economic interests of the United States."

The content is extraordinarily enlightening as to UN lingo: "It is vital that the effort to develop and strengthen a commitment on the part of LDC leaders not be seen by them as an industrialized country policy to keep their strength down or to reserve resources for use by the 'rich' countries," says the study. "Development of such a perception could create a serious backlash adverse to the cause of population stability.... The next page adds: "The US can help to minimize charges of an imperialist motivation behind its support of population activities by repeatedly asserting that such support derives from a concern with: (a) the right of the individual to determine freely and responsibly their number and spacing of children... and (b) the fundamental social and economic development of poor countries...." The study also argues for channeling population assistance through "other donors and/or from private and international organizations (many of which receive contributions from AID [Agency for International Development]).

Another source of pressure on our nations to abandon our morals and legalize abortion comes from none other than the august World Health Organization (WHO). WHO Regional Office for the Pacific published *Women's Experiences of Abortion in the Western Pacific Region*, [in] 1995, an aggressive pro-abortion piece which calls for the legalization of abortion throughout the world, advocates abortion services as an integral part of health services, and demands anonymity and confidentiality for adolescents seeking abortion—in other words that parents have no rights to be involved in whether their teen-age daughter gets an abortion or not. Our countries need more responsible parents, not more abdication of responsibility! After this entire booklet argues for "reproductive rights," "reproductive determination" and other euphemisms for abortion-rights, it actually has in its "Recommendations" section, a number of pro-abortion instructions which include: "Governments of countries where abortion is illegal should move towards the liberalization of these laws."

HOW THE UN FUNCTIONS AS AN ENABLER OF THE PRO-ABORTION IDEOLOGY

Population and Development: The Document

In spite of being held in the International Year of the Family the words "family" and "marriage" are not used in any positive context. Many attempts were made to include the concept of family, but it was always vetoed by the US, Canada or the Europeans.

Of the 100-some pages in 16 chapters, only 9 pages of the Cairo document are about development. The rest is trendy jargon, sprinkled with a collection of old-hat scare phrases of the '60's based on population theory proved wrong 30 years ago, and a truly amazing collection of linguistic exercises to try to camouflage from the public an effort to destroy, at an international level, all traditional moral beliefs and remodel society in the image of the radical far left, which to us is simply socialist atheism.

Even though all the reputable demographers and economists agree that the fast rate of population growth that has taken place in the past decades is due to longer life spans, not to increasing birthrates, UNFPA with the backing of the US government, has continued to function on the basis that the "world is over-crowded." This argument, although scientifically disproven by economists of the stature of Simon, Eberstadt, Ayrd and many others, has continued to be used, to advance their own ideologies, by extreme environmentalist, radical feminists and those who stand to make huge profits from programs pushed by the United Nations and paid for by the American Taxpayer.

The world has in fact been experiencing a great health explosion, due to increased levels of nutrition, sanitation and medical care. In the words of Economist Nicholas Eberstadt, of the American Enterprise Institute: "World population has increased rapidly, not because people are breeding like rabbits, but because they have stopped dying like flies." This is a one-time increase that cannot be duplicated unless life expectancy were again *doubled*, a most unlikely development.

As I am sure this Committee is aware, the number of children a woman has in her life time, or Total Fertility Rate, of 2.1 must be maintained by a nation to keep a level population. The citizens of Europe, the United States and Japan have failed to do this for decades, and thus the "graying of America" means that the ratio of workers to retired persons in the United States has changed from 16 to 1 in 1950, to 5 to 1 in 1960, to 3 to 1 today and in 15 years there will be only 2.2 workers to support each retiree. The consequences of this trend for the nation's economic future and for Social Security are frightening.

In Europe things are even worse, with Total Fertility Rates as low as 1.66 in France, 1.6 in Russia, 1.23 in Spain and 1.21 in Italy. In the last 5 years births have dropped 20% in Poland, 25% in Bulgaria, 30% in Estonia, 35% in Russia and, 60% in the former East Germany, which in 25 years will have lost a quarter of its population. What future is there for the economy of Europe in nations that will lose such a proportion of their population at each generation? What does that mean for trade? For strategic alliances? For the economies of the developed world and therefore our own economies? These are considerations which need to be addressed immediately and deeply

concern us in the developing world, and yet nothing of this was discussed in Cairo....

Prep Com III

In view of the gravity of the content of the Cairo document, there was strong activity by thoughtful people in several countries of Latin America, particularly Honduras, Guatemala and Nicaragua, El Salvador, Venezuela, and Argentina, which sent exceptional delegations prepared to fight what they saw as clear cultural imperialism. Nicaragua in fact, sent the Minister of Education, Humberto Belli and his assistant who together have been expunging from the text books of the whole school system the Sandinista propaganda which held sway for so long....

The Latin American delegations, encouraged by the Holy See, Argentina, Malta and Benin, made clear their concern about the pro-abortion contents of the document. Venezuela stated her constitutional limitations and the impossibility of accepting the pro-abortion parts of the document, as her Constitution protects life from the moment of conception. This lead was followed by others from Latin America and Africa, and the battle was joined.

Honduras was particularly eloquent and tenacious and the elegant young woman heading the delegation was called away a number of times to be grilled by the US delegation, as were others. The third time, she was alone and her knees were trembling, but she stated firmly to the effect that "It is not true that I am imposing my personal beliefs on the whole world. This is the position of my government and the one I was instructed to uphold.... And what is more, I am so glad to be here in the United States because I know that although I am here all alone, and you don't like my position, I know that nothing can happen to me." This brave attitude on the part of the Central American countries caused angry visits later to some of their Presidents, at least one of whom called in the head of delegation to say sadly that he would not be able to send them to Cairo: "It would cost our country too much!"

UN procedure is very interestingly devised in order to make it quite difficult for the press, and even the governments, to know what a delegation actually said. Thus the extraordinary situation occurred that 2 countries of Latin America, who were speaking often at Prep Com III and always in favor of abortion, homosexual rights, contraceptives for children and so on, turned out to be speaking contrary to the policy and Constitution of their governments. Thanks to NGO activity, their governments found out, both delegations were fired and in Cairo a different tune was heard.

At Prep Com III the Moslems were very silent, and evidently careful not to jeopardize the Cairo venue for the Conference by sounding too "fundamentalist." (Accusations of "fundamentalism" are a new, subtle way to blackmail those who defend their principles.) But even without them, 10% of the document was successfully "bracketed," meaning that these portions had to be hammered out in Cairo. This caused a lot of anger, and indeed unbelievable rudeness, on behalf of Timothy Wirth and Mrs. Sadik.

The pro-abortion bias of the UN was also made evident to all when Secretary General Nafis Sadik, seeing, on the last day, that "Safe Motherhood" was going to stay bracketed because of its ambiguity, could not contain her fury. When Bangladesh suggested that the wording be clarified slightly so that it would be plain that it did not include abortion, she said angrily "I would rather take the brackets to Cairo!" ...

In Cairo

Once in Cairo, the battle lines were precisely drawn. Clearly decided to defend their legal and cultural patrimony, were most of the countries of Latin America, with the exception of Mexico, Brazil and Colombia, who were outspoken allies of UNFPA. (These are the countries signaled in NSSM 200 as strategically the first where population control should be imposed, and where International Planned Parenthood has been the strongest for the longest.) In contrast, an admirable defense of family, the right to life and traditional morality was made by Honduras, El Salvador (represented by their First Lady), Guatemala, Dominican Republic, Costa Rica, Nicaragua, Ecuador, Peru, Argentina, Slovakia and Poland....

On the other side, with US and Norway leading, were Scandinavia, the Commonwealth countries, the European Community and the Asians in general. It was distressing to see that in the name of controlling population growth, these delegations made a shameless effort to force upon the world the whole radical feminist, pro-abortion agenda, regardless of the religious beliefs of the peoples concerned. The discussions seemed to take forever as those who controlled the Conference were determined to obtain certain wording, while the countries who were awakened to the dangers of that wording were prepared to fight to the last to remove it.

Tactics at Cairo and Beijing

The work in the Main Committee consisted of going through the "bracketed" parts and trying to reach agreement on them. One tactic on those occasions when many countries raised objections that a given phrase was obviously unacceptable, was that a "working group" would be assigned, always heavily weighted in UNFPA's favor, to hammer it out in a windowless little room. One incident lasted for 3 days even though it was obvious that they could never agree. It was on the issue of "fertility regulation" because, it was discovered, it is defined by the World Health Organization to include abortion. Finally, after a disgraceful verbal abuse of one of our particularly refined young women, our side was railroaded into agreement, with no possibility of returning to the Main Committee for an up or down vote. The Main Committee was paralyzed for this entire time, while this momentous point was decided in a lop-sided little "working group" rather than being decided by the entire body. Evidently "consensus," the unanimous agreement of all nations, was not the goal of the organizers.

More blatant, more serious and more successful were the tactics adopted in Beijing. Almost 30% of the outrageous document had been bracketed at the Prep Com, and it was unthinkable that it should all be negotiated in the 10 days allowed to finish it up and approve it. It was therefore rushed through, breaking the Main Committee up into many little "working groups" which met in hallways, without translation, and frequently the delegates were not even told where or when they would be held. As records were not being properly kept in these hallways, many instances of brow-beating and rudeness were experienced, while the text was pretty well dictated by the US and the European Union and the "chairwomen" chosen by the UN.

One European Union delegate described it perfectly when she said: "Last year at Cairo we took a back seat, but this year we are advancing with our knives out." The document was rushed through, frequently separating the delegates into smaller and smaller working groups, where they were rushed through the paragraphs, with no translation. The chairwomen were inexorable and would take up the points again in other groups if they didn't succeed in getting their points through, or would not take them up again if they did.

In this way, for example, parental rights, which had qualified 17 paragraphs on children's health in the Cairo document, was battled over for 4 days, and in the end pushed through with wording which left the actual words Parental Rights in, but effectively overshadowed by the "confidentiality and privacy" of the children. A definite loss over Cairo.

It is very important to note that 46 countries took "reservations" to this and other paragraphs on the closing day, which demonstrates a far cry from "consensus." But the document is what stands, the reservations have no binding status. The work of the International Agencies, and the financial Aid will be given in accordance with the "guidelines," the document, that the "whole world" agreed to.

Consensus
It is important to understand what has happened to the concept of the system used by the UN that is called "the system of consensus." This means that any word, phrase or terminology which is not satisfactory to one of the member states, is placed in brackets, and later negotiations are held until an alternative is found which suits everyone. It is

not a majority rule, but one which is supposed to respect the sovereignty of every country.

At the Earth Summit, in Rio, when the Holy See and a few other countries, notably Argentina, blocked some of the phrasing that the Europeans wanted to push through, the Prime Minister of Norway, Gro Harlem Brundtland, said ominously something to the effect that: "the UN will have to abandon the system of Consensus, as the slower countries are impeding the advance of all the rest." And they *have changed it*. But they never took a vote on that decision, and never announced it. We have simply seen it in action.

Procedures

The procedures used by the UN proved, as we know, highly arbitrary in the sense that when working groups were chosen, they were always heavily weighted in favour of the document, and their chairmen were always chosen by the Secretariat (invariably veteran members of IPPF), but during the discussion of "Fertility Regulation" this was taken to unacceptable lengths. That the working group remained stuck nearly 3 days, that the conditions in there were so uncomfortable and that abusive language was used toward the young women who defended their countries' position, was inexcusable....

It is possible to promote the ideology of sexual permissiveness through the UN because of its structure. The fact that the peoples of the many nations represented there are not consulted in any way, or even properly informed of the content of the documents, means that it is contrary to all democratic ideals. The individuals who represent each country have no accountability to the voters; they are appointees. Perhaps one of the most dangerous factors is that the usage allows that each Conference is to "Build on" the others, and *never* "go back." This actually means that those who control these conferences make sure that their ideological gains can never more be put to discussion. The points that they fail to win, however, are discussed at each meeting until they are won. It is a grossly unfair incremental method which works inexorably to their advantage....

After these conferences there is a final document, with "commitments," a "plan of action," "strategies for implementation," "task forces," (4 special task forces are already funded to enforce "mainstreaming the gender perspective"), a call to national governments to enact policy in accord with said documents, and require permanent funding for such "task forces" and other monitoring and implementing agencies. Taken altogether, this forms an overall family policy, promoted and supported with massive funding both by the UN and so-called NGO's which are mostly government funded.

The Imposition of Foreign Ideologies

In order to understand fully how this revered body actually functions, it is important to recall the words of Gunnar and Alva Myrdal, so important to the founding of the UN, and particularly to setting up the social policies which continue to this day. These Swedish socialists of the 30's and 40's and 50's were the champions and organizers of the "Swedish model" of free love and sex education which was exported unfortunately very successfully through many ways, but particularly enshrined as the social spirit of the UN where Alva Myrdal set up and reigned over the social policy for many years. On Population Control, economist

Gunnar Myrdal said: "the population question could be transformed into the most effective argument for a thorough and radical socialist remodeling of society." On the destruction of the Family, was Alva Myrdal's argument that the achievement of *gender equality* required the conscious dismantling of remaining traditional homes, through law and policy, and even coercion, to "eliminate" women's traditional roles.

As Michael Schwartz has so correctly summarized, "The 3rd Conference on Population and Development in Cairo would set the targets of birth-rate reduction and legalized abortion for the whole world. The world Summit on Social Development in Copenhagen would build the funding mechanism for carrying out the plan. And the 4th International Conference on the Status of Women in Beijing would be the great triumph of world feminism that would overturn established customs and institutions and replace them with the social vision of Bella Abzug."

However, at Cairo the insubordinate countries were able to de-rail a number of points which were of basic importance to the successors of these Swedish socialists. These were the points relating to the destruction of the family, which is so vital for a total reorganization of society, and so intensely desired by the UN bureaucracy and perhaps even by those who fund it....

Coercion in population policy is not only at the level of the World Bank. It appears to be United States policy. The National Security Study Memo 200 (NSSM 200) which was the response to the reluctance of many nations to adopt the proposals of the North regarding population control, details the perceived threat to US interests by the superior increase of other populations and their competition for resources, and so on, and states:

> "It is vital that the effort to develop and strengthen a commitment on the part of LDC leaders not be seen by them as an industrialized country policy to keep their strength down or to reserve resources for use by the 'rich' countries." "The US can help to minimize charges of an imperialist motivation behind its support of population activities by repeatedly asserting that such support derives from a concern with (a) the right of the individual to determine freely and responsibly their number and spacing of children... and (b) the fundamental social and economic development of poor countries...."

This same memorandum suggested that US officials "collaborate with other interested donor countries and organizations (e.g. WHO, UNFPA, World Bank, UNICEF)" in other activities which could include family planning. It particularly stressed the impact that could be made by the World Bank:

> "With greater commitment of Bank resources and improved consultation with AID and UNFPA, a much greater dent could be made on the overall problem."

The imposition of unpopular population policies on developing countries is more than a blatant violation of the principle of national sovereignty. Because of the extraordinary costs associated with supervision, these actions significantly increase the cost of development in general, add to the debt burden—which debt is to be paid by increasingly smaller generations—and thereby hinder still more the economic advancement of borrower countries....

Positions of Other Countries

The most vocal countries opposing these terms and concepts of ICPD document were: Argentina, Venezuela, Guatemala, Nicaragua, Morocco, Ecuador, Chile, Honduras, Benin, Malta, Iran, and several African nations.

Opposed, but less vocal were: Cameroon, Ivory Coast, Togo, Senegal, Lithuania, Mali, Algeria, Zaire, Croatia, Niger, Jordan, and all the other Moslem countries.

Countries vigorously upholding the US position were: Canada, Australia, New Zealand, Bolivia and Peru (until discovered by their respective governments during Prep Com III), Caricom, Bangladesh, Scandinavia, Mexico and Europe.

El Salvador and Brazil supported the US position in defiance of their own legislation.

World Wide Rejection of the Cairo and Beijing Documents

The degree to which women all over the world repudiate the contents of these 2 documents is illustrated by the work of 2 housewives. They collected in the space of six months, the notarized adherence of women's organizations from all over the world and representing a total of somewhere in the vicinity of 55 million women, to reject the main tenets of the documents. These notarized statements are at the disposal of this committee if desired.

POSTSCRIPT

Are UN-Sponsored World Conferences Beneficial?

The debate between Wirth and Vollmer highlights several important matters. The first is the growing trend toward global governance. The World Trade Organization (WTO) can, for example, make rulings that are binding on member countries whatever their national laws and regulations may be. Although world conferences do not make law, the concern that they are part of the process that can lead to international law is evident in Vollmer's charge that the conferences are trying to impose their will on countries. For more on international law, consult Jonathan I. Charney, "Universal International Law," *American Journal of International Law* (1993).

Concern about world conferences has to do with both democracy and sovereignty. For background, read Jens Bartelson, *The Genealogy of Sovereignty* (Cambridge University Press, 1995). The delegates to the official world conferences are appointed by national governments; the delegates and organizations that attend the parallel conferences are usually self-selected. But do these delegates, official and unofficial, represent the voice of, say, women at Cairo or Beijing? Vollmer thinks not.

It is also the case that national sovereignty is diminished to the degree that organizations such as the WTO can make authoritative rules or that conferences can impose their values on others. Vollmer is clearly worried that this is the case, and that concern touches on many other activities of IGOs. Some people, for example, see the rise in UN military activities as a threat to national sovereignty. Because the John Birch Society and some other right-wing fringe groups stress this issue, it is easy to write off the concern as paranoid ranting. That would not be accurate, however, because, in fact, many scholars view (and some welcome) the rapid growth of IGOs, of multilateral treaties, and other global processes as evidence that sovereignty as an absolute is being slowly eroded. All of this also touches on the value and future of nationalism.

None of this means, however, that the diminution of sovereignty, much less the specific work of the conferences, is not worthwhile. There are many observers who argue that the world cannot address common problems unless there is less policy "freelancing" by countries and more authoritative rule-making by IGOs. Many would also contend that the specific conduct and resolutions of world conferences allow voices to be heard that are often muted at the national level. Many women might reject the idea that the conferences at Cairo and Beijing were undemocratic and contend, instead, that they provided a chance for women to break free of the policies imposed on them by largely male-dominated national governments. More on this topic is available in Rebecca Cook, ed., *Human Rights of Women: National and International Perspectives* (University of Pennsylvania Press, 1994); Francine D'Amico and Peter Beckman, eds., *Women and World Politics* (Bergin & Garvey, 1995); and Martha Alter Chen, "Engendering World Conferences: The International Women's Movement and the United Nations," *Third World Quarterly* (1995).

ISSUE 16

Is Nationalism Destructive?

YES: John Keane, from "Nations, Nationalism and Citizens in Europe," *International Social Science Journal* (June 1994)

NO: Salvador Cardús and Joan Estruch, from "Politically Correct Anti-Nationalism," *International Social Science Journal* (June 1995)

ISSUE SUMMARY

YES: John Keane, director of the Centre for the Study of Democracy, condemns nationalism as a destructive force that makes people self-absorbed, gives them a false sense of being invincible, and too often leads them to attack others.

NO: Professors of sociology Salvador Cardús and Joan Estruch contend that those who condemn nationalism either do not understand it or approach the subject with an antinationalist bias.

Nationalism is perhaps the most powerful political idea in the world. It is, in essence, the connection between individuals and their country. To discuss nationalism adequately, it is necessary to understand three terms: *nation, state,* and *sovereignty.* A nation is a group of people who have some level of ethnic, religious, or other common characteristics, which makes them identify with one another and perceive themselves as different from others, and which urges them to govern themselves. This third characteristic leads to the state, also known as a country. A state is a sovereign political organization that governs territory. Americans are a nation; the United States is a state. The word *sovereignty* is important because it means that a state does not answer to any higher authority. Nationalism is the emotion that connects nation and state, creating the bond that holds individual members of a nation together to offer their primary loyalty (patriotism) to the nation and its state.

Nationalism has had many beneficial influences. One is that it has encouraged self-determination. Empires, where one people controlled others, were considered legitimate until not too long ago. That is no longer so. The twentieth century alone has seen the demise of, among others, the Ottoman, Austro-Hungarian, British, French, and, in 1991, the Russian Empires. Just 50 years ago, most Africans and Asians were ruled by white colonial powers; nationalism helped end that dominance. Nationalism has also created national strength. When World War II began, it would have been reasonable to predict that the Germans would defeat the British. Part of what saved Great Britain, however, was the strength of the British national spirit. "We shall defend every village, every town, every city," proclaimed Prime Minister Winston Churchill, echoing the nationalist sentiment of the British people.

There are also negative aspects of nationalism. One is that nationalism stresses differences. Nationalism is the chief ingredient in distinguishing "we" from "they." Therefore, it helps determine who is and is not in our zone of responsibility. Most developed countries spend huge amounts to support the welfare of their less fortunate citizens, while they spend a relative pittance to help poor people in less developed countries. Nationalism can also lead to discrimination, even hatred and oppression.

Another problem with nationalism is that the concept of the nation-state is more of an ideal than a reality. There are a few places that come close to the ideal. For example, people who live in the United States are Americans; most Americans live in the United States. But it is more common for states to contain more than one nation, for nations to overlap borders into two or more states, or even for nations to have no state of their own at all. In such cases, there is often instability and warfare as nations seek to establish a state of their own.

This urge for nations to have their own states brings up the issue of how much the world community should support self-determination. In the abstract, it is very difficult not to support self-determination. The idea dates back to the mid-1700s and the idea of popular sovereignty. This concept rejected the theory of the divine right of kings to hold power and to control, even own, the people within their realms. The theory of popular sovereignty rests on the idea that people should be free from outside control.

Yet, in the real world, self-determination has troubling consequences. If we can support the right of a Bosnia dominated by Muslims to secede from Yugoslavia, how can we deny the right of Bosnian Serbs to secede from Bosnia? And if there were other minorities in the Bosnian Serb territory, should they be allowed to secede in turn and establish their own country? In addition to the violence, the unhindered path of self-determination can lead to tiny political units, called microstates, which have neither a solid economic base nor any ability to defend themselves.

It is also possible to argue that nationalism prevents the world from cooperating to solve its common problems. Nationalism is what makes many Americans insist that U.S. soldiers only serve under U.S. commanders. If all countries took a similar stance, there could be no United Nations peacekeeping forces. The following two selections focus on Europe and the interplay between nationalism and the European Union. John Keane believes that nationalism is poisonous and that a new European citizenry will prove the best antidote yet. Salvador Cardús and Joan Estruch believe that nationalism plays a positive role and that we cannot hope for a stable future in a postnationalist Europe.

YES
John Keane

NATIONS, NATIONALISM AND CITIZENS IN EUROPE

EARLY MODERN ORIGINS

What is a nation? Do nations have a right to self-determination? If so, does that mean that the national identity of citizens is best guaranteed by a system of democratic government, in which power is subject to open disputation and to the consent of the governed living within a carefully defined territory? And what of nationalism? Does it differ from national identity? Is it compatible with democracy? If not, can its growth be prevented, or at least controlled, so as to guarantee the survival or growth of democracy?

These questions, pressingly familiar in contemporary politics although strangely neglected in contemporary political theory, have their roots in early modern Europe. With the decline of the Carolingian Empire [751–987], a new sense of collective identity, national awareness, began to emerge as a powerful social force. This process of nation-building was championed initially by sections of the nobility and the clergy, who used derivatives of the old Latin term *natio* to highlight their dependence upon a common language and common historical experiences. The nation' did not refer to the whole population of a region, but only to those classes which had developed a sense of identity based upon language and history and had begun to act upon it. Nations in this sense were seen as distinctive products of their own peculiar histories.

From the fifteenth century onwards, the term 'nation' was employed increasingly for political purposes.... Here 'nation' described a people who shared certain common laws and political institutions of a given territory. This political conception of 'the nation' defined and included the *societas civilis*—those citizens who were entitled to participate in politics and to share in the exercise of sovereignty—and it had fundamental implications for the process of state-building. Struggles for participation in the state assumed the form of confrontations between the monarch and the privileged classes, which were often organized in a parliament. These classes frequently designated themselves as advocates of 'the nation' in the political sense of the term. They insisted, in opposition to their monarch, that they were the representatives and defenders of 'national liberties' and 'national rights'. If the sovereign monarch came from a different nation—as in the Netherlands during the war against Habsburg Spain—then such claims were sharpened by another dimension: the struggle for privileged liberties was transformed into a movement for national emancipation from foreign tyranny.

During the eighteenth century, the struggle for national identity was broadened and deepened to include the non-privileged classes. Self-educated middle classes, artisans, rural and urban labourers, and other social groups demanded inclusion in 'the nation', and this necessarily had anti-aristocratic and anti-monarchic implications. From hereon, in principle, the nation included everybody, not just the privileged classes; 'the people' and 'the nation' were supposed to be identical. Thomas Paine's *Rights of Man* (1791–2) was the most influential European attempt to 'democratize' the theory of national identity....

[Paine] concluded that the struggle for representative government—for periodic elections, fixed-term legislatures, a universal franchise, and freedom of assembly, the press and other civil liberties —required recognition of the right of each nation to determine its own destiny. 'What is government more than the management of the affairs of a nation?', he asked. 'It is not', he answered. 'Sovereignty as a matter of right, appertains to the nation only, and not to any individual; and a nation has at all times an inherent indefeasible right to abolish any form of government it finds inconvenient, and establish such as accords with its interest, disposition, and happiness'.

Paine's thesis that the nation and democratic government constitute an indivisible unity subsequently enjoyed a long and healthy life. Nineteenth-century Europe saw, for example, the emergence of two great powers (Germany and Italy) based on the principle of national self-determination.... During our own century, especially after the First World War, the principle of 'the right to national self-determination' enjoyed considerable popularity among international lawyers, political philosophers, governments and their opponents, who supposed that if the individual members of a nation so will it, they are entitled to freedom from domination by other nations, and can therefore legitimately establish a sovereign state covering the territory in which they live, and where they constitute a majority of the population.

From this perspective, the principle that citizens should govern themselves was identified with the principle that nations should determine their own destiny, and this in turn produced a convergence of meaning of the terms 'state' and 'nation'. 'State' and 'nation' came to be used interchangeably, as in such official expressions as 'League of Nations', the 'law of nations' or 'nation-state', and in the commonplace English language usage of the term 'national' to designate anything run or regulated by the state, such as national service, national health insurance or national debt. Such expressions reinforce the assumption, traceable to the eighteenth century, that there is no other way of defining the word nation than as a territorial aggregate whose various parts recognize the authority of the same state, an assumption captured in [the] famous definition of a nation as 'a people who have hold of a state'.

The principle that nations should be represented within a territorially defined state echoes into our times. In the European region—to mention [one] example—... [t]he same powerful dynamic worked to secure the collapse of the Soviet Empire. The Soviet Union was an empire comprising a diversity of nationalities all subject to the political dominance of a Russian-dominated Communist party that ensured for seven decades that the federal units of the Union had no meaningful political autonomy and that demands for 'national communism' would trigger a political crackdown backed if necessary by military force....

NATIONAL IDENTITY AND CITIZENSHIP

The collapse of the Soviet Empire under pressure from struggles for national self-determination adds weight to the thesis that a shared sense of national identity ... is a basic precondition of the creation and strengthening of citizenship and democracy. Understood in ideal-typical terms, national identity is a particular form of collective identity in which, despite their routine lack of physical contact, people consider themselves bound together because they speak a language or a dialect of a common language; inhabit or are closely familiar with a defined territory, and experience its ecosystem with some affection; and because they share a variety of customs, including a measure of memories of the historical past, which is consequently experienced in the present tense as pride in the nation's achievements and, where necessary, an obligation to feel ashamed of the nation's failing.

National identity so defined is a specifically modern European invention and its political importance is that it infuses citizens with a sense of purposefulness, confidence and dignity by encouraging them to feel 'at home'.... That familiarity in turn endows each individual with a measure of confidence to speak and to act. Consequently, whatever is strange is not automatically feared; whatever diversity exists within the nation is more or less accepted as one of its constitutive features....

Whenever they are denied access to a shared sense of nationhood citizens tend to experience the world as unfriendly and alien—in the extreme case of enforced exile they experience the nasty, gnawing and self-pitying and self-destructive *Hauptweh*.... This renders them less capable of living democratically. After all, democratic regimes are the most demanding of political systems. In contrast to all forms of heteronomous government, democracy comprises procedures for arriving at collective decisions through public controversies and compromises based on the fullest possible and qualitatively best participation of interested parties. At a minimum, democratic procedures include equal universal adult suffrage within constituencies of various scope and size; majority rule and guarantees of minority rights, which ensure that collective decisions are approved by a substantial number of those expected to make them; freedom from arbitrary arrest and respect for the rule of law among citizens and their representatives; constitutional guarantees of freedom of assembly and expression and other civil and political liberties, which help ensure that those expected to decide or to elect those who decide can choose among real alternatives, and various social policies (in fields such as health, education, child care and basic income provision) which prevent market exchanges from becoming dominant and thereby ensure that citizens can live as free equals by enjoying their basic political and civil entitlements. Expressed differently, democracy requires the institutional division between a certain form of state and civil society. A democracy is an openly structured system of institutions which facilitate the flexible control of the exercise of power. It is a multilayered political and social mosaic in which political decision-makers at the local, regional, national and supra-national levels are assigned the job of serving [the public], while, for their part, citizens living within the nooks and crannies of civil society are obliged to exercise vigilance in preventing each other and their rulers from abusing their powers and violating the spirit of the commonwealth.

Although democracy in this sense does not require citizens to play the role of full-time political animals—too much democracy can kill off democracy—it is always difficult to generate or to sustain its momentum. That task is rendered even more arduous in contexts lacking traditions which are home to the virtues of democratic citizenship: prudence, common sense, self-reliance, courage, sensitivity to power, the knack of making and defending judgements in public, the ability to (self-) criticize and to accept criticism from others in turn, and the capacity to join with others in dignity and solidarity to resist the enervating miasma of fear. The last-mentioned quality is especially important in the democratic transformation of despotic regimes, when fear of power corrupts those who are subject to it and fear of losing power corrupts those who exercise it.

Shaking off fear is always a basic condition of democracy and it is normally assisted by citizens' shared sense of belonging to one or more ethical identities, national identity being among the most potent of these. Fearlessness is not a naturally occurring substance. It is a form of courage or 'grace under pressure' (Aung San Suu Kyi) developed wherever victims of political lies and bullying and violence make a personal effort to throw off personal corruption and to draw on their inner and outer resources to nurture the habit of refusing to let fear dictate their actions. Grace under pressure normally precedes and underpins attempts to institutionalize democracy. To be effective, it must be practised in small daily acts of resistance that in turn feed upon citizens' sense that they speak a common language and share a natural habitat and a variety of customs and historical experiences....

THE RISE OF NATIONALISM

The preceding analysis appears to confirm the eighteenth-century doctrine of national self-determination. It implies that Paine and others were correct in thinking that the defence of 'the nation' and the struggle for democracy against political despotism are identical, that when the winds of national feeling blow, the people, like beautiful birds, grow wings and fly their way to a land of independence. And yet the experience of the French Revolution, which inspired Paine's *Rights of Man*, casts doubt upon any such conclusion.... The Revolution destroyed forever the faith in the divine and unchallengeable right of monarchs to govern and it sparked a struggle against the privileged classes in the name of a sovereign nation of free and equal individuals. Those acting in the name of the sovereign nation were ever more tempted to emphasize faithfulness to *la patrie*, that is, citizens' obligations to their state, itself the guarantor of the nation, itself said to be 'one and indivisible'. The motto of the *ancien régime*, 'Un roi, une foi, une loi' ('One king, one faith, one law') was replaced by 'La Nation, la loi, le roi' ('The Nation, the law, the king'). Thenceforward the Nation made the law which the king was responsible for implementing. And when the monarchy was abolished in August 1792, the Nation became the titular source of sovereignty. 'Vive la Nation!' cried the French soldiers one month later at Valmy, as they flung themselves into battle against the Prussian army. Everything which had been royal had now become national. The nation even had its own emblem, the tricoloured national flag, which replaced the white flag of the house of Bourbon. The new spirit of *nationalism* had surfaced, bringing with it a lust for the power and glory of the nation-state which finally overwhelmed the democratic potential of the revolution. The first nationalist dictatorship of the modern world was born.

The formation of a despotic regime sustained by nationalist appeals to the nation was an utterly novel development—Europe's Greek gift to itself and to the rest of the world. Since that time, and despite its extraordinary global impact, the eighteenth-century doctrine of national self-determination has been subject to a smouldering crisis, whose contemporary resolution necessitates both a fundamental rethinking of that doctrine, a more complex understanding of the relationship between national identity and nationalism, and greater clarity about the nature of democratic procedures.

... Democratic procedures tend to maximize the level of reversibility or 'biodegradability' of decision-making. They invite dispute and encourage public dissatisfaction with currently existing conditions, even from time to time stirring up citizens to anger and direct action....

In fully democratic systems, by contrast, everything is in perpetual motion. Endowed with liberties to criticize and to transform the distribution of power within state and civil institutions, citizens are catapulted into a state of permanent unease which they can cope with, grumble about, turn their backs on, but never fully escape. The unity of purpose and sense of community of pre-democratic societies snaps. There is difference, openness and constant competition among a plurality of power groups to produce and to control the definition of reality. Hence there are public scandals which unfold when publics learn about events which had been kept secret because if they had been made public ahead of time they could not have been carried out without public outcries. Under democratic conditions the world feels as if it is gripped by capaciousness and uncertainty about who does and should govern. Existing relations of power are treated (and understood) as contingent, as lacking transcendental guarantees of absolute certainty and hierarchical order, as a product of institutionally situated actors exercising power within and over their respective milieux.

It is this self-questioning, self-destabilizing quality of democratic regimes which not only provides opportunities for the advocates of national identity to take their case to a wider public. It also increases the magnetism of anti-democratic ideologies such as nationalism. Democratic conditions can severely test citizens' shared sense of the unreal-ity of reality and chronic instability of their regimes, to the point where they may crave for the restoration of certainty about 'reality' by suppressing diversity, complexity and openness within and between the state and civil society. Democracies never reach a point of homeostatic equilibrium. They are dogged permanently by public disagreements about means and ends, by uncertainties, confusions and gaps within political programmes, and by hidden and open conflicts, and all this makes them prey to... morbid attempts to simplify matters, to put a stop to pluralism and to foist unity and order onto everybody and everything.

The events of the French Revolution revealed this dynamic for the first time, confirming the rule that whenever believers in a nation assemble they risk being seduced by the language and power fantasies of nationalism. The distinction between national identity and nationalism —overlooked by many commentaries on the subject... is fundamental in this context. Nationalism is the child of democratic pluralism, both in the sense that the existence of open state institutions and a minimum of civil liberties enables nationalists to organize and to propagate their nationalism, and also in the less obvious sense that democracy breeds insecurity about power and sometimes fear and panic and, hence, the yearning of some citizens to take refuge in sealed forms of life.

In the European region, nationalism is at present among the most virile and magnetic of these closed systems of life, or what I prefer to call ideologies. Like other ideologies, nationalism is an upwardly mobile, power hungry and potentially dominating form of language game which makes falsely universal claims. It supposes that it is part of the natural order of things and that the nation is a biological fact, all the while hiding its own particularity by masking its own conditions of production and by attempting to stifle the plurality of non-national and sub-national language games within the established civil society and state in which it thrives.

Nationalism is a scavenger. It feeds upon the pre-existing sense of nationhood within a given territory, transforming that shared national identity into a bizarre parody of its former self. Nationalism is a pathological form of national identity which tends... to destroy its heterogeneity by squeezing the nation into the Nation. Nationalism also takes advantage of any democratizing trends by roaming hungrily through civil society and the state, harassing other particular language games, viewing them as competitors and enemies to be banished or terrorized, injured or eaten alive, pretending all the while that it is a universal language game whose validity is publicly unquestionable, and which therefore views itself as freed from the contingencies of historical time and space.

Nationalism has a fanatical core. Its boundaries are dotted with border posts and border police charged with the task of monitoring the domestic and foreign enemies of the nation. In contrast to national identity, whose boundaries are not fixed and whose tolerance of difference and openness to other forms of life is qualitatively greater, nationalism requires its adherents to believe in themselves and to believe in the belief itself, to believe that they are not alone, that they are members of a community of believers known as the nation, through which they can achieve immortality.... This level of ideological commitment ensures that nationalism is driven by a bovine will to simplify things—by the kind of instruction issued by [Chancellor Otto von] Bismarck [1862–1890]: 'Germans! Think with your blood!'

If democracy is a continuous struggle against simplification of the world, then nationalism is a continuous struggle to undo complexity, a will not to know certain matters, a chosen ignorance, not the ignorance of innocence. It thereby has a tendency to crash into the world, crushing or throttling everything that crosses its path, to defend or to claim territory, and to think of land as power and its native inhabitants as a 'single fist'.... Nationalism has nothing of the humility of national identity. It feels no shame about the past or the present, for it supposes that only foreigners and 'enemies of the nation' are guilty. It revels in macho glory and fills the national memory with stories of noble ancestors, heroism and bravery in defeat. It feels itself invincible, waves the flag and, if necessary, eagerly bloodies its hands on its enemies.

At the heart of nationalism—and among the most peculiar features of its 'grammar'—is its simultaneous treatment of the 'Other' as everything and nothing. Nationalists warn of the menace to their own way of life by the growing presence of aliens. The Other is seen as the knife in the throat of the nation. Nationalists are panicky and driven by friend–foe calculations, suffering from a judgment disorder that convinces them that the 'other nation' lives at its own expense. Nationalists are driven by the feeling that all nations are caught up in an animal struggle for survival, and that only the fittest survive.... Croatian nationalists [for example] denounce Serbians as... butchers who murder their victims and mutilate their bodies; Serbian nationalists reciprocate by denouncing Croats as ... fascists who are hellbent on eliminating the Serbian nation. Both curse Muslims as foreign invaders of a land in which they have in fact lived for five centuries.

Yet nationalism is not only fearful of the other. It is also arrogant, confidently portraying the Other as inferior rubbish, as a worthless zero. The Other is seen as unworthy of respect or recognition because its smelly breath, strange food, unhygienic habits, loud and off-beat music, and incomprehensible babbling language places it outside and beneath us. It follows that the Other has few if any entitlements, not even when it constitutes a majority or minority of the population resident in the vicinity of our nation. Wherever a member of the nation is, there is the nation. It is true ... that nationalism can be more or less militant.... Yet despite such variations nationalists suffer from a single-minded arrogance. This leads them to [discriminate against and persecute] the Other... or even, in the extreme case, to press for the expulsion of the Other for the purpose of creating a homogeneous territorial nation....

NATIONAL SELF-DETERMINATION?

... As I see it, there is an urgent need to stretch the limits of the contemporary sociological and democratic imagination, to think differently about the intertwined problems of nationalism, national identity and democracy, and to consider how the limits of democracy can be overcome in practice by inventing new democratic methods of preventing the growth of democracy's own poisonous fruits.

Solving the problem of nationalism by democratic means is possible, but not easy. The thesis presented here is that since democratic mechanisms facilitate the transformation of national identity into nationalism, democracy is best served by abandoning the doctrine of national self-determination and regarding a shared sense of national identity as a legitimate but *limited* form of life. This thesis contains a paradoxical corollary: national identity, an important support of democratic institutions, is best preserved by restricting its scope in favour of *non-national* identities that reduce the probability of its transformation into anti-democratic nationalism.

In the European context it is now possible to envisage, by means of this thesis, a cluster of four interdependent mechanisms which together can curb the force of nationalism and at the same time guarantee citizens' access to their respective national identities:

1. The first of these remedies is to de-centre the institutions of the nation-state through the development of interlocking networks of democratically accountable sub-national and supra-national state institutions. Their combined effect, if rendered accountable to their citizens, would be to improve the effectiveness and legitimacy of state institutions and, more pertinently, to complicate the lines of political power, thereby reducing the room for manoeuvre of single nation-states and frustrating the nationalist fantasy of securing nations through strong, sovereign states that are prepared in principle to launch war on their neighbours or to crush their domestic opponents in the name of national preservation or salvation.

In effect, this remedy involves renewing—but at the same time democratizing—the more complex patterns of political power typical of the late mediaeval and early modern periods. The modern process of European state-building entailed the eclipse of numerous units of power —free cities, principalities, provinces, estates, manors, and deliberative assemblies—such that the 500 or so political units that dotted the region in 1500 were reduced to around 25 units in 1900. There are now signs of a reversal of this process of building centralized state institutions. One symptom of this 'scattering' of political power is the renewed interest in local government as a flexible forum for conducting local politics and competently administering local policies, partly in response to the declining effectiveness of macroeconomic management and the retreat of the national welfare state in western Europe.

The same decentring of the nation state 'downwards and sideways' is evident in the vigorous development of regional ideas and regional power in areas such as Catalonia, Wallonia, Emilia-Romagna, Andalucia, Scotland and the Basque region....

Finally, the trend towards a *Europe des régions* has been supplemented by the accelerating growth of supra-national political institutions such as the European Parliament, the Council of Europe, and the European Court of Justice....

... From standards of central heating and housing to the purity of beer and wine, the cleanliness of beaches and the conditions of women's employment, the populations of the EU are increasingly touched and shaped by European political integration. This process arguably hastens the decline of nation-state sovereignty and facilitates the birth of a post-national Europe, in the sense that it adds to the pressure on nationalist movements, parties, governments and leaders to recognize the fact and legitimacy of countervailing political powers, even in such sensitive matters as 'national economic policy' and the resolution of so-called 'national conflicts'.

2. The formulation and application of internationally recognized legal guarantees of national identity is a vital adjunct of the breaking down of the sovereignty of the nation-state. Such formal guarantees were pioneered in the four Geneva Conventions commencing in 1929 and expressed forcefully in the Universal Declaration of the Rights of Man ratified by the United Nations in December 1948: 'Everyone is entitled to the rights and freedoms set forth in this declaration, without distinction of any kind such as race, colour, sex, language, religion, political or other opinions, *national* or social *origin*, property, birth, or other status' (emphasis added).

... [An] EC report [on the Balkans] co-ordinated by the former French Justice Minister and President of France's Constitutional Court, Robert Badinter, ... has far-reaching implications for the subject of nationhood, nationalism and democracy. It supposes that governments have a primary obligation to respect the wishes of their populations, but it does not fall back on the old premise that each nation requires a sovereign state covering the territory in which it lives.... The Badinter report spots a murderous difficulty lurking in this early modern doctrine of national self-determination: if the political boundaries of the earth are to be fixed by the criterion of nationhood then, since nations do not see eye to eye ... and do not live in discrete geographic entities, then there will be no end to boundary disputes.... The report correctly understands that in the European context civil wars sparked off by nationalist pressures, rather than war between homogeneous nation-states, have become the major threat to regional stability.

The Badinter report also reminds Europeans of the increasingly multinational character of their states. Of course, most European states have always been multinational, but recently that fact has been accentuated by large-scale migrations. The permanent entry into western Europe of more than 15 million non-EU people during the past half-century has ensured that mononational states no longer exist, and that even the oldest and most culturally 'homogeneous' of civil societies in countries or regions such as Spain, England, Portugal, France and Germany are now vertical mosaics of nationalities which do not humbly accept their position as satellites of the currently dominant national identity. The report challenges the early modern assumption that national loyalties are exclusive, and that democracy is therefore only possible in a nationally homogeneous state.

The report calls instead for a new compromise between nations *within* states. It sees that the peaceful and democratic functioning of European states and societies necessitates reliance upon supranational monitoring and enforcement mechanisms and it urges recognition of the new principle that the various nations of any single state are entitled to their nationhood, and thus to live differently, as free equals. The Badinter report 'de-politicizes' and 'de-territorializes' national identity.... It sees national identity as a *civil* entitlement of citizens, the squeezing or attempted abolition of which, even when ostensibly pursued by states in the name either of higher forms of human solidarity or of protecting the 'core national identity' ..., serves only to trigger off resentment, hatred and violence among national groupings.

3. Of equal importance as a guarantor of national identity and democracy against nationalism is a factor that has been barely discussed in the literature on the subject: the development of a pluralist mosaic of identities within civil society. This third antidote to nationalism is as effective as it is paradoxical. It presumes that the survival and flourishing of national identity is only possible within a self-organizing civil society, which, however, provides spaces for citizens to act upon *other* chosen or inherited identities, thus *limiting* the probable role of national identity in the overall operation of state and civil institutions and political parties, communications media and other intermediary bodies. The paradox bears a striking parallel to the question of religious tolerance: the practice of a particular religion in a multi-religious society requires—if bigotry and bloodshed is to be avoided—the principle of freedom of religious worship, which in practice entails recognition of the legitimacy of *other* religions and, hence, the need for secularism which simultaneously guarantees the freedom *not* to be religious. The same maxim ought to be carried over into matters of national identity, for it is clear that to model either state institutions or civil society solely on the principle of national identity means privileging one aspect of citizens' lives, devaluing others, and contradicting the pluralism so vital for a democratic civil society, thus rendering those citizens' lives nation-centred and one-dimensional and, thus, susceptible to the rise of nationalism....

4. Perhaps the most difficult to cultivate antidote to nationalism is the fostering of an *international* civil society in which citizens of various nationalities can inter-mingle, display at least a minimal sense of mutual understanding and respect, and generate a sense of solidarity, especially in times of crisis, for example during natural disasters, economic collapse or political upheaval.

* * *

During the second half of the eighteenth century, this friendship among citizens of various nations was called cosmopolitanism.... There was seen to be no contradiction between feeling oneself to be a citizen of the wider world ... and wanting to enlighten and to transform that little corner of the European world where one had been born or had been brought by destiny to live, work, love and to die. The phase of early modern cosmopolitanism soon declined.... With the French revolution the era of cosmopolitanism declined and into its place stepped nationalism, nation-state building and nation-state rivalry.... [S]lowly and surely the word *patriot* became charged with all the hatred and love of modern nationalism, while the word *cosmopolite* became the symbol of an ideal political unity that in practice could never be achieved.

A pressing theoretical and political question in today's Europe is whether a new form of the old cosmopolitanism is developing in tandem with the process of supra-national political integration in the west and the attempted dismantling of totalitarian regimes in parts of central-eastern Europe. Is the growth of an international civil society in Europe possible or actual?...

[Those who answer 'no' do] not take account of the growth of multinational states and societies and the trend towards the definition of the rights of *European* citizenship, available to all who live within the European Union region. It and when the Maastricht Treaty of Union is finally implemented, this trend will be greatly strengthened. Citizens of any state resident in another Member State will be entitled to vote and to stand for office at the levels of local government and the European Parliament. Citizens will enjoy the rights to information across frontiers, to petition the European Parliament, and to make use of a Parliamentary Ombudsman. And they will be entitled, when travelling abroad, to full diplomatic protection by any other EU Member State.

These projected entitlements provide further evidence that Europe—at least the Europe of the European Union—is witnessing the slow, unplanned, blind and painful birth of a new species of political animal, the European citizen.... The habitat of the new European citizen is an emerging international civil society of personal contacts... [that] take advantage of new communications technologies—fax machines, answerphones, satellite broadcasting—which break down the apparently 'natural' barriers of geographic distance and state borders, increase the physical and cultural mobility of people, and even simulate the possibility of being simultaneously in two or more places. The new European citizens intermingle across frontiers for various purposes without making a cult of national origins, national identity, and 'foreigners'. These citizens... value nests, such as national identity, in which citizens are warmed and nourished and gain confidence in themselves. Yet they also recognize otherness as a right and a duty for everybody. These new citizens maintain that in the contemporary world identity is more a matter of politics and choice than fate.... European citizens are late modern cosmopolitans.

No doubt the internationalization of civil society is destroyed by nationalism and genocidal war, as in south-central Europe.... These social exchanges among a plurality of citizens can also be squeezed or suffocated by the power of transnational corporations... seeking to co-ordinate their national markets, to trim and discipline their workforces, and to dominate European social life through profit-driven matrix management and marketing. It is also true that xenophobes and other anti-democratic forces are taking advantage of the new European habitat. Nevertheless the long-term growth of European-wide exchanges among citizens whose social and political views are predominantly pluralist and republican is among the most remarkable features of contemporary Europe.... [T]here is an underlying belief that not only Europe from the Atlantic to the Urals, but indeed the world beyond, should be a coat of many colours, a region marked by a precarious, non-violent yet permanently contested balance between governors and citizens.

... [M]ost often the formation of a European civil society is an undramatic, nearly invisible process that seems unworthy of the attention of journalists, intellectuals and policy-makers. It clearly requires detailed sociological investigation. For could it be that this new European citizenry, providing that it is not stillborn and that it is nurtured with adequate funding and legal and political guarantees, will prove to be the best antidote yet invented to the perils of nationalism and the poisonous fruits of democracy?

NO

Salvador Cardús and Joan Estruch

POLITICALLY CORRECT
ANTI-NATIONALISM

INTRODUCTION

The history of the social sciences provides us with many examples of the use of terms which have the appearance of being neutral, objective instruments of analysis, but which are in fact used, deliberately or not, as ideological weapons intended to discredit the opponent at the same time as they disguise one's own standpoint. At the present moment, discussions on the issue of *nationalism* very often provide a perfect example of this careless, inexact and, in short, sloppy use of a concept which, because of the way it is ideologically exploited, eventually loses its value as an analytically useful concept in understanding the reality it is intended to designate.

Analyses of nationalism coming from the social sciences have indeed been generally very closely linked to political circumstances, which have given the national factor a central role in the great events of history. In the course of the twentieth century these have included the end of two World Wars, the decolonization processes in the Third World and, more recently, with the collapse of the Soviet empire, the resurgence of territorial strife in the areas formerly under its domain.

Similarly, there are concepts such as self-determination which cannot be looked at from a strictly juridical point of view, but must be seen in the framework of the political contexts which give them their practical signification: the founding of the modern states of Germany and Italy in the last century, the break-up of the Austro-Hungarian Empire at the end of World War I and the achievement of independence by the former colonies after World War II, for example.

But although both the analyses and the concepts depend on the political circumstances in which they arise and are used, many people writing on the nationalist issue and on the process of self-determination nevertheless claim to be ideologically and politically neutral, when the ideas they express in fact make them out-and-out critics of nationalism.

NATIONALISM AND PREJUDICE

On the simplest level, even the terminology used to refer to nationalist issues hints at this anti-nationalist bias. While one widespread image associates nationalist movements with the slow but unstoppable movement of the tides, very often in speaking of nations words like *tribe* have been used and national feelings have been compared with religious phenomena in their supposedly most *irrational* aspect. None of this, of course, takes into account the fact that, as [one scholar] pointed out, 'A thing is never "irrational" in itself, but only from a particular "rational" *point of view*'.

Disregarding the 'particular point of view' of the speaker is what allows the authors of many analyses of nationalism to appear to leave their own political prejudices to one side, or even claim to have immunity from them. Thus, to quote just a few examples from relatively recent and in this sense quite explicit studies, we could turn to Eric Hobsbawm's historic work *Nations and Nationalism since 1780*. In the introduction, after saying that 'no serious historian of nations and nationalism can be a committed political nationalist', Hobsbawm goes on to make the following declaration of non-nationalist faith: 'Fortunately, in setting out to write the present book I have not needed to leave my non-historical convictions behind'.

In the same way, but from a sociological standpoint, Anthony Smith, in the introduction to his summary *National Identity*—it is very often in introductions that authors' intentions are most clearly revealed—makes no attempt to conceal the fact that the interest of his work lies in its contribution to the future disappearance of nationalism: 'The final chapter looks at the possibilities of a new "post-national" world, a world without nationalism and perhaps without nations', though he admits that 'this will probably be a slow and uncertain process'.

More recently,... John Keane, in 'Nations, nationalism and citizens of Europe', made no bones about his belief that the doctrine of self-determination was one with anti-democratic consequences, that a stand had to be taken in favour of a 'post-national' Europe and that it was important to avoid the danger of nationalism, which he railed against on the grounds that 'nationalism is a closed system', which is 'fanatical', 'xenophobic', 'an oversimplification', 'macho', 'arrogant', etc. The argument of the central pages of Keane's article can be summed up in the words of [Spanish analyst] Mario Vargas Llosa when he says, 'Nationalism is an ideology that raises borders, excludes the *other* and looks down on what is the other's', because, to sum up, 'one is a nationalist against the others'.

Are we to believe from these examples and from a host of others that could be given that these analyses are really made leaving to one side their authors' political prejudices? Are we to believe that only those who are favourably inclined towards the national rights of certain peoples are *prejudiced*, while those who are in the comfortable position of belonging to a nation formally recognized by other states are not *prejudiced* in considering the claims of the former a threat to the future of democracy?

'One is a nationalist against the others', writes Vargas Llosa. Nationalism, says the former national secretary of the French Socialist party, Gilles Martinet, in a recent book, *Le réveil* [awakening] *des nationalismes français*, is 'an affront to reason', precisely because 'it feeds on hatred, contempt and the fear of others'. On the other hand, opposing nationalism there is—continues the same author, in a deliciously moving confession—*patriotism*, which is what one tends to call *l'amour des siens'* [the love of one's own people]. In short, the issue lies in knowing who has a right to describe himself as a 'patriot' and who is condemned to being a miserable 'nationalist'.

EPISTEMOLOGICAL CRITICISM

The lack of objectivity in the supposedly anationalist, post-nationalist—or openly anti-nationalist—theories predominating in work on nationalism in the social sciences could be debated from a strictly epistemological standpoint. For one thing, there is nothing new to be said about the central role played by nation-state frameworks in establishing the conditions of scientific production. Thus, to speak of French, German or North-American sociology is not an oversimplification, but a reference to geographical and political contexts that have been a decisive factor in the approaches and viewpoints of those countries' scientific output. In the same way, it is very difficult to imagine that these political frames of reference carry no weight in the analysis of national issues itself. We could, for example, speak from personal experience of the difficulty of obtaining funds for academically ambitious university research into nationalism in Catalonia and, in general, in the *Països Catalans* [Catalan nationalists], simply because this is not one of the priorities of the scientific policy dictated by the Spanish Government....

At the same time, it is a well-known fact that the framework of different scientific theoretical traditions is inseparable from the political and historical circumstances in which they have developed, circumstances which, once again, and whether we like it or not, have national borders. Cultural, linguistic, conceptual and other references are inevitable, though not necessarily explicit, elements which, by not being recognized, spread confusion or naiveness in a supposedly analytical discourse. A memorable example of this is J. Stuart Mill's [1806–1873] classic, 'Of nationality, as connected with representative government' in *Considerations on Representative Government*, in which, having stated the general principle that 'it is in general a necessary condition of free institutions, that boundaries of governments should coincide in the main with those of nationalities', he soon succumbs to prejudice and goes on to say: 'Nobody can suppose that it is not more beneficial to a Breton, or a Basque of French Navarre, to be brought into the current of the ideas and feelings of a highly civilized and cultivated people—to be a member of the French nationality, admitted on equal terms to all the privileges of French citizenship, sharing the advantages of French protection, and the dignity and prestige of French power—than to sulk on his own rocks, the half-savage relic of past times, revolving in his own little mental orbit without participation or interest in the general movement of the world. The same remark applies to the Welshman or the Scottish Highlander, as members of the British nation'.

We could say, then, that the greatest weakness of certain analyses of nationalism is that, though supposedly neutral, their authors show themselves to be at heart profoundly anti-nationalist with regard to the emerging nations and, without actually saying so, profoundly nationalist with regard to those that have already acquired political status. Thus the militant anationalism of some social scientists implies a reified view of national constructs and becomes the ideal foundation for a political discourse legitimating existing nation-states, whose nationalism is never questioned.

NATIONALISM AND SOCIAL CONFLICT

Even more interesting would be a debate going beyond the strictly epistemological terrain to discuss the premises forming the point of departure for an analysis of nationalism.

First of all, any criticism of nationalism that presents it as a disintegrative force is gratuitous. The social sciences do not seem to be the field in which to establish what 'degree' of disintegration is historically and presently recommendable to legitimate the diversity of the political processes leading to the category of an independent state. Not only because some artificial groupings, especially in the territories formerly colonized by Europeans, have given rise to regions of permanent political instability, but because in view of the diversity of real cases in history it is impossible to establish a standard measure of political unity. And needless to say, it would be even more preposterous to try to impose it by anti-democratic means. And if there is no 'recommendable' measure for the state and no democratic method of imposing arbitrary borders, on what principle can a nationalist trend emerging within a larger state be described as 'disintegrative'? In any case, all that would disintegrate would be the unity of the state to which that nation belonged, a territorial integrity which does not correspond to any form of national homogeneity, but nothing more. Simi-

larly, it does not seem that the social sciences can sustain that a state's territorial integrity is any more 'sacred' than the right of nations to self-determination!

Secondly, in a world dominated by a geometric progression in economic, political, cultural and social interrelations, this horror of national disintegration smacks of hypocrisy, with little basis in the objective likelihood or chance of a break in these interrelations, especially if we are talking about the situation in Europe. In other words, why should anyone assume that a nation's self-determination must necessarily involve an increase in political isolation? Has anyone studied objectively whether this break with the exterior generally takes place, excepting, of course, those cases of isolation provisionally imposed by the international community itself, in anticipation of formal recognition of the process of self-determination? Or would it on the other hand be easy to show that the result of this 'disintegration', as soon as it receives international recognition, is an immediate increase of exchanges in all fields?

Thirdly, perhaps one of the greatest difficulties in analysing nationalism, over and above the political motivations of research carried out with a thinly disguised animosity towards these processes, is that of finding a single model for analysis. In fact, nationalist movements are shaped by historical circumstances so specific that one cannot help feeling that general models, abstract typologies, are completely useless. Nationalism can hardly be studied other than on the basis of knowledge—and recognition—of the particular historical circumstances of the territory concerned. In some cases it will be the language, in others race; sometimes there will have been a long history of struggle, in others rapid economic growth; often an important part will have been played by the awareness of a clearly delimited geographical territory, but also on occasions a scattered nation with no territory will be in search of a place to settle down; here we find a leader who channels an essentialist concept of the nation, there an intellectual spirit gives support to a voluntarist concept of the national issue; in another case the population will belong to a single culture, and on the other hand, the same situation can arise in a territory in which intense immigration has created an inextinguishable melting-pot of cultures.... Is it possible, then, to establish a single concept of nation which is of use from an analytical point of view, so as to study the issue on a global basis? Frankly, no. Any attempt to do so is unacceptably reductionist. In just the same way that nationalist movements spring from a defence of the right to diversity, no homogenizing instrument of analysis can help understand the political, cultural and social keys to nationalist issues.

BETWEEN THE LINES OF THEORIES OF NATIONALISM

The global criticism aimed exclusively at nationalism that expresses a political wish for self-determination—forgetting that the dominant nationalism of established states does the same—seems, first of all, to arise from an implicit ideological principle that 'history has already passed sentence'. In fact, the principle by which existing political units should not be further broken up is a conservative one which attaches greatest value to the stability of political structures resulting from previous, generally random historical processes. According to this outlook, the main thing is stability, which, paradoxically, is maintained even when it is known that the price will be a long and permanent national conflict—in other words, the image of stability which is defended is directed at the exterior of the state, regardless of the interior political instability resulting from nationalist claims.

Secondly, these supposedly anational standpoints in fact overlook the objective fact that in many cases the constituted states do not respect the rights of national groups that do not belong to the nation with hegemonic pretensions. What is more, history has shown that in many cases it is the state and its policy of repression and even of cultural genocide that provokes a reaction by groups who see their collective identity threatened. Indirectly, therefore, the state itself often encourages or even provokes the emergence of a national awareness with a political scope where none existed before. The wish for a political voice on the part of certain cultural identities has in many cases been fed by this permanent aggression from the state in its search for national unification. On the other hand, what alternative is proposed for these threatened national identities by those who make non-disintegration a basic principle, knowing that since it is an 'internal' affair of the state, external intervention is impossible? Generally speaking, none.

Thirdly, and with regard to the intransigence of states wishing to reunify different national realities within a single territory, it may be worth mentioning something so obvious that it is often overlooked. This is the existence of a state nationalism whose absence from the concerns of the majority of writers on nationalism can only be explained by the 'naturalness' with which it manifests itself and with which it is recognized. Once more we must avoid the mistake of generalization: not all states are equally nationalistic, and their nationalism is not always expressed in the same way, nor does it show the same qualities. But there is no doubt that some manifestations of national pride by North Americans could seem exaggerated even to certain radical European nationalist movements, while, for example, a confederacy such as Switzerland—though for a series of exceptional reasons—does not apparently need to stimulate the adhesion of its citizens to a political structure with cultural and linguistic homogeneity (although it may have a certain homogeneous foundation in economic interests). State nationalisms, therefore, do not form a single model either. But the fact is, however, that state nationalisms exist which throughout history have competed with whatever other national expression might undermine their political legitimacy.

There still remains one issue which is manifestly difficult to understand for those minds comfortably installed in their own national reality, backed up by the power of their own state. This is that not all nationalist movements can be reduced analytically to 'national minorities'. The expression 'national minority' serves to identify groups of national origin different from that of the territory they occupy, who are obviously a minority in that territory, regardless of how long they have lived there. However, there are also cases in which certain national 'minorities' are in fact the national 'majority' in their own territory, and they only become minorities in the territorial framework of a state which they in no way claim as their own. In these cases it is impertinent, in every sense of the word,

to put forward policies for the protection of 'minorities' which are not in fact minorities at all. Once again we come up against an example of the term 'minority' used without any academic or scientific justification other than the unquestioning acceptance of a state's territorial limits, which are what can turn a true majority into a hypothetical minority. Once again, we see how an apparent neutrality, or even a laudable effort to understand the national rights of the supposed minority, can act as a smoke screen for the established state's interests in terms of territorial integrity.

'POST-NATIONAL' EUROPE OR THE ABSENCE OF ALTERNATIVE MODELS

Finally, a few words need to be said about processes of political integration, especially in the European case. Almost everyone agrees that at the present moment this process is very limited politically because of the so-called democratic deficit. This is a deficit which at the same time could well be a necessary condition for a certain period so that the process is not paralysed by the many misunderstandings resulting mainly from state nationalisms. Some states in the present European Union have managed to maintain their allegiance to Maastricht precisely by not submitting the decision to a democratic referendum. At the same time the European Parliament is maintained as a purely formal structure with hardly any true legislative capacity, when this is a *sine qua non* condition for formal democracy.

What is missing from the European Union? Apart from the logical difficulties resulting from the evasiveness of the states themselves as they jostle for positions of strength, what is most lacking as regards the process of unity is legitimacy. To put it another way, at this moment it would be untrue to say that the process was the expression of a solid 'wish of the people' of Europe, or that the decisions taken arise from a 'sovereignty of the people' of Europe. That this lack of legitimacy is no secret to anyone is shown by the fact that for some time now there have been constant pro-Europe campaigns aimed at countering this weakness and in part at fomenting legitimacy. This raises the question of the possibility of and need for a true *European nationalism*. Of course, in view of certain anti-nationalist conceptual susceptibilities, more than one intellectual and two social scientists might fall off their chairs on hearing this. Which is why people prefer to talk about the bases of a *post-national* Europe, which is also less taxing intellectually. Nevertheless, all the theoretical work of rethinking Europe with a view to breaking out of today's cramped framework of nation-states can only be understood politically as an undertaking of *national European construction*. All this in spite of those who prefer to call it, confusingly, a 'post-national' model, or who could speak of European 'patriotism' rather than European 'nationalism' or simply refer to a 'European vocation', as people call it.

One can certainly imagine—and there are empirically observable cases—the existence of collective identities definable at different levels of allegiance. One can have a local/regional allegiance, a national allegiance (if there is a desire for self-determination), allegiance to a state or higher. But in each case there is a need for a legitimating discourse, and stability depends on not having to define one's allegiance against any of the other levels, either higher or lower. It is in no way true that nationalism needs the image of a foreign rival to be able to survive, although it has been sought, at different times and in different places, throughout history (and still is, periodically, by constituted states).

Therefore, if we want to avoid the trap of terminological prejudice, in these last years of the century with the many varied processes of national emancipation that have so quickly succeeded each other in Europe, we must denounce any attempt to reify the national issue and any reductionist analysis, which both need to be revised precisely in the light of these changes. It is because these processes have followed so many different paths that we can no longer try to look for general theories, which for some reason are always so doom-laden. No-one today gives Slovenia as an example of disintegrative or conflictive nationalism, and the most ominous hypotheses have proved unfounded in Slovakia, to mention just two peaceful and unquestionably democratic processes. But there was no lack of pessimistic forecasts.... [O]f course, there is all the barbarism of Serbian expansionist nationalism, before which, incidentally, Europe has been unable to act intelligently and is perhaps once again—leaving aside political, financial and military interests—paralysed by patterns of mental analysis which have introduced fear where courage was needed.

In any case, the problem of national conflicts will not be solved by melting down separate national identities into a chimerical mixture, even in the unreal supposition that these identities can be shared. On the contrary, they need to be recognized and given a real part to play in the cementing of other identities at a higher level which in turn can help to guarantee the survival of the lower levels. Democracy is unimaginable without the notion of a sovereign people, and we need to establish a series of graded sovereignties and multiple complex forms of popular awareness, in which the interrelation of one with another has a positive effect; they should 'add up' rather than 'subtract'.

In short, we cannot hope for a stable future in what is referred to as a *post-national Europe*. Note that the very concept defines a negative Europe, which is against something previously existing, the nations. Instead, we need a Europe with a positive definition, such as the *Europe of peoples and nations*.

POSTSCRIPT

Is Nationalism Destructive?

Whatever you may think of nationalism, it remains a powerful force that dominates political identification and loyalty throughout the world. It is a key reason why humans divide themselves into nearly 200 states, with as many nations, each hoping to create their own state to add to that number. Nationalism is inculcated in children from a very early age. In the United States, nursery school children are taught to recite the Pledge of Allegiance, even though they do not know what the words mean. Patriotism is not only expected, but it is legally enforced. Murder is not proscribed in the Constitution; treason is.

Not everyone agrees with such nationalistic sentiments. Albert Einstein commented in 1921 that "nationalism is an infantile disease... the measles of mankind." Similarly, the French philosopher Voltaire lamented in *Patrie* (1764) that "it is sad that being a good patriot often means being the enemy of the rest of mankind." Speaking at the UN in October 1995, Pope John Paul II condemned extreme nationalism as a doctrine that "teaches contempt for other nations or cultures" and threatens "to give rise to new forms of the aberrations of totalitarianism."

Because most of us are so imbued with nationalism, it is difficult to imagine a different type of primary political loyalty. Yet political identification is learned. Therefore, it could change, and states and nations will not necessarily always be the way humans organize themselves politically. There are some analysts who believe that nationalism and its agent, the sovereign state, are doomed. Because the contemporary world is undergoing so many changes, this issue is widely discussed among scholars and others. A review of several of the more recent works on nationalism can be found in Yael Tamir, "The Enigma of Nationalism," *World Politics* (April 1995). Other excellent sources are John Dunn, ed., *Contemporary Crisis of the Nation State?* (Blackwell, 1995); Hendrik Spruyt, *The Sovereign State and Its Competitors: An Analysis of Systems Change* (Princeton University Press, 1994); and Montserrat Guibernau, *Nationalisms: The Nation-State and Nationalism in the Twentieth Century* (Polity Press, 1996).

You are left, then, with the question about where your loyalties should, and will, be placed in the future. Should you—will you—pledge allegiance to your nation and country? Or will you declare your loyalty to your cultural group, your region, or perhaps humanity and the global village?

ISSUE 17

Should Immigration Be Restricted?

YES: Yeh Ling-Ling, from "Legal Immigration Must Be Curbed, Too," *USA Today Magazine* (January 1997)

NO: Stephen Moore, from "Give Us Your Best, Your Brightest," *Insight* (November 22, 1993)

ISSUE SUMMARY

YES: Yeh Ling-Ling, founder of the Diversity Coalition for an Immigration Moratorium in San Francisco, California, argues that immigration should be curbed because it detracts from the economic opportunities available to Americans.

NO: Stephen Moore, an economist with the Cato Institute in Washington, D.C., maintains that the net gains that the United States reaps from the contributions of immigrants far outweigh any social costs.

The world is awash in refugees and immigrants, with some 125 million people living outside their native lands.

If all those people were grouped together to establish a single country, it would be the ninth most populous in the world. Whether those who are seeking new homes are actual refugees who have already fled their homelands or those who wish to leave, immigration has been a traditional path to seeking a new life in a new place.

The difficulty is that many countries are reacting to the increase in immigration pressure by closing, not opening, their doors. The United Nations estimates that since 1980, more than 15 million people have migrated to Western Europe. Three million of these asked for political asylum. There are now an estimated 2.8 million people living illegally in the countries of Western Europe.

The reaction of many countries has been to tighten entry policies. Germany's constitution once promised asylum to "people persecuted on political grounds." Germany eliminated that clause in 1993 and adopted a highly restrictive immigration policy. Similarly, France in 1994 changed its laws in a way that forced many foreign workers who had earlier entered France legally to leave. Most of these workers and their families came from former French colonies in Africa. President Jacques Chirac explained that "overall, the French are increasingly irritated by immigrants." He conceded that the feeling was "irrational and often unfair," but still held that a show of "firmness on the immigration issue" had been necessary.

Immigration has also been a significant part of American history. More than 65 million immigrants have come to the United States during its history. Measured in number of immigrants per 1,000 Americans, the highest rate of immigration occurred in the first decade of this century, when an annual average of 10.4 immigrants per 1,000 came to the United States. From 1970 to 1990 the annual rate averaged 2.6. The most recent data available shows that the rate in 1995 was 2.7. In all, there are 19.8 million legal and an unknown number of undocumented immigrants living in the United States.

As in Europe, legal and illegal immigration has become the subject of heated debate in the United States. There are numerous reasons why Americans tend to resist immigration. Many Americans believe that immigrants compete for jobs, a worrisome thought in an era of economic uncertainty. There is also a common notion that immigrants too often use expensive social services (such as education, housing, and health care) while paying little in taxes. There has been broad political pressure to reduce legal immigration and illegal workers. Legislation, such as Proposition 187 in California, has been proposed to deny services, including education for children, to undocumented aliens. New welfare changes by the federal government allow legal immigrants to be denied unemployment benefits and some other social services.

The demographic characteristics of immigrants have also been changing. Racial and ethnic data is not kept as such, but based on the immigrant's country of birth, it seems that the number of traditional immigrants from Europe and largely European-heritage countries (such as Canada) is declining as a percentage of U.S. immigrants, whereas the percentages from other areas are rising.

Racism may also play a part in the current debate over immigration policy. Some people argue that the shift away from what might be called Euro-white immigration to the increasing entry of Asians, Africans, Latin Americans, and West Indians (many with some combination of African/Spanish/Indian heritage) has increased American resistance to immigration based on open or latent racism. A national poll on immigration conducted in 1993 revealed that, of those Americans surveyed, half thought that it should be easier for people from Eastern Europe to emigrate to the United States. By contrast, 73 percent of the poll's respondents thought that it should be more difficult for Haitians to come to the United States, 59 percent favored making immigration more difficult for Africans, and 65 percent wanted to make it harder for Asians to seek residency and citizenship.

Should more immigrants be allowed into the United States? Or is fewer —even none—a better proposal? This is the issue taken up in the following selections by Yeh Ling-Ling and Stephen Moore. Yeh argues for a five-year moratorium on immigration. Moore asserts that by pursuing liberal immigration policies, the United States can ensure that the twenty-first century, like the twentieth century, will be the American century.

YES

Yeh Ling-Ling

LEGAL IMMIGRATION MUST BE CURBED, TOO

Year after year, presidential candidates and members of Congress from both parties repeatedly have promised to reduce budget deficits, strengthen the economy, create jobs for Americans, and put welfare recipients back to work. Yet, how can those goals possibly be achieved if the U.S. continues to allow an average of more than 800,000 legal immigrants to enter the country every year? These newcomers need jobs, education, welfare, health care, and many other services that can not even be provided to millions of native-born Americans.

As a naturalized citizen of Chinese ancestry with extensive professional experience preparing family- and employment-based immigrant petitions, I am disappointed over the lack of will in Washington to reduce legal immigration. This hesitancy continues despite the fact that even strong immigration rights advocates have admitted the adverse impact of mass immigration.

Antonia Hernandez, president of the Mexican American Legal Defense and Educational Fund, has stated that "migration, legal and undocumented, does have an impact on our economy.... Most of the competition is to the Latino community. We compete with each other for those low-paying jobs. There is an issue of wage depression, as in the garment industry, which is predominantly immigrant...."

Chinese-American Prof. Paul Ong of UCLA, a strong advocate of a liberal immigration policy, points out that, "In terms of adverse impact [of immigration] on wages and employment, the adverse impact will be most pronounced on minorities and established immigrants...."

Po Wong, director of the Chinese Newcomers Service Center in San Francisco, indicated in 1993 that, of the 11,000 new Chinese immigrants looking for work through his agency, just two percent were placed successfully. "I don't think our community is equipped to welcome this large a number.... It's very depressing to see so many people come here looking for work."

Dolores Huerta, co-founder of the United Farm Workers Union, testified before the California Select Committee on Immigration that, "With 1,500,000 legalized immigrants living in California, and only approximately 250,000 agricultural jobs in the state, there is no need for additional farm workers."

The pro-immigration Urban Institute has acknowledged that "less-skilled black workers and black workers in high immigration areas with stagnant economies are negatively affected [by immigration]."

Stanford University law professor Bill Ong Hing, author of a report on contributions of Asian immigrants, cites "a certain legitimacy to the view that parts of the country are being overcrowded with immigrants.... They affect growth, air pollution, water availability. It's not bogus for people to raise that issue."

The nation's leaders should be reminded that today's economy requires fewer and fewer workers due to automation, advances in technology, and corporate downsizing. Moreover, many jobs have been lost to foreign countries. If the Federal government continues to allow hundreds of thousands of low-skilled legal immigrants of working age to enter the U.S. every year, how can America's unemployed, low-skilled workers and welfare recipients be expected to find work? Rosy unemployment rates released by the Labor Department do not include millions of workers who are underemployed or never have found work.

U.S. immigration laws have a devastating impact on American professionals as well. In addition to 130,000 employment-based immigrant visas for foreign-born professionals being provided annually, virtually unlimited numbers of various types of "temporary workers" are permitted to enter to work in professional occupations for several years. "H1B [extraordinary ability] temporary workers"

alone are estimated to be around 400,000 in this country at any time.

Today's global economy requires highly skilled workers to prosper. If the U.S. does not have sufficient resources to prepare its children and existing legal immigrants to be tomorrow's productive workers, why should the nation invite hundreds of thousands of legal immigrant children to America's already overcrowded schools every year? Fiscally responsible politicians should bear in mind that the cost of educating a child in the U.S. runs about $5,000 a year. If an immigrant child needs an average of eight years of education, it will cost taxpayers $40,000.

In 1994, 740,000 elderly legal immigrants were on welfare, a 580% increase over 1982. (This number did not include the seniors who became naturalized citizens.) Bekki Mar, an immigration advocate working for Self-Help for the Elderly in San Francisco, indicated that 85% of the immigrant clients of her center were on welfare. If a senior immigrant receives welfare, Medicaid, food stamps, and government-subsidized low-income housing, he or she will cost taxpayers a minimum of $100,000 over a five-year period.

More than half of recent legal immigrants are low-skilled and therefore unlikely to pay enough taxes to cover the cost of educating their children. While many immigrants own businesses, they very rarely hire U.S.-born workers. The jobs they create usually are low-paying ones. These low-paying jobs frequently do not generate sufficient tax dollars to cover the cost of all the services rendered to the families of the immigrant employees and employers.

Pro-immigration libertarians argue that immigrants help stimulate the economy and create jobs by their consumerism. While immigrant students and welfare recipients are consumers, they require more teachers, classrooms, welfare, and health care. Who is paying the bills if not U.S. taxpayers? George Borjas, a Cuban immigrant and an economics professor at Harvard University, estimates that, in California, 40% of welfare benefits, cash and non-cash, go to immigrants.

Donald Huddle of Rice University projects that the *net* costs of legal immigration over the next 10 years will exceed $400,000,000,000 unless the numbers are reduced drastically. Studies claiming mass immigration to be an economic asset have not computed the cost of all services rendered to immigrants. Moreover, children born in the U.S. of immigrants are left out in their fiscal analyses. Can the U.S. ever balance its budgets without first addressing legal immigration? What price tag should be appended to the daily frustration of dealing with traffic congestion? How can one compute the loss to the U.S. of having a growing semi-illiterate workforce?

Proponents of mass immigration often claim that the nation's computer industry depends on immigration for its technological edge. However, reports on "60 Minutes," "48 Hours," and "CNN Presents" have shown that American computer professionals have been replaced with foreign-born workers because of companies' desire for a cheaper workforce. Sun Microsystems, a prominent company in California's Silicon Valley lobbying heavily for large-scale immigration, has boasted publicly that it has hired 50 Russian programmers at "bargain prices." Hewlett-Packard also has admitted under oath in court that their engineers from India are of lower quality.

Norman Matloff, former chairman of the Affirmative Action Committee at the University of California, Davis, points out that, out of 56 awards for advances in hardware and software by the Association for Computing Machinery, the nation's main computer science professional society, only one recipient has been an immigrant. Similarly, out of 115 awards given by the Institute of Electrical and Electronics Engineering, just nine recipients have been immigrants.

The large numbers of immigrants in American graduate schools often are cited by advocates to support their claim that immigration continues to be vital to the U.S. economy. Yet, this country has an oversupply of PhDs, as has been reported in many publications and a joint study by Stanford University and RAND Corp.

Even assuming that immigrants were more talented and productive than Americans, should the U.S. write off its own citizens and invest in those of other nations? If mass immigration is allowed to displace native workers, is it being suggested that unemployed Americans should join the welfare rolls or turn to crime to support their families? Do pro-family leaders realize that extended unemployment can lead to family breakdown?

A token reduction in employment-based visas or requiring employers to pay aliens prevailing wages merely would be a cosmetic change. Politicians truly concerned about protecting American workers at all levels must recognize that expansive family-based immigration, approaching 500,000 annually, and other categories of immigration, add hundreds of thousands of immediate and future workers to the labor markets each year. In addition, adjudicators at the U.S. Department of Labor simply do not have the technical knowledge to determine the actual prevailing wages of professional jobs. Furthermore, this country does not have a system to verify that employers actually will pay aliens the wages they claim in their petitions.

A 1995 audit by the Labor Department's Inspector General concluded that "the foreign labor programs... do not protect U.S. workers' jobs or wages from foreign labor." The report found that tests imposed on U.S. employers to prove a lack of qualified American workers were "perfunctory at best and a sham at worst."

George Borjas has estimated that immigration costs $133,000,000,000 a year in job losses and wage depression to native workers. Addressing corporate downsizing, which mercilessly sheds U.S. workers, without reducing immigration barely would curb corporate greed.

It is true that the U.S. is a nation of immigrants, many of whom have contributed to building this country. However, circumstances have changed drastically. The U.S. now is the greatest debtor nation on Earth. It has an oversupply of labor at all levels. Schools, jails, and freeways are overflowing. America still may have millions of acres of open space, but land area alone can not support human lives. Millions of prospective immigrants are awaiting opportunities, but there already are 39,000,000 poverty-stricken citizens who are not yet living the American Dream.

SAVING LIMITED RESOURCES

Many people love children, but very few want unlimited numbers of them. Wise and responsible parents want to limit their family sizes so that they can better provide for their existing offspring. Similarly, Washington should curb immigration in order to save limited resources and job opportunities for Americans of all racial backgrounds, as well as legal immigrants already in the U.S.

Reducing legal immigration simply requires an act of Congress signed into law by the President. Illegal immigration can be curbed significantly by taking away the job and benefit magnets in the U.S. through employer sanctions and tamper-proof documents to verify immigration status.

Mass immigration impacts minorities and the working class the most, the very people liberals want to protect. While it is not the cause of all of America's problems, mass immigration does make many of them much more difficult to solve. Because of the scarcity of jobs, mass immigration essentially means a greater demand on the infrastructure and, therefore, government budgets. Those who wish to provide health care and education to citizens of the poor nations should be aware that mass immigration is by no means cost-efficient. The expense of providing those services in developing nations would be a small fraction of what it costs in the U.S.

Liberals opposing immigration reduction must understand that they unintentionally help big businesses, which lobby vigorously for mass immigration, to exploit U.S.-born workers and existing immigrants. Many conservative pro-business politicians favor large-scale immigration because it keeps wages down. They overlook the real and total costs of services rendered to immigrants and their descendants, a burden unduly borne by taxpayers. Welfare legislation recently passed by Congress will continue to give naturalized citizens access to all assistance programs. Aid to legal immigrants is not limited to welfare, Medicaid, food stamps, and government-subsidized low-income housing. The government is required to provide public education from kindergarten to 12th grade; construction and maintenance of roads and bridges; and fire, police, emergency, park, prison, and court services.

Modern transportation and telecommunications can be used to link immigrants with their relatives separated by oceans within hours or minutes. Many countries in the Pacific Rim are experiencing tremendous economic growth. Yet, hundreds of thousands of nationals of those "emerging economies" have been admitted every year to an America that is struggling with economic woes and skyrocketing budget deficits. Meanwhile, many recent Chinese immigrants have *Hui Liu* (returned to Taiwan, Hong Kong, and China), saying that the U.S. has fewer opportunities than the Far East. They left their children behind for American taxpayers to educate, however!

In 1995, the United Nations recommended that all countries accept a combined total of less than 32,000 refugees. The U.S. alone admitted more than 110,000 immigrants that year as "refugees." In 1994, 112,573 "refugees" were welcomed to the U.S., though just one-sixth of them were recognized by the international relief community as "special needs refugees" requiring resettlement in a third country. Roger Winter, a refugee rights advocate working for the U.S. Committee for Refugees, has estimated that the cost of settling a refugee

in the U.S. would cover the expenses of helping 500 refugees abroad.

Clearly, current U.S. immigration policy needs to be overhauled. It is fiscally irresponsible toward U.S. taxpayers and economically unfair to American workers. It also is a disincentive for developing nations to learn to provide for their own citizens.

A study conducted by the Harwood Group showed that voters heading into the 1996 presidential election were more angry than ever with politicians in Washington for not addressing their major concerns—education, jobs, crime, and health care. According to a Roper poll released in February [1996], 54% of Americans want annual immigration to be less than 100,000 a year. That poll also showed the majority of blacks and Hispanics favor drastic reductions in immigration. A *Wall Street Journal*/NBC News poll published in March [1996] revealed that 52% of Americans favor banning all legal and illegal immigration for five years.

If the nation's leaders want to show the world that the U.S. practices democracy and if they are sincere about addressing voters' concerns, they immediately should support a five-year moratorium on legal immigration with an all-inclusive ceiling of 100,000 a year. The tens of billions of dollars saved annually in servicing fewer legal immigrants can be used to help balance budgets, fund measures to stop illegal immigration, invest in Head Start and public schools, and finance crime prevention programs. Such a moratorium would allow time to develop a long-term immigration policy that reflects economic realities and resource availability.

NO

Stephen Moore

GIVE US YOUR BEST, YOUR BRIGHTEST

For many Americans, the word "immigration" immediately conjures up an image of poor Mexicans scrambling across the border near San Diego to find minimum-wage work and perhaps collect government benefits. Recent public opinion polls confirm that the attitude of the American public toward immigration is highly unfavorable. Central Americans are perceived as welfare abusers who stubbornly refuse to learn English, Haitians are seen as AIDS carriers, Russian Jews are considered to be mafiosi, and Asians are seen as international terrorists. The media reinforce these stereotypes by battering the public with negative depictions of immigrants.

The conception of immigrants as tired, poor, huddled masses seems permanently sketched into the mind of the public, just as the words are sketched irrevocably at the feet of the Statue of Liberty. But the Emma Lazarus poem simply does not describe the hundreds of thousands of people who are building new lives here in the 1990s. It would be more appropriate if the words at the base of the statue read: "Give us your best, your brightest, your most energetic and talented." Why? Because in large part those are the people who come to the United States each year.

Before we start slamming shut the golden door, it might be worthwhile to find out who the newcomers are and how they truly affect our lives.

Anyone who believes that immigrants are a drain on the U.S. economy has never visited the Silicon Valley in California. Here and in other corridors of high-tech entrepreneurship, immigrants are literally the lifeblood of many of the nation's most prosperous industries. In virtually every field in which the United States asserted global leadership in the 1980s—industries such as computer design and softwear, pharmaceuticals, bioengineering, electronics, superconductivity, robotics and aerospace engineering—one finds immigrants. In many ways these high-growth industries are the modern version of the American melting pot in action.

Consider Intel Corp. With profits of $1.1 billion in 1992, it is one of the most prolific and fast-expanding companies in the United States, employing tens of thousands of American workers. It is constantly developing exciting, cutting-edge technologies that will define the computer industry in the 21st century.

And it is doing all of this largely with the talents of America's newest immigrants. Three members of Intel's top management, including Chief Executive Officer Andrew S. Grove, from Hungary, are immigrants. Some of its most successful and revolutionary computer technologies were pioneered by immigrants, such as the 8080 microprocessor (an expanded-power computer chip), invented by a Japanese, and polysilicon FET gates (the basic unit of memory storage on modern computer chips), invented by an Italian. Dick Ward, manager of employee information systems at Intel, says: "Our whole business is predicated on inventing the next generation of computer technologies. The engine that drives that quest is brainpower. And here at Intel, much of that brainpower comes from immigrants."

Or consider Du Pont-Merck Pharmaceutical Co., an $800 million-a-year health care products company based in Wilmington, Del., which reports that immigrants are responsible for many of its most promising new product innovations. For example, losartan, an antihypertensive drug, was developed by a team of scientists that included two Chinese and a Lithuanian. Joseph Mollica, Chief Executive Officer of Du Pont-Merck, says that bringing together such diverse talent "lets you look at problems and opportunities from a slightly different point of view."

Intel and Du Pont-Merck are not alone in relying on immigrants. Robert Kelley Jr., president of SO/CAL/TEN, an association of nearly 200 high-tech California companies, insists: "Without the influx of Asians in the 1980s, we would not have had the entrepreneurial explosion we've seen in California." David N. K. Wang, vice president for worldwide business operations at Applied Materials Inc., a computer-technology company in California, adds that because of immigration, "Silicon Valley is one of the most international business centers in the world."

Take away the immigrants, and you take away the talent base that makes such centers operate. Indeed, it is frightening to think what would happen to America's global competitiveness if the immigrants stopped coming. Even scarier is the more realistic prospect that U.S. policymakers will enact laws to prevent them from coming.

New research has begun to quantify the contributions of immigrants to American industry. The highly respected National Research Council reported in 1988 that "a large fraction of the technological output of the United States [is] dependent upon foreign talent and that such dependency is growing." Noting that well over half of all scientists graduating with doctorate degrees from American universities and one in three engineers working in the United States are immigrants, the report states emphatically: "It is clear ... that these foreign-born engineers enrich our culture and make substantial contributions to the U.S. economic well-being and competitiveness."

The United States' competitive edge over the Japanese, Germans, Koreans and much of Europe is linked closely to its continued ability to attract and retain highly talented workers from other countries. A 1990 study by the national Science Foundation says, "Very significant, positive aspects arise from the presence of foreign-born engineers in our society."

For example, superconductivity, a technology that is expected to spawn hundreds of vital new commercial applications in the next century, was discovered by a physicist at the University of Houston, Paul C. W. Chu. He was born in China and came to the U.S. in 1972. His brilliance and inventiveness have made him a top contender for a Nobel Prize.

Of course, if Chu does win a Nobel, he will join a long list of winners who were immigrants in America. In the 20th century, between 20 percent and 50 percent of the Nobel Prize winners, depending on the discipline involved, have been immigrants to the United States. Today there are more Russian Nobel Prize winners living in the U.S. than there are living in Russia.

Public opinion polls consistently reveal that a major worry is that immigrants take jobs from American workers. The fear is understandable but misplaced. Immigrants don't just take jobs, they create jobs. One way is by starting new businesses. Today, America's immigrants, even those who come with relatively low skill levels, are highly entrepreneurial.

Take Koreans, for example. According to sociologists Alendro Portes and Ruben Rumbaut, "In Los Angeles, the propensity for self-employment is three times greater for Koreans than among the population as a whole. Grocery stores, restaurants, gas stations, liquor stores and real estate offices are typical Korean businesses." Cubans also are prodigious creators of new businesses. The number of Cuban-owned businesses in Miami has expanded from 919 in 1967 to 8,000 in 1976 to 28,000 in 1990. On Jefferson Boulevard in Dallas, more than 800 businesses operate, three-quarters of them owned by first- and second-generation Hispanic immigrants. Just 10 years ago, before the influx of Mexicans and other Central Americans, the neighborhood was in decay, with many vacant storefronts displaying "for sale" signs in the windows. Today it is a thriving ethnic neighborhood.

To be sure, few immigrant-owned businesses mature into an Intel. In fact, many fail completely. Like most new businesses in America, most immigrant establishments are small and only marginally profitable. The average immigrant business employs two to four workers and records roughly $200,000 in annual sales. However, such small businesses, as President Clinton often correctly emphasizes, are a significant source of jobs.

It should not be too surprising that immigrants are far more likely than average U.S. citizens to take business risks. After all, uprooting oneself, traveling to a foreign culture and making it requires more than the usual amount of courage, ambition, resourcefulness and even bravado. Indeed, this is part of the self-selection process that makes immigrants so particularly desirable. Immigrants are not just people—they are a very special group of people. By coming, they impart productive energies on the rest of us.

This is not just romanticism. It is well-grounded in fact. Countless studies have documented that immigrants to the United States tend to be more skilled, more highly educated and wealthier than the average citizen of their native countries.

Thomas Sowell, an economist and senior fellow at the Hoover Institution in Stanford, Calif., reports in his seminal study on immigration, "Ethnic America," that black immigrants from the West Indies have far higher skill levels than their countrymen at home. He also finds that the income levels of West Indies immigrants are higher than those of

West Indies natives, American blacks and native-born white Americans.

Surprisingly, even illegal immigrants are not the poverty-stricken and least skilled from their native countries. Surveys of undocumented immigrants from Mexico to the United States show that only about 5 percent were unemployed in Mexico, whereas the average unemployment rate there was about three times that level, and that a relatively high percentage of them worked in white-collar jobs in Mexico. In addition, surveys have found that illiteracy among undocumented Mexicans in the U.S. is about 10 percent, whereas illiteracy in Mexico is about 22 percent.

Perhaps the greatest asset of immigrants is their children, who tend to be remarkably successful in the U.S. Recently, the city of Boston reported that an incredible 13 of the 17 valedictorians in its public high schools were foreign-born—from China, Vietnam, Portugal, El Salvador, France, Italy, Jamaica and the former Czechoslovakia. Many could not speak a word of English when they arrived. Public high schools in Washington, Chicago and Los Angeles also report remarkably disproportionate numbers of immigrant children at the top of the class. Similarly, Westinghouse reports that over the past 12 years, about one-third of its prestigious National Science Talent Search winners have been Asians. Out of this group might emerge America's next Albert Einstein, who himself was an immigrant.

So one hidden cost of restricting immigration is the loss of immigrants' talented and motivated children.

In the past century, America has admitted roughly 50 million immigrants. This has been one of the largest migrations in the history of the world. Despite this infusion of people—no, because of it

—the United States became by the middle of the 20th century the wealthiest nation in the world. Real wages in America have grown more than eightfold over this period. The U.S. economy employed less than 40 million people in 1900; today it employs nearly 120 million people. The U.S. job machine had not the slightest problem expanding and absorbing the 8 million legal immigrants who came to this country in the 1980s. Eighteen million jobs were created.

But what about those frightening headlines? "Immigration Bankrupting Nation." "Immigrants Displacing U.S. Workers." "Foreigners Lured to U.S. by Welfare."

Here are the facts. The 1990s census reveals that roughly 6 percent of native-born Americans are on public assistance, versus 7 percent of the foreign-born, with less than 5 percent of illegal immigrants collecting welfare. Not much reason for alarm. Because immigrants tend to come to the United States when they are young and working, over their lifetimes they each pay about $20,000 more in taxes than they use in services, according to economist Julian Simon of the University of Maryland. With 1 million immigrants per year, the nation gains about $20 billion more than cost. Rather than fiscal burdens, immigrants are huge bargains.

Nor do immigrants harm the U.S. labor market. A comprehensive 1989 study by the U.S. Department of Labor concluded: "Neither U.S. workers nor most minority workers appear to be adversely affected by immigration—especially during periods of economic expansion." In the 1980s, the top 10 immigrant-receiving states —including California, Florida, Massachusetts and Texas—recorded rates of unemployment 2 percentage points below the U.S. average, according to the

Alexis de Tocqueville Institution in Arlington, Va. So where's the job displacement?

We are now witnessing in America what might be described as the return of the nativists. They are selling fear and bigotry. But if any of their allegations against immigrants are accurate, then America could not have emerged as the economic superpower it is today.

In fact, most Americans do accept that immigration in the past has contributed greatly to the nation's economic growth. But they are not so sanguine in their assessment of present and future immigrants. It is strangely inconsistent that Americans believe that so long-standing and crucial a benefit is now a source of cultural and economic demise.

Shortly before his death, Winston Churchill wrote, "The empires of the future are the empires of the mind." America is confronted with one of the most awesome opportunities in world history to build those empires by attracting highly skilled, highly educated and entrepreneurial people from all over the globe. The Andrew Groves and the Paul Chus of the world do not want to go to Japan, Israel, Germany, France or Canada. Almost universally they want to come to the United States. We can be selective. By expanding immigration but orienting our admission policies toward gaining the best and the brightest, America would enjoy a significant comparative advantage over its geopolitical rivals.

By pursuing a liberal and strategic policy on immigration, America can ensure that the 21st century, like the 20th, will be the American century.

POSTSCRIPT

Should Immigration Be Restricted?

In New York Bay on Liberty Island stands a 152-foot-high, world-renowned statue of a woman facing seaward. The Statue of Liberty greets those entering the harbor from the Atlantic, and its torch is meant to symbolically light the way of immigrants to nearby Ellis Island, which long served (1892–1943) as the chief point of entry for immigrants to the United States. At the foot of the Statue of Liberty is a plaque with a sonnet by Emma Lazarus, "The New Colossus," whose most famous lines read:

> Give me your tired, your poor,
> Your huddled masses, yearning to breathe free,
> The wretched refuse of your teeming shore.
> Send these, the homeless, tempest-tost to me,
> I lift my lamp beside the golden door.

On the question of whether or not the words of the poet Lazarus should still govern U.S. policy, several points are important. The open door to immigration ended long ago. The decade 1911–1920 was the last, with an average annual rate of over 5 immigrants per 1,000 Americans. Since then the rate has risen and fallen; the 1931–1940 rate, at 0.4, was the lowest in history. Moore may be right that immigration should be encouraged, but those who argue that case need to account for changing conditions.

By the same token, those who oppose immigration also need to argue with care. Totaling up numbers of immigrants and quoting unemployment statistics are easy exercises in data collection. To say that A (immigration) causes B (unemployment) is another matter. They may not be related at all. Indeed, in a low-birthrate and graying America, it may be that immigrants provide new sources of labor for both high-skill jobs and those that many Americans disdain. Similar observations could be made about the logical validity of other pro and con arguments. The point is to be wary of inferences and illogical connections. For more discussions of the economic contributions of immigrants to the United States, read the companion articles by James C. Clad, "Lowering the Wave," and Michael Fix, "Myths About Immigrants," in *Foreign Policy* (Summer 1994). For a more extensive look at the data, consult Julian L. Simon, *Immigration: The Demographic and Economic Facts* (Cato Institute, 1995).Nathan Glazer, in "Immigration and the American Future,"

The Public Interest (Winter 1995), argues in favor of selective immigration that would allow only those with desirable skills into the United States. For a broader look at the global issues of immigration, see Wayne A. Cornelius, Phillip L. Martin, and James F. Hollifield, eds., *Controlling Immigration: A Global Perspective* (Stanford University Press, 1995).

ISSUE 18

Is There a Global Population Crisis?

YES: Al Gore, from "The Rapid Growth of the Human Population: Sustainable Economic Growth," *Vital Speeches of the Day* (October 1, 1994)

NO: Dennis T. Avery, from "The Myth of Global Hunger," *The World and I* (January 1997)

ISSUE SUMMARY

YES: Al Gore, vice president of the United States, contends that rapid world population growth is outstripping the globe's ability to sustain it.

NO: Dennis T. Avery, director of global food issues at the Hudson Institute, argues that increased agriculture yields and other technology-based advances mean that the globe can sustain a much larger population.

On July 11, 1987, the estimated world population reached 5 billion people. It took 100,000 years of human existence for the world population to reach that total. In just the next 8 years, the world population increased another 15 percent to its 1995 total of 5.75 billion people. The increase of 100 million people in 1995 alone is the equivalent of a new U.S. population every 2.5 years or a new Canadian population every 95 days. It is likely, the United Nations Population Fund (UNPF) predicts, that in the year 2000 the world population will reach 6.3 billion. Looking farther into the future, UNPF estimated in a November 1996 report that the world population will reach the 10 billion mark in the year 2071 and will not stabilize until it reaches about 10.7 billion people in 2200. Thus, the population continues to expand at a rapid pace and will in 1999 have doubled from what it was in 1960. There are approximately 30 countries with a population growth rate between 3.0 percent and 4.9 percent; they will double their populations in 14 to 22 years. About another 50 countries have population growth rates between 2.0 percent and 2.9 percent; they will double their populations in 23 to 34 years.

Several factors account for the rapidly expanding population. Fewer deaths is one. Infant mortality (annual deaths per 1,000 children through age five) has decreased, while adult longevity has increased. These two factors combine to mean that even in some regions where the birthrate has declined, the population growth rate continues to accelerate. Sub-Saharan Africa's birthrate declined from 47 births per 1,000 population in the early 1970s to 43 births per 1,000 in 1994, but during the same period life expectancy increased from 45 years to 52 years because of a decrease in the infant mortality rate from

135 children to 92 children. Furthermore, the region's overall crude death rate (annual death of people per 1,000) dropped from 21 to 15. The net result is that the rapidly declining death rates have more than offset the more slowly declining birth rates and have resulted in an annual population growth increase from 2.6 percent to 3.0 percent.

Another reason for the alarming population growth is the huge population base of 5.8 billion. This problem is, in a sense, a matter of mathematics. Although the global fertility rate (number of births per woman) has declined from 4.9 in 1970 to its current rate of 2.9 and continues to ebb, there are so many more women in their childbearing years that the number of babies born continues to go up. Moreover, this tidal wave of children will grow up, and most of them will one day become parents.

Poverty also spurs population growth. The least developed countries tend to have the most labor-intensive economies, which means that children are economically valuable because they help their parents farm or provide cheap labor in mining and manufacturing processes. Furthermore, it is the case that women in less developed countries (LDCs) have fewer opportunities to limit the number of children they bear. Artificial birth control methods and counseling services are less readily available in these countries. Additionally, women in LDCs have fewer opportunities than do women in economically developed countries (EDCs) to gain paid employment and to develop status roles beyond that of motherhood. The inadequacies in financial, educational, and contraceptive opportunities for women are strongly and inversely correlated to high fertility rates in LDCs.

Whatever its causes, with a population about to pass 6 billion and projected to reach almost 11 billion, there are many who worry about the ability of the biosphere to sustain that many people. People consume mineral resources, water, and other finite necessities. People use energy, which contributes to the carbon dioxide emissions that many believe lead to global warming.

Food and its continued adequacy to support the world population is a particular concern of Al Gore and Dennis T. Avery. In the following selections, Gore argues that the world may be reaching the point where it can no longer "carry" its population—that is, meet its food and other requirements. Avery disagrees and asserts that technology and science will increase agricultural yields and provide other advancements that will meet future population needs.

YES

Al Gore

THE RAPID GROWTH OF THE HUMAN POPULATION

Delivered before the National Press Club, Washington, D.C., August 25, 1994

I'd like to [address] population, sustainable development and the challenge of preparing for the 21st century. In the aftermath of the Cold War, the community of nations has been freed from many of the divisions of the past, and nations are moving ever closer together—economically, ecologically, and politically. In this transition period, the United States, and all nations, have an opportunity and responsibility to address long neglected future-oriented concerns that will determine what kind of world we leave to our children and grandchildren.

To make this transition successfully, we first must come to accept and understand the profoundly altered nature of the relationship between human civilization and the ecological system of the earth. Three factors have produced a radical change in this relationship, one philosophical and two physical. The philosophical change has to do with our attitude toward the earth and toward our own future: specifically, a habit of denying responsibility for the long-term consequences of our actions and behaviors. I have discussed this at length elsewhere and do not intend to go into depth here.... The other two factors are physical in nature. And while both of them have occurred in only a millisecond on the scale of geological time, both are unique to this century.

The first is the dramatic and unprecedented revolution in science and technology—still accelerating—which has enhanced our quality of life, but has also given us the power to alter the life-support systems upon which our communities, our economies, and our lives are based....

The second, of course, is the rapid growth of human population—the topic I want to address ... in the context of sustainable economic development.

If you were to draw a chart depicting the population of the earth over time, you would start in the beginning. For sake of argument, if you assume that the scientists are right, roughly 200,000 years ago, events took place which led to the emergence of modern Homo sapiens. The population slowly began to rise some 10,000 years ago with the agricultural revolution. By the birth of Christ, the population on earth had reached roughly 250 million. By the time Christopher Columbus sailed to the New World, it was roughly 500 million people. By the time the Declaration of Independence was written, it was roughly one billion people. At that point, during the scientific revolution, population began to increase dramatically. And by the end of World War II, when I was born, and many of you were born, the world had reached a population of two billion people.

Now, to recap, it took roughly 10,000 generations to reach a population of two billion. And yet in my 46 years, we have gone from a little over two billion to almost six billion. And if I'm fortunate enough to live another 46 years, the world's population will almost certainly go to nearly nine billion.

If it takes 10,000 generations to reach a population of two billion, and then we move in a single human lifetime from two billion to nine billion, clearly that is a dramatic change. Also, if you overlay on this same graph trends in deforestation, the accumulation of greenhouse gases, depletion of ozone levels, disappearance of living species, loss of top soil, and others, most of those trends show a sharp correlation to this underlying pattern.

To put it another way, global population is now growing by far at the fastest rate ever. It is growing by almost 100 million people every year. You could say we are adding the equivalent of another Mexico every 12 months, we are adding the equivalent of another China every ten years.

It's not so much the empirical data that is disturbing; it is the foreseeable consequences of such rapid population growth for tomorrow that should instill in all Americans and in all nations a sense of urgency and resolve to address these unprecedented developments. Let me just name a few:

- For the environment, of course, rapid population growth often contributes to the degradation of natural resources, as does the pattern of consumption in the more stable and more prosperous developed nations—it's important to add that.
- Economically, population growth often contributes to the challenge of addressing persistent low wages, poverty and economic disparity. While there are certainly some circumstances where rapid population growth can meet the need for unfulfilled demand for labor and become a positive factor, nevertheless, in the real world on which we live today, it almost always adds to the challenge of addressing low wages and poverty.
- Population trends also challenge the ability of societies and economies and governments to make the investments they need in both human capital and infrastructure.
- At the level of the family, demographic trends have kept the world's investment in its children low and unequal, especially where girls are concerned.
- For individuals, population growth and high fertility are closely linked to the poor health and welfare of millions upon millions of women, infants and children.

And population pressures often put strains on hopes for stability at the national and international level. Look, for example, at the 20 million refugees the world is now attempting to deal with.

The growing migration flows across international borders are often fed, in part, by unsustainable population growth.

It is impossible to say that rapid population is, ever, by itself, the cause of instability in a society. But neither is it irrelevant to note that last year in Africa, the nation with the highest population density of all was Rwanda. Nor is it irrelevant to note that the nation in Africa with the fastest rate of population growth of all was Somalia. While there is not a direct cause and effect relationship, common sense surely reveals that rapid, unsustainable population growth makes it more difficult for societies and nations to deal with the kinds of political and economic and other problems that all nations have to deal with.

On a global scale, the implications are ones which must be dealt with. But it is important to note that at the local and national level the implications also must be dealt with. There has been, for example, a great deal written recently about problems in countries like Nigeria. Nigeria has a population that has tripled in the past 40 years. The problems in a society like that of Nigeria have many causes. But when the population triples in 40 years it makes these problems more difficult for any society to deal with. Nigeria, to use that example again, is on a pathway that will lead its population to triple again in the next 40 years. It will have more people 40 years from now than the entire continent of Africa had in the 1950s. To take another example, the fastest growing country in the world is Afghanistan. It is on a trajectory that will double its population in only the next 10 years.

These snapshots of a world that is becoming increasingly complex point us toward the need for what I believe must be a centerpiece of international cooperation in the post-cold war period, realizing the vision of sustainable development. With courage, conviction, consensus and common strategies, we can no doubt rise to the great challenges of stabilizing global population and realizing sustainable development. These challenges have proven hard to accept, for there is nothing more difficult for individuals or societies than to change the way we think. And the issues we confront require, above all, new ways of thinking about our world and our relationship to it.

Of the various factors that have shaped this new situation, none is more difficult to discuss than the issue of rapid population growth. It is on our minds and our agenda as the third major world conference on population in this century nears early next month. Ten years ago, the U.S. delegation sat on the sidelines as nations met for the second world conference on population in Mexico City. This was not just a setback for America's long history of leadership, but also for progress and momentum in international population efforts throughout the 1980s.

Ten years later, change has come; the United States is back, and President Clinton has restored U.S. leadership on the critical challenges of population and sustainable development. The Cairo conference [in 1994], or the International Conference on Population and Development, as it is officially known,... is officially and, in fact, a conference on "population *and* development," and that linkage is crucial to the world's ability to forge a consensus that allows us to address both of these challenges in concert....

This conference seeks to affirm the inter-dependent nature of the world and the need for all nations to work together to sensibly stabilize global population;

to integrate economics, the environment and development; to reaffirm enduring values for the family, individual and collective responsibility, and to place priority on global education, health care and the empowerment of women and all people.

... [P]reparations for the Cairo conference have been most notable for the remarkable consensus that has formed around a comprehensive set of strategies to realize these goals. Where once there were a few who suggested that population growth was not a problem, now there is virtual unanimity about the need for all nations to address population and sustainable development on a priority basis....

Also, where once this discussion broke down on north-south lines, there is now agreement that cooperation is in the interest of all nations, north and south. Where once there was disagreement about whether family planning or economic progress was a prerequisite to progress in either area, there is now a broad recognition that both are important in their own right, but that they work best when pursued together. Where once there was a narrow focus on only one aspect of a global strategy, common cause has been forged around a comprehensive effort that links education, health, women's empowerment and economic progress to the dream of improving the quality of life for all people.

... I want to discuss movement toward consensus in the draft of the Cairo document for women, for children, for the environment and much else besides. But we must not allow this dramatic progress to be obscured by an issue rooted in deep moral, philosophical and religious differences—I'm referring, of course, to abortion.

In this area, more than in any other, full consensus is unlikely. Even among men and women deliberating in a spirit of candor and mutual goodwill. It is essential that the partial agreement that may be within reach not be thwarted by misunderstanding....

Just about everyone in every corner of the world wishes to make abortion rare,... though many of us pursue that goal in different ways. For example, I believe that when fewer women feel abortions are necessary, they will be less frequent. And that when women rarely feel they are necessary, they will be rare.... That is not the situation we face today; it is not rare. Around the world today, there are more than 25 million abortions annually. There are places where it is not uncommon for women to have seven or eight abortions in their lifetime.

In fact, there are entire nations, like the Russian Republic, where contraceptives are not easily and widely available, and where the average number of abortions a woman has in her lifetime is seven to eight. And for a variety of reasons, there are more than 200,000 women worldwide who die each year from medically unsafe abortions. We cannot sweep this situation under the rug or pretend that it does not exist, and no one is trying to.

One of the questions for those meeting in Cairo and for all the world's citizens is, what are we going to do about it? How can we make abortions rare? Our administration believes that it is desirable to make available the broadest possible range of health and reproductive options. But we are well aware that views about abortion are as diverse among nations as among individuals. Today, 173 nations have laws setting forth the circumstances in which abortion is permitted, and setting forth the manner in which it is restricted.

We believe that decisions about the extent to which abortion is acceptable should be the province of each government within the context of its own laws and national circumstances. Therefore, throughout these negotiations, we have supported language and sought to have added to the text, language that clearly establishes this principle for all of the Cairo recommendations. And we fully expect, and will insist at Cairo, that this principle be affirmed in the final document. Let me repeat, we have previously urged that it be added; we will continue to do so; we expect that it will be.

Respect for national sovereignty does not imply neutrality on this issue. We believe that the incidence of abortion must be reduced. Abortion is not the strategy by which the nations of the world can or should reduce population growth. We do not promote abortion. We abhor and condemn coerced abortions, whether the coercion is physical, economic, psychological, political or in any other way.

There have been allegations made that the United States has used undue influence related to the availability of development assistance to nations that do not support our population policies and programs.

That is unambiguously and absolutely wrong. We are aware that some statements have been made to this effect; we respect the fact that people of goodwill can have a misunderstanding about the truth, and we have requested specific information. No reasonable person would countenance such behavior. And I will say this: if there is evidence supporting the existence of this behavior at any stage in the preparatory process for Cairo, or at Cairo, or after Cairo, we will take im-

mediate and decisive disciplinary action. These allegations are outrageous. But if they were determined to be true, we would reinvent government right there on the spot.

We do not believe that abortion should be viewed as a method of family planning. It should not be and can not be seen as a method of family planning; although tragically, in countries where contraception is not readily available, it is today all too often used for this purpose. And we certainly do not regard abortion as morally equivalent to contraception. There is, as acknowledged by all participants in the debate, a different moral sensibility brought to a choice for one option as compared to all of the others.

Let me be clear, our administration believes that the United States Constitution guarantees every woman within our borders a right to choose, subject to limited and specific exceptions. We are unalterably committed to that principle. But let us take a false issue off the table: The United States has not sought, does not seek, and will not seek to establish any international right to an abortion. That is a red herring.

Now the principles I've just articulated represent the long-standing position of the administration and of the United States on this issue, on these points. In his authoritative speech to the National Academy of Sciences in June, President Clinton said this,

> "Now, I want to be clear about this, contrary to some assertions, we do not support abortion as a method of family planning. We respect, however, the diversity of national laws, except we do oppose coercion wherever it exists. Our own policy in the United States is that this should be a matter of personal

choice, not public dictation. And, as I have said many times, abortion should be safe, legal, and rare.... In other countries where it does exist, we believe safety is an important issue. And if you look at the mortality figures, it is hard to turn away from that issue. We also believe that providing women with the means to prevent unwanted pregnancy will do more than anything else to reduce abortion."

Since that speech, before that speech, but many times since that speech, the president has personally reaffirmed to me and others on numerous occasions that where abortion does occur, it should be safe. Each nation should determine it. We are opposed to coercion. We abhor it. And we should pursue other policies that reduce the number of abortions.

Let me repeat, we want to do everything we can to reduce the incidence of abortion around the world. And our view is that the most effective way to reduce population growth and abortion is through a comprehensive global strategy that makes family planning information and services as widely available as possible, that promotes sustainable economic development, that increases child survival rates and literacy, that fosters women's health, that strengthens families, and that focuses on the education and empowerment of women.

This is a conclusion brought home to us by hard experience. During the past generation, we have learned that family planning by itself rarely succeeds, and that economic development by itself does not automatically reduce population growth.

In fact, in my opinion, the real story of the preparatory process and the conference itself is the extent to which a new worldwide consensus has congealed

around this more sophisticated, holistic, richer view: that the means by which the world can stabilize population is a multifaceted strategy that includes making contraception available under appropriate circumstances—with respect for the cultures in which it is made available—putting emphasis on educating and empowering women to take part in the choices that relate to family size, sustainable and equitable economic development—which is historically associated with the demographic transition and the stabilizing of population, an emphasis on improving child health and child survival to influence the choices that parents make about the size of the families they wish to have—because when children survive, then the desire for much larger families is greatly diminished.

Let me read a communication which came last spring to Dr. Nafis Sadik, the Secretary General of the Cairo conference, from Pope John Paul II. He said this:

"There is widespread agreement that a population policy is only one part of an overall development strategy. Accordingly, it is important that any discussion of population policies should keep in mind the actual and projected development of nations and regions. At the same time, it is impossible to leave out of the count the very nature of what is meant by the term 'development.' All development worthy of the name must be integral—that is, it must be directed to the true good of every person and of the whole person. True development cannot consist in the simple accumulation of wealth, and in the greater availability of goods and services, but must be pursued with due consideration for the social, cultural, and spiritual dimensions of the human being. Development programs must be built of justice and equality, enabling people to live in dignity, harmony, and peace. They must respect the cultural heritage of peoples and nations, and those social qualities and virtues that reflect the God-given dignity of each and every person, and the divine plan which calls all persons to unity. Importantly, men and women must be active agents of their own development. For to treat them, men and women, as mere objects in some scheme or plan would be to stifle that capacity for freedom and responsibility, which is fundamental to the good of the human person."

How the world needs to hear that perspective. And how the world needs to hear what the great religions of the world have to say about all of the issues we confront.

The Catholic Church, as well as other Christian and non-Christian religions, have a mission that sometimes has to be distinct from that of the political authorities. The religious leaders try to encourage morally strong attitudes with respect to material goods and socioeconomic relationships. The political leadership has a responsibility to listen very carefully to what the religions are saying—even if they cannot always honor it. This dialogue is very important. We want to make Cairo a time of dialogue instead of a pre-fixed confrontation—especially since there is so much agreement on so much of the preparatory document.

We agree, also, with Pope John Paul II that these issues are the most important issues of the 21st century, and that they will determine the future of humankind. I have argued in the past that, in spite of the disagreements which persist, the broad nature and strength of what is *agreed* makes for a natural alliance between—on the one hand—those of us

serving in governments who believe we must stabilize population, protect the environment, promote sustainable development, and create a future that is worthy of our children and grandchildren—and the Catholic church, on the other hand, which despite its well-known opposition to contraception, historically, is one of the most forceful and effective advocates in the entire world, bar none, for literacy and education programs, for measures to dramatically reduce infant mortality, and for other steps that we now understand are in fact crucial in stabilizing population and producing a pattern of sustainable development.

The whole point is to build a humane and comprehensive strategy on the foundation of universal human aspirations. As one part of this comprehensive strategy, a goal at Cairo and beyond is to strengthen the ability of prospective parents to choose how many children to have and when to have them. Every country has a responsibility to determine the appropriate services that are necessary to prevent unintended pregnancies, ensure maternal health, and reduce the incidence of abortion. Every country should strive to make the services that it has chosen for itself available to all its citizens. And in those circumstances in which a nation chooses to make abortion legal, it should be medically safe.

If we can increase life expectancy and child survival rates, if we can improve people's lives through education and economic opportunity, if we can expand their aspirations and widen their horizons, we can reduce the forces that fuel population growth. Family planning, equitable and sustainable development, empowerment for all citizens—we now realize that these are not rival strategies, but rather crucial and mutually consistent elements of the comprehensive approach our common global future demands.

This is the framework that will guide us as we work toward common ground in Cairo. We do not imagine that we will ever put the abortion debate to rest—differences go too deep. But we believe that our approach maximizes the range of possible consensus and reduces the remaining disagreements to manageable proportions. After all, most of the Cairo document—more than 90 percent, in fact—has already been agreed to, far more than in previous international conferences. And many of the differences that remain can be resolved with hard work, respectful dialogue, and reasoned reconciliation, which we call for today.

We need not be and must not become adversaries in the course of this endeavor. We must, rather, be co-laborers and friends in this historic effort to forge policies that affirm the dignity and worth of every human being on Earth, and policies that affirm the importance of the family.

We believe family life is the initiation into a responsible life in society. For example, if you want an environmentally responsible society, you must strengthen the family. Governments have a duty to ensure the political freedom to establish a family and raise children in keeping with that family's religious faith. All governments need to protect the stability of marriage and the institution of the family, and to protect the health of the family. Stressing the family is critical, we believe, because issues such as women's health and women's education, in many countries, must be approached through the prism of the family.

If is in this context, then, that the Cairo conference is remarkable for its effort to define a global agenda of hope, opportunity, and progress. Already, even in the absence of agreement of all issues, this is—by far—the best population document ever developed. And let me say that these efforts, and the United States itself, have benefited greatly from the talent, creativity, and careful guidance of Tim Wirth, our Undersecretary of State for Global Affairs. Through Tim's work and that of others, this conference will make an historic embrace of the need for integrating, on a global scale, economic and environmental policies, and recognizing the relationship between sustainable development and population stability.

I also want to, in advance, thank President Mubarak who, as host, has made an immeasurable contribution to the successful outcome we expect in Cairo.

And like the Earth Summit in Rio, this conference recognizes the importance of engaging citizens and non-governmental organizations, elevating their role and contribution to the international dialogue. This is a conference noted for its unprecedented involvement of citizens —particularly women—on the road to Cairo. Their contribution has been historic and extraordinary.

The Cairo conference has also recognized that these are not solely the matters of poor countries. They affect and involve the citizens of developed countries as well. We are connected to our neighbors by concern and compassion. Rapid population growth is closely linked with poverty, injustice, and human suffering. Americans are not indifferent to these issues.

So, in closing, we know that the challenges are great, and that is why our commitment runs so deep. Integration of population, the environment, and development is an imperative for peace and national security, for human health and well being, and for the quality of life on Earth. The Clinton administration is determined to meet this need. And on the population and development issue, we are determined to help lead the way.

Thank you very much.

NO

Dennis T. Avery

THE MYTH OF GLOBAL HUNGER

Twenty-five years ago, an alarm was sounded: We faced a global food crisis. Many predicted that the world was entering an age of food shortages, high prices, and large-scale famines.

These dire forecasts were followed by a call for radical population-control programs, under the assumption that it would be difficult if not impossible to increase farming yields enough to feed the burgeoning population.

Lester Brown, for example, in his 1974 book *By Bread Alone*, warned ominously, "The choice is between famine and family planning."

But while the food-shortage and famine prophesies have yet to come true, recent years have seen a renewal of these predictions, spurred by two current trends:

- Global grain stocks, used as reserves in years of short harvest or high demand, fell to a near-record low in 1995–96 of only 45 days of consumption.
- The economic success of many Third World countries, especially in Asia, is giving large populations the individual incomes they need to upgrade their diets. As more people eat more meat, the world's demand for feed grains increases.

Are the famine forecasters correct this time? Or are they continuing to misread the world's rising ability to feed itself?

LOW WORLD GRAIN STOCKS

The fact that world grain stocks have reached a modern low point has little to do with population growth and has virtually no implications at all for famine.

In 1995, several factors led to the low-stocks situation. That year saw (1) poor harvests in America's grain belt, (2) an increase in feed grain use in China and other economically emerging countries, and, most important, (3) a change in U.S. farm policy.

For 60 years, American farm policy tried to keep world grain prices higher than the market would support. In most years, that stuck America with up to 400 million tons of "surplus" grain. The rest of the world benefited from U.S. carryover stocks but was all too willing to let America pay the costs. The only other significant grain stocks have been held by the European Union, which was also trying to keep its farmers' grain prices high.

Over the past several years, however, budget deficits have forced both the United States and the EU to cut back the amount of grain held in carryover stocks. In 1996, America finally took the radical step of scrapping its price-support system altogether. This would have triggered momentous change in world grain markets under any circumstances, but it happened right after America's 1995 grain crops were sharply reduced by both bad weather and millions of acres of ill-advised cropland diversion spurred by the government.

Nineteen ninety-six also happened to be the year that China's rising affluence (and thus rising meat demand) forced it to forgo its usual 10 million tons of corn exports and *import* 5 million tons of corn instead.

Added together, these factors have led to the current low grain stocks situation. The paucity is only temporary, however, because high prices have whetted the enthusiasm of farmers all over the world. Barring truly awful weather, optimists say, the 1997 crops will be bin busters and stocks will be at least partially rebuilt to comfortable levels.

Since there's no demonstrable negative trend in world weather (claims of global warming notwithstanding), a bad 1997 growing season will do no more than delay the rebuilding of the world's grain stocks by another season.

In the 1960s, when world population was rising by nearly 2.1 percent per year and crop production in the developing countries was barely gaining 1 percent annually, global food shortages were, perhaps, a plausible forecast.

These trends, however, have radically changed.

WORLD NEVER SO WELL FED

Even before the alarms were sounded, efforts were under way to improve the agricultural situation in the Third World. During the 1960s, an international network of agricultural researchers and research centers began extending across the globe the benefits of the green revolution: the scientific strides that have sent crop yields through the silo roof.

By the early 1970s, farm output in the Third World was rising at well over 2 percent annually, and the population growth rate was beginning to moderate.

The current world food situation is the best ever. Total calories per capita have risen by about one-third since 1960, and virtually everyone outside of Africa now has at least a minimally adequate calorie intake. (Africa's problem is bad government, not a lack of farming resources or even agricultural technology. Its current corn yields average less than 0.32 tons per acre but should be four times that high.)

This is not to argue that the food situation has been resolved for every person on earth. The world still has roughly 800 million chronically "food insecure" individuals, according to the International Food Policy Research Institute. However, this classification encompasses many degrees of food-access difficulty, and being moderately "food insecure" is much better than being an actual famine victim.

The famines of the last two decades have either resulted from civil war or been confined to the harshest, most uncertain, and thinly populated regions of Africa, or both.

The hunger remaining in the world is not due to distribution problems. Simple poverty is to blame. The bitter irony is that most countries have adequate agricultural resources to produce their own basic food supplies, *if* they use high-yield seeds and fertilizers (Africa mostly doesn't) and if they adopt effective government institutions that don't rob the people and discourage farmers and industries.

While acknowledging the success in overall world food production over the last 30 years, where is the world heading? Have the neo-Malthusians been right all along, only premature in their predictions? To answer this question, we need to evaluate trends in the components that contribute to food production and demand: crop yields, farmland availability, population growth, input constraints (for example, irrigation water), and food consumption patterns.

POPULATION STABILIZING RAPIDLY

The pessimists' biggest fear has been planetary overpopulation. The idea of growing beyond the carrying capacity of the planet originated with the concept of a limited food supply. Consequently, population control has been virtually their only policy solution.

The problem with population management is that it is nearly powerless to stop population growth suddenly. A growing population is like a long train with a lot of momentum. Contraceptives make only about a 10 percent difference in the effectiveness of families' birth-control decisions.

The good news is that, although the world has largely ignored the recommendations for drastic population-control programs, the World Bank notes that the world's population growth rate fell from 2.2 percent per year in the 1960s to 1.8 percent in the 1970s. The current growth rate is 1.6 percent per year.

Instead of world population spiraling ever upward, out of control, we are seeing a onetime surge—due to modern medicine and lower death rates—that is rapidly tapering off.

The main reason the world's population growth rate is declining so fast is that the average number of births per woman (bpw) in the Third World is down from 6.1 in 1965 to 3.1 today, according to the World Bank.

A population remains stable at an average of 2.1 bpw, which means the Third World has come three-fourths of the way to stability in one generation. Most affluent countries level off at 1.7 or 1.8 bpw, which means the world's population will eventually peak and then slowly decline.

The world's current population is estimated at nearly 6 billion. According to a recent study conducted by the Winrock Foundation, the peak world population will be less than 9 billion people, reached around 2040. We won't get more than that, because the brakes have already been applied on the population train. It just takes a while to fully stop it.

Besides population growth, one other major trend will add to the world's food demand: affluence. As free trade and economic growth spread around the globe, the world's poor are getting more affluent. Along with income growth comes the desire and purchasing power for more affluent diets: more meat, milk, eggs, and dairy products.

These foods take two to five times as many farming resources per calorie to produce as grains do. So when populations start eating more meat and milk, they are effectively consuming significantly higher quantities of grain and agricultural resources.

Combined, population growth and affluence will probably double the world's food demand and possibly triple it. Can countries meet this challenge?

FOOD PRODUCTION CEILING

The world's grain production has been increasing for over a century. According to U.S. Department of Agriculture statistics, world grain production has increased linearly since 1950.

Brown and other pessimists point to the last five years as evidence that production is reaching its upper limits. But they have made similar claims following periodic production drops in the past. Actually, this last production plateau is almost entirely due to the collapse of economic and farming systems in the former Soviet Union. The true trend has yet to be interrupted.

Pessimists such as Brown worry that humankind is losing farmland to roads, homes, and shopping malls. But the world will not suffer a food crisis because of urban development.

Cities currently occupy roughly 1.5 percent of the earth's surface. According to a World Bank study, even at the peak world population, cities will occupy less than 4 percent of the total land area. Considering the expected food needs, specialists would have to fail miserably in their efforts to increase crop yields and in the other agricultural policy areas for this small loss to push humankind over the brink into food crisis.

Moreover, the world has millions of acres of good farmland in the United States, Argentina, and western Europe that are underutilized or even wasted.

The doomsayers believe that the world won't be able to increase crop yields substantially. Nations are now experiencing the biological and practical limits to their ability to increase crop yields, the pessimists claim.

"Unfortunately, the inability of agricultural scientists to come up with a new formula to boost output means that production has stalled," says Brown in *State of the World: 1996.*

Actually, Brown made similar claims in 1989 and, remarkably, even way back in 1974. Yet grain yields have continued a steady and nearly constant increase over the last several decades in both the First and Third Worlds.

And the future looks bright for increasing crop yields. Traditional breeding techniques have been given new life by the science and tools of molecular biology. Using gene identification and marking techniques, tissue culture, and a host of other technologies, plant breeders can achieve years of traditional breeding advances in only a season or two.

Biotechnology holds even greater promise. Disease-resistant and drought-tolerant varieties are just the beginning. Researchers are redesigning virtually the whole layout of some plants, increasing the size of grain heads while shortening and strengthening the stalks to support them.

There is much reason for optimism.

SAVING NATURE WITH HIGH-YIELD FARMING

The real issue is not whether the world will experience massive food shortages in the future. According to the evidence, it almost certainly will not. The real question is whether humankind will spare room for nature as we feed ourselves.

This is actually one of the pessimists' major concerns. Paul Ehrlich, noted author of *The Population Bomb*, believes humankind has already surpassed the earth's carrying capacity. Yet his real concern is preserving habitat for wildlife.

The environmental movement is strident in its belief that population control is needed to save wildlife habitat from human encroachment. But if environmentalists are truly worried about wildlife and realize the realistic limitations on population-control measures, then maximizing land-use efficiency is essential. Nowhere is that more important than in agriculture.

According to the UN Food and Agriculture Organization, farming already occupies over a third of the earth's land area. In reality, modern, high-yield farming—which environmental activists ironically despise—has saved an enormous amount of the world's wildlife.

In recent decades, the world has lost hardly any of its wildlands to population growth, because nations have been increasing crop yields rather than plowing down wild forests. The world has been cropping nearly the same 5.8 million square miles of land since the end of World War II.

The world today still has about one-third of its land area in forests, just as it had 35 years ago, because nations haven't had to take more land for food. Without the higher yields produced with hybrid seeds, irrigation, fertilizers, and pesticides, the world would have already lost another 10–12 million square miles of wildlands. That's equal to the total land area of the United States, Europe, and Brazil combined!

Fortunately, the vast majority of the world's biodiversity is still out there to be saved—in the tropical forests and the mountain microclimates. The earth hasn't really begun to lose big tracts of wildlands yet.

Ultimately, the dilemma is that nations will have to either triple the yields on existing croplands or take huge tracts of land from nature.

If the world goes the route of increasing yields based on high-powered seeds, trees, and irrigation technologies, experts say 90-plus percent of the wildlands can be saved—and an even higher percentage of the wildlife species.

The food-supply pessimists have never wavered from their claims that humanity would soon hit the limits to the earth's bounty. Despite repeatedly failed predictions of disaster and continuing demonstrations of human ingenuity and adaptability, they believe the good times have passed.

Yet, looking at the trends in population growth, crop yields, land use, and food demand, the doomsday scenarios seem less likely with every passing year.

POSTSCRIPT

Is There a Global Population Crisis?

It is a matter of fact that the world population continues to grow rapidly. The most recent statistics can be found in the annual edition of *The State of the World Population* (United Nations Population Fund). But beyond sheer numbers, the population issue becomes much more controversial. Avery and many others argue that fears about the population overwhelming the Earth's resources are not well founded. They concede that there are some countries that cannot feed their populations. But, the argument continues, this is more a matter of poor agricultural practices and other local conditions, not a result of overpopulation. For a similar view, see Julian L. Simon, *Population Matters: People, Resources, Environment, and Immigration* (Transaction Press, 1990).

Population cannot be looked at just in the context of current resource utilization and economic patterns. There is a potential catch-22 in the "technology will meet population needs" argument. The catch is that the very technology that will expand agricultural yields and provide other benefits will also mean that as countries develop economically their resource utilization will grow exponentially, as will their pollution production. Now the vast majority of resource consumption and emissions are attributable to the small minority of people who live in industrialized countries. Once the LDCs (which contain 80 percent or so of the world's population) modernize, their consumption of resources and excretion of pollution will add considerably to the pressure on the biosphere. This conundrum of trying to develop economically while protecting the biosphere is termed the "sustainable development" issue. An excellent source of data is the annual publication of the World Resources Institute, *World Resources* (Oxford University Press). Another annual publication, and one that takes a dire view of sustainability, is Lester R. Brown et al., *State of the World: A World Watch Institute Report on Progress Toward a Sustainable Society* (W. W. Norton).

Yet another issue is what to do if, indeed, one decides to stem population growth. Some solutions, such as using artificial birth control devices or abortion as population control methods are highly controversial in many parts of the world. Other solutions—even relatively simple ones, such as distributing birth control devices or performing vasectomies—cost money. And perhaps the best solution, assisting poorer countries to develop economically, costs vast sums of money.

There are also some undesirable side effects from population control. For example, China imposes penalties on couples or individual women who have more than one child. The efforts to control population has also led to infanticide, with girl babies being killed (or female fetuses being aborted) in order to allow room for boy babies in a family. So, even if we can agree there is a problem, we are only part of the way to providing a solution. A study of those who become involved in seeking solutions can be found in Paul Wapner, *Environmental Activism and World Civic Politics* (State University of New York Press, 1996).

CONTRIBUTORS
TO THIS VOLUME

EDITOR

JOHN T. ROURKE, Ph.D., is a professor of political science at the University of Connecticut for campuses in Storrs and Hartford, Connecticut. He has written numerous articles and papers, and he is the author of *Congress and the Presidency in U.S. Foreign Policymaking* (Westview Press, 1985); *The United States, the Soviet Union, and China: Comparative Foreign Policymaking and Implementation* (Brooks/Cole, 1989); and *International Politics on the World Stage*, 6th ed. (Dushkin/McGraw-Hill, 1997). He is also coauthor, with Ralph G. Carter and Mark A. Boyer, of *Making American Foreign Policy* (The Dushkin Publishing Group, 1994). Professor Rourke enjoys teaching introductory political science classes—which he does each semester—and he plays an active role in the university's internship program as well as advises one of its political clubs. In addition, he has served as a staff member of Connecticut's legislature and has been involved in political campaigns at the local, state, and national levels.

STAFF

David Dean List Manager
David Brackley Developmental Editor
Ava Suntoke Developmental Editor
Tammy Ward Administrative Assistant
Brenda S. Filley Production Manager
Juliana Arbo Typesetting Supervisor
Diane Barker Proofreader
Lara Johnson Graphics
Richard Tietjen Publishing Systems Manager

AUTHORS

GREGORY ALBO teaches in the Department of Political Science at York University in Toronto, Canada.

MADELEINE K. ALBRIGHT is the United States secretary of state.

DENNIS T. AVERY is a former senior U.S. State Department agriculture analyst and a policy analyst in the Department of Agriculture. He is currently a director of global food issues at the Hudson Institute. He is the author of *Saving the Planet With Pesticides and Plastic: The Environmental Triumph of High-Yield Farming* (Hudson Institute, 1995).

DOUG BANDOW is a senior fellow of the Cato Institute in Washington, D.C., a public policy research foundation, and a member of the State of California Bar Association and the U.S. Court of Appeals for the District of Columbia. He is the author of *Beyond Good Intentions* (Crossway Books, 1988) and *The Politics of Plunder: Misgovernment in Washington* (Transaction Publishers, 1990).

TOM BETHELL is a *National Review* contributing editor and a visiting media fellow at the Hoover Institution.

GEORGE LEE BUTLER was commander in chief of the U.S. Strategic Air Command from 1991 to 1992 and the U.S. Strategic Command from 1992 to 1994, with responsibility for all U.S. Air Force and Navy deterrent forces. He was closely involved in the development of U.S. nuclear doctrine. General Butler has also served as deputy to General Colin Powell.

MARY CAPRIOLI was a graduate student in the Department of Political Science at the University of Connecticut, Storrs, when she wrote "Why Democracy?"

SALVADOR CARDÚS is a professor of sociology and an investigator in the Centre of Research in Sociology of Religion at the Autonomous University of Barcelona. He was vice-director of the *Avui* newspaper between 1989 and 1991.

WALTER C. CLEMENS, JR., is a professor of political science at Boston University. He is also an associate at the Center for Science and International Affairs and at the Davis Center for Russian Studies at Harvard University.

EDITORS OF *THE ECONOMIST* publish articles dealing with national as well as international affairs. Topics range from world politics and current affairs to business, finance, and science. *The Economist* is published weekly by The Economist Newspaper.

JOAN ESTRUCH is a professor of sociology and an investigator in the Centre of Research in Sociology of Religion at the Autonomous University of Barcelona. She recently published a study on the Opus Dei and its paradoxes.

FRANCIS FUKUYAMA, a former deputy director of the U.S. State Department's policy planning staff, is a senior researcher at the RAND Corporation in Santa Monica, California. He is also a fellow of the John Hopkins University School for Advanced International Studies' Foreign Policy Institute and director of its telecommunications project.

PATRICK GLYNN is a resident scholar at the American Enterprise Institute in Washington, D.C. He is the author of *Closing Pandora's Box: Arms Races, Arms*

Control, and the History of the Cold War (Basic Books, 1993).

AL GORE became the 45th vice president of the United States in 1992. Prior to that, he was a senator (D) from Tennessee. He has been acknowledged as a proponent of responsible actions toward the environment and the communication industries of the United States.

JAMES P. GRANT is executive director of the United Nations Children's Fund.

COLIN S. GRAY is a professor of international politics at the University of Hull in the United Kingdom. He is the author of *Explorations in Strategy* (Greenwood Press, 1996).

JOHN F. HILLEN III is a defense analyst at the Heritage Foundation and author of *Blue Helmets in War and Peace: The Strategy of UN Military Operations* (Brassey's, 1997).

ZACHARY KARABELL is a researcher in Harvard University's Kennedy School of Government.

JOHN KEANE is director of the Centre for the Study of Democracy and a professor of politics at the University of Westminster. His main publications include *Public Life and Late Capitalism* (Cambridge University Press, 1984), *Democracy and Civil Society* (Verso, 1988), and *The Media and Democracy* (Blackwell, 1991).

ANTHONY LAKE is the assistant to the president for National Security Affairs for the Clinton administration.

MARTIN LIBICKI is a senior fellow of the Center for Advanced Concepts and Technology at the National Defense University, where he specializes in the application of information technology to national security. His writings have focused on future battlefields, information warfare, and standards.

STEPHEN A. LISIO is an independent analyst affiliated with the law firm of Shearman and Sterling in Washington, D.C.

GREG MASTEL is vice president for policy planning and administration at the Economic Strategy Institute in Washington, D.C., an organization devoted to changing American attitudes on issues of trade, competitiveness, and economic policy issues that affect America's overall economic performance, the creation of good jobs, and the welfare of individual industries.

STEPHEN MOORE is director of fiscal policy study at the Cato Institute in Washington, D.C., a public policy research foundation.

ALBERTO J. MORA is a Cuban American and an attorney with a specialty in international law.

DANIEL PIPES is the editor of the *Middle East Quarterly* and the author of three books on Islam and politics.

MICHAEL POSNER is executive director of the Lawyers Committee for Human Rights.

JAMES LEE RAY is a professor of political science at Vanderbilt University in Nashville, Tennessee. He has also been a professor of political science and international affairs at Florida State University, and he is the author of *Democracy and International Conflict* (1995).

ROBERT S. ROSS teaches political science at Boston College and is a research associate at the John King Fairbank Center for East Asian Research at Harvard University. He is the author of *Negotiating Cooperation: U.S.-China Relations, 1969–1989* (Stanford University Press, 1995).

JOSEPH E. SCHWARTZBERG , primarily a South Asian specialist, has also taught political geography at the Universities of Pennsylvania and Minnesota since 1960. He is a national board member of the World Federalist Association (WFA) and president of WFA's Minnesota chapter.

ALAN TONELSON is the research director of the Economic Strategy Institute in Washington, D.C., which is a research organization that studies U.S. economics, technology, and national security policy. His essays on American politics and foreign policy have appeared in numerous publications, including the *New York Times, Foreign Policy,* and the *Harvard Business Review.* He is coeditor, with Clyde V. Prestowitz, Jr., and Ronald A. Morse, of *Powernomics: Eco-*

nomics and Strategy After the Cold War (Madison Books, 1991).

CHRISTINE VOLLMER is president of the Latin American Alliance for the Family.

MURRAY WEIDENBAUM is the Mallinckrodt Distinguished University Professor in and director of the Center for the Study of American Business at Washington University in St. Louis, Missouri. His publications include *Public Policy Toward Corporate Takeovers* (Transaction Publishers, 1987), coedited with Kenneth Chilton.

TIMOTHY WIRTH is a senator (D) from Colorado. He is a former chairman of the House Subcommittee on Telecommunications, Consumer Protection, and Finance, and he is interested in issues of energy policy and protection of the environment.

YEH LING-LING is the founder of the Diversity Coalition for an Immigration Moratorium in San Francisco, California.

INDEX